关于价格和货币流通状况的历史

A History of Prices, and of the State of the Circulation

（英）托马斯·图克（Thomas Tooke）
（英）威廉·纽马奇（William Newmarch） 著

中国财富出版社

图书在版编目(CIP)数据

关于价格和货币流通状况的历史．第四卷 = A History of Prices, and of the State of the Circulation Volume 4:英文 / (英)托马斯·图克(Thomas Tooke),(英)威廉·纽马奇(William Newmarch)著．—北京:中国财富出版社,2019.12

ISBN 978-7-5047-7107-0

Ⅰ. ①关…　Ⅱ. ①托…　②威…　Ⅲ. ①经济史—英国—1793-1856—英文
Ⅳ. ①F156.194.1

中国版本图书馆 CIP 数据核字(2019)第 270156 号

策划编辑	王　君	**责任编辑**	张冬梅　郭　莹		
责任印制	尚立业	**责任校对**	卓闪闪	**责任发行**	白　昕

出版发行	中国财富出版社		
社　　址	北京市丰台区南四环西路 188 号 5 区 20 楼	**邮政编码**	100070
电　　话	010-52227588 转 2098(发行部)		010-52227588 转 321(总编室)
	010-52227588 转 100(读者服务部)		010-52227588 转 305(质检部)
网　　址	http://www.cfpress.com.cn		
经　　销	新华书店		
印　　刷	北京九州迅驰传媒文化有限公司		
书　　号	ISBN 978-7-5047-7107-0/F·3133		
开　　本	710mm×1000mm　1/16	**版　　次**	2020 年 5 月第 1 版
印　　张	37	**印　　次**	2020 年 5 月第 1 次印刷
字　　数	515 千字	**定　　价**	198.00 元

TO

ALEXANDER BLAIR, ESQ.

TREASURER OF THE BANK OF SCOTLAND,
DRYLAW HOUSE,
NEAR EDINBURGH.

MY DEAR SIR,

As it was during a residence of some weeks under your hospitable roof, last autumn, that I began this work, I thus place your name upon its front, as a grateful acknowledgment, to you and Mrs. Blair, of the feelings of pleasure with which I shall always recur to that period. In the forenoon I was allowed the seclusion of a delightfully situated study; and my evenings were most agreeably passed in your family circle.

With the warmest wishes for the health and happiness of yourself and Mrs. Blair, and your amiable Daughter,

I am,

My dear Sir,

Your obliged and attached friend,

THOS. TOOKE.

PREFACE

The period comprised within the interval since the close of 1839, to which time my historical sketch of prices, and of the events connected with them, had been brought down, until the close of 1847, has been marked with extraordinary changes, affecting, in their most material interests, all classes of the community.

We have experienced great vicissitudes in the supply of food for the population, from dearth to abundance, and again from abundance to famine; succeeded, finally, by the return of comparative plenty. We have also witnessed the transition from distress and despondency, and a general prostration of the energies of the country, pervading all branches of industry, in the years 1840, 1841, 1842, and part of 1843, to a state of extraordinary prosperity, activity, and excitement, which prevailed through the three following years. While the last year of the series has been mournfully distinguished by a degree of commercial discredit, and by mercantile and banking failures, unparalleled, in number and extent, since 1825. And the variations in the rate of interest, especially in 1847, have been more frequent, and more violent, than any of which there is an example in the history of the commerce of this country.

During the same interval, great alterations have been made in the corn laws, in our commercial tariff, and in our banking system.

The great importance of these changes in the condition of the country, and of the alterations of our laws, in so far as these may be considered to be connected, would seem to call for a historical record of them, accompanied by such explanations derived from an extensive and connected view of facts, as might be calculated to throw light upon the phaenomena by which the period from the close of 1839 to that of 1847 has been signalised.

As, besides, the whole of this eventful period, and more especially the latter part of it, has been pregnant with facts calculated, in a striking manner, to exemplify and confirm the views which it was my object, in the "History of Prices", to set forth, it forms a fitting occasion for a continuation of that work.

Accordingly, I had it in contemplation last spring, when the state of the corn trade, and of the money market, invested the subject with considerable interest, to undertake the preparation of a fourth volume. But I recoiled at the idea of the labour it would entail. As the summer advanced, however, the motives which had led me to contemplate the undertaking acquired additional strength.

Notwithstanding the lull which followed the shock of April, I became strongly impressed with the opinion that there was reason to apprehend another period of pressure before the end of the year. It is well known that I entertained and expressed that apprehension; the grounds for it, it is not necessary now to state.

I mention my forebodings of a second crisis, chiefly for the purpose of observing that while it strengthened the motives which urged me to the task I contemplated, it added to the difficulty of my accomplishing it; for if my forebodings of commercial discredit, combined with what I considered was likely to be the operation of the banking act, should be realised, it was in the highest degree probable that the new parliament, on its meeting, would have its attention drawn to the general state of commercial credit, in connection with the act of 1844. This consideration rendered it important that whatever I might determine to publish should be completed by, or soon after, the meeting of parliament, at the usual time of its assembling; because if the information I had to impart was calculated to be of any use, it would be more especially so by being available in the discussions and inquiries to which, in the state of things which I contemplated, the subject would give rise.

But to accomplish such a work, doing any thing like justice to it, within so limited a time, (for I had not written a line, or made any other preparation for it, till near the middle of August,) would hardly have been within my power at any time, and must, at my time of life, have been out of the question. I should, therefore, have abandoned the attempt in despair, had not my friend Mr. Danson, while he strongly urged me to undertake the task, offered his assistance towards the performance of it.

Mr. Danson is advantageously known to those persons, and they are not a small number, who have had an opportunity of seeing, in the Journal of the Statistical Society, a valuable paper, drawn up and read by him before that Society, in January 1847, on the Accounts of the Bank of England, under the operation of the Act 7 & 8 Vict. c. 32.

Of his offer I gladly availed myself; and the assistance which he has afforded in enabling me to bring out this volume, has been, to me, of inestimable value.

He has supplied the whole of the elaborate and accurate statistical statements and tables in the work, with the exception of the small number in the 11th section of the third division of it.

Of the first division (namely, that on the seasons and the corn trade), the description of the character of the seasons, and their relative productiveness, and the conjectural opinion of the probable future range of prices are mine. For the statements of prices and quantities, and the reasoning upon these, I am indebted to Mr. Danson. To him, likewise, I owe the contribution of by far the greater part of the second division of the book, on the prices of produce other than corn. And he has afforded me the further essential service of conducting the whole of the work through the press.

To my friend, Mr. Newmarch, I have to express my obligation for important assistance which he rendered me in the general arrangement of the third division of the volume; and for his contribution of the statistical tables in section 11 of that division.

It will be observed, that in the argument on the act of 1844, there is a large number of extracts, some of considerable length, from my pamphlet of 1844, and from other publications.

The extracts from my own tract contain facts or reasonings essential to the argument. If to avoid the appearance of quoting from a work of my own, I had stated afresh the same views, I am not sure that I should have expressed them better; and I could ill spare the time for such additional labour.

And whenever, in the writings of others on the subject, I have met with passages confirmatory, or illustrative, of the views which it fell in the way of my argument to urge, I have not scrupled to avail myself of them largely. Independently of the support which my opinions were likely to derive from such eminent authority, (not to mention the consequent saving of my own time and labour,) I considered that my readers would be thankful to me for the opportunity thus afforded to them of seeing, in the forcible and eloquent language of Mr. Fullarton, in the philosophic exposition of Mr. Mill, and in the remarkably lucid style of Mr. Wilson, the arguments which I should be hopeless of being able to state with the same effect. Such extracts impart, moreover, some variety to the discussion of a subject which, at best, is any thing but attractive.

Just as the press is closing upon this volume a pamphlet by Colonel Torrens, which came out two days ago, has been put into my hands. It purports to be a defence of the act of 1844, against my objections, and those of Mr. Fullarton and Mr. Wilson.

I am glad to find that there is little, if any thing, in it which will not be found to be dealt with, and, I trust, sufficiently answered, in the following pages.

If the earlier volumes of the present work be critically examined, there will be found in them some remains (chiefly, however, in the phraseology) of my former attachment to the currency theory, as it was generally received, before it had been caricatured by the modern school.

In the correctness of the following sketch by the hand of Mr. Fullarton, of the progress of my opinions to those which I now entertain, I fully acquiesce, and lest his estimate of the value of my contributions to an extension of the knowledge of this subject, should be ascribed to the bias of friendship, I think it right to state that the distinguished author was unknown to me, except by name and reputation, till after the publication of his treatise, and that I had not the slightest previous knowledge of such a work being in preparation: —

"Mr. Tooke himself has been exceedingly slow in following out his original conclusions on the subject of price to all their consequences. The germ of his present opinions may be traced in the facts, which he collected and laid before the public in the first edition of his great work; but at the time of that publication, in 1823, Mr. Tooke's mind appears to have been still strongly imbued with the prevailing notions, that prices are liable to rise and fall with the increase or diminution of the amount of Bank notes in circulation, that banks have it in their power to increase at pleasure the quantity of paper money, and that the efflux and influx of gold are to be regulated by regulating the issues of the banks. He adhered to these doctrines even after he had refuted them by his discoveries, and seems to have parted with them at last only by degrees and with reluctance, under the pressure of his growing convictions. The progress of those convictions may be traced through their successive stages in his various publications, and in the evidence delivered by him before diverse Parliamentary Committees. His pamphlet on the Currency, published after the crisis of 1825, might, for aught to the contrary that can be gathered from its doctrines, have almost been the production of Mr. Loyd or Mr. Norman. It is in his examination before the Commons Committee of 1832, that we perceive the first decided indications of the revolution which was gradually taking place in his mind, though even then he had not yet brought himself to discard entirely the old theory of prices, but professed himself still ready to admit that prices are liable to be influenced by the amount of the circulating medium. The second and altered edition of his work on prices, published under a new title in 1838, exhibits in a more elaborate shape the conclusions to which his continued observations had led him; though, even in those volumes, passages of the original treatise have been retained, which do not seem altogether in harmony with the new doctrines which he had espoused. Nor was it till the appearance in 1810 of his 'History of

Prices in 1838 and 1839,' that the system which he had been so long maturing received its full development. These slight appearances of wavering, which, rightly viewed, ought rather to be considered as proofs of the caution and deliberation with which he formed his judgments, have been charged against him as inconsistencies, and advantage has been taken of them to detract from the weight of his authority."

The limits of time within which I have found it necessary to confine myself, have deterred me from entering upon some points which are, more or less, connected with the topics treated of in this volume. But I am the more reconciled to the necessity which compels me to abstain from touching upon these, because they will, doubtless, be among the objects to which the inquiries of the committees of the two houses of parliament will be directed, with the advantage of their being enabled to collect information which I have not the means of obtaining, and without which no judgment, entitled to much weight, could be formed.

London,
5th February, 1848.

CONTENTS

PART I ON THE PRICES OF CORN FROM 1840 TO 1847

APPENDIX

PART I

ON THE PRICES OF CORN FROM 1840 TO 1847

ON THE PRICES OF CORN FROM 1840 TO 1847

During the last few years a striking change has taken place in the degree of attention given to the effect of the seasons on the price of provisions. It is not now the farmer or the corn dealer only, who watches with painful anxiety the state of the weather at the several critical periods in the growth of the different descriptions of produce, and, from what he thus observes, infers the probable range of prices, and of his own fortune, in the ensuing year. Such anxious observation has of late been scarcely less common in the counting house and on the stock-exchange than on the farm and in the corn market. Every passing cloud, indeed, may at those periods be said to have had some effect on the prices of public securities, and of shares in railways, and other joint stock companies, in consequence of the apprehensions entertained of the unfavourable influence of high prices, and of large importations of corn, on the rate of interest, and on banking accommodation.

Any one who may recollect, or will be at the trouble of referring to, the city articles of the daily papers in June, July, and August of each year since 1839, will be sensible of the importance attached, in what is now called the money market, to the state of the weather. If any material variation occured in the price of the Government funds, or of shares, it was not unfrequently, or I should rather say it was generally, ascribed to the wet or fair weather of the day, modified more or less by the reports of the state of the growing crops in the earlier, and of their appearance in the later, stages of their growth. Nor is this increased attention given, as formerly, only for the time.

The effect of the seasons is now constantly regarded as a primary element in all well considered speculations touching the condition, past or present, of the numerous and various interests affected, directly or indirectly, by the prices of agricultural produce. It may even be doubted whether too much weight is not sometimes attached to this particular class of causes, to the exclusion of others, for the time being, less obvious, or less frequently adverted to. Be that, however, as it may, the change alluded to in the public mind affords me the advantage of not having to apologize, as I considered it incumbent upon me in the earlier volumes of this work to do, for attaching so much importance to the influence of the seasons. And the corn laws being, as I now believe, finally settled, I am also dispensed from discussing, as I had occasion to do when treating of the corn trade in connection with the seasons in 1838 and 1839, the merits of that vexata quaestio. My task therefore in the portion of my work which I am now entering upon will be more simply historical than it was in the previous volumes.

SECTION 1 *Character of the season of 1839-1840. Prices and estimated produce of wheat*

The history of the prices of corn in connection with the seasons and other circumstances affecting them, was, in the work of which this is a continuation, brought down to the close of 1839.

The season of 1839 had been the second of two, in immediate

succession, in which the harvests, especially as regarded the crops of wheat, were very unproductive, and nearly in the same degree.

The deficiency of the two successive crops of 1838 and 1839 entailed the necessity of very large foreign supplies. The quantity of imported wheat and flour entered for consumption between the 5th of August, 1838, and in the same period in 1840, while the produce of these two harvests may be supposed to have been in the market, was more than 5,300,000 quarters.[①] The average price of wheat had fluctuated in the same interval from 61*s.* 10*d.* to 81*s.* 6*d.*, and the duty on wheat imported, from 1*s.* to 20*s.* 8*d.*, while the average duty paid on the whole of the quantity entered for home consumption was under 3*s.* 7*d.* per quarter.

Though the deficiency of the crop of 1839 was supposed to be nearly if not quite as great as that of the crop of 1838, the foreign supplies to meet the deficiency in the year 1839, were much larger in proportion than in the previous year; and this, combined with a general inferiority of quality in the home produce, had the effect of causing a decline of the average price of wheat from 81*s.* 6*d.*, which it had reached in the second week of January, 1839, with no important oscillations, to 65*s.* 6*d.* in November following.

The whole of the Autumn, to the very close of 1839, was excessively

① The precise quantities entered, with their distribution over the period in question, were, according to the official accounts, as follows: —

	Quarters.
Foreign and colonial wheat, and flour entered for consumption in the United Kingdom from the 5th of August, 1838, to the end of that year	1,827,088
Entered in 1839	2,712,555
Entered in 1840 down to the 5th of August	784,528
	5,324,171

wet, so as almost wholly to prevent the sowing of wheat at the usual season. This extreme wetness continued (with the exception of two days of slight frost early in January) to the 17th of February, 1840; with occasional snow, which, however, did not lie. Thenceforward there was a succession of dry, cold, easterly winds, and night frosts (with occasional snow) to the second week of April. This interval of dry weather was highly favourable to farming operations, and admitted of a large breadth being sown with spring wheat.

In the first week of May, vegetation was more forward than it had been at that period in any of the four years preceding; and the whole of that month, and of June, had a fair proportion of seasonable weather.

July was, throughout, cold and wet. This unfavourable weather, combined with a general impression that the stocks of old wheat were low, and that the growing crop (a considerable proportion of it being spring sown) would not prove to be a large one, favoured the speculations for a rise of price. The weekly average consequently advanced to 72*s*. 10*d*. in the week ending the 7th of August, and the duty fell on the 28th to 2*s*. 8*d*. per quarter. But the weather in August proving generally favourable to the ripening and gathering of the crops, and the wheats being reported to be better than had been expected, there was no longer any speculative ground for anticipating a further advance of prices, and fall of duty. The whole stock of wheat, therefore, then in bond, amounting to about 1, 500, 000 quarters, was entered for home consumption. This quantity of foreign corn being suddenly let out just at the time that supplies of the new crop were coming forward in a condition for immediate use, caused a somewhat rapid fall of prices during the remainder of the year. From 72*s*. 10*d*., in August, the price fell to 58*s*. 10*d*. in the second week of December following; being a fall of 14*s*. in four months. As, however, the result of the harvest, on the further progress of threshing out, gave reason to suppose that there would not, with the foreign corn admitted, be more than sufficient to last till the ensuing harvest, the price thenceforward slowly advanced.

The total quantity of wheat and wheat-flour, (the latter being stated as wheat at the rate of 392 lbs. to the quarter) entered for consumption in the United Kingdom, between the 5th of August, 1839, and the same date in 1840, was 1,762,483 quarters. ① This, therefore, may be regarded as an approximation to the quantity of foreign and colonial wheat actually taken into consumption with the produce of the harvest of 1839.

The official average price of wheat for the year 1839 was 70*s*. 8*d*. per quarter, and for 1840 it was 66*s*. 4*d*. Neither of these, however, can be received as indicating the average price of the year during which the crop of 1839 was in course of consumption. The average price of the *harvest* year, computed from the averages of the fifty-two weeks following the first week in August, 1839, was about 68*s*. per quarter. ②

---

① See statement in detail in the Appendix.

② Though the actual date of the gathering of the wheat crop varies considerably between the northern and southern districts of England, in which the weekly averages above referred to are taken, and the commencement as well as the close of the harvest in the United Kingdom is not unfrequently hastened or delayed a week or two by the character of the season, these variations do not materially affect the computations in the text. The first week in August is probably a month earlier than the period at which any considerable quantity of the new crop usually appears in the market. But the estimated yield of the harvest operates upon prices for some time previously; and the annual fluctuations of the weekly average price, prove that the first week in August may, for all practical purposes, be taken as the period when prices cease to be influenced by the old and begin to be dependent upon the new crop. It should also be observed that the price stated in the text, as that of the harvest year, is only offered as an approximation to an accurate average. (See Appendix)

According to the best estimates, formed at the time, of the wheat harvest of 1840, the average yield per acre exceeded that of either of the two previous harvests by about one third. The breadth of land sown, however, (the autumn of 1839 having been extremely unfavourable for farming operations) was probably much less. The returns of the corn inspectors show that while the quantity of wheat sold in the inspected markets in England and Wales in the twelve months following the first week in September, 1839, was about 4,000,000 of quarters, the quantity sold in the same period of 1840-1841 was only 3,870,000 quarters; thus favouring the assumption, founded on the combined estimates of the breadth of land sown and the average yield, that the crop of 1840 did not, in fact, materially, if at all, exceed that of 1839.

SECTION 2 *Character of the season of 1840-1841. Prices and estimated produce of wheat*

The weather during the autumn of 1840 presented nothing remarkable. Upon the whole it was favourable to farming operations, till the month of December. The last three weeks of this month, as well as the first half of

---

The quantity of home-grown corn sold in the inspected markets in England and Wales, apparently the produce of each harvest, is computed from the first week in September forward, because a careful examination of the returns of the corn inspectors, in conjunction with contemporaneous reports from the chief markets, leads to the inference that that is the period at or about which the new wheat first appears at market.

The quantity of imported wheat entered for consumption is computed from the fifth of August, because the revenue return for the month ending the fifth of September, has hitherto commonly included the greater part of the entries of the current year; and any but a small quantity entered after the fifth of August must obviously be received as going into consumption rather with the new than with the old crop.

January, were characterised by a much lower temperature than usual: frost prevailing so severely as totally to impede the navigation of the Thames. In the night of the 7th and 8th of January the thermometer was lower than it had been since January, 1838; but the latter half of this month was comparatively mild. The first ten days of February were attended with frost of some severity, and occasional snow.

Thus far the winter of 1840-1841 may be considered to have been a rigorous one; but its rigour was not marked by such continuousness and severity of frost, nor did it extend so far into the spring, as some former ones; for after the second week of February there was very little of either frost or snow. It cannot, therefore, be classed among the more memorable instances of long and severe winters.

The weather in March was variable, but a large proportion of it was fine; and there was less of strong easterly wind than usual. Of the spring quarter, from Lady-day to Midsummer, the prevailing character was cold, gloomy and wet, with much wind: the number of fine days being very small.

From Midsummer to Michaelmas, embracing the important periods of the blooming, the ripening, and the gathering of the crops, the weather was for the most part cold, wet, and ungenial. On the 15th of July there was a remarkably heavy fall of rain; and on the 8th of August prayers were put up in the churches for fair weather. After the 14th of August there were somewhat longer intervals of fair weather; but not enough to redeem the general character of the summer, as decidedly wet and cold throughout.

The total quantity of imported wheat and flour entered for consumption in the United Kingdom between the 1st of August, 1840, and the same date in 1841 was 1, 925, 241 quarters. [①] The foreign supply taken into consumption with the crop of 1840 may therefore be estimated to have exceeded that so taken with the crop of 1839 (1,762,483 qrs.) by nearly 200,000 quarters.

The average price of wheat, in England and Wales, for the harvest year 1840-1841, was 63*s*. 6*d*. per quarter, or 4*s*. 6*d*. lower than that of the harvest year 1839-1840.

The backwardness of the season of 1840-1841, and the prevalence of rainy weather in the time of the flowering of the wheat, and during the progress of the harvest, favoured the speculation for a rise of prices and a consequent fall of the duty. Accordingly the weekly average reached 76*s*. 1*d*., and the aggregate average 73*s*. 2*d*., early in September, when, the duty having fallen to 1*s*., there were entered for home consumption in that month 2,178,966 quarters of wheat and flour.

The crop of wheat of 1841, though backward, and injured by the rains, was of considerable breadth, and of great bulk on the ground. The produce was at the time computed to be nearly an average in quantity, but very inferior in quality. This inferiority of quality, combined with the large foreign supply suddenly let in in September, caused a rapid fall of the weekly average, which got down to 61*s*. 6*d*. in the first week of October: being a decline of nearly 15*s*. within six weeks. The markets rallied a little thenceforward, till the close of the year, when the average was 62*s*. 10*d*.

There is reason to believe that the ultimate yield of the wheat harvest of.

---

① Of this quantity, the greater part (1,132,000 quarters) was entered in September, 1840, at an average duty, on the foreign portion of it, of 3*s*. 11*d*. per quarter.

1841 fell considerably short of the estimates made in the first instance. The official returns show an aggregate sale in the inspected markets in England and Wales, in the year following the first week in September 1841, of only 3,626,000 quarters. ① The supply by importation was very large, upwards of 2,900,000 quarters having been entered for consumption between the 5th of August, 1841, and the same date in 1842; fully four-fifths of it being entered within the last four months of 1841. The average price of the harvest year (1841-1842) having been, notwithstanding the absorption of this large foreign supply, and the general inferiority of the grain, no less than 63*s*. 4*d*., or very nearly as high as that of the previous year, the inference of a reduced home supply, in point of quantity, is almost irresistible; particularly as the year 1841-1842 was that in which the means of purchase, and consequently the demand, of the majority of the consumers was, probably, from the depressed state of trade, at its lowest point.

The season of 1841-1842 was the last of four in which the home supply of corn, generally, and of wheat more especially, was deficient in a greater or less degree. The prices of meat, also, were at a somewhat high range, the long prevalence of cold and wet weather having been injurious to the cattle and sheep; and the whole interval from the summer of 1838 to that of 1842 must be characterised as a period of dearth. The dawn of an improved prospect commenced with the season of 1841-1842.

---

① The number of markets from which returns were obtained was increased, by the act 5 & 6 Vict. c. 14., from 150 to 290; and the change appears to have affected the returns of the last nine or ten weeks of the harvest year 1841-1842. Had this change not been made, the quantity stated in the text would probably have fallen short of 3,500,000 qrs.

SECTION 3 *Character of the season of 1841-1842. Prices and estimated produce of wheat*

After a very rainy autumn, and a prevalence of wet weather to the close of 1841, which retarded the sowing of wheat, the winter of 1842 was favourable to farming operations; there being frequent frosts, but not severe, and occasional falls of snow, but not heavy, or remaining long on the ground. April was severely cold, with an almost constant prevalence of strong, dry, easterly winds; and the greater part of May was cold, showery, and windy. And at this period the crops of wheat were reported to be backward, and thin on the ground, with an appearance in every way unpromising.

The variations in the price of wheat, and in a lesser degree in the prices of other descriptions of grain, were, in the course of this year, greater than those which had occurred in any of the three preceding years. The average price of wheat in the first week of January was 63*s*. , from which it fell gradually to 57*s*. 8*d*. in April. This decline might be in some degree attributable to the change in the corn law, which was announced by Sir Robert Peel, in his speech on the budget, on the 1st of March. Some relaxation, however, had been anticipated; and the actual announcement of the proposed alterations in the import duties on corn did not appear to exercise any considerable influence on the markets. This comparative absence of influence from the alteration of the law would lead to the inference which, indeed, corresponds with the opinions then prevailing in Mark Lane, that the stocks of wheat on hand were within a moderate compass, and barely sufficient to supply the consumption till harvest.[①] The impression to this effect was strengthened as the spring advanced, by the cold and ungenial weather in April and May, which (apart from the reports prevalent of injury to the crops) was calculated to render the harvest a late one. A spirit of speculation hence arose upon the probability of the necessity for a foreign supply, which supposed such an advance of the average price as would reduce the duty to its minimum rate of 1*s*. per quarter. Under the influence of this spirit of speculation, in which the farmers seem to have participated so far as to abstain from supplying the markets freely, prices rose, so that the weekly average reached 65*s*. 8*d*. on the 16th of July.

In the mean time the speculation had a more important consequence in the shape of extensive arrangements with a view to a large importation of foreign corn.

But the weather becoming suddenly fine and warm in June, a great and most beneficial change took place in the appearance of the crops. Indeed so sudden was the change that I heard at the time, from persons who were among the best informed in the corn trade, that the alteration for the better caused by the bright and hot weather of the first fortnight of June might pass as something almost miraculous. Thenceforward the season continued to be of a favourable character: there being only so much rain as was calculated to improve rather than to injure the crops. And favourable as the season was in the southern division of the island, it was, if possible, still more so in the northern. In Scotland it was considered to be the finest and hottest summer that had been known there since 1826: and, accordingly,

① The whole quantity of foreign and colonial wheat in bond at the end of March, was 174,662 quarters.

their harvests were remarkably forward, the reaping of wheat having been general, and a good deal carried, in August. And the whole of the crops were secured in that and in all other parts of the United Kingdom in the best possible order. The quality was regarded as generally good, and the yield satisfactory; and on an average throughout the Kingdom the grain was housed about a fortnight earlier than usual.

The prices of corn had reached their greatest height by the end of June; but the average price of wheat regulating the import duty did not exhibit the full extent of the rise till the 28th of July, when it reached 64*s*. 7*d*. The duty was then 8*s*. per quarter①, at which rate it continued till near the middle of August. The subsequent fall of the weekly average price making it certain that the duty would immediately rise, and all chance of a rally of the markets being evidently hopeless, the whole of the wheat and flour at that time in bond, and the cargoes recently arrived, but not yet landed, amounting to about 2,000,000 of quarters, were entered for home consumption. ②

The sudden admission of so large a quantity of foreign corn, coincidently with the securing of a full crop, of good quality, of our own growth, and in such condition that the greater part was fit for being immediately brought to market, could not fail to cause a great reduction of price. Accordingly the

---

① This was the lowest point reached by the duty in the summer of 1842, being the rate fixed by the new tariff when the six-weeks average price should be 64*s*. and under 65*s*. The price reached 64*s*. 1*d*. on the 14th of July, and did not fall below 64*s*. until the 18th of August. The duty of 8*s*. thus remained in operation for five weeks.

② The quantity of wheat and flour entered for consumption between the 5th of August, 1841, and the same period in 1842, and so, apparently, taken into consumption, with the crop of 1841, had been 2,985,422 quarters; of which no less than 2,178,966 quarters were, as has been stated, entered in September, 1841. The entire quantity entered in the month ending the 5th of September, 1842, was 2,240,233 quarters; leaving only about 8,900 quarters in bond at the end of the month.

averages declined, rapidly and progressively, till they got down to 46*s*. 10*d*. in the week ending 24th December, being a fall of no less than 18*s*. 10*d*. from the weekly average in July. And the real fall was greater than appears by these figures; for the quality of the wheat of the harvest of 1842 was very superior to that of 1841. If allowance were made for this difference, the fall of price between July and December would be fully 20*s*.

The results of the large importations referred to proved to be most disastrous to the parties concerned. It was computed that the difference against the importer, between the cost, exclusive of the duty, and the net proceeds, could not, on the average, be less than 12*s*. per quarter: to which adding 8*s*. duty makes 20*s*. per quarter, as the lowest estimate of the loss sustained on the whole quantity imported. And as the importers and speculators for a rise were generally possessed of but little capital, compared with the credit they obtained, the failures were numerous, and the loss fell very heavily, in some part on the shippers abroad, but chiefly on the corn factors and dealers in this country.

The yield per acre of the wheat harvest of 1842 was estimated at the time to exceed, by fully one- fourth, that of either of the two years immediately preceding; and the opinion that the crop was an unusually large one is amply confirmed by subsequent events. The returns of the corn inspectors for the twelve months following the first week in September, 1842, exhibit an aggregate quantity of home-grown wheat brought to market exceeding 5,000,000 of quarters. ① The foreign supply entered for consumption in the year between August, 1842, and August, 1843, was about 2,405,000

① This quantity cannot be compared with that of any prior season, as the number of markets actually inspected was increased, about June 1842, under the corn law of that year.

quarters, or nearly 600,000 quarters less than in the year preceding. And the average price of the harvest year 1842-1843 was only 49*s*. 4*d*.: that of 1841-1842 having been 63*s*. 4*d*.[①]

SECTION 4 *Character of the season of 1842-1843. Prices and estimated produce of wheat*

The weather in the last three months of 1842 was seasonable. In November there was less fog than usual. The first ten days of December were attended with more or less of fog; but the whole of that month was marked by a higher temperature, and the last three weeks of it by a larger proportion of fine, bright, and mild days, than usual.

Altogether, the winter was an open one. There was occasional frost; but it was not severe or continuous; and there were several falls of snow, but it did not lie. Heavy gales of wind occurred in January; and on the 12th of that month there was a violent storm. February was very rough and raw, with alternations of frost and thaw, rain and snow.

The first fortnight of March was cold and dry. The rest of that month, and the whole of April, was variable; but generally seasonable.

The six or seven weeks extending from the beginning of May to the middle of June were marked by an unusual prevalence of wet, and by a temperature low for the season. The rest of June was fair, with the exception of one or

① Nor, in making this comparison, should it be forgotten that the crop of 1842 was brought somewhat earlier into consumption than usual; and, that that of the succeeding year being gathered late, the former must have supplied the current demand during somewhat more than a year; and, further, that from the spring of 1843 forward, the, revival of trade, by increasing the means of the consumers, doubtless tended to increase the quantity consumed.

two cold days. In July the weather was variable, with a good deal of rain, but not continuously; some days were of summer heat, and others, especially the 23rd, unusually cold.

The weather continued thus till the end of the first week in August. Apprehensions having been generally entertained of consequent damage to the harvest, the weekly average price had then risen progressively for some weeks; and on the 12th of August it reached 61*s*. 2*d*., and the duty fell, by the end of the month, to 14*s*. per quarter.

After the 6th of August, however, there was a general prevalence of fair summer weather. The only exceptions were thunderstorms on the 9th and the 16th, and three days of rain from the 21st to the 23rd of that month. From the 26th of August to the 25th of September, one entire month, the weather was extremely and uniformly fine, bright, and hot. Consequently, though the harvest was, in most places, ten days or a fortnight later than usual, the crops of corn were secured, even to the extreme north of the island, in the best possible condition.

The price of wheat declined about 10*s*. per quarter in the month following the middle of August; and all the wheat and flour then in bond (about 750,000 quarters) was entered for consumption, during the last days of August and the first of September, at an average duty of about 14*s*. per quarter. Thenceforward prices varied but slightly to the close of the year.

What has been said of the weather during the growth of the corn crops of 1843 sufficiently accounts for the description generally given of them when gathered. In the southern districts of England, which were most severely affected by the unfavourable weather prevalent up to the beginning of August, the yield was generally defective. In the northern counties, and in Scotland, where the fine weather of August and September came in time to exercise considerable influence on the last stages of growth, and the ripening; and also in Ireland, where the nature of the soil rendered the rains and low temperature of the earlier part of the year less detrimental than they were on the heavier lands of our southern counties, the crops were reported to be larger and of better quality.

The yield of the wheat harvest of 1843, both per acre and in the aggregate, was supposed, at the time, to be nearly the same as that of 1842. Nor is this estimate materially inconsistent with the inference to be drawn from a combined view of the quantities sold in the inspected markets, the amount of the foreign supply, and the range of prices, in the following year. The returns of the corn inspectors show a total quantity brought to market, in the fifty-two weeks following the first week in September 1843, of 5,213,000 quarters, against 5,078,000 quarters in the preceding year. The quantity of foreign and colonial wheat and flour entered for consumption between the 5th of August 1843 and the same date in 1844 was only 1,606,000 quarters, or about two thirds of the quantity entered in the year before. The average price of the harvest year 1843-1844 was 53*s.* 9*d.*, or 4*s.* 5*d.* higher than in 1842-1843. Thus, if some allowance be made for the effect on price of an increased rate of consumption (in connection with the increased prevalence of profitable employment) in 1843-1844, the equality of the home supply in the two years appears to be tolerably well proved.

SECTION 5 *Character of the season of 1843-1844. Prices and estimated produce of wheat*

From the last week of September 1843 forward, the weather was seasonably autumnal. In December it was unusually mild, resembling on some days the fine weather proper to October: there was but little wind, and the barometer was mostly high. This mildness continued through the greater part of January; being only occasionally interrupted by frost, and by slight falls of snow.

In February the cold increased considerably; and there was a good deal of frost and snow, with rain and wind; a severe gale occurring on the 23rd.

The weather in March was variable, but not unseasonable; and in April was generally fine, excepting the prevalence of cold easterly winds during the last fortnight. These winds continued almost without intermission till the 4th of June, when the wind shifted to the west. Excepting occasional showers, however, there was but little rain before the 25th of June, when it fell heavily; and during June, though the temperature was variable, there were several warm, and a few hot days.

Much rain fell in the first week of July; but afterwards the weather was variable, with several fine days, and a good deal of rain, but not so heavy or continuous as to be injurious to the crops.

The first fortnight of August was windy and wet. Afterwards the weather improved; but the temperature still continued low for the season. The first week of September was fine; but there was rain on the 8th and 9th, and again on the 15th, 16th, and 18th. The rest of the month was fair. Upon the whole, the two months of August and September, excepting about a week at the beginning of the former, were favourable for gathering and securing the crops of corn throughout the country.

The wheat crop of 1844 was computed to be in bulk and yield the largest of all since the harvest of 1834; and the state of the markets during the following year amply confirms this estimate. The quantity of wheat returned as sold in the inspected markets in England and Wales in the year following the first week of September, 1844, was no less than 6,664,000 quarters; and the average price of the harvest year was only 46*s*. 7*d*. per quarter. ①

SECTION 6 *Character of the season of 1844-1845. Prices and estimated produce of wheat*

The weather in October and November, 1844, was of the usual character; and sufficiently favourable for farming operations. But the whole of December was characterised by a low temperature. During the first three weeks there was severe frost; and the navigation of the Thames was impeded by ice. From the 30th of November to near the end of the year there was also a nearly constant succession of dry easterly winds.

In January the weather was mild for the season, with a good deal of rain, till near the end of the month. There was a return of frost, with slight falls of snow, from the 27th to the 31st.

During February there was more severe frost, and more snow, than had been experienced in the same month for some years before: the lowest point of temperature occurring on the 11th.

March brought no alleviation of this severity. The weather during the first three weeks of the month was marked by a lower temperature (the lowest occurring on the 13th), and, altogether, by greater inclemency, than had occurred since 1814. ② The rest of the month was comparatively mild.

---

① The quantity of foreign and colonial wheat and flour entered for consumption in the United Kingdom between the 5th of August, 1844, and the same date in 1845, was only 476,190 quarters; and the lowest duty paid upon any considerable portion of this was 18*s*. per quarter.

② In 1814 there was continuous frost, with occasional falls of snow, till the 21st of March.

The four months extending from the end of November, 1844, to the last week of March, 1845, may therefore be described as a long and rather rigorous winter. The mildness of the weather in January, however, deprives it of the character of extreme severity.

The spring quarter, throughout the greater part of it, was unseasonably cold. The first three weeks of April were dry and very cold; and drought was much complained of. The last week of the month was warmer; yet less warm than is usual at this season. May was cold and gloomy, with a good deal of rain, and very little sun: hardly one fine bright day occurring throughout the month.

In June the weather was fair, and in every respect seasonable.

The first three days of July were rainy: the next three fine, bright, and hot. But the rest of the month was unsettled, and generally cold; with a good deal of rain, and not one day of full summer heat. This cold and wet weather continued with little variation through the month of August.

The low temperature caused the ripening process of the grain crops to be very slow; but it also rendered the prevalence of wet less injurious, as it prevented the sprouting which might otherwise have been apprehended.

The first fourteen days of September were dry and generally cold, with north-east winds; and the rest of the month variable; but with a preponderance of wet; and was cold for the season.

The season of 1844-1845 is remarkable, and will long be memorable, as having been that in which an extraordinary disease first made itself generally manifest among the potatoes, not only in the United Kingdom, but over a great part of the Continent of Europe. When the extensive prevalence of this disease first attracted public attention it was attributed to the ungenial character of the weather which had prevailed from the planting to the gathering of the crop. But doubts were thrown upon this mode of accounting for the disease, when it was discovered to prevail equally in districts of the Continent of Europe, which had been exempt from unfavourable weather. And these doubts were strengthened when it became generally known that the very same description of disease had existed for some time before in the United States of America. The existence, and extensive prevalence, and the probable causes of the disease in that country, had been matter of public inquiry, and had formed the subject of an elaborate report from the Commission of Patents, in 1844; and, in that instance, neither the climate nor the weather (so different from those on this side of the Atlantic) could be brought to account for the phenomenon. And the renewed appearance, and still more extensive prevalence, of the disease in the country, in 1846, when, as I shall have occasion to show, the season was, in all essential particulars, very different from that of 1845, goes far towards putting an end to the hypothesis on which it has been attempted to account for this extraordinary visitation by reference to the weather. How it is to be accounted for, it is no part of my present plan to examine, or to attempt to explain. I have here only to mention the facts, — that, in August, 1845, public attention was first drawn to the existence of the disease; and that, as the autumn advanced, great and increasing alarm was excited by accounts from all parts of the kingdom, but particularly from Ireland, of the fearful extent to which it was spreading.

The alarm felt at the great, though still partial, failure of the supply of potatoes, was heightened by reports of a deficiency of the wheat crop. And the character of the season, cold from the beginning to its close, dry and harsh in the spring, and wet from the time of blooming to the period of the harvest, could not, in the nature of things, be otherwise than injurious. Nearly all accounts, accordingly, concurred in stating some deficiency as the result of the harvest.

Under the joint influence of the unfavourable weather, of the reports of failure of the potatoes, and of a deficiency of the wheat crop, the weekly average price of wheat rose from 45*s*. in March to 60*s*. 1*d*. in November, being an advance of nearly thirty-five per cent. But this advance was not maintained.

Experience has shown that the crop of 1844, large as the contemporary estimates of its produce were, exceeded the widest computation; and a considerable surplus from it went towards covering the deficiency of that of 1845.

The announcement, early in December, of the intention of the Government to assemble Parliament somewhat earlier than usual for the purpose of considering the Corn Laws with a view to their repeal, combined with the general impression that the stock of corn in the country, together with the foreign supply likely to be admitted, would prove more than sufficient, notwithstanding the partial failure of the potato crop, to supply the average rate of consumption till the next harvest, seems to have induced fanners to thresh out and send their corn freely to market; insomuch that, although no foreign wheat, or none worth mentioning, was entered for home consumption[①], the price fell through the rest of the year; the average in the week ending 27th of December having got down to 55*s*. 4*d*. And, as we are about to see, this fall of price continued through the following six months.

① The total quantity of wheat and flour entered for consumption between the 5th of August, 1845, and the 5th of January following, was 187,348 quarters.

The decline of the price of corn, which took place from November—when the movement for a repeal of the Corn Laws, which led to the act of the following session, was first made in the Cabinet by Sir Robert Peel—forward, through the greater part of the following year, has been used to support, against that minister, the charge of having exaggerated the prospect of scarcity, for the furtherance of a preconceived political purpose. But the charge of exaggeration, in cases like this, in which so much uncertainty necessarily exists, both as to present facts, and as to events contingent on the casualties of the seasons, is easily made. It is hardly possible, when a view must be taken of the future, that there should not prove, by the event, to have been an exaggeration on one side or the other. Under the peculiar circumstances of the disease of the potatoes, and the deficiency of the wheat crop, both in this country and on the Continent of Europe, in the autumn of 1845, I think the only safe course was to contemplate the more adverse contingencies. And if this be admitted, there cannot, I imagine, be a reasonable doubt, that Sir R. Peel was perfectly right in the view which he adopted of the course a government ought to take on such an occasion.

The produce of the wheat harvest of 1845 was undoubtedly deficient, as well in bulk on the ground, as in the ultimate yield, and in quality; and the same cause—the low temperature and wetness of the latter part of the season—appears to have injured, more or less, every other description of corn. The average yield per acre over that portion of England south of York was estimated, at the time, upon tolerably safe data, to fall short of the average of the three previous years by about one-seventh. Over the whole of the United Kingdom it probably ranged nearly at the level of the harvest of 1840. The extent of the deficiency was not, however, fully apparent in the state of the markets during the following year. The harvests of 1842-1843-1844 having each, but especially the last, been unusually large, there would appear to have been, during the three corresponding harvest years, a gradual increase of the stocks on hand; and all attainable evidence favours the belief that at the harvest of 1845 there was a larger quantity of home-grown corn in store in this country than had been so held at the same period of the year, since the harvest of 1835.

It is also to be considered that, partly from the lateness of the harvest, and partly from the damp and defective condition of the grain, the crop of 1845 was not brought into consumption for three or four weeks after the usual period; and also that the harvest of 1846 occurred rather earlier than usual; so that the home supply of 1845 had not, in fact, to meet the demand of an entire year.

On the other hand, the rate of consumption of wheat in the harvest year 1845-1846 was undoubtedly enhanced, as well by the very general prevalence of profitable employment among the labouring classes, as by the failure of the potato crop.

With due allowance for the disturbing causes here indicated, the produce of wheat may be estimated upon the same data as before. The total quantity of wheat returned as sold in the inspected markets in England and Wales, in the fifty-two weeks following the first week in September, 1845, was very nearly 5,700,000 quarters. The quantity of foreign and colonial wheat and flour entered for consumption between the 5th of August, 1845, and the same date in 1846 was 2,732,000 quarters, or only about 250,000 quarters less than was entered in 1841-1842; and the average price of the harvest year was 54*s*. 8*d*.

SECTION 7 *Character of the season of 1845-1846. Prices and estimated produce of wheat*

The weather in October and November, 1845, was mild and seasonable. In December it became very wet, and continued so throughout the month; with much wind, mostly from south-west to north-west. This wet weather continued, with scarcely any cessation, during January and February; and was accompanied with a temperature unusually high for the season. In short, the winter extending from the commencement of December, 1845, to the close of February, 1846, was the mildest which had occurred in this country since that of 1821-1822. ① And the spring months of April and May were of corresponding mildness. A few days in the latter end of April, of cold easterly winds, formed the only exception to the general character of the season worthy of notice.

The extreme mildness of the winter of 1845-1846 is not only remarkable as an extraordinary fact in meteorology, but also as having had an important influence in mitigating the effects of the partial failure of the potato crop, and of the deficiency of the wheat crop. But little consideration is needed to show how great a saving of potatoes and corn is caused by an open, as contrasted with a severe, winter. In the former, cattle, sheep, and pigs, may be kept out and subsisted on green food and turnips so much longer. It

① In both these winters there was no native ice, not, at least, in the southern division of the kingdom. And it was the total absence of a provision of this luxury for the coming spring and summer that led, in the early part of 1822, to the importation of two or three cargoes from Norway. Ice has since become an article of regular import into this country, not only from Norway, but now, in even larger quantity, from Boston in the United States, known as the Wenham Lake ice.

is also to be observed that in the winter of 1845-1846, though potatoes were scarce and dear, turnips, and all other esculents, were abundant, and cheap. Indeed, it was with difficulty that the turnips could be fed off in the course of the spring; and it was said that, in several instances, farmers allowed their neighbours to send in sheep to assist, gratuitously, in feeding off the surplus stocks. The abundance of turnips, and of beetroot, and cabbages, and turnip-tops, also added to the supply of human food, in aid, and to the great saving, of the consumption of bread. It is just that these circumstances should be borne in mind in judging of the conduct of Sir Robert Feel with reference to the food question in the autumn of 1845. He has been charged with having, in November and December, exaggerated the extent of the scarcity. If, however, instead of a remarkably open winter, and a forward spring, the winter had been one of such severity as has sometimes been known, and, as an almost necessary consequence, the spring had been cold and backward, the period would have been one of dearth; and ministers, had they remained passive, would have been fairly blamed by their opponents for not having adopted measures of precaution against so obvious a contingency.

In the two last days of May, and the first three weeks of June, there prevailed the greatest degree and the longest continuance of hot weather that have occurred in the present century at so early a period of the summer.

The latter part of June and the whole of July were variable, and of a lower temperature, but with a full proportion of fair and seasonable weather. There were some very heavy storms of thunder and lightning, hail and rain, in different parts of the country; but these were generally confined within narrow limits.

The wetness of the autumn of 1845, and of January, and a part of February, 1846, had very much interfered with the sowing of wheat; and, so far, rather impaired the prospect of a large crop. But the forwardness, and the genial character of the spring, and the generally favourable appearance of the plant, combined with the prospect of the admission at a low duty of all the corn then in bond, had the effect of depressing the markets as the season advanced. The Corn bill received the Royal Assent on the 26th of June; and immediately on the new duties coming into operation, the whole quantity of foreign and colonial wheat and flour then in bond, amounting to more than 2,000,000 quarters, was entered for home consumption. In the third week of June the weekly average price was 52*s*. 2*d*., and in the week ending the 15th of August it had fallen to 45*s*. 1*d*.

On the 1st of August, 1846, London, and its immediate vicinity, were visited with the most violent and long-continued and destructive storm of hail and rain, of which there is any record. The weather in the remainder of the month was favourable to the ripening and securing of the crops of grain in the southern division of the kingdom. But during the first three weeks of August the weather in Yorkshire and to the northward of that county was wet and close, and there were, in consequence, complaints, in those districts, of the sprouting of the wheats.

Early in August the failure of the potato crop was again apprehended; and as the season advanced the worst apprehensions were more than realised. This circumstance was of itself calculated to enhance the value of wheat. At the same time the results of the corn harvest of 1846 were variously reported.

For the last ten days of August, and through the greater part of

September, the weather was generally fair, and admitted of the crops in the northern districts of the country being secured in good order.

As the autumn advanced the impression that the yield of the wheat harvest was, on the whole, deficient to a considerable extent, became very general. In some districts the produce, per acre, was estimated to be very large, in others it was said to be miserably deficient; and the common average, according to the best estimates, but little exceeded the yield per acre in 1841. The aggregate produce, in bulk, probably fell short of that of the harvest of 1845; but the grain being of a much better quality, it commanded a higher relative price, apart from measurement.

The comparative deficiency of the stock on hand, the prospect of a large extra demand, to supply the deficiency of the potato crop, and the improved quality of the grain, combined to raise the price, till, in the week ending the 7th of November, the weekly average reached 62*s*. 3*d*. But though the failure of the potato crop, to a very great extent, was, by that time, placed beyond doubt, this advance was not quite sustained; and the price declined during the next few weeks, and afterwards ranged at about 60*s*. down to the close of the year: when it was 61*s*. 6*d*.

The state of the markets for grain in the ensuing year leads to the conclusion that the actual deficiency of the supply of wheat in the autumn of 1846 was much greater than was generally supposed at the time. During the first four months following the first week in September, the quantities of home-grown wheat returned as sold, weekly, in the inspected markets in England and Wales, were greater than during any similar period before. Thenceforward, however, they dwindled rapidly; and in the last three months of the harvest year were extremely small. The following comparison of the quantities sold, and the average prices, in each of the four periods, of thirteen weeks each, extending from the 29th of August, 1846, to the 28th of August, 1847, will show how irregularly the home supply was distributed over the whole period.

			Quantity returned as sold in the inspected markets.	Average Prices.	
			qrs.	s.	d.
1st quarter, to	28th Nov. 1846.	–	1,891,561	56	9
2nd quarter, to	27th Feb. 1847.	–	1,618,773	67	10
3rd quarter, to	29th May, 1847.	–	1,258,383	80	6
4th quarter, to	28th Aug. 1847.	–	594,479	79	5

The aggregate quantity thus sold was 5, 363, 000 quarters; and the quantity of foreign and colonial wheatand flour imported between the 5th of August, 1846, and the same period in 1847, was 2,458,000 quarters. The foreign supply of bread-stuffs, however, during this period (particularly in the shape of Indian corn, and the meal of that grain, and of barley and oats) was much greater than might be inferred from this statement. A more particular account will be found in the Appendix.

The average price of the harvest year 1846-1847, computed from the weekly averages, was 68*s*. 9*d*.

The apprehended approach of scarcity in the autumn of 1846, from a cause (the potato failure) common to the United Kingdom and a great part of continental Europe, tended to direct public attention, somewhat more strongly than usual, to the result of the harvest in the neighbouring countries. It soon became apparent that in the central and southern parts of Europe the corn crops were generally deficient; and that they were especially so in France, Holland, and Belgium.[1] In these countries, also, the potato disease was prevalent, though less so than in the preceding year; and thus the demand for grain food was, as in our own case, increased concurrently with a reduced supply. The prices of corn consequently rose, in the continental markets, soon after the conclusion of the harvest, and ranged, during the autumn, higher than in this country.

SECTION 8 *Character of the season of 1846-1847. Prices and estimated produce of wheat*

The weather during October, and nearly the whole of November, 1846, was favourable to farming operations. In the last few days of November, and during the whole of December, it was extremely cold: the winter setting in early, and with much severity.

In January, the temperature became rather higher; and, though there were occasional falls of snow, it did not lie, and the frost was neither severe nor continuous.

From the end of January to the middle of March the cold increased, attaining its greatest intensity in the first fortnight of March; and during this period some heavy falls of snow and severe frosts occurred.

The latter half of March, and the greater part of April, though cold,

---

[1] The deficiency was materially augmented in the centre, west, and south-west of France, in October 1846, by floods, arising from heavy and continuous falls of rain in the upper districts of the country. The inundation seems to have followed, chiefly, the valley of the Loire. That river was said to have risen as much as twenty feet in one night; and the bridge at Orleans, as well as an extensive viaduct, then recently erected between Orleans and Vierzon, were swept away. The total loss sustained by these floods, principally in agricultural produce, was estimated at nearly 4,000,000*l*. sterling.

were fair and seasonable. Down to the 26th of April there was not a single day of such warmth as is sometimes felt even in March; and during the same period there was little or no rain. Thenceforward, till about the middle of May, much rain fell; the temperature continuing low for the season.

In the third week of May, the weather became fair, and improved rapidly; and towards the end of the month the heat was greater than I remember it to have been in any previous year at the same period. The weather was less warm after the first two or three days of June, but continued dry till the 14th of that month. It then became variable; but, on the whole, not unseasonable; and July may be fairly described as a month of fine summer weather, with many bright, and some hot days.

With the exception of a few days of unsettled weather in the last week of July, and the first of the following month, and a diminished temperature, the weather continued to be generally favourable till the end of August; and the crops of corn were secured in good condition, in nearly every part of the southern division of Great Britain.

In September there was rather more wind than usual, and occasionally strong gales; but the weather was generally dry, and, altogether, was favourable to the harvest in the northern division of the island.

The great rise of prices at the commencement of the harvest year 1846-1847 (as marked by the advance of 18*s*. per quarter between the weekly average of the 15th of August, and that of the 7th of November), though caused chiefly by the estimated deficiency of the home supply in proportion to the probable demand, was undoubtedly accelerated by the state of the corn markets on the Continent, and by the indications of approaching scarcity afforded by the acts of the French, Dutch, and Belgian governments. Early in the autumn, the ports of those countries were opened for the importation of all kinds of grain, free of duty. It also became known, about the same time, that the French government had given orders for large purchases of corn abroad. Hence their prices and ours rose nearly on a level.

The upward tendency was checked in France, in November, by a public statement, in a report by the Minister of the Interior, that there was no sufficient ground for the prevailing alarm, and the consequent high prices, and that large supplies by importation would shortly be forthcoming. In this country the progress of the advance was arrested partly by the effect of this announcement on the continental markets, and partly by the accounts received about the same time from the corn exporting countries, and particularly from the United States of America, of enormous supplies being available at the prices then current.

Before the close of the year, however, the deficiency of the wheat crop in the south of Europe, and particularly in the south of France, and, in a still greater degree, of rye, and the spring corn, generally, on the Continent, gave a fresh impulse to the rise of prices there. This renewed rise in the continental markets, combined with the alarming accounts from Ireland, and also from Scotland, of the necessity for large importations of grain and meal to avert impending famine, caused a further advance of the average price in this country; and in the week ending the 1st of April, 1847, it reached 77*s*.; when there was again a pause, and a slight recession during the four following weeks. But about the end of April, the smallness and diminishing amount of the supplies from our own farmers began to excite much attention; and the backwardness of the spring, together with accounts from France and Belgium of a further rise in their markets, such as placed their prices above ours, and the receipt of numerous orders for purchases in this country for shipment to the Continent, combined, with fears of the exhaustion of the home supply, to produce considerable excitement in the corn trade: insomuch that, notwithstanding the extreme pressure on the money market at that time, the weekly average price of wheat rose rapidly till the last week in May; when it reached an average of 102*s*. 5*d*. ①

The more favourable weather of the latter half of May, and the arrival of large foreign supplies, caused a gradual fall of prices from the beginning of June to the middle of July, when the weekly average price of wheat had declined to 74*s*.

The averages rose, a few shillings, under the threatened change of weather at the end of July; but the importations continuing on a scale beyond precedent, and the weather and the growing crops resuming a better appearance, prices again declined.

About the middle of August, favourable accounts being received of the harvest in most parts of the kingdom, and on the Continent, the quantity of corn imported also continuing to be very great, and the reports concerning the potato crop agreeing as to a general and decided diminution of the disease, the fall of prices became more rapid; and on the 18th of September the average had got down to 49*s*. 6*d*. ② It rose in the following week to 53*s*. 6*d*., and has ranged nearly at that level thenceforward to the present time.

---

① During the height of the excitement a sale was made in the Uxbridge market at 124*s*. and, in Mark Lane, one at 115*s*. per quarter.

② The difference between the highest and the lowest weekly average price of the year was 52*s*. 11*d*., and the fall took place in sixteen weeks: the average of the 29th of May having been 102*s*. 5*d*., and that of the 18th of September, as above stated, 49*s*. 6*d*.

The most careful estimates of the wheat crops of 1847 lead to the inference that the yield per acre was somewhat greater than in the two previous years; and was rather over than under an average. In point of bulk and tallness of the straw, and consequent weight of the sheaves, in some considerable districts, it was very remarkable, and, perhaps, never surpassed. Hence the produce in yield of flour was likely to be overrated, for, as usual in such cases, the size of the ears was not equal to what it sometimes is, when the plant is thinner on the ground, and shorter.

The breadth of land sown, particularly with spring corn, under the influence of the high prices prevailing at that season, would appear to have been greater than in any previous year. In Ireland, and in those districts of England and Scotland in which the consequences of the potato failure of the two previous years had been most severely felt, corn was extensively substituted for potatoes.

The quality of the grain has been reported to be generally good, with the exception of that raised in some parts of the south of England, where blight was complained of a week or two before the harvest, and the grain, when cut, appeared thin in the ear, and prematurely ripe.

From the first week in September the weekly returns of the quantities sold in the inspected markets in England and Wales exhibited a gradual increase, as compared with the small supply of home-grown corn brought to market in June, July, and August. The average quantity sold, weekly, in the aggregate, as returned during those three months, was about 45,600 quarters, or considerably less than during any similar period since these returns have been made. In the first week of September the sales amounted to 55,427, and in the fourth, to 96,895 quarters; and the average of four consecutive weeks in October was upwards of 112,000 quarters weekly. In November the average did not exceed 90,000 quarters. Afterwards the importations fell off, and the quantity of home-grown wheat brought to market again increased.

It would appear, from the great reduction of the home supply during the last quarter of the harvest year, that the stocks of wheat in this country were much more nearly exhausted at the period of the last harvest than in any previous year of which we have a record sufficient to afford a comparison; and this inference is confirmed by the opinions most prevalent in the corn market.

It is obvious, however, if only from the experience of the year before, that the extent of the subsequent increase of the weekly sales of home-grown wheat cannot be held to afford any definite indication of the actual results of the last harvest. For though the crop of 1846 was undoubtedly deficient, the quantity of wheat sold in the inspected markets in the first three months after the harvest was much greater than in any similar period before; and, as has been shown, actually comprised more than one-third of all that was so sold during the harvest year.

On the other hand, it is to be observed that the quantities of imported wheat and flour introduced into the home market in the first three months after the harvest were very much larger in 1847 than in 1846[①]; the difference being sufficient, indeed, together with the range of prices, to

① The quantity of foreign and colonial wheat and flour imported at eleven of the principal ports of Great Britain only, according to the weekly returns from the Custom House, during the thirteen weeks ending the 24th of November, 1847, was 1,709,400 quarters. The quantity of home-grown wheat returned as sold in the 290 inspected markets of England and Wales in the thirteen weeks ending the 27th of November was 1,243,700 quarters; and the aggregate average price for the quarter about 53*s*. 8*d*.

afford support to the inference that the home supply has been, in the present year, held back, to some extent, in the expectation that when these large importations should cease, prices would assume a higher level.①

Dec. 6. 1847.

SECTION 9 *On the variation of the supplies of wheat from Ireland*

There was a remarkable deficiency in the quantity of wheat imported into Great Britain from Ireland in 1839, and the three following years, as compared with the years immediately preceding and following these.

Of the precise causes of the deficiency we have no direct evidence. But if the annual official returns, as made up in the ordinary manner, be converted into returns for the harvest years, by adding the importations during the last quarter of each astronomical year to those of the three first quarters of the year following, it becomes apparent that the deficiency has relation to the Irish harvests of the four years from 1839 to 1842 inclusive.

The following were the quantities of wheat, apparently of the produce of each year's harvest, imported from Ireland into Great Britain during the ten years preceding the 5th of October, 1845, with the average prices of the harvest year (computed from the first week in August forward), in England and Wales:—

---

① For further information, down to the close of the year, see the Appendix.

		qrs.	s.	d.			qrs.	s.	d.
1834-1835	–	625,567	41	5	1840-1841	–	192,885	63	6
1835-1836	–	705,593	42	8	1841-1842	–	216,204	63	4
1836-1837	–	457,435	55	0	1842-1843	–	310,344	49	4
1837-1838	–	590,842	57	10	1843-1844	–	467,800	53	9
1838-1839	–	332,270	71	8	1844-1845	–	729,812	46	7
1839-1840	–	174,650	68	0					

The average annual quantity of wheat of Irish growth added to the British supply in the first four years was, therefore, about 594,600 quarters.

In the second period of four years the annual average was reduced to 229,000 qrs.

If the two years, 1836-1837 and 1837-1838, immediately preceding this period of deficiency, be regarded separately, it will be observed that the supply from Ireland and the price in England varied nearly together; and if the comparison be extended to the two years, 1842-1843 and 1843-1844, immediately following that period, it will be seen that there is a similar correspondence: the amount of the supply, and the average price in the market to which it was brought, rising and falling together, with remarkable regularity.

The reduction of the supply, when contrasted with the concurrent high range of prices in England, during the four years intervening (1838-1841), leads irresistibly to the conclusion that the wheat crops of those years were deficient in Ireland as well as in Great Britain; and thence tends to support the inference that the causes of the deficiency are referable to the character of the seasons; which would thus appear to have been similar in their nature, and to have operated with nearly equal effect in both countries.

It will also be observed, that the two years 1835-1836 and 1844-1845 agree in the coincidence of an unusually large supply from Ireland with an unusually low price in this country. Hence it would appear, that in those years, also, the general character of the Irish harvests was nearly the same as that of our own.

Were the common cause of fluctuation, thus apparently in operation simultaneously in both countries, to be found in a variation of the breadth of land sown with wheat, corresponding fluctuations of an opposite character would be observed (or at least might be fairly expected) in the Irish supplies to this country of other descriptions of grain. But an examination of the official returns as to the only other descriptions of grain imported from Ireland during the ten years referred to, in any considerable quantity (oats and barley), affords no confirmation of any such surmise: the supplies of other grain having, in fact, exhibited variations similar to, though within a narrower range than, those already observed as to wheat.

Annual average.	Quantities imported from Ireland into Great Britain.	
	Oats.	Barley.
	Qrs.	Qrs.
In the two years 1837-1838.	1,790,353	181,970
In the four years 1839-1842.	1,417,817	70,868
In the two years 1843-1844.	1,535,933	100,551

It would therefore appear, upon the evidence afforded by these returns, that the wheat crops in Ireland were not only generally as deficient in the four years 1839-1842 as those in this country, but that the deficiency was due to a similar cause: a succession of unfavourable seasons.

SECTION 10 *On the probable future course of the prices of wheat in the United Kingdom*

The future course of prices is dependent on contingencies of such magnitude and uncertainty, that any one, however extensive his experience or means of information, would justly be open to the charge of presumption if he were to offer a confident opinion. Too great allowance can hardly be made for the possible influence of the seasons. The effect of a single season like that of 1816, the inclemency of which extended over nearly the whole of Europe, and rendered the crops of corn of all kinds greatly deficient, and raised the price of wheat both in this country and in the principal consuming countries of the Continent above 100*s*. per quarter, is scarcely susceptible of previous estimate. So also the singular and afflicting visitation of the potato disease (which is obviously a casualty connected with the season, however it may be accounted for) has had the effect of raising the price of wheat nearly as high as it was in 1816-1817. The occurrence of such casualties must necessarily disturb and defeat all attempts at reasoning, with much probability of proving to be right, on the course of future prices. If the potato disease should continue, although in a mitigated form, it will exercise more or less influence on the prices of corn by the extra consumption thus thrown on wheat and other bread-stuffs, and thus counteract, possibly for some time, the tendency to cheapness which may be anticipated from more propitious seasons, combined with the improved and extended cultivation to which recent high prices will have offered an inducement.

If, however, barring the occurrence of such extraordinary visitations as occurred at the close of the last and in the early part of the present century, and in 1816, and more recently in 1846-1847, I were called upon to hazard a conjecture as to the probable range of the prices of wheat, it would be to this effect.

Assuming the weekly averages to be collected as at present, I should expect that the whole fluctuation would range between 60*s*. and 30*s*. per quarter.

My reasons for assuming this as the probable range of fluctuation are: —

1. As regards the maximum.

This is derived from a careful view of the prices of corn, and the circumstances connected with the corn trade, in the interval between 1818 and the close of 1846. Taking into consideration the peculiar operation of the corn laws, which made an advance to 80*s*. till 1828, and to 73*s*. till 1846, the condition of our receiving a foreign supply, in the event of a decided deficiency of the home growth, it appears to be a reasonable conjecture that, but for that peculiar operation, and supposing that the ports had been open for importation at the duty of 1*s*., there was no one occasion on which the price would have risen above 60*s*.

2. As regards the minimum.

In the interval between 1831 and 1836 the crops of corn on the continent of Europe were (with the exception of a deficiency of the rye crops in Russia in 1835) generally abundant, as they also were in this country; and if, under those circumstances, our ports had been open for importation at 1*s*. duty, I think that the price, instead of 36*s*. at which it stood in the last week of December, 1835, and the first week of January, 1836, might have fallen to 30*s*. Lower than that it would hardly have gone. The country being then in a flourishing state, the population fully employed, manufacturing profits unusually large, and the rate of interest low, the probability is that the fall would have been checked by speculative investments; by which I mean that capital from sources extraneous to the corn exchange would have been embarked in it; distinguishing such investments from ordinary speculative purchases on credit, which could only be held till the limits of credit were reached, when sales, made of necessity, would entail a fall greater than the rise which had been caused by the purchases.

The medium or pivot price would thus be 45*s*. At any thing materially below this rate there would be a tendency to accumulate stocks in the hands of farmers, and importers, and speculators; and this accumulation would have a strong tendency to check any considerable advance from deficiency of crops, unless of an extraordinary character.

Taking the question of conjectural price in another point of view, it appears to me that there are the strongest grounds for believing that an average of about 45*s*. may be considered as a rate which will be consistent with keeping up and gradually extending cultivation in the United Kingdom, and at the same time admitting of such an importation of foreign corn as, with our own growth, will fully meet the wants of an increasing population.

There is, however, one other consideration which must not be lost sight of in any view to future prices; and that is the value of gold. I believe that the circumstances operating upon the supply of gold, relatively to the demand for it in the markets of the world, have been for many years past such as to preserve it at a nearly constant value. At least there have been no indications, taking the ordinary tests, of any material variation. But there are in prospect causes which may produce a considerable alteration.

The most important of these is the extraordinary production of gold in Russia. In the Appendix will be found the latest account that I have been able to obtain of the quantity produced in that empire.

If the produce should continue only to be annually what it has been in the last year, and still more if it should increase in any thing like its recent rate of progression, while other sources of supply may be assumed to be not likely to fall off, there can hardly fail to be, ere long, a sensible change in the value of money, properly so termed—though not in the stock-exchange sense of the word.

If the quantity of gold relatively to its uses should increase so as sensibly to affect its value, while the production of silver should be comparatively stationary, the diminished value of gold will be perceived not only in an increased price of corn, and of labour, and of commodities generally, but in an increased price of silver, and our par of exchange will be reduced with foreign countries whose standard is silver. At the same time it is not unreasonable to contemplate the probability, on general grounds, of an increase of the production of silver from the American mines, which might keep pace with the increased produce of gold in Russia. In this case there might be no very perceptible difference in the relative value of the two metals, and our par of exchange with the states of the Continent of Europe would not be sensibly varied.

These are considerations, however, which it is not within the scope of my present purpose to pursue.

PART II

ON THE PRICES OF PRODUCE OTHER THAN CORN

Since the previous volumes of this work were written, much additional attention has been given by mercantile men to its subject; and the result is seen in a diminished tendency to refer general fluctuations of the prices of produce to changes in the amount of the circulation, or in the rate of interest. The large class of circumstances affecting prices, apart from the state of the circulating medium, and arising from variations of the relation of supply to demand, are now commonly and justly regarded as of primary importance. But the errors which it has been the principal purpose of this work to expose, are still entertained by a large part of the mercantile community, as portions of a once generally prevalent theory of the currency; and have, therefore, still sufficient importance to warrant a careful consideration of them in a history of prices during the eight years extending from the close of 1839 to that of 1847.

It need scarcely be remarked that the period referred to is one of considerable interest. Besides the abolition of the law limiting the importation of foreign corn, which belongs to the preceding part, and the repeal or reduction of the duties levied on the importation of most articles of foreign produce entering largely either into the food of the people or the materials of our principal manufactures, changes have taken place in the monetary and commercial affairs of the country, of a character perhaps more important in reference to the investigation of the laws governing the relation of the currency to prices, than are embraced in any similar period since 1819; previous to which period the connection of the currency with prices was complicated by reference to the supposed influence of the war, and the Bank restriction. How these changes bear upon the subject will become apparent as I proceed.

SECTION 1 *On the concurrent variations of prices, the circulation, and the rate of interest, from the close of 1839 to the autumn of 1844*

Notwithstanding the extreme depression which had marked the closing months of 1839, the year 1840 opened with some slight symptoms of returning prosperity.

On the 10th of January the Bank of England reduced its rate of discount from 6 to 5 per cent.

This expansion of the currency, as it was called, gave a temporary animation to the markets for manufactures and other produce, under the influence of the common opinion of the connection of the money market with the prices of commodities. But it turned out, as usual, that there was no ground for that opinion; and as the spring advanced the aspect of affairs was materially altered.

The high prices of food, of nearly every description in ordinary use, but particularly of bread, meat, sugar, and tea, already limited very considerably the demand for manufactured goods in the home market; and as the year advanced, the additional exports to the countries whence we had recently drawn supplies of grain were found quite insufficient to fill up the vacuum thus created.

Early in the summer the prospect of hostilities with the United States, and, somewhat later, the threatening aspect of our relations with France, tended strongly to increase the prevailing disposition of mercantile men to contract their engagements. This disposition was probably further increased by the circumstance that on the 15th of October the Bank of England, not finding the reflux of bullion to be so great as had been expected, reduced the date of bills admissible for discount from ninety-five to sixty-five days. And a review of the year at its close exhibits, on the whole, throughout its course, a decided increase of the depression observed during the two previous years.

With the exception of the speculation in tea, noticed in the last volume, which began in 1839, and may be said to have reached its climax about the middle of January, 1840, and an enormous increase in the price of sugar available for consumption in this country, resulting from the failure of the supply from the West Indies, the markets for produce were dull, and prices, generally, declining, under a diminished demand, during the whole year.

The circulation of the Bank of England was lower in 1840 than it had been for some years before. The amount scarcely exceeded 18,000,000*l*. even for a single week after the payment of the dividends in January and July; and the general average of the year was not more than 16,800,000*l*., or about half a million less than that of 1839, and fully two millions less than that of 1838.

If we compare the prices of the principal articles of produce other than corn in 1840, with the prices of 1838, we find a considerable diversity of movement; but no part of it is explicable by reference to any supposed influence of the currency. Some articles of importance, as hemp, tea, coffee, sugar, and rum, had risen in price, and others, as cotton and indigo, had fallen; while timber, tallow, raw silk, and wool, were nearly the same as in 1838. To explain these changes by reference to corresponding changes in the amount of the circulating medium would be impossible, for according to the Currency theory, seeing that the circulation had been reduced, prices should have fallen, while, if there be a preponderance, it is decidedly in favour of higher prices. But a reference to each article in the relation of supply and demand will account for them at once.

1841.—In the first months of 1841, as in the preceding year, there was a somewhat general feeling of hope prevalent that a revival of trade was about to take place. The raw materials of our manufactures, generally, were observed to be low in price; the manufacturers on the continent were known to be even more depressed, and more crippled in their resources, therefore less capable of meeting efficiently any revival of the usual demand in markets open to both, than our own; and the demand for manufactured produce, both at home and abroad, had been so long below an average level, that its increase, at no distant period, was deemed almost certain. Commercial credit had everywhere been brought within narrow limits; and there seemed to be no longer any sufficient ground for the prevailing want of confidence in the results of commercial transactions conducted with ordinary prudence.

On the 3rd of January, 1841, the Bank of England withdrew the restriction imposed in October, 1840, upon bills admissible for discount, and restored the term to ninety-five days.

The quarterly accounts of the Bank, made up to the end of January, exhibited a remarkable coincidence with those of the previous year at the same period; but they were in so far improved that, in the interval, the debt to the bankers of Paris had been liquidated.

The stock of corn in the country at this period was considered to be much larger than it had been in January, 1840.

The receipt, in April, of news of Captain Elliott's preliminary arrangement with the Chinese authorities at Canton, promising a speedy and satisfactory conclusion of hostilities, with the consequent fall in the price of tea; and a fall, nearly simultaneous, of some 20 per cent in the prices of sugar and coffee; together with the pacific tone of the inaugural address of General Harrison, and its repetition, soon afterwards, by Mr. Tyler, were all circumstances calculated to encourage hopes of the approach of an improved state of things.

But as the summer advanced it became evident that the continued high price of corn and cattle, together with the general scarcity of employment for the labouring population, precluded any material improvement for the present; and the reports from the manufacturing districts grew gradually more gloomy than ever. Towards the close of the summer, it was ascertained that the consumption of raw materials in our principal manufactures was proceeding at a rate considerably lower even than that of the previous year.

During the latter half of 1841 the general depression rather increased than diminished; and at its close, though the pressure upon commerce had not then reached its maximum, the distress experienced by almost every class of producers, and more particularly by the operatives in the manufacturing districts, was probably greater than at any other period, as being yet wholly unrelieved by any definite prospect of improvement.

The circulation of the Bank of England was, on an average, rather higher in 1841 than in 1840; being about 17,000,000*l*.

The Bank rate of interest, for discounts and advances, was kept, throughout the year, at 5 per cent; and the market rate for the best bills ranged from $4\frac{1}{4}$ upwards to that point.

The markets for produce presented, all through the year, a dull uniformity of appearance: want of confidence in the future, even for a few months, preventing all speculation, and prices, generally, tending downwards, under the influence of a still further reduced demand for nearly every article of common use.

1842.—The most remarkable circumstance to be observed in the first months of 1842 was a strong tendency to a further reduction of the rate of interest. In January the brokers' rate of discount, for unexceptionable bills, was about $4\frac{1}{2}$ per cent; and in March it had fallen to $3\frac{1}{2}$. The Bank of England, by the usual notice in February, offered advances at 4 per cent; and early in April this rate was extended to discounts.

During the first months of the year several important branches of our foreign trade were held in suspense by the uncertainty attending the fate of the tariff proposed by Sir R. Peel at the opening of the session.

Towards the close of the spring some signs of returning prosperity became distinctly visible. It was evident that commercial operations were again being extended—slowly, and for some time with but little effect on the apparent condition of the community—but the movement was observable in several directions; and especially in a gradually increasing demand for capital. And when, as the summer advanced, it became generally known that the harvest was likely to prove better than any that had been gathered in this country for several years, the improvement was perceptibly though slightly accelerated.

As the result of the harvest became more certain corn fell considerably in price; and large orders begin to come in to the manufacturing districts.

The supply of floating capital became at this unusually large. For a week or two in August the best bills were readily discounted at $2\frac{1}{4}$ per cent. And there was a general feeling of confidence in an approaching termination of the period of general depression.

This confidence was checked and diminished for a time by the disturbances in the manufacturing districts, which, beginning in the midland counties in June, had spread, before the first week in August, to Lancashire, Yorkshire, and the west of Scotland. But these were not of long continuance, and were suppressed with little if any violence. And when tranquillity was restored in the disturbed districts, the work-people, — their means being entirely exhausted by want of employment, and the long previous high prices of food, and other necessaries, — readily met the renewed offers of employment which the manufacturers, finding their stocks materially reduced by the increasing demand and the long cessation from work, were enabled to offer.

These circumstances, if taken in combination with the assurance of abundant grain crops, the news of the Chinese Treaty, the settlement of the corn laws and the tariff, and a great fall in the prices of cattle, may be regarded as having opened, in the last quarter of 1842, the prospect of revived prosperity which was realised in the spring of the following year.

Excepting a few weeks at the end of 1842, the markets for produce other than corn may be said to have retained, during the whole of the year, the quiet and drooping character observed in those of the previous year. The only striking exception was seen in the article of indigo, the price of which, in consequence of reports from India of a deficient crop, rose considerably during the autumn.

The market rate of discount for unexceptionable bills fell, steadily, with the exception of the temporary decline in August, already mentioned, from $4\frac{1}{2}$ per cent in January, to about $2\frac{1}{2}$ per cent in December; and during the same period the interest charged upon the periodical advances of the Bank was reduced from 5 to $3\frac{1}{2}$ per cent.

The note circulation of the Bank of England, for the year, averaged about 19,000,000*l*., or fully two millions higher than in the previous year. But, what is, perhaps, more important with reference to the present subject, it was increased to a greater extent, and more rapidly, during a few months of this year, than in any similar period before. The average circulation, taken upon a period of four weeks in January, was, in round numbers, about 16,000,000*l*.: in November it had attained an average level scarcely short of 20,000,000*l*.

It is particularly remarkable, in reference to so sudden and large an increase in the amount of Bank of England notes in circulation, that a comparison of the prices of all the more important articles of produce in January, with the prices in November, shows only two, worthy of notice, which had risen in price in the interval. Excepting indigo and cochineal (the latter an article of comparatively small value), the prices of produce, home and foreign, were lower, and in most cases considerably so, in November, 1842, when the circulation had for four or five months averaged 20,000,000*l*., than in the preceding January, when it was, and for some months had been, scarcely over 16,000,000*l*. And the exceptions, though too trifling, under any circumstances, to afford material support to the currency theory, are at once explained by the anticipation, in both cases realised, of a diminished supply, concurrently with an increased demand, in the following year.

1843. — The hopes of renewed prosperity commonly indulged during the last months of 1842 having, as is usual in such cases, been pitched rather too high, were followed by some degree of disappointment—not so much at any reversal of, or even check to, the progress of the improvement, as with its slow advance, as experienced in the first months of 1843. The prices of food, and the current rates of discount, were lower, and the foreign exchanges were higher, than they had been for several years; and there was no ground for reasonable doubt of the continuance of these favourable circumstances; but as the demand upon the manufacturing districts for the home market did not meet the expectations entertained at the close of the previous year, there was, in January and February, a very general disposition to despond; and the prices of manufactured goods, which had in most cases slightly risen, again declined.

In March, however, matters assumed a better aspect, particularly in the manufacturing towns of Lancashire and Cheshire. Thenceforward the improvement was steady and constant; and though still slow, was sufficiently perceptible to inspire very general confidence in its continuance. In April it was agreed that the Manchester trade was in a better condition than it had been in for some years before. It was observed, too, that good bills, of the scarcity of which brokers had hitherto complained, now became much more numerous. About the opening of the summer quarter, money, which at the beginning of the year had been but little in demand for commercial purposes at 2 per cent, was taken up rather freely; and a slight advance was even made in the current rate of discount.

Early in May the revival of business had extended from the cotton to the woollen trade; and before the end of the summer the hardware manufactories and potteries of Warwickshire and Staffordshire were again in motion, and sharing the general increase of employment.

And here it is worthy of observation, that as commercial confidence rose, and the number and extent of the daily transactions involving the payment of money increased, the amount of Bank of England notes in circulation was not increased, but diminished. In the week ending the 4th of February the amount was 21,344,000*l.*; and in the corresponding week in August, only 20,247,000*l.* Similarly, in the fourth week after the dividend day in April it was 20,294,000*l.*; and in the corresponding week at the end of October, only 19,563,000*l.*

In July 1842 the decline of prices, generally, as caused by the absence of a demand equal to the supply, or any immediate prospect of it, may be said to have reached nearly its lowest point. It has been observed that at the same period a large increase was taking place in the amount of bank notes in circulation. This increase continued with little variation till the complete restoration of confidence, in the spring of 1843; and for the year ending July 1843, the amount of Bank of England notes in circulation ranged at an average level between three and four millions above the average of the three years extending from July 1839 to July 1842. During nearly the whole of the three years last mentioned, the current rate of discount on unexceptionable bills varied from $4\frac{1}{2}$ to 6 per cent[①]; while, in the year ending July,

① The current rate of discount for unexceptionable bills did not fall so low as four per cent till about the end of February, 1842.

1843, it scarcely exceeded 2 per cent.

An entire year of increased circulation, increased so rapidly, and to such an extent, following three years during which it had been so much reduced, and accompanied by so great a fall in the current rate of interest, might, if either the amount of the circulation, or the rate of interest, or both, exercised on prices any such influence as is often ascribed to them, be reasonably expected to have exhibited some signs of this influence in July 1843. But no such signs are apparent.

It has already been stated that the general tendency of prices down to near the close of 1842 was a declining one. And if the price-currents of July 1843 be compared with those of the same period in 1842, it will be observed that, with few exceptions, and those of little importance, prices were even lower in July 1843 than they had been a year before.

From the summer of 1843, forward, the general aspect of commercial affairs was one of decided prosperity.

And now, before proceeding further, it may be useful to revert to the most prominent of the apparent causes of the change observed to have taken place at this period, as well on account of the interest attaching to all such changes in this country, as in relation to the bearing this change in particular may be fairly supposed to have had upon the course of prices, and the state of the circulating medium, in succeeding years.

The long duration of the season of depression and want of confidence which set in in 1839 had, in 1842, prepared all parties to expect a change for the better immediately on the occurrence of favourable circumstances. And in the year last mentioned events concurred, in a manner somewhat remarkable, first to encourage, and afterwards to aid in realising, the hopes which were thus indulged.

The most important of these events, as affecting the range of prices, not only of food, but of most articles of general consumption, was, undoubtedly, the abundant harvest of 1842, which was anticipated early in the summer, and got in about a fortnight earlier than usual. The home supply of corn was also aided in its effect upon prices, as has been stated in the previous part, by a large foreign supply.

Nearly simultaneously, and producing effects of a similar character, came the general fall in the prices of cattle. This was widely attributed at the time to apprehensions, entertained in the home market, of the probable effect of the removal of the prohibition of, and the levying of a moderate duty on, the importation of foreign cattle, by the Tariff of 1842. Fears of this kind no doubt existed, and must have had some effect; but the true cause of the great reduction in the prices of cattle in 1842 was of a much more substantial description—there was a very considerable increase of the home supply. In that year, the disease which had prevailed among cattle in this country, during the three or four previous years, gradually and completely ceased. In September 1843 the stock of sheep in Great Britain was stated, and generally believed, to be unusually large; and that of horned cattle and pigs to exceed, materially, the average of past years; and all were declared, in the agricultural reports of the time, to be, with few exceptions, in remarkably good condition.

Nor were bread and meat the only articles of food of which this year brought renewed abundance: the supplies of tea, coffee, and sugar were also very much increased; and the prices reduced in proportion.

And when it is added that the supplies of nearly all the more important of the raw materials of our principal manufactures, as cotton, flax, hemp, timber, tallow, and iron, were larger in 1842, and their prices lower, than they had been for several years immediately preceding, and it is remembered that the satisfactory settlement of the Chinese war opened to us, in the last quarter of 1842, the double prospect of an addition to the revenue①, and of new and extensive markets for the sale of our staple products, the rapid revival of the home trade during the eight or nine months following will appear anything but inexplicable.

The equally rapid reduction of the rate of interest from $4\frac{1}{2}$ per cent in the spring of 1842, to barely 2 per cent in the spring and summer of 1843, appears to be sufficiently explained by the accumulation of surplus capital necessarily accompanying the scarcity of profitable employment for it in previous years, by the release of hoards, and by the revival of confidence in commercial prospects, as the return of comparative prosperity became evident.

The average amount of Bank of England notes in circulation in 1843 was about 19,500,000*l*.; the highest (monthly) average occurring in January, when it was 21,100,000*l*., and the lowest in June, when it was 18,400,000*l*. The average amount of Bank notes in circulation in the United Kingdom, for the year, was about 35,700,000*l*. (or about 1,000,000*l*. higher than in 1842); and its highest and lowest points also occurred, respectively, in January and June; being 36,900,000*l*. in the former, and 33,400,000*l*. in the latter month.

1844.—Excepting the dullness usually attending the close of the year, the general increase of profitable employment for labour and capital, the increase of the revenue, and the improvement of the condition of the

① By the 21,000,000 of dollars stipulated to be paid by the Chinese within the three years following August 1842.

people, which marked the summer and autumn of the year 1843, were continued with out abatement thenceforward, and during the whole of the following year.

In the first months of 1844 the prices of the raw materials of our chief manufactures were in most instances lower, and in the rest quite as low, as they had been at the same season for many years before. There was a brisk and increasing demand for manufactured produce, at home and abroad; and the prevalence of full employment in every branch of industry, with moderate prices for all the principal articles of food, increased very considerably the demand for consumable commodities of every description. Abroad, the trade opened with the four new Chinese ports, the renewal of commercial intercourse with the United States upon a sounder basis of credit, and an increase of British exports to Brazil, in view of the expiration of our commercial treaty with that country in November, together with the improved state of our commerce with the continental countries of Europe, (resulting from their having experienced a renewal of internal prosperity in many respects similar to, and nearly simultaneous with, our own,) produced a rapid and steady growth of every branch of the export trade.

The only movement observable in the markets for produce during the earlier months of the year was a tendency to advance in the prices of those articles the consumption of which had been materially augmented in the latter months of 1843. The renewed activity of our manufacturers, and the consequent increase of the amount of capital currently devoted to the payment of wages, and thence conveyed through the hands of the retail dealers in payment for increased supplies of food, clothing, household furniture, &c., the demand for which had been reduced much below the ordinary level during the previous years of depression, may be distinguished as the most general of the causes of this movement. The consequent rise of prices in this direction, however, was but slight, and was anything but universal.

It was in the markets for colonial produce, where, in the first months of 1844, deficiency of supply, actual or prospective, combined, in several prominent instances, with the increasing demand, to cause an advance, that the upward tendency of prices was most remarkable, and attracted most attention.

The brokers' circulars of the period contained, as of course, the usual references to the increased amount of the circulation; but the accompanying statements of the altered relation of supply to demand afforded, in almost every instance, a much more ready and simple, and undoubtedly a much more correct explanation of the phenomena adverted to.

With a single exception, that of the China trade, there was no appearance of speculation in the markets for produce in 1844. Nor was the exception referred to palpable at the time, otherwise than as a disposition to rely somewhat confidently upon an immediate extension of the China trade greater than, to the few persons in this country well informed as to the probabilities of the subject, seemed likely. So little to the purpose, however, was really known in the commercial world, with any degree of certainty, that those who embarked at once and largely in the export trade to the new ports, could scarcely have been said to hope too much, until the experience and better information of the two following years proved that they had done so. This exception should therefore, perhaps, be referred to rather as an illustration of the prevailing soundness and legitimacy of the commercial transactions of the period, than as indicating anything of a contrary character.

In the condition of the people, notwithstanding a degree of improvement in the mass which made itself palpable through every medium of observation and inquiry available to the public, there was still, even at the close of 1844, a melancholy and painful exception presented by the state of the labourers in the agricultural districts. This was of course attributed to the abatement of protective duties on agricultural produce in 1842; and more particularly to the low range of the prices of corn during the two following years. But it may be much more clearly traced, in the first instance, to the accumulating results of the interruption of the customary migration from the agricultural to the manufacturing districts, during the long and severe depression of the latter; and secondly, though in a much less degree, to the disheartening effect upon the agricultural mind, of the prophecies of ruin uttered by the advocates of protection, confirmed, as to persons of limited observation these apparently had been, by the fall in the prices of both corn and cattle immediately after the session of 1842.

It is now abundantly obvious, as well from the Annual Reports of the Poor Law Commissioners, as from other and not less trustworthy sources of information, that while the manufacturing districts were being again (in 1843-1844) brought into a busy and prosperous condition, the purely agricultural parts of the country were still burdened with the population raised to supply the usual stream of migration to the Towns, and not drawn off during the three or four previous years.

The low prices of agricultural produce were, as has been shown, caused entirely by its comparative abundance in the home market. And as neither the system nor the extent of cultivation were materially altered, and the improved state of trade had certainly enlarged the general demand for food, it is clear that if employment was more scarce than usual for farm labourers, its scarcity must have arisen from an increase in their numbers;

and that if their wages were insufficient to procure the ordinary means of subsistence, the prices of food being lower, there must have been a reduction in the rate of wages. That their numbers had increased in every agricultural locality, there are good reasons for believing; and that the low prices of produce may have induced many farmers, pressed by high money rents, to pay to those they selected from the crowd competing for employment lower wages than usual, is more than probable. But of the assertion, common at the time, that the distress prevalent in the agricultural districts in 1844 was caused by the reduced prices of corn and cattle, there is really no evidence whatever.

The complaints of want of employment for agricultural labourers would probably have been even louder and more frequent, as they would undoubtedly have been longer continued, than they were, had not a new demand for field labour gradually arisen during the summer and autumn of 1844, from the construction of new railways, consequent upon the speculations of that year. This additional demand does not seem to have had much effect upon the purely agricultural districts, whence, chiefly, the complaints were heard, until the beginning of 1845; but after that period these districts appear to have shared completely the renewed activity previously displayed elsewhere.

With some exceptions, already referred to, and of minor importance in a general review of the principal markets for produce, prices were in most instances even lower at the end of the first six or eight months of 1844, than at its commencement: the supply of the more important articles of consumption being found to be very generally beyond the demand; although the latter had materially increased.

In the last three or four months of the year a tendency to higher prices was observable in several directions; but was, in each, readily traceable either to a rapid consumption having much reduced the stocks on hand, or to the prospect of a diminished supply in the year ensuing. In short, the relation of supply and demand, actual or anticipated, affords, at this as at former periods, an ample explanation of all changes in the market prices.

Of the supposed influence of an expanded, currency in raising prices, there was at this time certainly no trace whatever. On the contrary, it would be difficult to conceive an array of facts better calculated to disprove the existence of any such influence, than that presented by a statement of the prices of produce, of the amount of the Bank note circulation, and of the rate of interest, concurrently, either in 1844 in particular, or during the five years I have now passed in review; or even during any one or two of these years, in the course of which any material change took place, either in the circulation or the rate of interest, or in the general level of prices. Indeed, to any one regarding the facts by themselves, and altogether independently of any preconceived theory—and not indisposed to deduce a general conclusion of so much importance from a range of observation so limited as that presented by a period of five years —the facts would rather suggest the converse of the currency theory, exhibiting, as they almost invariably do, prices rising coincidently with the reduction of the circulation, and as regularly falling when its amount is increased.

By way of placing in the clearest light the results of a comparison of the prices and the circulation of the period referred to, and more particularly of the earlier and the later parts of it, it may be useful to present somewhat more in detail the condition of each in 1841 and in 1844.

The average amount of Bank of England notes in circulation in 1841 was about 17,000,000*l*. ; and the average amount of the bank note circulation of the United Kingdom in the same year was probably about 35,800,000*l*. ① In 1844 these average amounts were increased respectively to rather more than 21,000,000*l*. in the one case, and 38,800,000*l*. in the other.

The Bank rate of interest in 1841 was 5 per cent; and in 1844 it varied from 4 down to $2\frac{1}{2}$ per cent.

The market rate of interest, on discount of unexceptionable bills, ranged in 1841 from 5 to $4\frac{1}{2}$ per cent, and in 1844 from $1\frac{3}{4}$ to $2\frac{1}{2}$ per cent.

The following were the prices of the principal articles of produce, other than corn, in July and November in each year.

		1841.		1844.	
Prices in		July.	November.	July.	November.
Ashes, Canadina pearl	– *cwt.*	28*s*. @ 29*s*. 6*d*.	32*s*. 6*d*. @ 33*s*.	27*s*. @ 30*s*.	26*s*. @ 26*s*. 6*d*.
Coffee, St. Domingo, in bond	*cwt.*	42*s*. 6*d*. @ 45*s*.	40*s*. @ 40*s*. 6*d*.	31*s*. @ 34*s*.	26*s*. @ 34*s*.
— B. P. –	– *cwt.*	62*s*. @ 128*s*.	62*s*. @ 147*s*.	34*s*. @ 156*s*.	18*s*. @ 132*s*.
Cochineal – – –	– *lb.*	3*s*. 10*d*. @ 6*s*. 3*d*.	3*s*. 9*d*. @ 6*s*. 3*d*.	4*s*. 4d@ 6*s*. 3*d*.	4*s*. 1*d*. @ 5*s*. 9*d*.
Copper, British, in cakes	– *ton.*	98*l*.	98*l*. @ 99*l*.	84*l*. 10*s*. @ 85*l*.	84*l*.
Cotton wool, bowed Georgia	– *lb.*	$6\frac{1}{2}d.$ @ $7\frac{5}{6}d.$	5*d*. @ $6\frac{1}{2}d.$	5*d*. @ 6*d*.	$3\frac{1}{2}d.$ @ $5\frac{1}{4}d.$
— East India	– *lb.*	$4\frac{1}{2}d.$ @ $5\frac{5}{8}d.$	$3\frac{3}{4}d.$ @ $5\frac{1}{6}d.$	3*d*. @ $4\frac{1}{2}d.$	$2\frac{1}{2}d.$ @ $4\frac{3}{8}d.$
Hemp, St. Petersburg, clean	– *ton.*	38*l*. 10*s*. @ 39*l*.	36*l*.	33*l*.	27*l*.
Lead, British, in pigs –	– *ton.*	20*l*. 5*s*.	20*l*. 5*s*.	17*l*.	16*l*. 10*s*.
Indigo, East India – –	– *lb.*	2*s*. @ 8*s*. 6*d*.	1*s*. 6*d*. @ 8*s*.	2*s*. 7*d*. @ 6*s*.	2*s*. 4*d*. @ 5*s*. 10*d*.
Iron, British, bars –	– *ton.*	7*l*. @ 7*l*. 5*s*.	6*l*. 15*s*.	6*l*. @ 6*l*. 5*s*.	5*l*. 15*s*. @ 6*l*.
Iron, Swedish, in bond	– *ton.*	14*l*. 5*s*. @ 14*l*. 10*s*.	11*l*. 15*s*. @ 12*l*. 5*s*.	9*l*. 5*s*. @ 9*l*. 10*s*.	9*l*. 10*s*. @ 9*l*. 15*s*.
Oil, Southern fishery –	– *ton.*	26*l*. @ 29*l*.	32*l*. @ 36*l*. 5*s*.	31*l*. 10*s*. @ 32*l*.	27*l*. 10*s*. @ 33*l*.
Butter, Waterford –	– *cwt.*	4*l*. 10*s*. @ 4*l*. 16*s*.	4*l*. 12*s*. @ 4*l*. 15*s*.	2*l*. 16*s*. @ 83*l*. 10*s*.	3*l*. 18*s*. @ 4*l*. 6*s*.
Beef, prime mess –	– *tierce*	6*l*. 12*s*. 6*d*.	6*l*. 2*s*. 6*d*.	5*l*.	4*l*. 15*s*.
Saltpetre, rough, in bond	– *cwt.*	27*s*. @ 29*s*. 6*d*.	26*s*. @ 28*s*. 6*d*.	23*s*. 6*d*. @ 27*s*. 6*d*.	23*s*. @ 27*s*.

① This is the average of the last six months of the year; the returns not extending to an earlier period. See Appendix.

Continued

		1841.		1844.	
Silk, East India, raw –	– *lb.*	10*s.* 6*d.* @ 19*s.*	9*s.* @ 21*s.*	9*s.* 6*d.* @ 20*s.*	8*s* 6*d.* @ 20*s.*
— Italian, raw – –	– *lb.*	18*s.* @ 33*s.*	13*s.* 6*d.* @ 26*s.*	15*s.* @ 28*s.*	15*s.* @ 26*s.*
Cinnamon, Ceylon, Ist quality	*lb.*	6*s.* 4*d.* @ 7*s.* 9*d.*	6*s.* 4*d.* @ 7*s.* 1*d.*	4*s.* 5*d.* @ 6*s.* 7*d.*	3*s.* 8*d.* @ 5*s.* 5*d.*
Pepper, black – –	– *lb.*	$3\frac{1}{2}$*d.* @ $4\frac{1}{4}$*d.*	$3\frac{1}{2}$*d.* @ $4\frac{1}{2}$*d.*	$3\frac{1}{4}$*d.* @ 4*d.*	3*d.* @ 4*d.*
Rum, Jamaica – –	– *gall.*	4*s.* 11*d.* @ 5*s.*	4*s.* @ 4*s.* 2*d.*	2*s.* 6*d.* @ 2*s.* 9*d.*	2*s.* 9*d.* @ 2*s.* 10*d.*
Sugar, Muscovado, in bond	*cwt.*	44*s.* $10\frac{1}{2}$*d.*	34*s.* $4\frac{1}{2}$*d.*	34*s.* 10*d.*	31*s.* $0\frac{3}{4}$*d.*
— Havanna. white –	– *cwt.*	30*s.* @ 33*s.*	24*s.* @ 33*s.*	25*s.* @ 32*s.*	25*s.* @ 32*s.*
Tallow, Russian candle	– *cwt.*	48*s.*	49*s.*	42*s.* 6*d.*	43*s.*
Tar, Stockholm –	– *barrel*	22*s.* 6*d.*	18*s.* 6*d.*	11*s.* 9*d.*	15*s.* 6*d.* @ 16*s.*
Tea. Congou – – –	– *lb.*	1*s.* 8*d.* @ 2*s.* 7*d.*	1*s.* 10*d.* @ 3*s.* 2*d.*	1*s.* @ 2*s.* 5*d.*	$10\frac{1}{4}$*d.* @ 2*s.* 6*d.*
Tin, Engligh, in bars –	– *cwt.*	4*l.* 4*s.* 6*d.*	4*l.*	3*l.* 14*s.*	3*l.* 13*s.*
Tobacco, Virginia, inbond	– *lb.*	$3\frac{3}{4}$*d.* @ $7\frac{1}{2}$*d.*	$3\frac{1}{2}$*d.* @ $6\frac{1}{2}$*d.*	2*d.* @ 5*d.*	2*d.* @ 5*d.*
Wool, sheep's, Sp., Leonesa	– *lb.*	2*s.* 1*d.* @ 2*s.* 6*d.*	2*s.* @ 2*s.* 6*d.*	2*s.* @ 2*s.* 6*d.*	1*s.* 9*d.* @ 1*s.* 11*d.*
Logwood, Jamica –	– *ton*	6*l.* 10*s.*	5*l.* 5*s.*	5*l.* 5*s.*	1*s.* 9*d.* @ 1*s.* 11*d.* 5*l.*

The change which had taken place in the state of the money market during the three years separating the points of comparison in the foregoing table, may be more completely illustrated by the difference in the prices of Consols, Bank Stock, and other securities, in the state of the foreign exchanges, and in the amount of bullion held by the Bank of England.

	In the third week of Nov. 1841.	In the third week of Nov. 1844.
Price of consols – – – – – – – –	89	100
— Bank stock – – – – – – –	163	206
Exchequer bills – – – – – –	$2\frac{1}{2}$*d.* per diem	$1\frac{1}{2}$*d.* per diem
Railway shares. —Great Western £ 100 Shares.	12*s.* pm.	60*s.* pm.
London and Birmingham –	£ 65 pd. 77	£ 75 pd. 139
	£ 90 pd. 155	Stk. 219
Exchange on paris, short. for bills and money –	25. 45	25. 65
— on Amsterdam – – – – – –	12. 2	12. 3
Bullion in the Bank of England – – – –	£ 4,700,000.	£ 14,300,000.
Bank of England notes in circulation – – –	£ 16,300,000.	£ 21,000,000.

Thus, when the amount of bank notes in circulation had been reduced to the narrowest limits, when the exchanges were low, and the bullion in the Bank at a minimum, and when credit was most restricted, and the rate of interest unusually high, prices, which, by the currency theory, should have been forced down, were, generally, higher than ordinary. And when the former conditions were all, without exception, reversed—when the bank note circulation had been increased by the addition of more than one third to its previous amount[①], when the exchanges were high, and rising, the bullion in the Bank greater in amount than it had been for many years, and still increasing, when credit was almost unlimited, and the market rate of interest had for two years barely exceeded 2 per cent per annum, or less than half its previous amount, prices, instead of being higher, were, with hardly a solitary exception, considerably lower than at the former period.

No amount or ingenuity of comment could add to the force of the argument against the supposed influence of the amount of the bank note circulation, or of the rate of interest, upon prices, conveyed by a simple statement of these facts.

---

① The actual difference between the amount of Bank of England notes in circulation in 1841 and in 1844, was, in fact, greater than that shown by the returns, by nearly 700,000*l*. Between the 4th of March, 1843, and the 5th of January, 1844, the Directors of the Bank excluded from the returns of its circulation notes to the amount of 507,279*l*. 19s. 2d., on the ground that they had been outstanding more than thirty years, and were therefore supposed to be lost; and a further sum of 188,299*l*. was, during the same period, similarly excluded, on the ground that the notes composing it had been outstanding more than fifteen years, and were therefore considered to be out of circulation. The total sum thus excluded (695,578*l*.) must therefore be added to the apparent, in order to exhibit the actual difference between the amount of the circulation as it was before and after the period within which, as above stated, the exclusion occurred. To make the preceding comparison in the text accord strictly with the facts, the circulation of November, 1841, should be stated at 15,600,000*l*.

SECTION 2 *On the same phenomena, from the autumn of 1844 to the close of 1847*

On the 2nd of September 1844 the Bank Act of that year came into operation. The reasons offered for imposing the peculiar restrictions embodied in this measure will be considered in the next part. It need be noticed here only with reference to one of its most obvious practical effects, as seen in the subsequent operations of the Bank.

It was a favourite boast of the advocates of this measure, frequently reiterated at the period of its discussion in parliament, and which at the time made no slight impression upon the public mind, that its immediate result would be to deprive the Bank at once of the power and the responsibility of "regulating the currency." The issue of notes being placed under the new restrictions, the Bank was to be placed, with reference to all its other business, in a position as free as that of any other banking company: the only responsibility of the Directors, thenceforward, being to the proprietors of bank stock; and their only duty "to make as much as they could" of the capital at their command.

That the Directors were prepared to carry out the spirit of the Act by the line of conduct so authoritatively pointed out to them, became apparent very soon after the Act came into operation. A few days afterwards (on the 5th of September) they issued a notice offering to discount bills of the highest class not having more than ninety-five days to run, at $2\frac{1}{2}$ per cent, and notes at 3 per cent.

In March 1845 the rate was announced to be $2\frac{1}{2}$ per cent for both bills and notes: a rate lower than they had ever before adopted.

At the same time (March 1845) another change was made, small in itself, but highly significant of the altered position of the Bank under the Act of 1844. The rate of interest announced was declared to be a *minimum* rate; and this form of notice has been adhered to ever since.

The importance of these steps in the reduction of the rate of interest, and of the subsequent conduct of the Bank in the same direction, with reference to the state of the circulation during the following years, will be abundantly manifest as we proceed.

When the Act of 1844 came into operation the market rate of discount for commercial bills of the highest character was about $2\frac{1}{2}$ per cent; but it then exhibited a tendency to rise. The Bank, therefore, under the notice of the 5th of September, came into open competition with the large bill-brokers; and the immediate effects were, first, a decided check to the increase of the market rate of interest, already begun, and, secondly, a considerable addition to the amount of private securities in the banking department.

One of the most important circumstances bearing upon the state of the money market at this period was the commencement of that disposition to speculate in the construction of new railways which was carried so far in the following year. Early in 1844, when the restored prosperity of trade was no longer doubtful, and the rate of interest had for about a year and a half, been under 3 per cent, the attention of the public was strongly attracted to the favourable results of the investments made in the principal lines of railway then in operation. That the system might be extended with equal profit seemed highly probable, particularly when regard was had to the unusually low prices of iron, and other needful materials, and when it was also considered that the experience gained in the construction of the existing lines had suggested improvements likely to reduce, considerably, for the future, the outlay in the first instance. Accordingly, during the spring and summer of that year, while the shares in most of the old lines rose considerably in value, many new companies were projected. In September 1844 prospectuses of more than ninety new schemes were before the public, avowedly requiring for their completion an aggregate amount of capital not much short of 100,000,000*l*. sterling; and the number continued to increase down to the end of the year.

1845.—In the last months of 1844, and for some time afterwards, frequent complaints were heard of losses incurred upon importations from abroad. The commodities imported in that and the previous year, in exchange for the increased quantity of goods exported, were found, with one or two exceptions (among which were timber and sheep's wool), so far to exceed the demand for them, home and foreign, that in very many instances the prices obtainable not only left no profit to, but entailed a loss upon, the importer; and hence, notwithstanding an increased rate of consumption, prices at the opening of 1845 ranged, generally, quite as low as, or even lower than, at the beginning of the previous year.

Early in the spring the commencement of several new lines of railway, in different parts of the country, gave additional employment to the class of agricultural labourers; and thus silenced the last complaints of want of work resulting from the past season of depression.

When Parliament met, the petitions for the requisite powers for the proposed new railways served to give further publicity to the schemes themselves. The uncertainty attending the passage of the bills through the ordeal of legislative discussion, while it strongly excited the hopes and fears of those immediately concerned, seemed also to impart a new charm to the speculation itself. The number of speculators increased rapidly; and as the demand for shares thus increased, the number of new lines projected kept pace with it, till, as the summer advanced, nearly every part of the country was intersected with imaginary lines, and almost every person who had either capital or credit engaged in the purchase and sale of railway shares.

In August, after the fate of the bills before Parliament had been decided for the session, the speculation assumed all the apparent characteristics of a mania. Symptoms of an approaching revulsion were, however, then clearly discernible. It was remarked by the least observant, that the lapse of a few months had introduced among the speculators a great number of persons who acted without reference to any hope of profit on the completion of the undertakings in question, or, indeed, to anything whatever but the speculative opinions concerning them most current, for the moment, in the share market. Thus shares were commonly, indeed almost invariably, bought, not for permanent investment, but with a view to a speedy sale at an inordinate profit. And there is reason to believe that almost the only real buyers of shares after the middle of August, and during the few weeks in which the speculation rose to its climax, were persons of limited means, and of still more limited information on the subject, who were tempted to speculate by instances of enormous gain apparently realised by the fortunate adventurers who had been earlier in the field.

From this point forward the speculation degenerated, as might be expected, into a variety of the worst species of gambling. As long as the class of persons last referred to continued to come forward, the prices of shares continued to rise; and if we may rely, with any degree of confidence, upon numerous subsequent revelations, the inflated condition of the share market was at this time very extensively sustained by the report of transactions either entirely fictitious, or designed only to deceive ignorant and unwary speculators.

During the first six months of 1845 every item in the accounts of the Bank of England had presented a remarkably regular and satisfactory appearance. The bullion increased steadily from 14,800,000*l*. in the first week of January, to 16,600,000*l*. in the last week of June; while the circulation, with the exception of the usual expansion after the payment of the dividends, varied but little from an average level of about 21,000,000*l*. And the Bank note circulation of the United Kingdom was similarly undisturbed.

The Bank rate of interest remained at $2\frac{1}{2}$ per cent, and that current in the market, for first class bills, was nearly the same, being occasionally a trifle lower.

About the middle of September there was a perceptible, though slight, rise in the current rate of interest, and it continued till about the middle of October; when the rate of discount for first class bills ranged from $3\frac{1}{4}$ to $3\frac{3}{4}$ per cent. On the 16th of October the Bank rate was advanced to 3 per cent.

The general increase of the rate of interest at this time was attributed, and not without apparent reason, partly to the arrangements in progress for providing the large amount (about 14,600,000*l*.) required to be deposited with the agents of the Government in London, Edinburgh, and Dublin, on behalf of the subscribers to the numerous railway schemes about to be submitted to Parliament, and partly to the first pressure of the additional calls made on account of the lines which had been sanctioned in the previous session.

The rise went on till, in November, the current rate was $4\frac{1}{2}$ per cent. On the 6th of that month the Bank rate was raised to $3\frac{1}{2}$ per cent.

But the crisis of the railway fever had already come.

The first increase of the Bank rate of interest in October, though it left the rate still somewhat below the general level of the market, excited much attention, and some uneasiness. Before the end of October an anxious desire to realise at the high prices then current, manifested itself among the shareholders in railways to an extent that was termed a panic. Prices declined; great numbers of persons who had bought only in the expectation of a still further rise, and who had no guide in their speculation but the share lists of the day, hastened to sell; and the decline increased in rapidity, till, in less than a fortnight, the prices of shares in most of the lines, old and new, were reduced below the level at which they had stood two or three months before; and the share markets established in every large town in the kingdom, which had for several months been filled with crowds of eager speculators, were almost entirely deserted.

It was at this period, when public confidence in the permanence of the value of railway shares was shaken and declining, and speculation had ceased, that the circulation of the Bank of England, and that of the Country Banks, reached respectively their highest points during the year.

The markets for produce in 1845 did not share, in the slightest degree, the speculative spirit so prominently displayed in the markets for railway shares, and also, though in a minor degree, in some other and similar fields of enterprize. The price of iron, indeed, and of some other articles of less general importance, required in railway construction, rose steadily, and somewhat rapidly, from the autumn of 1844, when the ascertained and probable demand began to exceed materially the means of supply at the command of the producers, till the summer of the following year, when, under the stimulus (continued during some six months) of high priccs, and a very large prospective demand, the means of supply had been very much extended. In September 1844, the current price of British bar iron was 5*l*. 5*s*. to 5*l*. 10*s*. per ton; and the price had not varied materially from this level during the two years previous. In March 1845 the price had risen to 10*l*. 10*s*. per ton. At this point it remained for a few months, and then declined, ranging during the remainder of the year at from 8*l*, to 9*l*. , per ton. There was also a slight general tendency, during the latter half of 1845, to an advance of the prices of some of the raw materials of our manufactures the consumption of which had most rapidly increased, and also in the prices of some of the principal articles of colonial produce, more particularly sugar and coffee, the quantities of which entered for consumption in 1845 greatly exceeded those of any former year. The price of tea would doubtless have been similarly affected had not the importations been enormously increased by the inability of our merchants to obtain any other eligible return for the additional quantity of British goods recently exported to and sold in China, or had the home demand not been checked by a high duty.

The Bank note circulation reached in November 1845 the highest weekly average amount it attained during the eight years under review. The markets for produce, generally, at this period, exhibit, however, nearly as many instances of the fall as of the rise of prices; and in every instance of movement, in either direction, the amount of the stocks on hand, the prospects of their renewal, and the extent of the current demand, will be found to afford, when taken together, a complete explanation of the changes observed.

1846.—The increased price of the most necessary articles of food during the autumn and winter of 1845-1846, and the uncertainty prevalent as to the adequacy of the supply of corn in the country to meet the additional demand thrown upon it by the failure of the potato crop, checked, for a time, the demand for articles of secondary necessity. The markets for produce were, during the winter and spring, remarkably quiet: buyers and sellers being alike unwilling to act upon the future, and prices varying but slightly, and only in accordance with immediate and tolerably well founded anticipations.

The terms of the advances by the Bank remained unaltered (the minimum rate of interest being $3\frac{1}{2}$ per cent), while the rate current out of doors continued to advance, till about the end of February 1846, when the process of collecting and paying in the deposits on account of projected railways was completed, and when the current rate reached 5 per cent.

From June till November 1845, the exchanges with the continent were gradually and on the whole considerably depressed; and the bullion in the Bank fell during the same period from 16,500,000*l.* to 13,000,000*l.* But during the four months extending from the beginning of November 1845 to the beginning of March 1846, the exchanges were rising; while the amount of bullion in the Bank slowly increased; and the circulation, allowing for periodical variations, was steadily falling.

After March 1846, the current rate of interest for first class bills declined gradually, till in September it scarcely exceeded the Bank rate of 3 per cent. At the same time the bullion was increasing rather rapidly (reaching 16,200,000*l.* in the first week of September); while the circulation preserved, with but little variation, the lower level it had fallen to early in the year.

The following figures show the amount of the circulation and the bullion, in the fourth week after each dividend day, from the summer of 1845 to that of 1846.

		Circulation (including Post Bills).	Bullion.
1845. Week ending	Aug. 9th.	£ 22,500,000	£ 15,600,000
	Nov. 15th.	22,500,000	13,500,000
1846.	Feb. 7th.	21,300,000	13,300,000
	May 9th.	21,300,000	13,800,000
	Aug. 8th.	21,200,000	15,900,000

The progressive decline of the rate of interest, between the spring and autumn of 1846, from 5 to 3 per cent, with the accompanying, though comparatively slight, diminution of the amount of Bank notes in circulation, seems, however, to have had no more effect upon prices than similar changes are observed to have had before.

The markets for produce, generally, during the spring and summer of 1846, were in a remarkably quiet and uniform condition, the consumption of nearly all articles of common use being fully sustained at the high level reached in the previous year.

In the autumn of 1846 circumstances arose which in a few weeks materially changed the aspect of commercial affairs at home and abroad.

The almost total failure of the potato crop, the deficiency of the grain crop on the Continent, the comparatively small stocks of grain in this country, and the rapid rate at which the consumption had been proceeding for more than a year, combined to render it extremely probable that a large foreign outlay would be necessary to secure an adequate supply of food during the coming year.

The uneasiness created in the public mind by the anticipation of such an outlay, and its probable consequences, had a depressing effect upon the markets for produce during the last two or three months of the year.

From the middle of September to about the first week in November the exchanges were depressed, and the bullion in the Bank fell from 16,200,000*l*. to 14,700,000*l*. The exchanges then became more favourable, and the stock of bullion increased, though not more than is usual during the last few weeks of the year. The change, however, served to allay the uneasy feeling with which the public had begun to regard the previous drain; and, as the demand in the home market for articles of general consumption was found not to be nearly so much affected as the high prices of food had led importers and producers to expect, the markets assumed a more animated appearance as the opening of the new year approached.

The prospective scarcity of cotton led, in December, 1846, to some considerable purchases being made on speculation; but an advance of price commensurate with the estimated deficiency of the supply having been established, and the rate of consumption proportionately checked, the movement quietly subsided. One or two other articles of importance, as tallow and hemp, of which the supply, already short, was deemed likely to fall much below the current demand in the ensuing year, also rose considerably in price during the last months of the year; but in no instance did the advance exhibit any symptoms of what is usually termed speculation. In every instance it was gradual; and in most it was amply justified by the event.

1847. —In January 1847 a variety of circumstances combined to induce a pressure upon the money market. Railway calls upon British lines, and on foreign lines, shares in which were extensively held in this country, were becoming immediately due to an amount estimated, in the aggregate, at not less than 6,000,000*l*. The exchanges with the continent, and especially with Russia, again showed a decidedly adverse tendency. Difficulties which had for some time previously beset the Bank of France had now come to a crisis; and the measures found requisite to sustain the credit of that establishment began to operate upon this country. And at the same time the prospect of still higher prices for corn, and of very large importations before the next harvest, with the ascertained deficiency of the supply of cotton, and the expectation, at this time becoming general, that the drain of floating capital for railway construction would eventually prove too heavy for the diminished resources of the country, tended strongly to produce among the mercantile classes a vague feeling of apprehension.

On the 14th of January the minimum rate for discounts at the Bank was raised from 3 to $3\frac{1}{2}$ per cent, and on the 21st to 4 per cent. The rapid diminution of the bullion, and the higher rate of interest current out of doors, afforded an abundant explanation of these steps; yet they excited considerable alarm.

The bullion, which at the end of January had fallen to 12,900,000*l*., continued slowly to decrease, chiefly by exportation to France and the United States, during February and the first three weeks of March. Thenceforward the drain proceeded more rapidly till the week ending the

24th of April, when the bullion in the two departments had fallen to 9,200,000*l.*: showing a loss of nearly six millions in four months.①

Between the 2nd of January and the 24th of April, the reserve in the banking department was reduced from 8,920,000*l.* against liabilities to the amount of 18,795,000*l.* to 3,383,000*l.* against liabilities exceeding 12,600,000*l.*

The market rate of interest continued to advance. On the 8th of April the minimum rate at the Bank was raised to 5 per cent; and during the latter period of the drain the terms of the advances and discounts were gradually restricted, till in the third week of April it was understood that only bills of the

---

① Here it may be useful to advert to certain financial operations on the part of the Russian government, which had the effect of relieving, in some degree, the monetary pressure prevailing in this country, and in France, in the spring of 1847.

The only securities of a nature readily available, held by the Bank of France pending the embarrassment of that establishment in the last months of 1846, consisted of 3 percent. rentes to the amount of 50,000,000 of francs. These were not sold, the influence of the government having, it is supposed, been used to avert the sale, as likely to affect injuriously the terms of a public loan then in contemplation. Early in March, an offer was received by the Bank of France from the Russian government, to purchase the whole of these securities. A conference took place between the Russian Chargé d'Affaires, the minister of France, and the Conseil Général, and a transfer was accordingly made, on the 11th of that month, at the price then current. At this time, a loan of a million sterling granted by the Bank of England to the Bank of France in January, still remained due; and the credit thus raised at St. Petersburgh in favour of the latter (upwards of 1,500,000*l.*) became conveniently available for meeting heavy drafts from the north of Europe upon France and England, for corn supplied to both, as well as for large supplies to the latter, at unusually high prices, of hemp, flax, and tallow, the stocks of which articles in this country were much reduced at the end of 1846.

The operation above described would appear, however, to have been only a part of one much more extensive, and having for its object the substitution of interest-bearing securities for a portion of the large stock of bullion held in reserve against the government paper money of Russia. About the end of April, there was received in this country a copy of an imperial ukase (dated 31st March 1847) by which it was dcereed that of the 114,000,000 of silver rubles then forming "the bullion capital of the department of credit billets,"— "a sum should be set apart to the extent of 30,000,000 of silver rubles for the gradual purchase of public securities, Russian and foreign, at home and abroad."

first class, due in May and June, were discountable at so low a rate as $5\frac{1}{2}$ per cent; those running into July being charged 6 per cent, and many being altogether rejected: the Directors having determined that only a limited amount should be discounted, however unexceptionable the bills, and however high the credit of the party offering them. This last circumstance—the entire rejection of bills without reference to their character—it was, which brought on the extreme severity of the pressure in April.

During the first four months of the year the markets for produce (excepting the districts of the cotton manufacture, in which business was checked by the high price of the raw material) were, generally, in an active and prosperous condition, the demand for home consumption being, throughout, well maintained.

The pressure upon the money market in the spring of 1847 may be said to have attained its greatest severity in the last week of April. At this time the effect of the violent contraction of its advances by the Bank was seen in the stoppage of the transmission of bullion to America. A considerable amount in gold, which was on the point of being shipped (and even some that had been actually placed on board) was withdrawn, and applied to the making of payments in this country.

In the following week, however, it was observed that the bullion in the Bank was increasing; and it was understood that the Directors were affording increased accommodation—making advances on Stock and Exchequer Bills, and discounting bills not having more than ninety-five days to run, at 5 and $5\frac{1}{2}$ per cent.

Thenceforward, during May, the pressure gradually abated; and at the end of that month the bullion had risen to 10, 100, 000*l*., while the circulation, which at the end of April had been 20,600,000*l*., had fallen to 19,400,000*l*.

On the 7th of May the Chancellor of the Exchequer announced that the rate of interest on the Exchequer Bills falling due on the 21st (amounting to 9,000,000*l*.) would be raised from 2*d*. to 3*d*. per diem, and that a discount of 5 per cent would be allowed upon so much of the remaining instalments of the Irish loan (of 8,000,000*l*. contracted for at the beginning of the year) as should be paid up before the period stipulated. During the greater part of the month of May the discounts and advances of the Bank were made freely at rates varying from 5 to 5 $\frac{1}{2}$ per cent; but the rate current out of doors, which had been since January higher than that charged by the Bank, ranged, for short bills of the highest character, at about 6 per cent. On the 4th of June the Chancellor of the Exchequer announced that payments on account of the Irish loan had been made in anticipation to the extent, in the aggregate, of 2,678,000*l*. Thenceforward the rate of interest declined; and the money market remained in a comparatively quiet condition; the Bank extending its advances as usual before the dividend day in July, and discounting short bills freely at 5 per cent.

Early in July the exportation of bullion to America was renewed; and about the same time a considerable fall took place in the exchanges with the continent; and the repayment of the advances made by the Bank during the previous six weeks having increased the demand for accommodation, the rate of interest again rose, and continued to rise, though slowly, during the remainder of the month.

The accounts of the Bank for the week ending the 31st of July showed a diminution of the bullion, during the four weeks preceding, of about a million: and on Monday the 2nd of August it was resolved, at an extraordinary meeting of the Directors, that only bills having less than one month to run should be discounted at 5 per cent, those having not more than two months to run at $5\frac{1}{2}$, and all of longer date (not exceeding ninety-five days) at a minimum rate of 6 per cent. On the following Thursday the minimum rate was raised to $5\frac{1}{2}$ per cent.

At the beginning of August, though the drain to America continued, the exchanges with the continent were, and had been for a week or two, improving; and during the three following weeks the bullion remained very nearly stationary at 9,200,000*l*.; that being also about the lowest amount it had fallen to in April.

The market rate of interest continued to range, with little variation, about one per cent higher than the minimum rate at the Bank.

Before the end of August the high rate of interest was very severely felt by all whose current business required the aid of credit; and as it became evident that no relief was to be expected even from the assurance of an abundant harvest, complaints became general as to the large amount of capital being sunk in the construction of new railways; and various propositions were made and discussed for reducing the demand in this direction; but without any practical result.

The markets for produce remained undisturbed from the beginning of the year down to the month of September: the demand for home consumption continuing rather active than otherwise, and the deficiency of the foreign demand in Europe for articles of export from this country being largely made up by increased orders from America and the Mediterranean.

Besides the commercial failures which took place during August in connection with the sudden fall in the price of corn, and which are adverted to in the previous chapter, several other large failures occurred early in September, among which were those of Gower, Nephews and Co., and Reid, Irving and Co.; and before the end of the month, five or six other firms of scarcely inferior magnitude, besides many houses of less importance, in London and the country, were added to the list.

On the 2nd of September the minimum rate of interest at the Bank had been reduced, preparatory to the usual advances at this period, from $5\frac{1}{2}$ to 5 per cent; and in the following week the circulation was at the lowest point it reached during the year, viz. 18,600,000*l.*; the bullion being 8,900,000*l.*

In the second week of September affairs in the money market assumed an appearance of much doubt and alarm; and the failures before mentioned were followed by others, in rapid succession, down to the end of November.

And here, after nearly twelve months of monetary pressure, gradually increasing during the greater part of the time, and at the commencement of some six weeks of the utmost discredit and distrust, with the circulation lower in amount than it had been at any time since the summer of 1842, and a rate of interest current higher than had prevailed at any former period within the eight years now under review, it may be worth while, once more, to refer somewhat particularly to the state of prices. The following table contains the prices, in London, of all the most, important articles of produce in the second week of September 1847, and also at the same period in each of the two years immediately preceding. With the apponded statement of the concurrent variations of the Bank of England circulation, and the rate of interest, it may be left to speak for itself.

		1845. September.	1846. September.	1847. September.
Ashes, Canadian, pearl –	*cwt.*	24*s.* @ 24*s.* 6*d.*	25*s.* @ 25*s.* 6*d.*	37*s.* @ 38*s.*
Timber, fir, Dantzic and Memel	*load.*	3*l.* 17*s.* @ 4*l.* 10*s.*	4*l.* @ 4*l.* 10*s.*	4*l.* @ 4*l.* 10*s.*
— Queber yellow pine	*load.*	3*l.* 10*s.* @ 4*l.*	3*l.* 10*s.* @ 4*l.*	3*l.* 10*s.* @ 4*l.*
Hemp, St. Petersburg, clean	*ton.*	27*l.* @ 27*l.* 5*s.*	30*l.* @ 30*l.* 10*s.*	38*l.*
Flax, Riga, P. T. R. – –	*ton.*	46*l.* @ 51*l.*	46*l.* @ 52*l.*	46*l.* 54*l.*
Tar, Stockholm – –	*barrel.*	15*s.* 6*d.*	16*s.* @ 16*s.* 6*d.*	17*s.* 3*d.* @ 17*s.* 6*d.*
Tallow, St. Petersburg, New Y. C. – – – –	*cwt.*	41*s.* @ 41*s.* 6*d.*	42*s.* 3*d.* @ 42*s.* 6*d.*	46*s.* 6*d.* @ 46*s.* 9*d.*
Iron, British, bars – –	*ton.*	8*l.* 5*s.*	9*l.* 10*s.* @ 9*l.* 12*s.* 6*d*	9*l.* 15*s.*
— Swedish, in bond – –	*ton.*	10*l.* 10*s.* @ 11*l.*	11*l.* @ 11*l.* 10*s.*	11*l.* 5*s.* @ 11*l.* 10*s.*
Copper, in tongh cake –	*ton.*	88*l.* 10*s.*	88*l.* 10*s.*	98*l.*
Lead, British, in pigs – –	*ton.*	19*l* 5*s.* @ 19*l.* 10*s.*	18*l.* 10*s.* @ 18*l.* 15*s.*	18*l.* 15*s.*
Tin, English, bars – –	*ton.*	91*l.* 10*s.*	93*l.* 10*s.*	86*l.* 10*s.*
Cotton, bowed Georgia – –	*lb.*	$3\frac{2}{4}$*d.* @ 5*d.*	4*d.* @ $5\frac{1}{2}$*d.*	6*d.* @ $7\frac{3}{8}$*d.*
— Surat – – – –	*lb.*	$2\frac{5}{8}$*d.* @ $3\frac{3}{4}$*d.*	$2\frac{7}{8}$*d.* @ $3\frac{7}{8}$*d.*	$4\frac{3}{8}$*d.* @ $5\frac{3}{8}$*d.*
Woll, English. fleeces – –	*lb.*	12*s.* 10*d.* @ 17*s.*	11*s.* 10*d.* @ 15*s.* 10*d.*	10*s.* @ 13*s.* 10*d.*
— Spanish, Leonesa –	*lb.*	2*s.* @ 2*s.* 3*d.*	1*s.* 8*d.* @ 2*s.*	1*s.* 8*d.* @ 2*s.*
Silk, East India – – – –	*lb.*	9*s.* @ 19*s.*	8*s.* @ 17*s.*	6*s.* 6*s.* @ 15*s.*
— Italian – – – –	*lb.*	21*s.* @ 30*s.*	18*s.* @ 26*s.* 6*d.*	16*s.* @ 22*s.*
Coffee, St. Domingo – –	*cwt.*	31*s.* @ 35*s.*	28*s.* @ 32*s.*	28*s.* @ 32*s.* 6*d.*
— Jamaica – – –	*cwt.*	30*s.* @ 136*s.*	28*s.* @ 115*s.*	25*s.* @ 128*s.*
Tea, Cougon – – – –	*lb.*	9*d.* @ 2*s.* 6*d.*	$8\frac{1}{2}$*d.* @ 2*s.*	$9\frac{1}{2}$*d.* @ 2*s.*
Tobacco, Virginia, in bond –	*lb.*	$2\frac{1}{4}$*d.* @ $5\frac{1}{2}$*d.*	$2\frac{1}{4}$*d.* $5\frac{1}{2}$*d.*	$2\frac{1}{4}$*d.* @ $5\frac{1}{2}$*d.*
Indigo, East India – – –	*lb.*	1*s.* 10*d.* @ 5*s.* 9*d.*	1*s.* 6*d.* @ 6*s.*	1*s.* 8*d.* @ $6\frac{1}{2}$d.
Cochineal – – – –	*lb.*	5*s.* @ 6*s.* 7*d.*	4*s.* 11*d.* @ 6*s.* 9*d.*	4*s.* 9*d.* @ 7*s.*
Logwood, Jamaica – –	*ton.*	4*l.* 5*s.* @ 5*l.* 7*s.*	4*l.* 5*s.* @ 4*l.* 10*s.*	4*l.* 5*s.* @ 4*l.* 5*s.*
Saltpetre, East India – –	*cwt.*	23*s.* 6*d.* @ 27*s.* 6*d.*	23*s.* 6*d.* @ 27*s.* 6*d.*	27*s.* 6*d.* @ 30*s.*
Sugar, Mnsov, average –	*cwt.*	35*s.* 1*d.*	32*s.* 5*d.*	26*s.* $4\frac{1}{2}$*d.*
Rum, Jamaiea – – –	*gall.*	3*s.* @ 3*s.* 2*d.*	2*s.* 11*d.* @ 3*s.* 2*d.*	3*s.* 4*d.* @ 3*s.* 10*d.*
Beef, Amcrican and Canadian	*tierce.*	68*s.* @ 77*s.*	78*s.* @ 105*s.*	95*s.* @ 102*s.* 6*d.*
Butter, Cork – – –	*cwt.*	80*s.* @ 82*s.*	92*s.* @ 96*s.*	92*s.* @ 96*s.*
Bank of England.—Circulation.		£ 21,719,484.	£ 21,465,605.	£ 18,655,017.
Bullion.		£ 15,426,858.	£ 16,273,827.	£ 8,915,072.
Market rate of interest on first class bills.		$2\frac{1}{4}$ to 3 per cent.	3 to $3\frac{1}{2}$ per cent.	6 to 7 per cent.

From the second week of September, to near the close of November, the ordinary course of commercial transactions in this country was so much deranged by the violent contraction of credit, that the state of prices during that period cannot be regarded as otherwise than exceptional.

If the price-currents of November be compared with those of June or July, it will be observed that the price of nearly every article of any importance had fallen in the interval, though in various degrees. If particular attention be given to the instances in which the fall was greatest, it will be observed that they are all comprised in one or both of two classes: that they were either articles, the prices of which had been declining for some timc previously, from an excess of supply, as compared with the current demand (and therefore could not but continue to fall, when the general demand was still farther diminished), or such as, having been largely held upon credit, were forced upon the market, in considerable quantities, under the monetary pressure. The instances of lower prices not obviously comprised in either of these classes are less remarkable; and they are clearly traceable either to a corresponding change in the relation of supply to demand, or to the necessity to raise money by extraordinary methods for immediate purposes which has lately been felt by wholesale dealers of every denomination.

But, however the general reduction of prices during the period in question was actually brought about, it is abundantly evident that it cannot be attributed, in any degree, to a diminution of the amount of bank notes in circulation: for this amount was considerably greater in October and November, than in July and August. If the average amount of the notes of the Bank of England, or of all the banks of issue in the United Kingdom, in the hands of the public in any given number of weeks following the dividend day in July, be compared with the average in a similar period after the dividend day in October, it will be seen that the latter was, by much, the higher of the two. ①If the range of prices were dependent upon the amount of the Bank note circulation, thc former should have been higher, not lower, in November than in July; whereas the fact is to the contrary.

6th Dec. 1847.

① The average amount of Bank of England notes in circulation in the six weeks ending the 14th of August 1847 was 19, 600, 000*l*. ; and in the six weeks ending the 20th of November it was 20,900,000*l*. There was a corresponding variation in the aggregate Bank note circulation of the United Kingdom; which, in the month ending the 14th of August, amounted to 34,500,000*l*. , and in that ending the 6th of November, to 36,700,000*l*.

PART III

A GENERAL REVIEW OF THE CURRENCY QUESTION IN ITS VARIOUS PHASES FROM 1797 TO THE CLOSE OF 1809

INTRODUCTION

There cannot be a stronger proof of the difficulties which surround the subject of the currency, than that which is afforded by the present state of the controversy relating to it. After all the discussion the topic has undergone during the half century which has elapsed since the suspension of cash payments, it presents, apparently, as wide a field as ever of debateable ground. There are still the following vexed questions—the meaning of the words "money" "currency" "depreciation" "excessive issues" the test or standard by which excess and depreciation are to be determined and measured; the power of over-issue of a note circulation by the country banks and the Bank of England; and the causes which influence the foreign exchange, — or, in other words, whether an adverse balance of foreign payments has its origin in, and is indicative of, a redundancy of the currency, or is to be accounted for on mercantile grounds, irrespective of the amount of the circulation, and, mutatis mutandis, of the opposite state of things. On all these points, and some minor ones, there exists still as wide a difference of opinion as prevailed in the earlier discussions on the subject. Of those discussions, and of the circumstances which gave rise to them, an account has been given in the former volumes of this work; but a brief recapitulation of some of the principal points raised by them will be found to be desirable, as being calculated to throw light upon the present state of the controversy; and, indeed is, in some degree requisite, for reasons which I shall have occasion to advert to presently.

Previously to the suspension of cash payments, by the Bank of England in 1797, questions of money and currency, in their more general bearings, had been very little a subject of public interest or discussion. On the occasion of the great recoinage of silver, in 1696, there was an animated controversy between Mr. Locke and Mr. Lowndes as to what should be the denomination and standard, when Mr. Locke's opinion in favour of the maintenance of the standard at its full weight of metal, according to the Mint regulations then existing, prevailed, and was acted upon. For some years afterwards, difficulties arose in adjusting the relative value of the gold coins to the silver; and Sir Isaac Newton, the master of the Mint, made an elaborate report, according to which the value of the guinea was finally fixed at 21 shillings, or as 1 to 15. 07. In the middle of last century, Hume's Essays on Money and Trade were published; and being written with all the charms of his popular style, and presenting, as they did, new and philosophic views of the nature and functions of money and paper credit, they attracted attention at the time, and have ever since been occasionally referred to, as authority, on some of the topics discussed in them. But the opinions expressed in them are for the most part crude, and the conclusions are in many instances very loosely drawn. Sir James Stewart's treatise on Political Economy, published in 1767, contained a great deal of miscellaneous information relating to the circulation of coin and paper, both in this country and abroad; but it disclosed no general views of the principles upon which variation in their value depended.

It was reserved for Dr. Adam Smith to lay down and explain, in an admirably lucid style, the fundamental principles by which the value of coins and paper credit is determined, and ought to be regulated. The doctrines on the subject developed in the great work entitled "the Wealth of Nations" were at once received, and formed the established creed, leaving little room for dissent or discussion, till the great disturbing causes towards the close of last century came into operation. Under the pressure of those disturbing causes, (which have been detailed in the first volume of this work,) the Bank of England was compelled to suspend its payments in cash, and the controversy arose which with few intervals has continued to the present time.

CHAPTER I
THE PERIOD FROM 1797 TO 1819

SECTION 1 *On the progress of the discussion from 1797 to 1809*

It is a prevalent opinion among those who have of late years taken part in the currency controversy, that little of public notice or attention was directed to the state of the circulation from the date of the Bank restriction till the occurrence of the circumstances that gave rise to the appointment of the Bullion Committee in 1810.① The impression to this effect is, however, hardly correct.

The fact of the suspension of cash payments in 1797, and the restriction bill then brought in, naturally gave rise to animated debates in parliament, and to a host of pamphlets. When, however, it was found, not only that no depreciation had taken place as an immediate consequence of that measure, but that the exchanges were more in favour of this country than they had been at any former period of the century, and that the Bank was in a condition, if required or allowed, to resume its payments in cash,

① Sir R. Peel, in his elaborate speech of the 6th of May 1844, on the occasion of introducing the Bank bill of that year, observed, that "from 1797 to 1810, public attention was not much directed to this important subject."

little or no further attention was directed to the subject.

On the occurrence of a combination of circumstances at the close of 1799, which I have in a former volume described, and which had the effect of producing a sudden and great fall in the exchanges, and a low range of them for two years, the attention of the public was again strongly drawn to questions on the state of the currency. Mr. Boyd, at the close of 1800, published a letter addressed by him to Mr. Pitt, ascribing the whole of the fall in the exchanges, and the rise in the price of provisions, to excessive issues of Bank of England notes. This publication excited considerable notice, and gave occasion to a great deal of discussion. It drew forth answers, among others, from Sir Francis Baring, and Mr. Henry Thornton. The treatise by the latter, entitled "An Inquiry into the Nature and Effects of the Paper Credit of Great Britain," is in every way a remarkable work. It was the subject of an article by the late Mr. Horner, in the Edinburgh Review for October 1802; and the tribute therein paid to the great merit of Mr. Thornton's tract, and the prefatory remarks by which the notice of it is introduced, have so direct a bearing upon the present discussion, that I am induced to insert the following extracts.

"The progress of commercial philosophy has been much accelerated by the writings of practical men of business. In that, as well as in the other departments of civil knowledge, it is only from the actual course of affairs that the statesman can derive his maxims of policy, or the speculative enquirer deduce the conclusions of his science; but the habits of both are incompatible with a personal knowledge of detail. It is necessary that the labour of accumulating particular facts should be separated from the more liberal task of generalising these into principles; and that they who are qualified to combine larger views should be furnished by the minute accuracy of others, with descriptions in which they may confide. In England, which is the native country of political economy, works contributed by professional men form a large deposit of authenticated facts. For these we are primarily indebted to that diffused literature which multiplies the demand for varied information, and has already liberalized the practitioners in almost every work of industry. But the greater number of these publications have been suggested by such occasional events in the fluctuation of our commercial prosperity, as rouse a general interest and direct the curiosity of the public to that quarter of the great machine in which the derangement is supposed to have taken place. It is in this manner that every period of dearth has contributed, in some degree, to alleviate subsequent years of scarcity by the instruction which it yielded against popular prejudice. More numerous tracts, in which alone the detailed history of our foreign commerce can be traced, at least during its earlier progress, appear to have been prompted by the frequent disturbance which the balance of exchanges suffered from the alternatives of war and peace. The immediate consequences of the South Sea scheme, and of the many wild projects that raged about the same time, were somewhat compensated by the more distinct knowledge which they ultimately furnished with respect to the bounds of commercial adventure. It was in a similar manner, from the embarrassments occasioned in the reign of King William, by the reformation of the coin, that our politicians first derived a clear and steady light on the subject of metallic circulation. And the operations of that curious system, by which the use of precious coin is now almost superseded, remained in a great measure unknown to all but the bankers and traders of London, until the suspension of cash payments at the Bank of England produced that copious information which, in various forms, has been communicated to the public. Of all the publications which that momentous event has occasioned, the most valuable, unquestionably, is this of Mr. Thornton. With no ostentatious professions, and with no admixture of superfluous matter, it contains the largest portion of new information that has for a long time been offered to them, who, either for the pleasures of speculation, or with a view to public life, are engaged in the researches of public economy." —(*Edinburgh Review*, No. 1, Oct. 1802, p. 173.)

The concluding sentences of the article are peculiarly entitled to attention, as conveying, in language the most clear and definite, an anticipation of the course of events which, after an interval of several years, rendered the subject of the currency permanent among the questions of the time.

"We have expressed ourselves," says the reviewer, "with unaffected doubt with regard to this alleged dependence of the present rate of prices on the present state of the paper currency, because it appears to us a problem of which a satisfactory solution has not yet been offered. According to that view of the question, indeed, which seems to us the most correct, as well as the most simple, a sufficient answer will be assigned, if the excess of the market price of gold above its Mint price shall be found to continue, notwithstanding the permanent restoration of the balance of trade to its accustomed preponderancy in our favour. In the meantime we should be glad to see the fact itself, of which the origin and cause are thus anxiously sought, perspicuously stated under its necessary distinctions and limitations. It may, perhaps, be in the power of those who have paid attention to such minute but valuable details, to date the first appearance of this recent increase of prices, and to trace its progressive diffusion over all the relations of internal exchange. In such a statement it would be necessary likewise to specify in what proportion this rise is locally confined to our own island, or common to us with the Continent of Europe; and to distinguish in what proportion that local rise consists of a real increase in the bullion price, and of a nominal increase only in the currency price."

The whole of the article evinces a degree of knowledge of the subject quite extraordinary, considering the period at which it was written. This, with the comprehensive views unfolded in the paper, and the philosophic spirit which pervaded it, gave promise of the eminence which the writer of it subsequently attained. While, however, offering my humble tribute to the great merit of the publications here referred to, I must guard myself against being held to agree with all the doctrines of any of them.

A work of considerable importance on the subject , by Lord King, appeared not long after these. It is entitled, "Thoughts on the Effects of the Bank Restriction," and was published in May 1803. There is in the Edinburgh Review for October, 1846, a very able and interesting article on "Lord For tescue's Memoir of the Speeches and Writings of the late Lord King." In referring to the above – mentioned treatise, the reviewer, Mr. Senior, observes:

"When this publication appeared, we had not the report of the Bullion Committee. We had not Mr. Bicardo's pamphlets. The subject had not been considered year after year, in and out of parliament, by the ablest men, theoretically and practically, in the kingdom; and, above all, we had not the experience of the sixteen years which followed." And he adds, "It contains so full and, in the main, so true an exposition of the theory of paper-money[①], that, after more than forty years of discussion, there is

① I shall have occasion hereafter to notice the use of the term paper-money.

little to add to it or to correct."

With some qualifications and reservations, I am disposed to concur in the praise bestowed by the reviewer on this work. It was, with the other two publications here noticed, far in advance of the knowledge of the public on the subject. Each of these three writers affirms the principle of a metallic standard; and their doctrine of the circumstances affecting the foreign exchanges agrees, in the main, with that which is now generally received.

The subject was again comparatively little attended to in the interval between the spring of 1803 and 1809, because, during that period, notwithstanding the renewal of the war between this country and France, the currency was in a quiescent and apparently satisfactory state; there being little, if any, depreciation indicated by the price of gold, or by the foreign exchanges. This state of things is referred to and correctly described by the very able writer of the article in the Edinburgh Review, on the Speeches and Writings of the late Lord King, before referred to.

The reviewer, while justly extolling Lord King's general views on the subject of the currency, and on the objectionable character and *tendency* of the act for the restriction on cash payments, questions the reasons assigned by the author for affirming the existence of a depreciation; namely, the price of bullion and the foreign exchanges.

"Lord King then proceeds to state two reasons for affirming the existence of a depreciation. These are, the price of bullion and foreign exchange.

"The argument founded on the price of bullion is the least satisfactory part of the work. In the first place, he takes the price of silver instead of gold as the test of depreciation; but silver is not the English standard. When Lord King wrote, it could be legally tendered only in payment of sums under 25*l*. ; and in fact it never was so abundant as to be employed, except as small change. To state that the Mint price of silver was 5*s*. 2*d*. , and the market price was 5*s*. 7*d*. , was merely to state that the relative values of silver and gold had altered since they were assumed by the Mint. A rise in the price of gold bullion might have been really important; but Lord King does not seem to have perceived, or, if he perceived, he has not clearly stated, that when we speak of the value of the metal which is itself the standard of value, we, in general, merely express the number and weight of the pieces into which a given quantity of it is coined. When we say that gold sells for 3*l*. 17*s*. $10\frac{1}{2}d$. an ounce, we do not mean that it sells for that amount of gold, of silver, and of copper, but that in return for forty pounds of gold, the Mint gives 1869 pieces of equal fineness, weighing also forty pounds; or, in other words, that forty pounds of gold are coined into 1869 sovereigns. This is the state of things when coin and bullion are equally exportable by law, — when the coin is of full weight, and the Mint charges nothing for coinage. Coin and bullion must then be of precisely equal value, and cannot measure one another. We might as well talk of the weight of water in water, or of the value of lead in lead, as of the price of gold in gold. Were an ounce of gold to fall one-tenth of its present cost of production, or to cost ten times as much labour as it does now, still, while the regulations of the Mint are unaltered, it will be worth 3*l*. 17*s*. $10\frac{1}{2}d$.

"Of course, laws may be enacted by which coined money may be made more or less valuable than bullion. If the Mint demand a seignorage, it may be more valuable. If it be forbidden to melt or export it, it may be less valuable. This was the law in 1803, and had been so for centuries before. Whenever, therefore, the exchanges were against us sufficiently to allow the export of specie, bullion became rather more valuable than coin. In 1810, the difference was about 4*s*. per ounce. The market price of exportable gold was 90*s*. per ounce, and that of gold the product of British coin, and therefore not exportable, 86*s*. In May, 1803, and for more than a year before, and a year after, no prices of gold are returned by the Mint: but on the 13th of April, 1804, the first quotation which occurs after the date of Lord King's publication, when the notes of the Bank of England amounted to 17,494,640*l*., the price of foreign, and therefore exportable, gold was 4*l*. per ounce, and does not appear to have risen above that price for several years. Now, as the difference between 4*l*. and 3*l*. 17*s*. 10 $\frac{1}{2}$*d*. is less than the difference between the value of exportable and non-exportable gold, we are inclined to consider the price of gold between 1804 and 1808 as evidence rather against than in favour of depreciation.

"We now come to Lord King's other ground for affirming an existing depreciation — the state of the foreign exchanges. The second edition of his work is dated the 20th of March, 1804; the exchange on Hamburgh was then 35.4.; that on Paris was 25.2. Now, these rates deviate so little, if indeed they deviate at all, from par, that they offer in themselves no evidence of depreciation.

"Lord King, therefore, was forced to argue, that, unless our currency were depreciated, the exchanges between England and the Continent must be in our favour, and that their being so low as par, therefore, was evidence of depreciation."

"But though Lord King's general views were sound, and in some respects original, the inference which he drew, in the case before him, was manifestly unwarranted. The reader will recollect, that, when he wrote, the exchange on Hamburgh was 35. 4. , and on Paris 25. 2. But 25.2. was higher than it had ever been since the autumn of 1790, and 35.4. was higher than that of 1792, which averaged little above 34, and higher still than that of 1795, which was below 33. As there could have been no depreciation before the Restriction Act, the comparison of the exchanges of 1804 with those of 1791, 1792, and 1795, though it may not exclude the possibility of depreciation, is certainly unfavourable to it.

"The last evidence of depreciation mentioned by Lord King, is, 'the general increase of prices, and diminution of the value of money.' He does not dwell on it, but rather alludes to it as a well-known fact, than as a premise requiring to be proved. Many commodities must at that time have risen in price, if our currency had continued metallic. Some, in consequence of their having been made the subjects of specific taxation, others from the interruption of commerce diminishing the supply, and others from the wants of war, or of preparation for war, increasing the demand. Such a rise, however, would have been partial. On the other hand, a rise of price, occasioned by a depreciation of the currency, must of course have been general: it must have added a per centage to all the other causes of price. At the time of which we are speaking, many important commodities were *below* their average price. Wheat, for instance, was, —

January 1. 1803,	–	–	57*s*. 1*d*.
July 1. 1803,	–	–	60*s*. 4*d*.
January 1. 1804,	–	–	52*s*. 3*d*.
July 1. 1804,	–	–	52*s*. 1*d*.

To show the reduction of prices of other commodities in 1803 and 1804, the reviewer refers to quotations from vol. ii. of this work, "History of Prices," and then goes on to observe: —

"The reader will suspect, from all that we have said, that we do not admit the generally received doctrine of a depreciation of British currency, coexistent with the whole period of the restriction of cash payments. We believe, with Mr. Tooke, that depreciation did not begin until the latter part of the year 1808. The merits of Lord King's work are, that he early perceived the tendency of the Restriction Act. That he saw the inadequacy of the limits which the Bank directors assigned to their issues. That he urged, with a force and a clearness which have not been surpassed, the necessity of returning to cash payments; and that he based his practical recommendations in theories generally sound, and frequently original; and that he did this at the age of twenty-eight. Its defects are, that he was too ready to believe that what was probable must also be true. That, finding that certain effects were likely to be produced, he inferred, on insufficient evidence, that they had been already produced. In short, that he turned what ought to have been merely a prophecy, and as a prophecy was an instance of great sagacity, into a positive statement.

"As we cannot explain the moderation of the Bank during the first five years of the restriction, by imputing to its directors a knowledge of the principles by which their issues ought to have been regulated, we think that Mr. Tooke's mode of accounting for it must be adopted: namely, that they adhered to the routine of their establishment, and that that routine accidentally preserved them from a conduct to which they were exposed by their neglect of the foreign exchanges and the price of bullion."

"This routine was to discount, at five per cent., first-rate bills having a short period to run, and founded, as we have seen, on a real transaction. But on such bills five per cent. discount was a very high rate of interest. In ordinary times they may be discounted at three or two and a half, or even two per cent. The public therefore did, in the words of the directors, control the issues of the Bank, on the terms imposed by the Bank; it did not ask for more than the Bank could supply, without materially affecting the value of its notes." — (*Edinburgh Review*, No. 170, p. 315.)

I have been induced to insert this long extract, not only because it conveys, as far as it goes, an accurate description of the state of things in the interval under consideration, but also because it confers the sanction of the high authority of the reviewer in favour of the correctness of the account of it contained in the earlier part of this work. There will be occasion for me to notice hereafter some views of the writer of the article just quoted regarding the state of things between 1808 and 1814, as to which I cannot concur with him. In the mean time, reverting to the period from the first suspension of cash payments to the latter months of 1808, being an interval of nearly twelve years, there are one or two other considerations bearing on the question of the currency, which it may here be proper to touch upon.

SECTION 2 *On the steadiness of the exchanges, and on the variations in the prices of commodities, during the first twelve years of the restriction*

It certainly is a striking fact, that for so long a period after the

Restriction Act, so uniform a value of the currency and of the amount of the circulation should have been preserved. The exchanges were (with the exception of two years from the autumn of 1799 to that of 1801, when the most violent disturbing causes acted upon them—large importations of corn, and an enormous expenditure abroad by the government) as high as they had been on an average of the 96 years, or of any consecutive ten years, of the last century, preceding 1797. The price of gold, with the same exception, did not exceed 4*l*.; being a depreciation, according to the strict definition which I admit, of between 2 and 3 per cent. Even this small difference, which, in a practical point of view, is hardly worth mentioning, would not have existed if the Bank had not needlessly held out 4*l*. as its minimum price for all the gold that might be offered.

This, of itself, is a curious fact; and no attempt has ever been made to explain it by the vast majority of those who, under the influence of the currency theory, or of the Birmingham school, write or talk of the period of the Bank restriction as having been characterised in its whole course by abundant or excessive issues of paper money, and consequent depreciation.

Another fact, which is partially noticed in the preceding extract, relating to the prices of commodities during the interval in question, is, that sugar and coffee, and other articles of colonial produce, and of Baltic produce, wheat, and provisions of all kinds, attained very high prices between 1795 and 1801; and that these and all other articles had experienced nearly if not quite their greatest elevation of price before the end of the first six months of 1809. I shall have occasion to notice this fact more at large a little further on. In the mean time, I may quote, as a striking instance of the profound want of knowledge which prevails, as to the state of things at that period, among persons who, from their station and their having occasion to speak on the subject in Parliament, might reasonably be expected to have at least some little information about it, the following passage in the speech of Mr. Goulburn, in answer to Mr. Hawes's motion of amendment on the second reading of Sir Robert Peel's Bill (13th June, 1844.)

"At the time that the suspension of the Bank first took place, there was *not at first a perceptible rise in prices*: *it came gradually on. The rise in the prices of articles was not perceivable*; but at length *the value of gold, from the redundancy of the paper circulation*, rose in price; so that, instead of its being 3*l*. 17*s*. 10*d*., it was at last above 5*l*."

That the Minister of Finance should know so little, or absolutely nothing, of the real state of things, or should have the impression of a state of them so opposite to that which really existed, must be matter of just surprise; especially seeing that the phenomena of the period in question are fertile in considerations and suggestions relating to finance.

SECTION 3 *On the comparative magnitude of the advances by the bank to the government during the same period—(1797-1809)*

There is yet one more fact to be observed upon in connection with the period now under consideration, viz., *that the excess of the advances by the Bank to the Government, over and above the amount of Government deposits, from the period of the suspension of* cash payments *in* 1797, *to the year* 1811, *was actually smaller in amount than the same excess during the seven years preceding that event*. The following figures, founded upon official returns①, represent the average surplus of public *securities* over public *deposits*, during the years indicated.

Years, both inclusive.		Average Surplus of Public Securities over Public Deposits.
		£
1780 – 1784	–	4,841,000
1785 – 1789	–	2,335,000
1790 – 1796	–	5,664,000
1797 – 1803	–	5,364,000
1804 – 1810	–	4,146,000

In the Bullion Report of 1810 is the following passage: —

"Your Committee have had an account laid before them of advances made by the Bank to Government on Land and Malt, Exchequer Bills, and other securities, in every year since the suspension of cash payments; from which—as compared with the accounts laid before the Committees of 1797, and which were then carried back for twenty years—it will appear that the yearly advances have, upon an average, since the suspension, been considerably lower in amount than the average amount of advances prior to that event; and the amount of those advances in the last two years, though greater in amount than those of some years immediately preceding, is less than it was for any of the six years preceding the restriction of cash payments."

① There is no specific return of the private deposits prior to 1807; but it is known that up to, and for a long time subsequent to that date, they did not exceed about 1,000,000*l*.

This fact is partially referred, to in the Lords' Report of 1819. But the comparison there instituted is between the amount of the *securities* and the amount of the circulation. The passage is as follows: —

"From the year 1790 to the year 1797, when the Restriction Act passed, the amount of advances made by the Bank to Government, and of the notes outstanding on the 25th of February in each year, was as follows: —

	Bank Notes.		Advances.
1790 –	10,217,360	–	7,908,968
1791 –	11,699,140	–	9,603,978
1792 –	11,349,810	–	9,839,338
1793 –	11,451,180	–	9,066,698
1794 –	10,963,380	–	8,786,514
1795 –	13,539,160	–	11,114,230
1796 –	11,030,110	–	11,718,730

"The amount, therefore, of advances to Government does not appear to have borne, for some time previous to the Restriction Act, a much less proportion to the total amount of notes outstanding, than the advances since 1814 have borne to the notes issued in corresponding periods."

The following statement of the amount of the Government deposits, or balances in the hands of the Bank, I received, in 1829, from my late lamented friend, Mr. Pascoe Grenfell, who had been at some trouble to prepare it from documents previously laid before Parliament; and I took occasion to insert it in a letter to Lord Grenville, which I published in that year: —

In 1800, the aggregate average was	£ 6,251,488
In 1806, the ditto auerage was ······························	12,197,303
From 1806 to 1817, the amount fluctuated between ··	11 & 12,000,000

Now the average of the advances by the Bank to Government, from 1806 to 1810, both years included, amounted to ······	14,492,970
Average of public money in the hands of the Bank, about 11,500,000*l.*, from which are to be deducted about 500,000*l.* for unclaimed dividends, these having been deducted from the amount of the Bank advances ······	11,000,000
Leaving the actual cash advance only about ······	3,500,000

This comparative smallness of the advances to Government completely negatives the supposition, so commonly entertained and reasoned upon as a point beyond doubt, that the Bank was rendered, by the restriction, a mere engine in the hands of Government, for facilitating its financial operations. And whether this moderation in the amount of advances resulted exclusively from the forbearance of Government in not requiring, or from the firmness of the Directors in refusing, such accommodation, it equally tends (especially when combined with the consideration of the large amount of treasure in possession of the Bank during the greater part of the restriction) to strengthen the presumption, that the Government and the Directors of that period were sincere in the declaration, that there constantly existed, on the part of both, a reference to the eventual resumption of cash payments.

It is only one, but not the least important, of the instances of the unaccountable ignorance which prevails, as to the circumstances of that period, that this fact, of the comparative moderation of the amount of the public securities for so long an interval seems to have been almost wholly overlooked; and that persons, otherwise well informed, still declaim upon the assumed fact of the Bank having, by excessive issues, afforded undue facilities to Government during the whole period of the suspension of cash payments. And we constantly hear such persons talk of a depreciation of bank notes of 20 or 25 per cent. As characterising the whole or the greater part of that period. It is in truth only to the interval between the autumn of 1808 and the summer of 1814 that the most striking phenomena of the great depression of the exchanges, and of the high price of bullion, were confined; with the exception, which I have before alluded to, of the two years from the close of 1799 to that of 1801.

SECTION 4 *On the progress of the discussion from 1809 to 1811*

Towards the close of 1808, and through the whole of 1809, the exchanges fell, and the price of bullion rose considerably, under the combined influence of large importations of corn, and raw materials of manufacture, and naval stores, and of remittances of an unusual amount to the continent of Europe for subsidies, and for the maintenance of our own armies abroad. This great fall in the exchanges, and consequent rise in the price of bullion, naturally attracted attention; but was not brought prominently into notice till the appearance of Mr. Ricardo's first pamphlet, "The high Price of Bullion a Proof of the Depreciation of Bank Notes."①

Early in the session of 1810 the subject was brought under the consideration of the House of Commons, and a committee, afterwards known as "The Bullion Committee", was appointed to inquire into the

① The introduction to the first edition is dated Dec. 1,1809.

causes of the high price of bullion. The appointment of this committee is thus noticed by Sir Robert Peel, in his Speech of the 6th of May, 1844: —

"In 1810 men of sagacity observed that the exchanges had been, for a considerable period, unfavourable to this country—*more unfavourable than could be accounted for by the balance of trade, or the monetary transactions of the country.* A committee was appointed to inquire into the subject."

This passage of Sir Robert Peel's Speech is here quoted, as leading, by the words which I have marked in italics, to the inference, that he adopted not only the general principles laid down in the Report, establishing *the fact* of depreciation, but the reasoning in it, tending to show that that fact could not be accounted for by the balance of trade, or the monetary transactions of the country. Now this is the point which was and is still contested by those who, agreeing in the general principles laid down in that report, deny that there were circumstances *corroborative* (*in addition to the high price of bullion*) of the fact of depreciation.

The Report of the committee was printed, and presented to the House of Commons on the 20th June, 1810, the day before the prorogation, and consequently too late to admit of the subject being then discussed.

A very able pamphlet, on the bullion side of the question, by Mr. Huskisson, entitled, "The Question respecting the Depreciation of our Currency stated and examined," appeared soon after.

There was a host of publications, as might naturally be supposed, in opposition to the Bullion Report; not only dissenting from the explanation therein given of the cause of the fall in the exchanges, and the high price of bullion, hut denying the principle of a metallic standard—denying consequently the existence of depreciation, and maintaining the doctrine contended for by the Bank Directors, that their issues could not be in excess as long as they were confined to the discount of bonâ fide bills not having more than sixty-one days to run. The only pamphlet, however, of any importance, or that attained any considerable circulation on the side opposed to the Bullion Report as to all points, was entitled, "Practical Observations on the Report of the Bullion Committee, by Charles Bosanquet, Esq."

The Report of the Bullion Committee was made the ground for a set of sixteen resolutions, moved in the House of Commons, on the 6th May, 1811, by Mr. Horuer, the chairman of that committee; the last of these resolutions being, in pursuance of the recommendation in the Report, to make it imperative on the Bank to resume cash payments at the end of two years. A counter-set of resolutions was moved by Mr. Vansittart; the third of them being the memorable one, "That the promissory notes of the Bank of England have hitherto been, and are at this time held to be, equivalent to the legal coin of the realm." The rival resolutions of Mr. Vansittart, including this last, which has been a standing topic of ridicule ever since, were carried, on the 9th of May, by a majority of 151 to 75; and in the division on the sixteenth resolution, proposed by Mr. Horner, affirming the necessity of resuming cash payments within two years, the numbers were still more in favour of the Government; being 180 to 45.

In the House of Lords a discussion on the currency took place in consequence of steps that had been taken by Lord King, requiring his tenants, holding leases granted before the assumed beginning of the depreciation, to pay their rent either in guineas or in Portugal gold coin of equal weight, or in Bank-of-England notes sufficient to purchase the weight of standard gold requisite to discharge the rent. This proceeding of Lord King was made the ground for a bill brought in by the late Lord Stanhope, making it illegal to pay or to receive gold at more or less than its nominal value. The bill passed both Houses in July, 1811; and thus terminated, as far as regarded any particular interest taken in it at that time by the public, the controversy relating to the currency, till 1819.

SECTION 5 *On the opinions of the bullion committee on the phenomena of the circulation in 1809-1811*

As the Bullion Report was noticed by Sir Robert Peel, in his introductory Speech in May, 1844, and as the state of things connected with the currency, at the period of the Report, was referred to and commented upon by Mr. Hawes, and by some of those members who followed him in the debate on his motion of the 13th of June, 1844, it may be worth while to make a few remarks on the controversy to which that Report and the pamphlets of the time gave rise in 1810 and 1811.

Mr. Ricardo's pamphlet preceded the Report. His exposition of the theory of the currency was that upon which the more scientific part of the controversy turned; and as the theory so expounded seems to have been implicitly adopted by Sir Robert Peel (with an exaggeration, however, in supposing the possible depreciation of strictly convertible paper), an examination of it is of importance with reference to the views which led to the measure of 1844.

There is, in the *Edinburgh Review* for February, 1811, an article, written, I have reason to believe, by the late Mr. Malthus, under the title "Depreciation of the Currency," containing a critique, in my opinion, so just, as far as it goes, of Mr. Ricardo's theory, that I am induced to insert here some extracts from it.

"The great fault of Mr. Ricardo's performance is the partial view which he takes of the causes which operate upon the course of exchange. He attributes a favourable or unfavourable exchange exclusively to a redundant or deficient currency, and overlooks the varying desires and wants of different societies as an original cause of a temporary excess of imports above exports, or exports above imports.

"To point out more explicitly the effects of these partial views on the reasoning of Mr. Ricardo, we will quote his criticism on a passage in Mr. Thornton's work on paper credit, in which the error of his principles appears in a very striking light: —

"Mr. Thornton had stated, in substance, that a very unfavourable balance of trade might be occasioned in this country by a bad harvest; that there might be, at the same time, an unwillingness in the country to which we were indebted to receive our goods in payment, and that under these circumstances the balance due must be paid for in part by bullion. On this statement Mr. Ricardo observes, that 'Mr. Thornton has not explained to us why any unwillingness should exist in the foreign country to receive our goods in exchange for their corn; and it would be necessary for him to show, that if such unwillingness were to exist, we should agree to indulge it so far as to part with our coin. If we consent to give coin in exchange for goods, it must be from choice, not necessity. We should not import more goods than we export, unless we had a redundancy of currency which it therefore suits us to make a part of our exports. *The exportation of coin is caused by its cheapness, and is not the effect, but the cause, of an unfavourable balance.* We should not export it if we did not send it to a better market, or if we had any commodity which we could export more profitably. It is a salutary remedy for a redundant currency; and as I have endeavoured to prove that redundancy or excess is only a relative term, it follows that the demand for it abroad arises only from the comparative deficiency of the currency of the importing country which there causes its superior value.' This reasoning Mr. Ricardo applies equally to the stronger case of the payment of a subsidy to a foreign power.

"Now, we would ask what necessary connection there is between the wants of a nation for unusual importations of corn, occasioned by a bad harvest, or its desire to transmit a large subsidy to a foreign power, occasioned by a treaty to that effect, and the question of redundant or deficient currencies? Surely such wants or desires might occur in one or two countries, where immediately previous to their existence the precious metals circulated, as nearly as possible, on a level. And the unwillingness of the country to which the debt is owing, to receive, in payment, a great quantity of goods beyond what it is in the habit of giving orders for, and consuming, stands much less in need of explanation than that a bad harvest, or the necessity of paying a subsidy in one country, should be immediately and invariably accompanied by an unusual demand for muslins, hardware, and colonial produce, in some other. We know indeed, that such a demand will to a certain degree exist, owing to the fall in the bills upon the debtor country, and the consequent opportunity of purchasing its commodities at a cheaper rate than usual. But if the debt for the corn or the subsidy be considerable, and require prompt payment, the bills on the debtor country will fall below the price of the transport of the precious metals. A part of the debt will be paid in these metals, and a part by the increased exports of commodities. But, as far as it is paid by the transmission of bullion, this transmission does not merely originate in redundancy of currency. It is not occasioned by its cheapness. It is not, as Mr. Ricardo endeavours to persuade us, the cause of the unfavourable balance, instead of the effect. It is not merely a salutary remedy for a redundant currency: but it is owing precisely to the cause mentioned by Mr. Thornton — the unwillingness of the creditor nation to receive a great additional quantity of goods not wanted for immediate consumption, without being bribed to it by excessive cheapness; and its willingness to receive bullion — the currency of the commercial world — without any such bribe. It is unquestionably true, as stated by Mr. Ricardo, that no nation will pay a debt in the precious metals, if it can do it cheaper by commodities; but the prices of commodities are liable to great depressions from a glut in the market; whereas the precious metals, on account of their having been constituted, by the universal consent of society, the general medium of exchange, and instrument of commerce will pay a debt of the largest amount at its nominal estimation, according to the quantity of bullion contained in the respective currencies of the countries in question. And whatever variations between the quantity of currency and commodities may be stated to take place subsequent to the commencement of these transactions, it cannot be for a moment doubted that the cause of them is to be found in the wants and desires of one of the two nations, and not in any original redundancy or deficiency of currency in either of them.

"The same kind of error which we have here noticed pervades other parts of Mr. Ricardo's pamphlet, particularly the opening of his subject."—(*Edinburgh Review*, Feb. 1811, pp. 343-345.)

And, a few pages further on, the same line of criticism is thus continued:—

"One of the principal faults which we have remarked in almost all the writers who are unfavourable to the Bank Restriction is, that they have not made sufficient concessions to the mercantile classes, in some points, where they appear to have truth on their side. We have already adverted to the error (confined, however, principally to Mr. Ricardo, and from which the Report is entirely free) of denying the existence of a balance of trade, or of payments not connected with some original redundancy or deficiency of currency. A practical merchant must, to be sure, be extremely surprised at such a denial, and feel more than ever confirmed in his preference of practice to theory. But there is another point in which also almost all the writers on this side of the question concur, where, notwithstanding, we cannot agree with them, and feel more inclined to the mercantile view of the subject. Though they acknowledge that bullion occasionally passes from one country to another, from causes connected with the exchange, yet they represent these transactions as quite inconsiderable in degree. Mr. Huskisson observes, that 'the operations in the trade of bullion originate almost entirely in the fresh supplies which are poured in from the mines of the New World, and are chiefly confined to the distribution of those supplies through the different parts of Europe. If this supply were to cease altogether, the dealings in gold and silver, as objects of foreign trade, would be very few①, and those of short duration.'

"Mr. Ricardo, in his reply to Mr. Bosanquet, refers to this passage with particular approbation. Now, though we are perfectly ready to acknowledge, that an unfavourable exchange has a tendency to right itself, without the transmission of the precious metals, and that the transmission of a moderate quantity has a considerable effect, yet we cannot believe that these transactions are altogether either few in number or small in amount.

① The experience of 1828-1829, 1830-1832, 1839, and 1847, abundantly disproves the correctness of this remark.

If the precious metals did not pass from one country to another, in consequence of the state of the exchange, the varying necessities of these countries would frequently raise the rate of the exchange very far above the expense of transport; and it would be impossible for the debtor country to make its payments at the time promised. But if the precious metals *do* pass readily from one country to another from this cause, we cannot help thinking that the same varying desires and necessities must render these transactions not very unfrequent. Every peculiar failure or peculiar abundance of produce, in any of the states of the great mercantile republic, every subsidy to be paid or received, and every movement of a considerable army from one country to another, must almost inevitably give some employment to the bullion trade: and when the level of the precious metals has been in some degree destroyed by these necessary operations, the bullion dealer is again called into action to restore the balance. But not only on such occasions as these does bullion pass from one country to another, but it is well known that most states, in their usual relations of commercial intercourse, have an almost constantly favourable exchange with some countries, and an almost constantly unfavourable one with others. And Dr. A. Smith has justly observed, that bullion forms, in general, the most convenient medium for carrying on the various roundabout foreign trades of consumption which a country finds it necessary to engage in, and is, in consequence, greatly used for this purpose. It appears, then, that in the most permanent and ordinary relations of countries with each other, the bullion trader will always have something to do." — (*Edinburgh Review*, Feb. 1811. pp. 361, 362.)

Mr. Ricardo, in an Appendix to a new edition of his Pamphlet, wrote an answer to the article (here quoted) of the Edinburgh Review. This answer, however, contains little more than a repetition, in varied forms of expression, according to the phraseology peculiar to the theory in question, of the axiom that gold will not be exported unless it is cheaper than any other commodity; assuming, consequently, the fact to have been, that all commodities were at that time dearer in this country than they were abroad, relatively to gold. The misapprehension of the facts of the case, involved in this view of them by Mr. Ricardo, was participated in by the other eminent persons who took the same side in the controversy. Mr. Huskisson, for example, in his Pamphlet, which was published soon after the appearance of the Bullion Report, assumes, as implicitly as the rest of the Bullion Committee, the existence of a fact not only not true, but the reverse of the truth, viz. that prices of commodities had risen in the two years preceding the date of either the Report or the Pamphlet. This assumption he makes in arguing against the assertion of the antibullionists, that gold had become dearer on the Continent; and he asks,

"Dear in exchange for what? For the gold coin of the Continent? Such an assertion would be ridiculous. Dear in exchange for any depreciated paper? This is very probable in several parts of the Continent, but is surely not the criterion to which wo shall be referred. Dear in exchange for all other commodities? Is this a fact? Where is the evidence of it? Are cloths, corn, iron, or any other leading articles, twenty per cent, cheaper on the Continent than they were if paid for in gold? Certainly not. And if they were so on the Continent, has not the drain lasted long enough to bring matters to a level, and produce the same effect in this country? *Has the price of commodities in this country fallen within these two years? Is not the contrary notoriously the fact?*"—(*Questions concerning the Depreciation*, &c., 1831, p. 90.)

This total misapprehension, and consequent misrepresentation, of the actual state of things connected with the prices of commodities at that time has been forcibly pointed out by the late Mr. James Deacon Hume, in one of the letters under the signature H. B. T., which he addressed to the editor of the *Morning Chronicle* in January 1834, and which were afterwards published as a pamphlet. Mr. Hawes (who alone, of all those members who took part in the debate on his motion of the 13th June, appears to have possessed any accurate knowledge of the state of things connected with the currency at the period of the Bullion Report), when questioning the correctness of the prevalent notion of the depreciation of Bank notes during the suspension of cash payments, referred, in support of his view, to the opinion of Mr. J. D. Hume on the subject, and gave a short extract from that publication. As the authority of Mr. Hume, who was contemporary with and an accurate observer of events connected with the commerce of the country at that period, is entitled to carry great weight on this point, I am induced to quote from his letters the following passage: —

"It may be observed, that no statistical tables or accounts have been introduced into these letters. There has been no need of them, because I have founded all my positions upon great leading facts which are notorious to all the public. The fact I am about to bring to the recollection of the reader is of this description, — *I mean the ruinously low prices of our manufactures and of our colonial productions under the operation, against England, of the 'Continental system' during the last six years of the war.* Prices are high or low only by comparison; but then it is material to consider what are the proper objects of comparison according to the purpose of the inquiry. For our present purpose we are to compare the English prices with the contemporaneous foreign prices①; and, in doing so, we need not aim at any great accuracy, because the foreign prices of all those descriptions of goods which we held in the greatest abundance were so much *above* the English prices, that if we were to take them at only half the amount, the excess would still be enough to have given the exporter an enormous profit over and above what he got by taking gold, even if he could have bought gold with his Bank notes at the Mint price. *I mean to assert that the prices of sugar② and coffee, for instance, on the Continent, computed in gold, were four or five times higher than their prices in England computed in Bank notes.* I am speaking of the times of the Berlin and Milan decrees and the British orders in council — of the times of the licence system and of the blockade system — of the times in which the French chemists discovered sugar in beet-root, and a substitute of coffee in chicory, and when the English grazier tried experiments upon fattening oxen with

① No mistake can be greater than comparing the prices of those times with subsequent prices. —Note by Mr. Hume.

② Mr. Hawes having, in his speech of the 13th June, 1844, quoted this passage, Mr. Goulburn, as Chancellor of the Exchequer, considered it incumbent on him to reply; but the only point of the quotation that he seems to have caught was the word "sugar" and his answer, according to the report in the "Times" was to the following effect: — "The honourable gentleman (Mr. Hawes) agreed with the principles laid down by the Bullion Committee; but then he did not agree with them in their opinions respecting prices; and he referred to the price of sugar, at the time the Bullion Committee made its report, for the purpose of showing that the paper at that time was not in excess. Let them, he said, see what was the price of sugar at that time. In consequence of the naval predominance of England at that very time, this country had the command of the sugar market. To show this, he need but refer to the fact, that at the time the English at my entered into France—'the English and sugar'—it was expected by the people in the South of France that the advance of the English would have brought to them a reduction in the price of sugar". A precious specimen of the knowledge and reasoning of some of the prominent supporters of Sir Robert Peel's measure!

treacle and molasses — of the times when we took possession of the island of Heligoland, in order to form there a depôt of goods, to facilitate, if possible, the smuggling of them into the north of Europe, and when the lighter descriptions of British manufactures found their way into Germany through Turkey. It will be remembered that the French decrees declared, on one hand, that no vessel should enter a continental port if she came from England, or even had touched at England , on the other hand, our orders in council declared that no ship should go to the Continent unless she came from England. Whatever might be the military merit of this mode of retaliation, its commercial effect against ourselves was most pernicious. Our fleets had complete possession of the seas at that time, and they compelled every ship they met to make for a British port. *The consequence was, that almost all the merchandise of the world accumulated in our warehouses, where they became impounded, except when some small quantity was released by a French licence*, for which the merchants of Hamburgh or Amsterdam had, perhaps, given Napoleon such a sum as forty or fifty thousand pounds. *They must have been strange merchants, according to the bullionists, to have paid so large a sum for liberty to carry a cargo of goods from a dear market to a cheap one.* What was the ostensible alternative the merchant had? Literally this — either to buy coffee at 6*d*. per pound in *Bank notes*, and send it to a place where it would instantly sell at 3*s*. or 4*s*. a *pound in gold*! or to buy gold with Bank notes at 5*l*. an ounce, and send it to a place where it would be received at 3*l* 17*s*. 10 $\frac{1}{2}$*d*. an ounce. A man might as well pretend to deny all Buonaparte's victories. or even that there ever was such a person, as attempt to deny that such was the state of our intercourse with the Continent during the reign of the decrees. It is too absurd, of course, to say literally and distinctly that the gold was remitted instead of the coffee, as a preferable mercantile operation; *and yet if it was not so, under some explanation which I am totally unable to conjecture, what becomes of Mr. Huskisson's advice to the Bank, to draw in a number of their notes, in order to reduce the price of the coffee to the sum at which it would be a preferable remittance to gold.* I have never been able to extract out of all the writings of the bullionists but one description of reasoning which could even seem to approximate to the shadow of an answer to this objection. I will state it, and expose its futility. They began by showing that all the human laws that ever were made have proved ineffectual in preventing the precious metals from finding their way *out* of the country, which debases its circulating medium; or into the country, which contracts its circulating medium, in even a small degree, within the amount which is consistent with the preservation of its intrinsic value. This is perfectly true; and, in proof of it, it would be easy to show that the natural tide of the precious metals did really set in strong upon England through the whole of the time in question. There was not a place in the globe at which we could gain access with some goods, as a valuable consideration, from whence the gold and silver did not spontaneously flow to us; *and there was not a country in the world in which so large a quantity of desirable goods could be obtained for an ounce of gold as in England.* But the error which these good people have fallen into is this —*they are thinking of the facility of smuggling gold, and forget the difficulty of smuggling goods.* The gold, of course, will not come if the goods cannot go; and that the goods could not go at the time in question, is sufficiently proved by their current market prices on different sides of the channel.① The impediment was the resistance of bayonets and cannons; and the efficacy of the impediment is undeniable. I remember well to have heard it frequently said of Buonaparte, at the time all this was going on, that he was constantly examining the English Price Current, in order to ascertain whether, and with what degree of success, his decrees were enforced by his own troops and obeyed by his allies. So long as he saw that gold was dear, and coffee was cheap, in England, he was satisfied that his continental system worked well. The English could see nothing in these documents but proof that the Bank was shamefully extending the issue of its notes."—(*Letters on the Corn Laws, by H. B. T.* London, 1834. pp. 29-31.)

And, after discussing at some length several other points of the controversy, Mr. Hume concludes this section of his Pamphlet thus:—

"In the quotation I have given from Mr. Ricardo, he says, and says most truly, 'The only proof which we can possess of the relative cheapness of money in two places is by comparing it with commodities in these two places.' Our money at that time (1808-1814) was wholly paper, unchecked by gold as its test or regulator: it was therefore peculiarly fit to be tested by the prices of commodities in countries where money was subjected to the ordeal of the precious metals. Now I mean to assert, that from this trial of its value our currency of that day will come out triumphant. It is a positive fact that England was the cheapest country in

① If 60,000 tons of coffee, held here unsaleable at 6*d*. per pound while coffee was 4*s*. or 5*s*. a pound on the Continent is not evidence that the impediment was more than all the subtlety of mercantile men could overcome, it is in vain to look for proof of such a fact. ——*Note by Mr. Hume.*

the world during the time when gold was 25 per cent and upwards above the Mint price. I am told that if I admit the possibility of disturbance by physical force, I deny the theory of money. Then the surgeon who recognises the power of the tourniquet denies the theory of the circulation of the blood." — (*Ibid*, p. 37.)

The following passage from the Speech of Mr. Huskisson, already quoted, may be adduced as one corroboration out of the immense number which exist, that Mr. Hume has not overstated the degree of misapprehension which prevailed even among the most eminent of the bullionist party, as to the real nature of the vital facts of the question.

"And here he must be permitted to notice, in passing, a very extraordinary statement made by a right honourable gentleman (Mr. Rose), who spoke before him in the debate — a statement not more singular in its nature than contradictory in itself, and wholly subversive of the object for which it was made. In his endeavour to account for the rise of the value of all articles in this country, without reference to a depreciation of the existing currency, that right honourable gentleman had adverted *to France, and to the apparent rise of prices which had, according to his assertion, taken place in that country*. The right honourable gentleman had contended that the price of labour was dearer in France than it was in England during the last year[①]: and thence he inferred that gold was cheaper in France than it was in this country.

① Not only labour, but nearly all articles of general use (wine and a few exportable articles excepted) had risen in France, from the date of the revolution there, to the time here referred to, in the full proportion of their rise in this country; and colonial produce was even tenfold higher. But it was quite in vain that facts like these were stated; not the slightest attention was paid to them. The high price of gold was the invariable answer.

Now, granting all this to the honourable gentleman, he would ask him, how he could reconcile such a statement with the fact admitted on all hands, that there was a profit of 20 *per cent. made by the exportation of gold to France?*"—(*Speech*, *7th May*, 1811—*Speeches*, vol. i. p. 202.)

The assumption by the framers of the Bullion Report and their partisans, of the relative state of prices at that period, so contrary to the actual facts of the case, is quite astounding; for, in reality, there had been a ruinous *fall* of prices in 1810, as compared with 1808 and 1809: and, so far from its being true, as affirmed in the Report, that "the prices of all commodities have risen, and gold appears to have risen in price in common with them,"— all commodities, provisions alone excepted (these being scarce from the effects of bad seasons, combined with obstructions to importation), were *actually falling*, *while gold was rising*.

I have always admitted that a difference between paper and its metallic standard, from whatever cause arising, establishes the fact of depreciation; because the promise to pay in coin ought to be equal in value to the actual payment. But the framers of the Bullion Report have not been satisfied with confining themselves to this test. Mr. Horner said, on introducing his resolutions, founded on the Bullion Report, —

"But it is not alone from the extraordinary rise in the market prices of the precious metals in this country—a rise not to be accounted for on the ground of any correspondent rise in the markets of Europe—that the depreciation of our currency is demonstrable. The equally extraordinary rise in the *price of the necessaries of life*, not as compared with the precious metals, but as compared with the actual circulation, affords a clear and convincing proof of its depreciation. *The great and paramount standard of all value, Sir, is corn*: and in order to enable the Committee to form an estimate of this standard, I shall beg leave to call the attention of gentlemen to the *extravagant rise which has within the last few years taken place in the prices of that articler*"—(*Mr. Horner, as quoted in Mr. Howes' Speech of* 13*th June*, 1844, p. 9.)

Precisely the same views were entertained by Mr. Huskisson. In the speech which he delivered in support of Mr. Horner's resolutions, already more than once referred to, there is the following passage: —

"But here he could not help asking, though the price of gold was so increased, was there such a great scarcity of the article? Where were the proofs of this scarcity? He was aware of none; but of this he was confident, that where gold was scarce other commodities must become cheap. Would gentlemen try the question by this test? *Was it the fact that other commodities had become cheap*? But if they were to entrust to the Bank this fearful discretion of countervailing the effects of the rise of the price of gold and silver, he thought *that then the best criterion of the required standard would be found in taking the average price of corn for a given period jointly with the average value of labour.* (Here he read a statement of the average price of wheat imported for the fourteen years since the Bank restriction in 1797.) *Throughout this period the progressive rise in the average price of wheat, at stated periods, proved the gradual depression of our domestic currency.*"—(*Speech*, *7th May*, 1811—*Huskisson's Speeches*, vol. i. p. 201.)

Here Mr. Horner and Mr. Huskisson both affirm that "corn is the great and paramount standard of value." And yet, at the very time that they were speaking (May 1811) the price of corn was falling; the average price of wheat, which in August 1810 had been as high as 116*s*., having declined to 86*s*. 11*d*.: being a fall of nearly 30*s*. a quarter.① And I would refer to a former volume of this work for a more detailed account of the decline in the prices of corn which then occurred, and of the extraordinary error into which Mr. Horner seems to have fallen respecting it.

Mr. Henry Thornton appears to have participated in the same distorted view of the facts as that under the influence of which Mr. Horner made the remarks above referred to. To go further, here, in exposing the utterly unfounded assumption as to the relative prices of gold and other commodities, hazarded by the ultra-bullionists on that occasion, would occupy too much of this portion of my work. The errors in Mr. Thornton's comparison of the prices of 1800 with those of 1811 have been pointed out at some length (*History of Prices*, vol. i. p. 310.) I will here only, in proof of my assertion of the total misapprehension of the real state of facts on the part of the Bullion Committee and its supporters, in the assumption (in their Report and in the debates that followed it in the session of 1811) of a general rise of prices in the two years immediately preceding, during which the exchanges had fallen, and the price of gold had risen, subjoin the following table, showing the highest prices which various articles of merchandise and produce had attained before the summer of 1809, and their depression in the early part of 1811.

---

① It is to be borne in mind that the charges on importation were in 1810-1811 immoderately high. The freight and insurance alone on wheat from the Continent of Europe amounted to from 30*s*. to 50*s*. per quarter.

ARTICLES.		Prices before the Period of the assumed Depreciation.		Prices during that Period.	
Ashes. Barilla, Carthagena, in bond	– *cwt.*	1808. Apr.	75*s.* @ 80*s.*	1811. Apr.	35*s.* @ 39*s.*
Coffee, St. Domingo, in bond	*cwt.*	1808. Apr.	80*s.* @ 90*s.*	1811. Apr.	58*s.* @ 68*s.*
British plantation, superior, in bond – –	– *cwt.*	1808. Apr.	95*s.* @ 120*s.*	1811. Apr.	75*s.* @ 95*s.*
British plantation, inferior, in bond – –	– *cwt.*	1808. Apr.	66*s.* @ 94*s.*	1811. Apr.	38*s.* @ 74*s.*
Cochineal, Spenish garbled, in bond	– *lb.*	1708. Apr.	52*s.* @ 54*s.*	1811. Apr.	31*s.* @ 35*s.*
Copper, British, in cakes –	– *cwt.*	1808. July.	200*s.*	1811. July.	140*s.* @ 146*s.*
Cotton wool, bowed Georgia	– *lb.*	1807. Apr.	1*s.* @ 1*s.* 2*d.*	1811. Apr.	7*d.* @ 9*d.*
Flax. St. Petersburg. 12 head	– *ton.*	1808. July.	140*l.* @ 142*l.*	1811. July.	100*l.* @ 105*l.*
Fleme, St. Petersburg. 12 head	– *ton.*	1808. Apr.	117*l.* @ 118*l.*	1811. Apr.	68*l*@ 70*l.*
Lead, English, in pigs – per 19 $\frac{1}{2}$	*cwt.*	1806. Apr.	41*l.*	1811. Apr.	33*l.* @ 34*l.*
Indigo, East India, superior	– *lb.*	1807. Apr.	11*s.* 6*d.* @ 14*s.* 6*d.*	1811. Apr.	8*s.* @ 9*s.* 6*d.*
Iron, Russia, in bond –	– *ton.*	1801. Apr.	23*l.* 10*s.* @ 26*l.* 10*s.*	1811. Apr.	14*l.* 10*s.* @ 18*l.* 10*s.*
Oil, Northern fishery –	– *tun.*	1801. Apr.	49*l.* @ 50*l.*	1811. Apr.	42*l.* @ 46*l.*
Gallipoli. in bond –	– *tun.*	1808. Apr.	84*l.* @ 85*l.*	1811. Apr.	57*l.* @ 59*l.*
Provisions. Butter, Waterford	– *cwt.*	1807. Apr.	108*s.* @ 110*s.*	1810. Apr.	90*s.* @ 95*s.*
Riee, Carolina – –	– *cwt.*	1808. Apr.	45*s.* @ 52*s.*	1811. Apr.	23*s.* @ 27*s.*
Saltpetre, rough, in bond –	– *cwt.*	1799. Jan.	140*s.* @ 143*s.*	1811. Jan.	76*s.* @ 80*s.*
Spices, Cinnamon, Ceylon, lst quality, in bond – –	– *lb.*	1796. Apr.	12*s.* @ 14*s.*	1811. Apr.	8*s.* @ 9*s.*
Pepper, E. I., black, in bond	– *lb.*	1801. Apr.	18*d.*	1811. Apr.	7*d.*
Spirits, Rum, Jamaica, proof	– *gall.*	1805. Apr.	5*s.* @ 6*s.* 6*d.*	1811. Apr.	4*s* 2*d.* @ 5*s.* 3*d*
Sugar, Havanah, white –	– *cwt.*	1806. Jan.	66*s.* @ 87*s.*	1811. Apr.	36*s.* @ 51*s.*
Museov. Gazette average	– *cwt.*	1804. Apr.	52*s.* @ 66*s.*	1811. Apr.	34*s.* 11*d.*
Tallow, Russia, Y. C. –	– *cwt.*	1808. July.	110*s.* @ 112*s.*	1811. July.	74*s.* @ 75*s.*
Tea. Congou – –	– *lb.*	1808. Apr.	3*s.* 2*d.* @ 3*s.* 8*d.*	1811. Apr.	2*s.* 11*d.* @ 3*s.* 6*d.*
Timber, Memel fir – –	– *load.*	1808. July.	15*l.* @ 17*l.*	1811. Apr.	10*l.* @ 11*l.* 10*s.*
Tobacco, Virginia, in bond	– *lb.*	1808. July.	16*d.* @ 24*d.*	1811. Apr.	4*d.* @ 9*d*
Sheep's wool, Spanish –	– *lb.*	1809. Apr.	22*s.* @ 26*s.*	1811. Apr.	7*s.* @ 8*s.*
Logwood, Jamaica – –	– *ton.*	1803. Apr.	24*l.* @ 25*l.*	1811. Apr.	16*l.* @ 17*l.*

With reference to the rival resolutions of Mr. Horner and Mr. Vansittart, it was only the concluding resolution of the latter set, and the third resolution of Mr. Vansittart's set, that had any practical importance or application. That of Mr. Horner proposed to make it imperative on the

Bank to resume cash payments at the end of two years; while that of Mr. Vansittart affirmed the equality of value of the paper and the coin.

But it required more than the mere affirmation, by a vote of the House of Commons, of this equality, to counteract the tendency of such a proceeding as that of Lord King in his notice to his tenantry. The Gold Coin Bill introduced by the late Lord Stanhope, and passed in July 1811, gave the weight of law, and penalties on its infringement, to the dictum of that resolution.

Mr. Canning voted for all Mr. Horner's resolutions except the last, while he poured an irresistible torrent of ridicule upon the expression "sense of value," which Lord Castlereagh made use of in his vindication of the resolutions of Mr. Vansittart.

SECTION 6 *On the policy of the government in rejecting the recommendation of the bullion committee for a speedy resumption of cash payments*

Taking a careful and impartial view of the circumstances of those times, as they then presented themselves, I cannot but think that the Government and the House of Commons were right in negativing the resolution making it imperative on the Bank to pay in gold at the end of two years. ①

① When treating of this period in a former volume of this work (Vol. I.), I expressed a very strong opinion that at the time when Mr. Horner's proposed resolutions were debated in May 1811, it would have been quite impracticable for the Bank to have been placed in a position to resume cash payments within two years from that time, in pursuance of the recommendation of the Bullion Report. But I took occasion to add that, although it would have been impracticable for the Bank to have been placed in such a position at that time, it might be questioned whether in 1808; when the exchanges and the price of gold were nearly at par, it would not have been in the power of the Directors, by timely precaution,

But the argument for the continuance of the restriction might and ought to have been placed on its proper footing of expediency, under the extraordinary circumstances, political and commercial, of the time; which were palpable enough; and which were appreciated by the public generally; although the ultra-bullionists seemed blind to them. And this might have been done without affirming a resolution so absurdly worded as the third of Mr. Vansittart's set.

If, however, a view of the circumstances of the time leads to the conclusion that it would have been inexpedient to prescribe, peremptorily, a return to cash payments within two years, still more directly does it lead to the conviction that it would have been in the highest degree impolitic on

---

to have resisted the effect of the violently depressing causes which operated on the foreign exchanges towards the close of 1808; and so to have preserved the exchanges and the price of gold at nearly their par value. And I leaned to the opinion that the attempt, if so made, might have been successful, and thus have averted some part of the calamitous events which burst over the commercial community towards the close of 1809, and marked the interval from that time to the summer of 1811 as one of the most disastrous on record to the mercantile, manufacturing, and banking interests of the country. But on carefully going over the ground again, and reconsidering the circumstances of that time for the purpose of this review, I see reason to doubt whether, if even the Directors had been able in the early part of 1808 to foresee the extraordinary events, political and commercial, which arose suddenly in the latter part of that year (all combining to cause an urgent necessity for immediate transmission of immense sums for foreign payment) they could have counteracted the effect upon the exchanges without a greater convulsion than occurred, and greater than would have been borne. The doubt I now entertain on this score has been strengthened by witnessing the great difficulty (increased, no doubt, by the unwise and mischievous Act of 1844) which the Bank has recently experienced in counteracting the large balance of foreign payments caused by the failure of the potatoe-crops; although the difficulty so caused has not been aggravated, as was then the case, by the exigences arising out of the stupendous political events which signalised that period. But in truth the supposition that the Directors might have foreseen the events calculated to bear on the exchanges is a superfluous hypothesis; for it has been their professed system, as stated by Mr. Palmer in 1832, not to anticipate; but to await the actual demand on their coffers. And even had that not been their system, they could not in reason be expected, in the early part of 1808, to foresee, what probably no one then living did foresee, as being likely to occur before the close of that year.

the part of the Government not to have taken measures to prevent the consequences which must have followed if Lord King had not been prevented, by the interference of Parliament, from acting upon the notice which he had given to his tenants. However great, therefore, the deference I feel for the opinion of the distinguished writer of the article in the Edinburgh Review for October 1846 (whom I have been glad to find concurring with me in his view of the state of the currency during the first twelve years following the suspension), I cannot agree with him in the regret he expresses at Lord King's not having been allowed to act upon his notice; supposing, as the reviewer does, that the example would have been followed by other landlords, and that eventually there would have been two prices, a gold price and a paper price.

SECTION 7 *On Lord King's requisition to his tenants to pay in gold*

In the passage from the Edinburgh Review which I here extract, there is much that is questionable.

"At the time when this resolution was carried, the price of gold had risen to 4*l*. 16*s*. an ounce, and the exchange on Hamburgh had fallen to 24*s*. and on Parts to 17. 16.

"Under such circumstances Lord King resolved to show that *he* did not hold the promissory notes of the Bank of England to be equivalent to the legal coin of the realm. He sent a circular to his tenants holding leases granted before the beginning of the depreciation, or when it was less than at the date of the notice, requiring payment of the rent either in guineas or in Portugal gold coin of equal weight, or in Bank of England notes sufficient to purchase the weight of standard gold requisite to discharge the rent.

"It is very seldom indeed that the single act of an individual can do so much good as would have been effected by this notice of Lord King's if parliament had allowed him to act on it. It suggested a safe mode, and that the only mode, by which the public could to a considerable extent correct the errors of the government, and obtain, if not a convenient, at least a steady measure of value. Had not the legislative interference which we have to relate occurred, the example must have been followed. Some difficulty would have arisen at first; all landlords and creditors would not have moderated their legal rights as equitably as Lord King, but this must have been set right by the courts of equity or by law. As to subsequent contracts there could have been no real difficulty: two prices, a gold and a paper price, would have been established, and one understood where the other was not specified. The Bank Directors must have admitted that their notes were of less value than the coin which they promised to pay. They would have maintained, probably, that the variation was occasioned not by the fall of their paper, but by the rise of gold. But however they accounted for the difference, they must have been anxious to remove it. Though they could neglect the foreign exchange, they could not have borne to see their paper in the British market at an open discount. Not long before, between February and August 1795, they had reduced their circulation from 14,017,510*l.* to 10,862,200*l.*, and in August 1796 to 9,246,790*l.* a much smaller proportionate reduction would now have been sufficient to raise it to par. But even if they had persisted in their wild course, if they had increased their issues until, as was the case in 1814, they amounted to nearly twenty-nine millions, and gold lose to 5*l.* 10*s.* an ounce, still the mischief would have been much less than what really followed. The public credit' loss would not have been greater, though it would have been more evident; but it is probable that the government would have been obliged in its subsequent loans to borrow and pay in gold, and the national debt would now be less by many millions. The foreign exchanges would have been quoted in gold, and could not have risen or fallen beyond the expense of transmission. We should have saved in our imports and in our foreign expenditure the additional price which the foreign producer and merchant were forced to put on their commodities in order to indemnify themselves against the contingency of a fall in the value of the unsubstantial paper pound in which our contracts were actually made, and above all we should have escaped all that part which was nominal of the enormous rise of agricultural produce, of rents, and of incumbrances on landed property that were the pretext for the Corn Laws, which have oppressed us for the last thirty years."

I apprehend that it would have been quite impossible that two prices could have been allowed to subsist—a gold price and a paper price. The inconveniences and anomalies attending such a state of things would have been innumerable, and among these not the least would have been an increased difficulty in the eventual return to cash payments. Indeed so many and so great would have been the inconveniences and anomalies, that, if Government had not interfered, the Bank Directors must, as one of the alternatives suggested by the reviewer, have felt, themselves bound to take immediate measures for the removal of the causes of difference. But the effect of the measures requisite for that purpose would, in my opinion, have been infinitely more severe than he seems to imagine.

SECTION 8 *On the possibility of the bank counteracting the fall of the exchanges in 1809-1811*

It is to be borne in mind that the year 1811 was one of extreme pressure and intense commercial distress and discredit; insomuch that Parliament sanctioned, in May of that year, an issue of 6,000,000*l*. of Exchequer bills, by way of loan, to merchants and manufacturers. Now, under the measures of violent contraction of mercantile and financial accommodation which must have been resorted to by the Bank in the supposed case, these Exchequer bills must have been unsaleable, or, if saleable at all, only at an enormous discount. As to getting advances upon them, that must have been out of the question; and as the Bank would have closed its doors to discounts, the merchants holding even short bills would have had scarcely any resource. The real rate of interest being above 5 per cent, and the usury law preventing all loans or discounts above that rate, few private lenders would have been found, except upon annuities, or with heavy commissions, or by such other contrivances as were occasionally resorted to at times when the market rate of interest was above the legal rate. And in all such cases the usury law operated as a great additional burthen upon borrowers. Under these circumstances, and at such a time of unprecedented political difficulties, I am perfectly convinced that if the attempt alluded to had been made there would have been a moment of total stoppage of business, something very like a general suspension of all payments, except for retail purposes, and of all business excepting retail trade.

In the passage quoted in the last section from the Edinburgh Review, it is assumed that a much smaller proportionate reduction of the circulation would have been found effectual to raise the exchange to par, in 1811, than that which had been effected by the Bank between February and August 1795, when the reduction was from 14,017,510*l*. to 10,862,200*l*., — and in August 1796 to 9,246,790*l*.

Upon this assumption I have two remarks to make: —

1. The relative amounts of the circulation, as here presented, do not afford a correct view of the actual circumstances. The amount in Feb. 1795, must be taken as a mere casual occurrence; and I have no doubt that, if explained, it would be found to have arisen from some peculiar transactions, probably between the Exchequer or the Treasury and the Bank, which caused the employment of some of the larger notes and the detention of them out of the usual course. The reason for supposing so is, that there was a sudden increase in the amount between the beginning of January, when it was 10,891,220*l*., and the 14th of March, when it reached 14,876,580*l*. And on the 21st of March it was still more suddenly reduced to 9,928,140*l*. It is not at all probable that the general circulation of notes can have experienced that increase of four millions, and the sudden diminution by no less an amount than nearly five millions within one week. The whole variation, therefore, in that interval ought to be excluded from the view taken of the effort of the Bank to counteract the fall of the exchanges by a contraction of the circulation.① But, admitting the facts stated, without any such qualification, they embrace an anomaly which would militate no less strongly with the assumption of the reviewer. If the reduction from 14 millions to 10 millions was calculated to raise the exchange, the previous advance from 10 millions to 14 millions, in the preceding six months, ought to have

① There is reason to believe that this extraordinary variation arose from some peculiarity in the mode of payment, by the Treasury, of the bills drawn upon it on account of the Austrian Loan.

depressed it. But how stand the facts? —

Aug. 30	1704,	circulation	10,286,780*l*.	Exch.	on Hamburg	35
Feb. 28	1795,	-	14,107,510*l*.	-		36
Aug. 31	1795,	-	10,862,200*l*.	-		32,6

2. The other remark suggested by the assumption of the reviewer is, that the view presented leads to a conclusion directly opposite to that which he attempted to draw from. it. The reduction, carried further than even the lowest amount there stated, — for by February 1797 the circulation had been reduced to 8,640,250*l*., — had not been effectual to restore the exchanges so as to stop the drain, and prevent the suspension which we know took place precisely at the time of that extreme reduction. And it was the inefficacy of the great efforts made by the Bank to contract its liabilities that led Mr. Henry Thornton to contend that the attempt at contraction had been carried too far; and that the catastrophe might have been averted, if the Directors had been more liberal in their accommodation, and had enlarged the circulation, instead of reducing it to so low an amount.

A reference to the state of things attending the efforts of the Bank Directors, in the years 1795-1796, to resist the tendency to a fall of the exchanges (in consequence of the large foreign expenditure, and the extensive importations of corn at that time) tends, therefore, to render it in the highest degree improbable that a less effort on the part of the Bank, or one attended with less pressure on the commerce and finances of the country, would have been more effectual in 1811 than it had been found to be in 1795 and 1796 — when it was not effectual.

It may here be worth while to consider what was the commercial and financial condition of the country consequent upon those efforts of the Bank in 1795-1796.

In a former volume of this work I have given the particulars of a meeting of merchants, in April 1796, at which resolutions were passed stating the alarming scarcity of money that existed in the city of London at that time. The reviewer inserts a copy of resolutions to a similar effect in March 1797.

There were extensive failures of banks in the North of England, and great mercantile discredit prevailed. The pressure on the money market was very severe; more particularly, as may be supposed, at the close of 1796, and the commencement of 1797. Exchequer bills bearing interest at $3\frac{1}{2}d.$ per cent per diem were sold at 3*l.* and 3*l.* 10*s.* discount. And it was said that, in some instances, sales were made at 5*l.* per cent discount. Navy and victualling bills were also at an enormous discount. Mercantile bills, excepting such as came within Bank time and conditions, were hardly negotiable at all, or were subject to heavy commissions by way of evading the operation of the usury law. So depressed were the public funds, that Mr. Pitt, finding there was no prospect of obtaining a loan by contract in the usual way, except at an enormous sacrifice, resorted to the expedient of a loan by subscription from the public to the amount of 18,000,000*l.* It was called the Loyalty Loan, and books were opened at the Bank for the purpose of receiving subscriptions on the following terms.

Subscriptions opened 1st December, 1796, and closed on the 5th.

"For every 100*l.* advanced, 112*l.* 10*s.* 5 per cent, irredeemable till the expiration of three years after the 5 per cent existing at the time this loan was made shall have been redeemed or reduced; with an option to the proprietors to be paid at par, on giving three months' notice at any period not less than two years from the conclusion of a definitive treaty of peace, in money or in 3 per cent valued at 75."

The subscription was filled in three days; but favourable as the terms were to the subscribers, the loan was at a discount for some time after it came out.[①]

Now what was the state of things in 1811, that in order to restore the exchanges to par and to bring in gold, should have required less effort than was found ineffectual in 1795 to resist the tendency to a fall in the exchanges?

I have already alluded to the extreme degree of commercial distress and discredit which prevailed in 1810; a detailed account of it is given in the earlier part of this work; and I will here only repeat the brief general description which I have there given of the state of things in the commercial world at that time.

"So many circumstances on so large a scale, combining in the same direction, the fall of prices, the reduction of private paper, and the destruction of credit, were greater and more rapid than were ever before, or have since been known to have occurred within so short a space of time. A general dismay prevailed throughout nearly all branches of trade during the last six months of 1810 and the first few months of the following year."

Seeing that this was the state of things at the period referred to by the reviewer, I would ask whether it is conceivable that the Bank could then have taken measures for *forcibly* reducing its liabilities by

---

① Credit continued to be much restricted for a considerable time afterwards; and the next loan was contracted on still more unfavourable terms, viz. —

Loan for 17,000,000*l*. — 1798.

For every 100*l*. advanced, 150*l*, 3 per cent consols; 50*l*. 3 per cent. reduced, and 4*s* 11*d*. annuity for $61\frac{3}{4}$ years.

contracting its loans and discounts, with a view to restore the exchanges. There can be but one answer. Such an attempt, at that time, would have been an intolerable aggravation of the prevailing commercial distress and public difficulties; and Government, if not so disposed of its own accord, would have been forced by the public voice, to interfere.

The Bank, on the contrary, was enabled, by the existence of the Restriction Act, to relieve the distress as much as could be done consistently with its rules. The Directors extended their discounts very considerably in 1810; and a strong presumption that they thus only filled the vacuum in the circulation caused by the numerous failures of the country banks is afforded by the circumstance, that coincidentally with the large discounts in 1810, the exchanges rose, and the price of gold fell to 4*l*. 4*s*. towards the end of that year, while the prices of commodities experienced a very considerable fall.

With regard to the effects on our financial state, the reviewer observes, that had the Government been obliged to borrow and to pay in gold, the national debt would now be less by many millions. This may well be questioned. The contrary would be the more reasonable conjecture. I have already shown the depressed state of public securities, and the disadvantageous terms on which, consequently, the loan of 18,000,000*l*. in 1796 was contracted; and I have no doubt that the difference of the rate of interest at which a loan must have been contracted in the case supposed in 1811, compared with that at which it was actually concluded, would have been little, if at all more favourable, and would consequently have entailed an increased rather than a diminished burthen from it at this time.

SECTION 9 *On the alleged excessive issues by the bank, 1808-1814; and on the distinction between small and large notes*

Mr. Senior, in giving credit to Lord King for having in 1803, pointed out, as the consequences of the Restriction Act, the dangers which burst upon England between 1808 and 1814, thus describes them: —

At length the dangers which Lord King had pointed out, burst also upon England. The bad harvests of 1808, 1809, and 1810— the vast foreign expenditure of the Government — the exclusion of British manufactures from the Continent, and of British shipping from the continental ports — the enormous freights and insurance at which we were forced to import in foreign bottoms — the sudden opening of the South American markets, and the mistakes of our merchants as to the extent and the nature of the new demand — these causes created an amount of speculation, of failure, of discredit, and of commercial embarrassment, which had never been incurred before, and is not likely to be ever undergone again. The interest of money lose, and the Bank, following their routine, went on increasing their discounts. Their private securities, consisting almost exclusively of discounted bills, on the 29th February, 1808, were 13, 234, 569*l.*; at about which amount, they had averaged for the previous six years. They now lose as follows: —

31st August, 1808,	–	–	£ 14,287,696
28th February, 1809,	–	–	14,374,775
31st August,1809,	–	–	18,127,597

28th February, 1810,	–	–	21,055,946
31st August, 1810,	–	–	23,775,093

The issue of notes exhibited a nearly proportional increase. On the 28th May, 1808, it was 16,899,970*l*., being also about the average of the previous six years. It rose as follows: —

27th May, 1809,	–	–	£ 18,252,780
26th May, 1810,	–	–	21,073,580
31st August, 1810,	–	–	24,446,170

The price of gold lose, in the beginning of 1809, to 4*l*. 11*s*. an ounce. The exchange on Hamburgh sunk from 35*s*. 5., its rate in July, 1808, to 26*s*. 6., its rate on the 28th December, 1810, and that on Paris, from 23*s*. 16. to 19*s*. 8.

The description here given of the circumstances existing at that time would amply account for the depression of the exchanges and the rise in the price of bullion, without ascribing these effects to the conduct of the Bank as an originating cause; and the statement of the progressive increase of the securities, and of the circulation, is calculated, if unexplained, to convey a very erroneous impression of the working of the Bank system under the Restriction Act.

The figures are correctly given; and, viewed in connection with the facts, the great increase of private securities serves to illustrate an observation which I have more than once had occasion to make in reference to this subject: namely, that applications to the Bank for extended discounts occur rarely, if ever, in the origin or progress of extensive speculations in commodities. These are entered into for the most part, if not entirely, in the first instance, on credit for the length of term usual in the several trades; thus entailing on the parties no immediate necessity for borrowing so much as may be wanted for the purpose beyond their own available capital. This applies particularly to speculative purchases of commodities *on the spot*, with a view to resale. But these generally form the smaller proportion of engagements on credit. By far the largest of those entered into on the prospect of a rise of prices are such as have in view importations from abroad. The same remark, too, is applicable to the export of commodities, when a large proportion is on the credit of the shippers or their consignees. As long as circumstances hold out the prospect of a favourable result, the credit of the parties is generally sustained. If some of them wish to realise, there are others, with capital and credit, ready to replace them; and if the events fully justify the grounds on which the speculative transactions were entered into (thus admitting of sales for consumption in time to replace the capital embarked) there is no unusual demand for borrowed capital to sustain them. The term speculation, in its obnoxious sense, is not, in such cases, applied to the transaction; and the parties engaged have the credit of superior sagacity.

It is only when, by the vicissitudes of political events, or of the seasons, or other adventitious circumstances, the forthcoming supplies are found to exceed the computed rate of consumption, and a fall of prices ensues, that an increased demand for capital takes place; the market rate of interest then rises, and increased applications are made to the Bank of England for discount.

The whole process is strikingly exemplified in the figures here given. It was in 1808, and the early part of 1809, that speculations in purchases of commodities on the spot, and in orders for imports from abroad, and in exports to newly-opened markets, were entered into on a most extensive scale. The grounds on which these were entered into have been described at some length in a former part of this work, and the table which I have given exhibits the prodigious fall of prices which commenced in the spring and summer of 1809, and continued into the spring of 1811. Now it will be seen, by reference to the amount of private securities held by the Bank, that the increase of them was coincident with the fall of prices. A part of the very great increase observable in August, 1810①, was the consequence of extensive failures which were just then occurring among the country banks. If the reviewer had continued the figures for the succeeding twelvemonths, it would be seen that, when the emergency and the pressure on credit subsided, the securities declined to within a trifle of what they had been at in 1808. Thus they were reduced:—

February, 28th, 1811, to £ 19,920,550.

August, 31st, 1811, to 15,199,032.②

The reviewer observes, that the notes exhibited a nearly proportional increase; but it should have been added, that a proportional variation between the amount of private securities and of the note circulation is rather the exception than the rule. In this instance, the increase of the note circulation is accounted for by the circumstance, already mentioned, of the

---

① In order to save the trouble of reference to a former volume of this work, I here transcribe a part of a note of Vol. I. "Mr. Manning, a director of the Bank, and member of parliament, when replying to some observation in the House of Commons on the Bank circulation, 8th December, 1812, said, 'In July or August, 1810, it would be remembered that the number of notes in circulation was about 25 millions. But this excess was occasioned by the failure of two large houses in London, which produced a considerable sensation in the country. Bankers, in the various principal towns, then made demands upon the Bank to insure themselves against a run upon their firms; *but within six months the greater part of three millions teas returned to the Bank of England without having been employed.*'"

② In February, 1813, the private securities were only 12,894,324*l*.

extensive failures of the country banks causing a vacuum in the circulation requiring Bank of England paper to supply it, in part at least; less being wanted in consequence of the great fall of prices. And in proof that this increase of Bank of England notes was not a case of excessive issues, causing depreciation, there is the fact that simultaneously with it the exchanges rose and the prices of bullion fell. The prices of commodities, likewise, were falling rapidly.

There is, moreover, a fallacy in the view presented of the increase of the note circulation, by taking the total amount, without distinguishing the notes under 5*l*. The distinction referred to is of the utmost importance in discussions of this kind; and the suppression of it is a favourite practice with the Birmingham School, whose constant purpose it is to lead to the inference of a more abundant circulation having existed during, than after, the suspension. There can be no doubt that the notes under 5*l*. served almost exclusively as substitutes for the coin that was exported, and hoarded. The increase, therefore, of that portion of the circulation ought not to be considered as added, but rather as replacing what would otherwise have remained in use. In the instance under consideration, the comparison would stand thus:—

	5*l*. and upwards.	Under 5*l*.
31st August, 1808,	12,993,020[①],	4,118,270.
31st August, 1810,	17,570,780,	7,223,210.

But while the small note circulation continued to increase till it reached

① This amount is less by two millions than it had been on the 31st August, 1807, and *less* by the very large sum of 3,764,000*l*. than it was on the 31st August, 1806.

The amount issued in August, 1810, about three millions returned to the Bank without having circulated at all.

9,000,000*l*. and upwards, the notes of 5*l*. and upwards were reduced, 31st August, 1811, by nearly 2,000,000*l*., namely, to 15,692,490*l*., and did not again reach 17 millions before the end of the war. And here it may be observed, that while the retail trade required a progressively increasing amount of Bank of England notes, the immensely increased transactions, financial and commercial, in the interval of four years following, were conducted through the medium of a diminished amount of the larger notes.

Before quitting this topic I would notice, as connected with it, Mr. Senior's remark upon what he terms the wild course of the Bank in increasing its issues until, as was the case in 1814, they amounted to nearly 29 millions, and gold rose to 5*l*. 10*s*.

Here the omission to distinguish the small notes causes the view to be most fallacious and exaggerated. The total amount on the 31st August 1814 was 28,368,290, of which 18,703,210 were of 5*l*. and upwards, and 9,615,030 under 5*l*.

And there is a very material error in the passage above quoted, where it is said that the price of gold rose to 5*l*. 10*s*. The context leads directly to the inference that the rise of price was coincident with the increase of the circulation. But this is the reverse of the fact. The price of gold was at 5*l*. 10*s*. on the 28th February 1814; but the gross amount of the circulation was then only 24,801,080*l*. or 3 millions and a half less than in August following; and coincidently with the subsequent increase of the circulation the price of gold fell rapidly. On the 19th July it was quoted at 4*l*. 12*s*.

SECTION 10 *On the re-adjustment of the relative values of gold and paper between 1814 and 1819*

Mr. James Deacon Hume has blamed the conduct of the Bank in 1814, in having then greatly extended its securities and circulation. I do not justify it. I think that both the Government and the Bank acted injudiciously: the one in requiring, and the other in granting, a large increase of advances on Exchequer bills immediately after the peace of 1814. But the effect was only that of retarding the final improvement of the value of the paper. And it is among the innumerable instances of the nonsense that has been talked about the restriction, and the resumption of cash payments, that in the great majority of pamphlets and speeches on the subject it is affirmed, or taken for granted, that a preparation, on the part of the Bank, for the resumption of cash payments, commenced with the peace in 1814, and was the principal *cause* of the fall of prices which then took place; whereas the blame really attaching to the Bank, at the period referred to, is for not having made any preparation whatever with that view.

The highest quotation of gold was 5*l*. 11*s*. at the close of 1813. At the nearest date of that year, on which there is any account of the amount of the circulation (November 27) it was (exclusive of the notes under 5*l*.) 15,775,640*l*. In February 1814 it was 16,455,540*l*., and standard gold was then quoted at 5*l*. 8*s*., and silver at 6*s*. 11 $\frac{1}{2}$*d*. per oz.

It is also important to observe, that when the price of bullion was at the highest point, the securities were scarcely, if at all, increased in amount.

On 31st August 1813 they amounted to 40,105,000*l.*, and the price of gold was then 5*l.* 10*s.*; at the close of 1810, when gold was at 4*l.* 4*s.* an ounce, the securities were 40,973,000*l.*, and in August 1814, when the price appears to have been also 4*l.* 4*s.*, they were 48,345,000*l.* These opposite movements of the two phenomena may reasonably excite some doubt as to the accuracy of the hypothesis which regards them as mutually dependent.

In October 1816 the price of gold had fallen to 3*l.* 18*s.*; and that it had not fallen to the Mint price was only because the Bank had fixed this as its minimum rate. That gold might have been had at the Mint price of 3*l.* 17*s.* $10\frac{1}{2}d.$ can hardly be doubted, because, at that time, the price of standard silver was 4*s.* $11\frac{1}{2}d.$, and the exchange on Hamburgh 37. 10. to 38., and on Paris 26 10. The amount of Bank notes on the nearest dates was, on August 30th, 1816, 17,666,510*l.*, and on 20th February, 1817①, 19,261,630*l.*

① The late Mr. Samuel Turner, formerly a director of the Bank of England, in a pamphlet published in 1822, in which he had occasion to remark upon a statement by Mr. Ricardo, in his pamphlet "On Protection to Agriculture", "referring to the amount of Bank notes in circulation, observed, It is true I have placed out of consideration the years 1817 and 1818, and I have done so, because it would be inconsistent with any degree of fairness to calculate upon those years (I rather think that Mr. Turner's remark cannot apply to 1818, because the discredit and failure of country banks did not extend begond the summer of 1817.) as showing the extent of the demand for Bank notes. It is quite notorious that in those years a large number of country banks failed, and a run took place upon many of the most respectable establishments; so that they were obliged to convert a considerable portion of their floating securities into Bank notes, in order to guard against a sudden panic. It has so happened, however, that many of the notes issued in those years from the Bank, in consequence of this unusual demand, never got into general circulation, and, in many instances, they have been returned precisely in the same state they went out of the Bank, without having passed into any other hands than those of the country banker and his town agent." — (*Consideration*, *&c.* by Samuel Turner, Esq., F. R. S., pp. 41, 42.)

Hence it appears that this re-adjustment, for it was completely such, of the value of the paper, took place without the slightest observable effort on the part of the Bank to reduce its securities or circulation with that view. Gold was flowing in largely, and the bullion in the Bank had, by August, 1817, reached the large amount—then without precedent—of 11,668,266*l*.①

There can be no doubt that the Bank was then in a condition to have resumed cash payments; and, indeed, it did actually make a beginning, by issuing sovereigns in exchange for its smaller notes. In the very able report of the Lords' Committee on the Resumption of Cash Payments, the following statement is made of the expectations entertained by the Directors at that time that the resumption of cash payments would take place prior to the period then fixed by Parliament, viz., the 5th of July, 1818.

"The Bank more than doubled its treasure during the last eight months of 1815, and the fall in the price of gold and the favourable turn of the exchanges enabled the Directors to raise it by January, 1817, to more than quadruple what it had been in the beginning of 1815. At this period the Directors felt so confident of being able to comply with the injunctions of Parliament, even before the period at which the restriction was to expire, that they issued a notice for the payment in cash of all the one pound and two pound notes bearing date prior to January 1816. Finding little or no demand for cash in consequence of this notice, and their treasure having continued during the course of the year to increase to an amount far exceeding what it had ever reached, and, with few

① The circulation being then 29,503,000*l*.: nearly the highest amount attained by the outstanding notes of the Bank of England.

exceptions, bearing a larger proportion to the extent of their issues than it had ever borne before, the Directors issued a second notice in September 1817, for the payment in cash of all notes bearing date before the 1st January in that year. This measure has been stated to the Committee to have been undertaken in the hope that if it proved successful, that is, if the gold so tendered were not demanded, or, if when demanded, it remained in the country, *the complete resumption of cash payments would take place gradually, and as it were insensibly, even prior to the period then fixed by Parliament*, viz. *5th July*, 1818." — (*Lords' Report*, 1819, p. 3.)

It may here, towards the close of this portion of my review of the state of the currency during the restriction, be advisable to repeat a general remark which I have had occasion to make in former parts of this work. The repetition is the more called for, because, while the facts to which I refer have a most important bearing on the question, how far the depreciation could with propriety be said to have been caused by over-issues of paper, I am not aware that any notice has been taken of them, or of the conclusions deducible from them, by those who affirm against the Bank the charge of constant over-issues.

The facts I allude to are these. That whenever there was a pause or cessation of the unusually large foreign expenditure by the government, or of unusually large importations of corn, there was also a tendency to a restoration of the value of the paper, by a rise in the exchanges, without any contemporaneous or immediately preceding reduction in the amount of Bank notes; and that a complete restoration of the value of the paper took place in the spring of 1817, coincidently with a *larger* amount of the circulation of the Bank of England than had existed at any former period.

But, in the latter part of 1817, the large loans required by the governments of France, Russia and Austria, to which considerable sums from this country were subscribed, combined with an extensive importation of foreign corn, depressed the exchanges, so as to cause a drain upon the Bank coffers. Under these circumstances the Directors abandoned the expectation they had before entertained of being able to resume cash payments before July, 1818; and an act was passed continuing the restriction to the end of the next session of Parliament. When that period approached, the application by ministers for an extension of the period of restriction was accompanied by a proposal for a committee of inquiry by both Houses of Parliament. The result of the inquiry by those committees was the Act of 1819.

What is particularly worthy of notice is the fact, of which the events of the time, if duty regarded, leave no doubt, that but for the disturbing causes operating on the exchange in the autumn of 1817, the Bank would have resumed cash payments in 1818.

It is impossible to conceive any evidence more complete of the principle of self-adjustment of the value of the currency inherent in the management of the Bank at that period (when not exposed to the disturbance of an unusual demand for foreign payments), than is supplied by this unquestionable fact. Not an effort had been made for the purpose by either the Bank or the Government — and the public were all the time unconscious of the process, or the effect. For whatever there may have been of distress or discredit in 1816 and the commencement of 1817 had entirely ceased before the close of the hitter year, which, taken with the commencement of 1818, was considered by the Birmingham school as a period of abundant currency, and consequently of halcyon days.

Had it not been for the casual occurrence of the disturbing causes already referred to, we should have had no committees of inquiry, and no Peel's Bill of 1819. Indeed, nothing but the disinclination of Lord Liverpool's government, at the commencement of the session of 1819, to apply for a further prolongation of the Restriction Act without inquiry, prevented the resumption being a spontaneous, or rather a necessary, consequence of the state of things at the close of 1819. In August of that year the price of gold was 3*l*. 17*s*. 10 $\frac{1}{2}$*d*.; the price of standard silver 5*s*. 2*d*., and of dollars 5*s*. per ounce; and this without the smallest effort on the part of the Bank or of Government. The proof of it is this. The only part of its position on which the Bank can operate, as is now well understood, is the amount of its securities. These stood —

		£	£
1817, Aug. 30.	Public	27,098,238	
	Private	5,507,392	
			32,605,630
1818, Aug. 30.	Public	27,257,012	
	Private	5,113,748	
			32,370,760
1819, Aug. 31.	Public	25,419,148	
	Private	6,321,402	
			31,740,550

Is it possible to conceive any thing more equable in the management of the Bank, or in the requirements of the Government for accommodation, than is shown in this statement? Although in the intermediate time the exchanges had fallen, and there had been a great drain on the coffers of the Bank, and the price of gold had risen to 4*l.* 3*s.* for a short time, yet, immediately upon the cessation of the disturbing causes, the tide of the precious metals turned, and the tendency to influx in the two following years was fully as strong as had been the tendency to efflux in the two preceding years. So strong indeed was the tendency to influx in the two years following August 1819①, that nothing short of a degradation of the standard, or a very violent effort on the part of the Bank in reducing its rate of interest much below the market rate, would have prevented or materially abated that influx. And yet there have been, and are, writers and speakers who, professing to be friendly to the principle of the Act of 1819, countenance the cry of the Birmingham school by contending that the measure was too hasty a one.

If it be objected that I have not, in the view here given of the amount of the circulation in 1819, included the country bank notes, without which, it may be said, no fair view of the operation of the Restriction Act on the amount of the currency can be taken, my answer is—that the issues of country notes, during the whole period of the suspension (as regards the

---

① Bullion: —

31st August, 1819,	-	-	£ 3,595,360
31st August, 1820,	-	-	8,211,080
31st August, 1821,	-	-	11,233,250

But the Bank had, in 1821, anticipated the requirements of the Act of 1819, by which it was not obliged to pay in gold, except by progressive stages, till 1823, and began paying in coin in May, 1821. The issue of sovereigns by the Bank, from May to August, 1821, inclusive, amounted to 5,657,053*l.*, which makes the whole *influx* in the two years, to 31st August, 1821, 13,295,283*l.*

provincial banks in Great Britain, and, after 1804, as regards the banks in Ireland) were limited as completely by the notes being convertible at the will of the holder into Bank of England notes, as the Bank of England notes were before the Restriction, and have been since 1819, by their being convertible into coin. This point cannot be fortified by higher authority, or expressed in clearer language, than is found in the following passage from Mr. Huskisson's pamphlet before referred to.

"A country bank, from its being liable at all times to pay its notes in those of the Bank of England at the option of the holder, is placed precisely in the same situation by this check upon the amount of its issues as the Bank of England itself was by the necessity of paying in guineas before the Restriction; " and again, "the circulation of Country Bank paper being therefore in exact proportion to that of the Bank of England, it follows," &c.

But admitting that the country note circulation had undergone a diminution in more than its usual proportion to that of the Bank of England, it is still clear that such relative reduction had no reference whatever to any preparation for cash payments. Nor was it caused by any contraction of accommodation by the Bank of England.

SECTION 11 *On the uniform coincidence of the periods of improved exchanges and diminished foreign expenditure*

The remarkable and uniform coincidence of the variations in the state of the foreign-exchanges with the course of the Government continental expenditure, the importations of grain, and the other causes which violently interfered with the ordinary state of the foreign commerce of the country, bears so intimately upon the controverted question of depreciation of the paper from excessive issue, that I am induced to allude to it at further length.

I subjoin a tabular summary of the periods of comparative depression and recovery of the quotations on the principal foreign places, and I venture to affirm that in every instance here given (and the whole period of the operation of the restriction is embraced in the table), there are abundant means of fully accounting for the phenomena upon purely mercantile grounds.

DEPRESSED.			RESTORED.		
	Years.	Months.		Years.	Months.
1794 May to 1796 May	2	0	1796 May to 1799 June	3	1
1799 June to 1802 April	2	10	1802 April to 1805 Oct.	3	6
1805 Oct. to 1805 Dec.	0	2	1805 Dec. to 1808 Sept.	2	10
1808 Sept. to 1811 Jan. ①	2	4			
1811 Jan. to 1812 Jan.	1	0			
1812 Jan. to 1814 May	2	4	1814 May to 1815 March	0	10
1815 March to 1815 July	0	4	1815 July to 1817 Nov.	2	4
1817 Nov. to 1819 Feb.	1	3	1819 Feb. to 1825 Jan.	6	0

① The year 1811 was that in which the depression was greatest, and it is important to bear in mind, that at the periods of the most depressed quotations, the transactions were so few, so irregular, and for sums so insignificant, as to form no fair criterion for judging of the relative value of the currencies. In point of fact, it can hardly be said that at that time there was any exchange business, properly so called, with Germany or France. There was no communication by post; the only intercourse was by bye-boats chiefly employed in smuggling, and the transmission of letters and documents by them was attended with great uncertainty, difficulty, and hazard.

Further, the negative proof afforded by mercantile considerations is confirmed by the positive evidence that these expansions of the circulation, and those operations of the Bank which are described as "occasioning" the fall of the exchange could not have had any such consequence, unless it can be shown, that the date of a cause may be subsequent to the date of its effect.

The evidence upon which this statement rests, is so easily accessible in the valuable Appendices to the Reports of 1819, and the Bank Charter Report of 1832, that I may safely spare the patience of my readers the task of accompanying me through an examination of every case, and content myself with one or two leading examples.

Thus, to take the severe depression which occurred between June 1799 and April 1802—what are the facts? There was, in the first place, in the two years 1800 and 1801, an importation of grain to meet the deficiency of our own very deficient harvests to the extent of nearly *twenty millions* sterling. The precise figures were:—

Years.	Estimated Cost of Grain Imported.	Yearly Average Price of Wheat.
	£	*s.* *d.*
1800	8,755,955	127 0
1801	10,149,098	128 6

Then there was a considerable continental expenditure in the year 1800, and also, though upon a less scale, in 1801. It is unfortunate that no official documents have hitherto appeared which enable us to state precisely the magnitude of that expenditure. Now, the decisive fall in the exchange took place in the summer of 1799, when the amount of the Bank circulation had been remarkably stationary, and the extent of the private securities had been actually diminishing, during the preceding year and a half; as the following account will show:

CIRCULATION.		PRIVATE SECURITIES.	
Dates.	£ 5 and above.	Quarters ended.	Average Amount.
	£		£
28 Feb. 1798	11,617,000	31 March 1798	5,077,000
31 Aug. 1798	10,639,000	30 June 1798	4,099,000
28 Feb. 1799	11,494,000	30 Sept. 1798	4,337,000
31 Aug. 1799	12,047,000	31 Dec. 1798	4,448,000
		31 March 1799	4,618,000
		30 June 1799	4,162,000

It is true that when the difficulties arising out of the adverse balance of payments had fairly set in, the advances by the Bank were greatly increased. But that circumstance does not in any way help the argument of the ultra-bullionist party. They have to show that these expansions took place *before* and not *after* the fall in the exchange.

I may next refer to the important and prolonged recovery of the par of exchange, and the price of gold, which took place between April 1802 and September 1808, and which was only interrupted for about two months at the close of 1805, by subsidies to Austria and Russia. During the whole of this period, the importations of corn were on a very limited scale; our continental government expenditure was also moderate, because the character of the war was decidedly naval rather than military; the impediments to commercial intercourse were not greater than in former periods of war; and the yearly subsidies to foreign powers were not large. These circumstances appear to be quite sufficient to account for the steady character of the exchanges, and the undisturbed prices of the precious metals. And yet, during the whole of this period, the private securities were, on an average, about *four* millions higher than in 1800 and 1801, and the circulation was undergoing a gradual expansion.

The facts connected with the great and continuous decline of the exchanges, and the important rise in the price of gold which took place in the autumn of 1808, are equally conclusive. It was in the summer of that year that the first opening occurred fur opposing the enemy in the Peninsula; and the effect of the enormous expenditure then incurred in the maintenance of the troops and the provision of military chests was almost immediately perceptible in the quotations of the exchange and the price of gold. There were also considerable importations of corn in 1800 and 1810. Mr. Vansittart, in the Appendix to his Speeches of 1811, states the expenditure and the cost of corn to have been as follows①:

Years.	Foreign Expenditure.	Cost of Corn Imported.
	£	£
1808	9,552,000	336,460
1809	10,235,000	2,705,496
1810	12,372,000	7,077,885

① These figures have been already noticed by me (Vol. I.), but I insert them again for facility of reference.

But, besides these direct causes, there was an indirect cause of depression in existence, scarcely less powerful. I allude, of course, to the very serious, and in many instances complete, impediments to the commercial intercourse between Great Britain and the Continent, which arose out of the Berlin and Milan Decrees of Buonaparte, and our own Orders in Council. ① These are the circumstances referred to by Mr. J. D. Hume in the passages already given from his Pamphlet. The difficulty was not merely that we were importing an extra quantity of corn, and remitting an enormous amount for our foreign expenditure, but that there was also the physical impossibility, in many cases, of obtaining admission into any part of continental Europe for the merchandize intended to balance the claims against us.

It will be worth while again to extract the figures which prove that the great fall of the exchange in 1808 could not arise from any previous over-issue of notes or lavish extension of discounts:

CIRCULATION.		PRIVATE SECURITIES.	
Dates.	£ 5 and above.	Quarters ended.	Average Amount.
	£		£
30 May 1807	12,320,000	30 June 1807	13,572,000
28 Nov. 1807	11,678,000	31 Dec. 1807	12,991,000
28 May 1808	12,982,000	31 March 1808	13,009,000
26 Nov. 1808	13,462,000	30 June 1808	12,369,000
		30 Sept. 1808	13,182,000

① The Berlin Decree was dated 21st November, 1806, that from Milan on 17th December, 1807, and the more important Orders in Council on the 11th and 21st November, 1807. The American embargo appeared on the 22nd December, 1807.

I do not know that it is needful to pursue the subject further, or I might refer to the conclusive nature of the facts connected with the period from 1812 to the close of the war; but, beyond adducing one or two of the more remarkable of them, I feel that I may safely leave this part of the subject to be elaborated by other hands.

It was during the year 1813 that the price of gold reached its highest point, and that the exchange, after 1811, was the most depressed. The following figures, compiled from the Commons' Report of 1819, will convey some idea of the prodigious extent of the disturbing causes then in action.

Years.	Bills on the Treasury.	Paid by Commissariat.	Coin, &c. remitted by Government.
	£	£	£
1813	19,092,521	2,724,792	3,371,825
1814	20,932,326	5,562,701	1,410,141
1815	9,108,892	11,019,225	2,182,014
1816	4,881,072	2,921,284	58,148

Without committing myself to the assertion that the price of gold, at this time, invariably rose and fell with the extent of the Government demand for coin and bullion for remittances, I may observe, that during the four years above referred to (1813-1816), there is a very close correspondence between the magnitude of the Government purchases and the published market prices.

CHAPTER II
THE PERIOD FROM 1819 TO THE CLOSE OF 1847

SECTION 1 *On Sir Robert Peel's speeches of May 1844. The rationale of a fixed metallic standard*

I have given the foregoing sketch of the controversy upon the state of the currency and the causes influencing it, as it existed during the period of the Bank Restriction, because it appears to me, that the subject is very imperfectly understood by the majority of those who have taken part in the discussion to which the Act of 1844 has given rise, and that it is wholly unknown to the greater part of the public who have, or fancy that they have, an interest in the question. A review of the various phases of the currency question since the resumption of cash payments will naturally come under consideration in the examination which I now propose to enter upon of the grounds on which the new Banking Act was brought forward and passed. ①

① One of these phases, indeed—that, namely, which arose on the remarkable (but, as regards the currency, purely accidental) coincidence of a general fall of prices with the resumption of cash payments (1819-1822)—and a misapprehension of which gave rise to what is now termed the Birmingham School — I have dealt with so fully in the previous volumes of this work, that I cannot but deem further reference to it unnecessary.

The measure was introduced into the House of Commons by Sir Robert Peel, on the 6th May, 1844, when he made an elaborate speech explanatory of the views by which he had been influenced in bringing it forward; and on the 20th, when moving the House to go into committee on the bill, he went into a further explanation of the principles on which it was founded.

There were two distinct objects proposed by the bill: the one to secure the general solvency of banks, whether issuing or non-issuing; the other to restrict the amount of notes in circulation of all issuing banks, those of Ireland and Scotland excepted[①], but inclusive of the Bank of England.

Now these very distinct purposes are unfortunately blended and confounded in Sir Robert Peel's Speech. Whether this proceeded from a consciousness on his part that his case was weak, and was, therefore, an adroit mode of evading a difficulty, or from an indistinct view of his subject in its general bearings, it detracts very much from the merits of the exposition. The Speech is altogether very imperfect and confused,—most unlike the luminous exposition of which upon many important occasions he has shown himself capable.

Sir Robert first addressed himself to pointing out the errors of the Birmingham school, and may be said to have devoted an undue portion of his speech to it. But even on this, which seemed a favourite topic, he hardly did justice to the argument in favour of a metallic standard. The reference which he made to the Mint proportions between gold and silver was wholly irrelevant to the main point to be established. He was perfectly

① The regulation of these having been postponed till the session of 1845, when the Irish and Scotch Bank Acts were passed.

right, although he dwelt upon the point at unnecessary length, in showing that a *pound*, when speaking of a metallic standard, means a certain quantity, a definite weight, of metal of given fineness; and he justly ridiculed the notion involved in some of the definitions of a standard of value proposed by the opponents of a metallic one.

The first was, "that a pound might he defined to be a sense of value, in reference to currency, as compared with commodities." This was the definition given in a speech by Lord Castlereagh, in 1811; and was the occasion of a cutting answer by Mr. Canning, from whose speech I have given an extract before.

Another of the definitions which Sir Robert Peel alluded to, without naming its author, appeared in a pamphlet by Mr. C. Bosanquet, in the following terms: "There is a standard and there is an unit which is the measure of value, and that unit is the interest of 33*l*. 6*s*. 8*d*. at 3 per cent, that being 1*l*., and being paid in a Bank note as money of account." This definition also was naturally exposed to ridicule.

The various arguments adduced in opposition to a metallic standard were answered in a pamphlet by Mr. Ricardo. I shall have occasion further on to notice these pamphlets, only observing here, by the way, that both Mr. Bosanquet and Lord Castlereagh, while lamentably and ludicrously in error about a standard of value, were full of information, extensive and accurate, as to the disturbing forces which, at the period to which their attention was more particularly directed, were operating on an enormous scale in depressing the exchanges.

Sir Robert Peel quotes a third definition. "The standard is neither gold nor silver, but it is something set up in the imagination to be regulated by public opinion."

These definitions are all confused and ridiculous enough; and the speaker succeeded in amusing the House with them. But in stating and proving that a standard meant a certain quantity of gold, he stopped short of showing an important distinction between two functions of money: the one, that of serving as an instrument of exchange; the other, that of being the subject of contracts for future payment. It is in the latter capacity that the fixity of a standard is most essential.

As a mere instrument or medium of exchange, at the same time and in the same place, invariableness of value, though desirable, is not of so much importance; the immediate purpose of money in this capacity being to serve as a point, or rather a scale, of comparison more convenient than actual barter between any two commodities or sets of commodities. It is in the latter capacity, that is to say, as the subject of engagements or obligations for future payment, that in every view of justice and policy, the specific thing promised, in quantity and quality; should be paid at the expiration of the term.

Thus the seller of a quantity of goods of any kind, on six months' credit, of the agreed value in gold, at the time of sale, of 46*l.* 14*s.* 6*d.* is, or ought to be, entitled to receive, at the expiration of the term, the specific quantity of gold coined into that sum: namely, one pound weight of a given fineness of the metal, which is the present standard. If he receives Bank notes instead of gold, it is because he prefers them for convenience.

Or suppose a person to lay out 934*l.* 10*s.* in a loan on mortgage at 5 per cent equal to 46*l.* 14*s.* 6*d.* per annum in half-yearly payments—the rationale of the transaction is, that having the command of twenty pounds' weight of gold, he lends it on the consideration of receiving, half-yearly, half a pound of gold, and also of receiving, at the expiration of the time, the quantity, twenty pounds' weight, which he had lent; unless he should prefer, as he probably would, Bank notes or a cheque on a banker, in either case equal in value to that quantity of gold, and more convenient to him, for otherwise he would have no motive for giving it the preference to gold.

Both the seller and the buyer of the goods, and the lender and borrower on mortgage, are willing to take their chance of what the value of gold may be at the expiration of the term. It is true that gold may vary in value; but there is no other commodity, silver perhaps alone excepted, so little liable to vary. And there is, accordingly, no other commodity than gold, or silver, which it would suit both parties to look to for eventual payment.

Suppose, in the case of the seller and buyer of goods, that these consisted of a quantity of copper, say ten tons, which, at the agreed price on six months' credit, amounted to 934*l*. 10*s*., it could not equally suit both parties to look to a repayment of the same quantity of copper, instead of twenty pounds of gold, which were of the exact value of the copper at the time of sale, inasmuch as that, at the expiration of the term, the price or value of copper might, as compared with all other commodities and with gold, have risen or fallen 10 or 20 per cent, and to the buyer (if a rise), or to the seller (if a fall), a loss to that extent would ensue, if the stipulation were to be by a repayment in copper. But copper is much less variable in value than iron. If the transaction, therefore, were to be in purchase of the latter article on six months' credit, the repayment, if it were stipulated to be by an equal quantity of iron, might vary in a much greater degree in the value. And still greater would be the liability to variation in value if the contract were for repayment at the end of six, or even three months, in wheat.

The case is hardly conceivable, in which it should equally suit both the seller and the buyer of any merchandize on credit, that the repayment at the expiration of any given term should be by an equal quantity of the thing sold; but it does invariably suit both parties equally that the repayment should be in a quantity of gold equal to the quantity which the subject of sale would have commanded at the time of the bargain.

So, and still more strongly, would this reasoning apply to the loan on mortgage. It could not equally suit both parties to look to eventual repayment in any other way, in any other commodity, or in the value of any other commodity, than gold.

The same reasoning applies, and in a still greater degree, to a payment stipulated to be made in Bank or Government notes at the expiration of six months or six years, if the notes be not payable at the will of the holder in a specific quantity of gold, or so regulated as to be equal in value to the specific quantity of the metal in which they purport to be payable.

This view of the rationale of what the Birmingham school, in their peculiar phraseology, are pleased to call the fixity of the price of gold, is explained so clearly, and illustrated so aptly, by a very accomplished writer, Mr. Bailey, in the tract entitled "Money, and its Vicissitudes in Value," that I am glad to be relieved from the necessity of urging further arguments or illustrations of my own, by laying before the reader the following extract from that work: —

"The simplest pecuniary contract which is entered into, and which may be considered as virtually representing all others, takes place when one man lends another a sum of money to be returned to him at some future period, as for instance at the end of twelve months.

"In this case the nature of the transaction is really this: The lender grants the use of a certain number of pieces of metal of given weight and fineness during a definite period, on condition that an equal number of pieces of the same weight and fineness, shall be restored at the expiration of the time. If we simplify the matter by putting aside the consideration of the circumstances attaching to corn, which are not essential to our purpose, it is the loan of a definite quantity of gold or silver on condition that an equal quantity be returned.

"Now, let it be observed, that there is here no question of *value*, or what quantity of commodity or set of commodities the gold will command in exchange. This has no part in the contract. The agreement respects the quantity and not the *value* of the gold; it has nothing to do with the purchasing power of gold in the market. The owner of the gold allows the borrower the use of the metal just as the owner of a spade or a plough might lend the implement to a neighbour, on condition of its being restored in the same state. It is true the owner of the gold does not require the return of the same identical pieces of metal as the owner of the spade would probably insist on the restoration of the identical spade, and for the reason before mentioned, that one pound of gold is precisely like another, or one piece of good money resembles in every respect others of the same denomination, and therefore, to exact a return of the pieces actually lent would be perfectly useless to the lender, while it would be incompatible with the object for which all money is borrowed, viz the power of transferring it to some one else. Should the transaction be somewhat more complex—should there be a stipulation that interest should be paid for the use of the money—still the nature of the contract would remain the same. It would be merely requiring that in addition to the restoration of the original quantity of gold a certain smaller quantity should be given to the lender for its use. There would still be no consideration—no question about value—but simply about quantity. The bargain would in no respect differ from one which had wheat for its subject instead of money, or a spade, or a plough. It would be an analogous case if one farmer lent another a plough on condition of receiving back not only the plough hut a new handle or a new share.

"This is a correct representation of the nature of all mere pecuniary bargains, whether loans or annuities, and it is so particularly desirable to notice that in such bargains the question is not at all of *value*, but of *quantity*, that the reader will pardon a little repetition. When I lend a sum of money I make no reference at all to its *value*—that is, of the relation of money to other articles — I never think of them; I stipulate only for the return of the quantity of money lent, along with such an additional quantity for its use as may be agreed upon. If I referred to the value of the sum lent, it would be necessarily its value in some one thing or in several things, and then my bargain would be in effect for a return of certain *quantities* of these things. We must come to a quantity of something at the last.

"*A steady application of this simple principle would remove many of the difficulties which are generally considered to embarrass this question.*"

"It is true that contracts may be made which shall have reference to the value of gold or silver as well as to its quantity; and in some cases very properly, I may with great propriety stipulate, that, inasmuch as the 100*l* which I lend when wheat is at 50*s* per quarter is equal to forty quarters of wheat, the value of forty quarters of wheat shall be returned to me when the loan is repaid. In effect this is, as already remarked, lending the wheat. In the same way any other commodity may be lent, or any other stipulation may be made. The freedom of bargains is and ought to be quite unrestricted; but, where no express condition of this sort is made, the contract amounts to what I have before stated it to be, *a loan of quantity without reference to value*, and the loan is fully repaid when the original quantity is restored, with the additional portion contracted for as interest This is the only construction that can be put upon a pecuniary contract; for if any one insists that it is a contract for a certain value, he is bound to show in relation to what commodity this value is to be, and then the matter would be reduced into a bargain for a quantity of that commodity. Thus he would be maintaining that a pecuniary contract does not relate to a quantity of money as expressed on the face of it, but to a quantity of some commodity of which no mention is made. This view is undoubtedly very different from that which has been frequently entertained. It has been usually assumed that in cases of loans an injustice is committed if the same value is not restored, as well as the same quantity. It has been considered, that is to say, that the sum paid back should enable the owner to command neither more nor less than the quantity of commodities in the market which he could have commanded when the money was originally lent.

"How far this might be a desirable circumstance, if it could be effected, is questionable; but it is certainly not required by justice or equity. It is not just that the man who borrows a spade from another when it is 5*s*. in price, and restores it when it is 2*s*. 6*d*. should be obliged to return two spades, unless a special agreement to that effect has been made. Neither can it be just that a man who borrows a pound of gold should be obliged to restore two pounds, on the ground that a pound of gold will, at the time of payment, purchase only half the quantity of wheat or other commodities that it could have purchased when the loan was advanced."

"The matter would be perfectly plain if the use which is made of gold permitted the identity of the individual pound borrowed to be preserved. No one in that case would think of any thing more than the restoration of the original gold. An instance closely analogous occurs when, as is by no means uncommon, a service of plate is lent by one individual to another for a specified compensation. The lender, on receiving back his plate at the end of a dozen months or a dozen years, would make no claim on account of the altered relation of the metal to other commodities. All that he would look for would be the restoration of the original articles in an uninjured condition" —(*Money and its Vicissitudes in Value, by the Author of a Critical Dissertation on Value*, &c. 1837, pp. 100-105.)

It will be observed that this view of the rationale of pecuniary contracts constitutes an insuperable objection to what is called a double standard of gold and silver.

In the interval between Sir Robert Peel's two Speeches of the 6th and 20th of May there had been some criticisms on the former. These were contained in an article of *The Times* newspaper. ① They were noticed by Sir

① In the 2nd edition of my pamphlet "on the Currency Principle", which had been published and was in the hands of some of the Members on the day of the debate of the 20th May 1844, I introduced an extract from the article in the *Times* in the following terms: —

The policy in pursuance of which the measures of government were proposed was developed in a speech on the 6th of May of some length by Sir Robert Peel. The merits of that speech have been described in a manner perfectly accordant with my estimate of them in a leading article of the *Times*; and as, agreeing in the view thus taken, I should fail of conveying it in language of my own so characteristically clear and appropriate as that in which it is there expressed, I am induced to give the following extract, premising that in the part immediately preceding, the proposed arrangements are spoken of as meeting with general approbation, in which the writer of the article concurs.

Robert, in his second Speech of the 20th of May. "I am told," he said,

---

"Sir R. Peel's speech was, we think, scarcely so good as his propositions. His premises were excellent; his conclusions admirable: all that was wanting was a connection between the two. The speech failed precisely in that which he professed, with some parade to have accomplished. It failed in developing clearly the principles on which the proposed changes were based. It had a beginning and ending, but seemed to have lost its middle in the delivery. He laid his foundations deep and palpable in the gold mines of Mexico; his towering results are those which have long furnished a landmark to the sagacious speculator on agios and exchanges; but there was a large intervening space of impenetrable and unmeaning cloud, displaying no visible or intelligible form to any imaginations but those which have already mastered the intricate and perilous ground which lies beneath. Sir Robert Peel expends much time in a true, ingenious, and very complete demolition of the Birmingham financiers. One-third part of his speech is occupied in showing that gold the money of this country is, and that gold it ought to remain—an exposition which, however valuable in itself, might, we think, without any serious loss to the argument, have been deferred till it was more distinctly called for. He proceeded to prove that an interference with promissory notes, which were the substitutes for gold, did not involve him in the necessity of meddling with bills of exchange or checks upon bankers—that convertibility was not alone a sufficient guarantee against over-issue—that country bankers did not regulate their issues by the foreign exchanges — and that a government bank was politically dangerous. Thence he unceremoniously leapt to his practical conclusions. 'This brought him,' he said, 'to an explanation of the practical measures which he proposed for the regulation of the matters he had submitted to the consideration of the House.'

"These measures we have said are just and sagacious; but they are scarcely justified by the speech by which they are introduced. The local banks of issue, for instance, are to be extinguished. Why? We gather from Sir Robert Peel's speech that it is because 'they do not control their issues according to the state of the foreign exchanges.' And why should they so control them? Because the omission to do so is the cause of over issue. And how so? Alas, in this, the very heart and root of the question—the moot point of the whole—Sir Robert leaves us in the dark. The connection between foreign exchanges and English circulation is an interesting and most important subject; it lay directly between Sir Robert Peel and his conclusion—nay, was the very ground on which that conclusion rested; and though to a certain extent intricate, is not too abstruse to be handled briefly and conclusively by the first financier of the day. Why, instead of grappling with it, did he spend time in proving what none but a few enthusiasts deny —the inexpediency of a return to paper payments? Equally chary is he of reasons for the proposed separation of the issue and deposit departments of the Bank of England. Those indeed who arc familiar with the opinions of the principal mercantile men of the day, or have even mastered the lending pamphlets on those subjects, will be at no loss to divine the principles on which he is proceeding. But this does not meet the wants of the wholly ignorant world, or even, we fear, of the half-informed House of Commons; and we therefore regret that such an occasion as the present has not drawn from the Premier a fuller and more instructive exposition of those views of currency on which he intends himself, "that my chain of argument the other night was incomplete; that there was no necessary connexion between my premises and my conclusions; that I did not show the necessity of interfering with the circulation of joint-stock banks or country banks; that I did not establish the policy of giving an increased control to the Bank of England over other banks. Now, I am not conscious that any link in the chain of argument was wanting."

With all due deference to such an authority, I have now to submit some considerations which may tend to show that *there is not one link in his chain of argument that will hold to warrant his conclusion.*

Sir Robert Peel's argument, as far as the immediate purpose is concerned, must be confined strictly to the question of the regulation and limitation of the amount of the note circulation. To provide for the solvency of banks, whether issuing or non-issuing, is a totally different question, although Sir Robert Peel, for the purpose apparently of producing an effect, thought proper to dwell upon the horrors of insolvent banks as a prominent reason for *restricting the amount of the circulation.* This question of insolvency is a

---

and should persuade his successors, to regulate the circulation of the country."

Unquestionably it is not easy to conceive a more defective or less instructive exposition of views which were destined to have so important a practical application.

Sir Robert Peel had evidently adopted the doctrine of the currency principle in its fullest extent, according to the exposition of it by Mr. Norman and Mr. Lloyd; but in his endeavours to explain it to the House, and to show the connection of it with the measure he was proposing, he failed in a degree which is surprising in a person so gifted, and so generally clear in his statements.

The truth is, that he laboured under the disadvantage of having embraced, without sufficient examination, a theory of the currency which is not accordant with, or explanatory of, the working of the actual system, or calculated to give any distinct insight into the probable effects of the intended change; and more especially of that part of it which relates to the separation of Issue and Banking. This measure of separation, for instance, may be the best possible, but if so, it could not be admitted to be so for the reasons stated by Sir Robert Peel. —

Inquiry into Currency Principle, *Supplementary Chapter*, 2nd edition, p. 148-151.

point to which I shall have occasion to advert hereafter. In the mean time it cannot be too strongly enjoined on the reader not for a moment to lose sight of this distinction, which Sir Robert seems constantly intent upon escaping from.

SECTION 2 *On Sir Robert Peel's definition of "money"*

The commencement of Sir R. Peel's exposition of the principles of the Act of 1844 is, as it ought to be, with a definition of the word *money*.

This definition, among ordinary disputants, would be a mere question of language, and would involve no interest except to those who were disposed to take part in what might be deemed a scientific controversy; but, in the instance of Sir Robert Peel's definition, the case is different. *Words*, with him, were *things*. Upon his understanding and assumption of the meaning of the word "Money," he has based a great part of his argument for restraining the circulation of that description of paper credit which, in obedience to the tenets of the currency theory, he considers to come within the definition of "Money." The definition by Mr. Norman and Mr. Loyd, and their deductions from it in favour of their theory would, however questionable, be harmless; but when adopted by Sir Robert Peel, and made the ground of a legislative measure, it has been far otherwise.

"I must state," he says, "at the outset, that in using the word 'money', I mean to designate by that word the coin of the realm and promissory notes, payable to bearer on demand. In using the word 'paper currency', I mean only such promissory notes. I do not include in that term bills of exchange, or drafts on bankers, or other forms of credit. There is a material distinction in my opinion between the character of a promissory note payable to bearer on demand, and other forms of paper credit, and *between the effects which they respectively produce upon the prices of commodities, and upon the exchanges*. The one answers all the purposes of *money*, passes from hand to hand without endorsement[①], without examination, if there be no suspicion of forgery; and it is what its designations imply it to be, currency or circulating medium."

Here the first link in the chain, or rather the ground-work of the argument, by which it is sought to show that Bank notes, possessing properties which apply to no other description of circulating medium, require regulation as to the quantity allowed to be issued, will be found to fail. The definition of money, as including promissory notes strictly payable in coin on demand, is not warranted by any recognised authority, or by any legitimate process of reasoning.

First, as to authorities.

In Johnson's Dictionary the definition of Money is, "Metals coined for the purposes of commerce."

In no instance, I believe, will it be found that Mr. Locke or Mr. Harris, or even the first Lord Liverpool, included promissory notes, issued by banks and returnable to the issuers at the will of the holder in exchange for coin, in their use of the word "Money".

The Bullion Report of 1810 affords no sanction to the definition of the word by Sir Robert Peel. The phraseology of the Report, on this important point, is remarkably guarded and uniform. "Paper currency" is the term employed, and the words "paper money" do not occur in more than one or

---

① If endorsement is an essential distinction, whence the *threat* to country bankers to deter them from any attempt at circulating short dated bills of exchange as substitutes for Bank notes?

two instances; and in these the immediate context fixes the acceptation in which they are used. So also Adam Smith occasionally speaks of paper money when meaning paper credit, that is, Bank notes payable in coin on demand. The same use of the term may doubtless be found in other writers; and I have so used it myself. But it will be found, I apprehend, that it has only been so employed as one among the several current modes of expression in which the term has been variously applied. And it is only as a matter of strict and scientific definition, in the nature of one of the postulates for the basis of a theory, and as a ground for its practical application, that I deny the existence of any sufficient authority for such use of the term.

Mr. Huskisson, in the following extracts① from his pamphlet, seems to have taken considerable pains in marking the distinguishing features of money and paper currency properly so called.

"It is," he observes, "of the essence of money to possess intrinsic value."

"Paper currency has obviously no intrinsic value."

"A promissory note, under whatever form, or from whatever source it may issue, *represents* value. It does so inasmuch as it is an undertaking to pay *in money* the sum for which it is issued."

"The *money* or coin of a country is so much of its capital. Paper currency is no part of the capital of a country; it is so much circulating credit."

"Whoever buys gives — whoever sells receives, such a quantity of pure gold or silver as is equivalent to the article bought or sold. Or if he gives or receives *paper* instead of *money*, he gives or receives that which is valuable

① *The Question concerning the Depreciation of our Currency stated and examined*, 1810, pp. I, 2.

only as it stipulates the payment of a given quantity of gold or silver. So long as this engagement is punctually fulfilled, paper will of course pass current with the coin with which it is constantly interchangeable. Both *money*, however, and paper *promissory* of money, are *common measures*, and *representatives* of the value of all commodities. But *money* alone is the *universal equivalent*: *paper currency* is the representative of that money."

Then as to the process of reasoning by which Sir Robert Peel classes Bank notes under the designation of *money*. He assumes that there is a distinction not only between the character of a promissory note payable on demand, and other forms of paper credit, but between the effects which they produce respectively upon the prices of commodities, and upon the exchanges. This assumption of the peculiar influence of Bank notes on prices, and on the exchanges, is unsustained by fact or argument. But of this ground of distinction, more hereafter.

The only other ground of distinction stated by Sir Robert Peel is that of their "passing from hand to hand without endorsement and without examination, if there be no suspicion of forgery." These differences are the most trivial imaginable. With reference to these and other distinctions that have been set up between Bank notes and bills of exchange, the following remarks by Mr. Fullarton have my entire concurrence: —

I am aware, indeed, that by those who can perceive no difference, between a Bank note and a sovereign, in respect to their several capacities of ministering to the offices of exchange, and yet are unwilling to allow the bill of exchange or the banker's cheque to rank on a parity with the Bank note as money, certain small and irrelative points of distinction have been suggested and insisted upon, as affording legitimate ground for the peculiar estimation which they claim for the Bank note. With regard to bills of exchange, for instance, we are told, that they are not entitled, like Bank notes, to the designation of money, for these among other reasons, namely, that they are "payable at a *fixed place* (!!), are drawn for amounts inconvenient for the general purposes of pecuniary affairs, require a knowledge on the part of those who receive them as to the solidity of the names which appear on them, and, in most cases, can only be transferred by an indorsement, which involves the credit of the indorser."①

Now, in the first place, it is not in point of fact true, that the circumstances here enumerated as peculiar to bills of exchange constitute any real distinction between those bills and promissory notes. If bills of exchange are payable at a *fixed place*, every Bank note, I apprehend, is the same; though how its being so or otherwise should be a matter of the slightest importance, I own I am quite unable to conjecture. The sums for which bills of exchange are usually drawn, may be more unequal, and less convenient for pecuniary purposes, than the sums imprinted on Bank notes; but this is an inconvenience easily obviated, wherever bills of exchange come extensively enough into use as a substitute for money to make it worth the trouble, and it proved no obstacle to their being employed during a long series of years, and to the almost total exclusion of notes, as the currency of all Lancashire, of the West Hiding of Yorkshire, and a large portion of the other great manufacturing districts in the heart of England. In those districts, we are told, that bills were then to be had for all sums from five pounds to ten thousand, and at all dates not exceeding three months. It may no doubt be very desirable that the party receiving a bill of exchange should know something "of the solidity of the names which appear on it;" but it

① See Mr. Norman's Letter to Charles Wood, Esq. M. P., p. 43.

cannot be more so, than that the taker of a Bank note should know something of the solidity of the banker who issues it. And, with respect to the alleged peculiarity attaching to bills, that "in most cases they can only be transferred by an indorsement which involves the credit of the indorser", it may be sufficient to answer, that, though an indorsement may in the first instance be required to render a bill of exchange negotiable, that negotiation need not involve the responsibility even of the first indorser, unless he pleases; and a bill once indorsed in blank may afterwards pass through a hundred hands by delivery, just as a Bank note does. ①

These *essential* distinctions are in truth worth absolutely nothing, and most assuredly they do any thing but prove that Bank notes can, with propriety, be included in the definition of *money*, to the exclusion of bills of exchange.

It will have been observed that, in the passage I have cited, Sir Robert Peel slides from contending that Bank notes are money into considering them only as *currency* or *circulating medium*, but still to the exclusion of bills of exchange. He, in a subsequent passage of his Speech, refers to the first Lord Liverpool, whom he had before quoted, and proceeds to remark: —

"There is a passage in the work to which I have before referred, the Treatise of Lord Liverpool, which draws the just distinction between paper credit and paper currency, and exposes the fallacy of those who deprecate any attempt to regulate by law the paper currency on the ground that it is not distinguishable from paper credit."

"Lord Liverpool observes: — It has been a common artifice practised by those who have written on paper currency, to confound paper credit with

---

① *On the Regulation of Currencies*, pp. 38, 39.

paper currency, and even the higher sorts of paper currency with the inferior sorts, such as immediately interfere with the use of the coins of the realm. Paper credit is not only highly convenient and beneficial, but is even absolutely necessary in carrying on the trade of a great commercial kingdom.

"Paper currency is a very undefined term as used by speculative writers. To find arguments in its support, at least to the extent to which it is at present carried, they have been obliged to connect it with paper credit; so that the principles on which the use of paper credit is truly founded may be brought in support of a great emission of paper currency. Paper currency, strictly speaking, consists only of bills or notes payable or convertible into cash on demand by the person who issued the same at the will of the holder."

Lord Liverpool's book, published in 1806, consequently during the Bank Restriction, treats almost exclusively of the professed object of it, as indicated by its title, "The Coins of the Realm." And a most valuable treatise it is on that subject. A distinct examination, however, of the nature and functions of the different forms of paper did not enter into the purpose of the writer, and consequently he can hardly be considered as an authority for the distinction set up by Sir Robert Peel. Lord Liverpool nowhere sanctions the definition of "*money*" as including Bank notes. But he incidentally notices a distinction which it would have been well that Sir Robert Peel should have been aware of. The distinction I allude to is that between the higher denominations of Bank notes and the lower. Lord Liverpool says, in the passage cited, it has been a common artifice among writers on paper currency "to confound the higher sorts of it with the inferior sorts, *such as immediately interfere with the use of the coins of the realm.*"

Adam Smith is the first, I believe, who pointed out the distinction between Bank notes of the lower denominations, which served chiefly for the purposes of retail trade, and the higher, which were in use principally between dealers and dealers. The higher ones do not now circulate even among dealers, excepting cattle dealers and horse dealers, having been superseded by a general use of banking accommodation, and consequently by cheques and book credits. I am not aware that this distinction between the two denominations of notes had been remarked upon by any writer since Adam Smith, excepting this slight incidental notice by Lord Liverpool, till I had occasion, in a pamphlet which was published a few weeks before Sir Robert Peel brought forward his measure, to call attention to the important bearing which the difference between the two sorts of paper is calculated to have upon the question of the currency theory. The confounding of them Lord Liverpool considers to be "an artifice" practised by those who have written on paper currency. I consider it to be nothing more than a gross mistake. It confuses and vitiates the reasoning on which the main conclusions of the currency theory are made to rest; and it involves the further mistake of confounding currency and capital.

Sir Robert Peel, after referring to the above passage from Lord Liverpool, says, "That appears to me to be the true definition of paper currency as distinguished from paper credit. It is the substitute for and immediate representative of coin, *and with coin constitutes 'money'*." Now Lord Liverpool justly observes that it is the lower sorts only that interfere with the coins of the realm: by *interfering with*, meaning, obviously, serving *as substitutes for them*; and nowhere does he sanction a definition by which even these notes of inferior denomination could be considered as paper "money".

Sir Robert Peel's definition of money is identical, however, with that which had been propounded and explained by Mr. Norman and Mr. Loyd in their evidence and their pamphlets.

The mistake on which this definition proceeds of confounding the two distinct functions of Bank notes, and considering both of them as substitutes for coin, and consequently as *constituting money*, is so important in its bearing upon this first link of Sir Robert Peel's argument, that I trust to be excused for here inserting the following extract from my pamphlet in which the distinction between the two kinds of circulation is pointed out: —

"Mr. Norman, after noticing what he calls the contrivances usually resorted to for the purpose of either dispensing with the use of money altogether, or of diminishing the quantity of it, which are absolutely required for the adjustment of existing transactions, observes —

'On these contrivances one general remark may he made, as it affords a ready and practical, if not a strictly scientific distinction between such substitutes for money, and that which, as I conceive, really constitutes money, viz. coin and bank notes. If bank notes are withdrawn from circulation, their place must necessarily be supplied by an equal amount of coin; but the abolition of any, or of all of the contrivances for dispensing with the use of money, will not necessitate the introduction in their place of an equal amount of coin or bank notes.'—(*Letter to C. Wood, Esq.*, p. 34.)

"In dealing with this proposition, let us try it by putting the case in the strongest way, and suppose that the Bank of England has the power, and is disposed, to withdraw all its notes from circulation; or, in order to obviate the objection, that in such case other banks might supply the vacuum, let us suppose that all promissory notes, payable on demand, were suppressed by act of Parliament, Would Mr. Norman contend, that the whole amount must of necessity be replaced by coin?

"Most assuredly such would not be the effect.

"A moment's consideration must be sufficient to satisfy any one that it would only be the smaller denomination of notes, which, if suppressed, would require to be replaced by coin; the whole of the 1*l.* notes, which still circulate in Ireland and Scotland, would require to be so replaced; and the greater part of the 5*l.* notes, and a small part of the 10*l.* notes, in the United Kingdom.

"All the larger amounts might be, and most probably would be, supplied by cheques, and bills of exchange, and settlements.

"The employment of the higher denominations of Bank of England notes is chiefly for the following purposes: —

"1. Collection of the public revenue, and the payment of it into the Exchequer.

"2. Payments on sales and mortgages of landed and other fixed property. Till lately the rule in transactions of this nature was almost uniformly that the payment, on conveyance of the deeds, should be made in Bank notes. But there has of late been a tendency to relax this rule, and cheques are now not unfrequently received in payment on such occasions.

"3. Dividends and rents received by persons who do not employ bankers.

"4. Payments for debts in cases in which the debtor has not a banker, or in which he would not be trusted so far as to have his cheque received in satisfaction of the claim.

"5. Payments into Court in litigated claims.

"6. Reserves held by bankers, and especially those of the west end of the town, and by the joint-stock banks in the city who are not admitted to the clearing-house.

"7. Settlements at the clearing-house.

"Now these are peculiar purposes, most or all of which might be answered by other means than Bank notes, and most assuredly not by supplying their place by coin.

"1. The public revenue is, in an increasing number of instances, paid into the Exchequer by drafts on the Bank of England.

"2. Payments for landed and fixed property are in an increasing number of instances paid by cheques.

"3. Dividends to persons not keeping bankers might be retained by them in the shape of warrants.

"4. and 5. Involve so small an amount, as not materially to affect the question.

"6. The circulation of Bank of England notes among bankers, whether between the Bank of England and the west end bankers, and the city joint-stock bankers, and the circulation of country Bank notes, in settlements among each other, are mere conventional transfers of capital.

"7. The clearings among the bankers of the city of London might all be effected either by Exchequer bills, as in the case of the banks of Edinburgh, or by cheques on the Bank of England.

"The country bank notes above the lowest denominations (which are in use in the retail trade, and in the payment of wages) are mostly employed in the provision markets, and in cattle and horse fairs, purposes for which bills of exchange were formerly, and might be again, very extensively employed."①

It appears, then, that there is neither authority nor reasoning in favour of the definition which invests Bank notes with the properties of money, or paper currency, *to the exclusion of all other forms of paper credit*. So that the first link of the argument of Sir Robert, Peel, or, rather, the groundwork of it, utterly fails. But even if he had established his definition of Bank notes, as constituting money, or even paper currency, exclusively of all other forms of paper credit, so that the distinction, instead of being a mere unsupported dictum of the currency theory, were admitted as an axiom beyond doubt or dispute — it does not follow that this description of paper obligations, or promises, should require more of regulation, as regards the issue or the quantity of them, than other obligations, merely because they are payable on demand. There is no more reason, derivable from the exposition which assumes this particular property of Bank notes as constituting them to be money, for compelling the issuers of them to limit their quantity, than for compelling the issuers of bills of exchange to do so.

But it seems there is another link in the argument which takes Bank notes out of the category of other forms of paper credit. Sir Robert Peel admits that other forms of credit have some effects in common with Bank notes, but he adds — "I think experience shows that the paper currency, that is, the promissory notes payable to bearer on demand, stands in a certain relation to the gold coin and the foreign exchange in which other

① It was a great omission on the part of the Committee on Banks of Issue in 1840 and 1841, not to have inquired of the bankers who were examined what were the purposes for which the different sorts of bank notes were required.

forms of paper credit do not stand." What this different relation may be is not, upon the bare enunciation of the proposition, very obvious, nor is it rendered much more so by the illustrations offered in elucidation of it. "There are," says Sir Robert Peel, "striking examples of this adduced in the Bullion Committee of 1810, in the case both of the Bank of England and of the Irish and Scotch banks." He then goes on to give the examples, which are —

1. The Bank of England in 1696, when it had suspended its payments in cash, and when its notes were at a discount of 17 per cent.

2. The Bank of Ireland in 1804, when its notes were not only inconvertible into gold, but were not convertible, as the English and Scotch bank notes were, into Bank of England notes.

3. The Scotch Banks about the middle of last century, which issued notes with an *optional clause*.

To Mr. Fullarton[①] we are indebted for a very clear exposure of the utter inapplicability of these examples to the elucidation of the very obscure proposition which they were called forth to illustrate. I regret that the length of this very striking passage compels me to refrain from inserting it. I will only here repeat the concluding sentence of it: —

"Really, to anticipate any effect from illustrations like these, is presuming somewhat far on the ignorance of those to whom they are addressed."

How Sir Robert Peel could venture to adduce examples so inappropriate to any legitimate purpose of his argument, is not easily to be accounted for, unless he acted upon the presumption — perhaps a fair one — that he

---

① *Regulation of Currencies*, 2nd edition, pp. 176-184.

was addrassing an auditory profoundly ignorant of the subject, and a public little less so.

Sir Robert Peel concludes the citation of these singularly inappropriate examples with the remark, "In all these cases *the action* has been upon that part of the paper credit of the country which has consisted in promissory notes payable to the bearer on demand."

It appears from this passage that Sir Robert Peel, assuming that the Bank, in those far-fetched cases of inconvertible paper, acted directly upon the amount of their out-standing notes, inferred, and desired those he was addressing to infer, that the Bank of England and the country banks, in modern practice, and in a strictly convertible state of the paper, have also a direct power over the amount of their circulation, and thence an influence on the total quantity of *money*; and, consequently, on prices, and on trade and credit.

SECTION 3 *On the currency principle*

Sir Robert Peel, in ascribing these exclusive properties and functions to bank notes, and in maintaining, as he did, that the amount of them ought to be regulated by immediate reference to the foreign exchanges, had become, in the fullest sense of the word, a proselyte of the "Currency principle"①school.

And as it was in accordance with the tenets of that school that his

---

① It has been supposed that the use of the- expression "Currency Principle" to designate the set of opinions here alluded to was first used by me. This is a mistake: it was first used, I believe, in the evidence of Mr. Norman, before the Committee on Banks of Issue in 1840. After a question and answer relating to the circulation of the country banks, he is asked,—

banking measure of 1844 was framed, it is necessary, in the examination of the merit of the scheme, here to give some account of them. This I cannot do better than by the following description of them, given by me when writing on the subject, before I was at all aware, *or thought it within reasonable probability*, that the theory of that principle was destined to form a basis for the regulation of our paper currency.

"It was held by most writers of any authority on the subject of the currency, till within the last few years, that the purposes of a mixed circulation of coin and paper were sufficiently answered, as long as the coin was perfect and the paper constantly convertible into coin; and that the only evils to be guarded against by regulation, were those attending suspension of payment and insolvency of the banks, a large proportion of which blend an issue of promissory notes with their other business. This,

---

"Q. 2018. Do you conceive that their circulation is at present regulated in any way consistently with the variation which would take place in a metallic currency? —No; I think not: it seems to me that their circulation is varied upon what I should call *Banking principles*: that is to say, that it increases with the rise of interest and prices, and that it decreases with the fall of interest and prices, *in opposition to what I should call Currency principles, according to which it would increase or decrease with increase or decrease of bullion*; and the only limitation that I can perceive, is the ultimate necessity which the private issuers are placed under of discharging their notes in gold or Bank of England notes."

There is another answer or two by Mr. Norman, in the same evidence, in which the term is so used. And in his letter to Charles Wood, Esq., in 1841, page 30, the term "Currency Principle" is again used in opposition to the "Banking Principle".

Mr. Gilbart, in the course of his examination before the same Committee in 1841, having made use of the terms Currency principles and Banking principles, was asked:—"Q. 932. What do you mean by the expression 'Currency principles?' — I mean by the phrase 'Currency principles' a bank which shall do nothing else but issue notes for gold, and gold for notes. Q 933. What do you mean by the expression, 'Banking principles?' —I mean by 'Banking principles' notes that are issued in the repayment of deposits, or in the discount of bills, or in the making of loans; at the same time, I would state that I merely used those words in the sense in which they are used by the writers who advocate those peculiar principles which they call Currency principles. I do not at all admit that those are the correct principles upon which the currency should be administered."

in point of fact, is what is understood in general terms as the ' Banking principle,' and is that upon which our system of currency is constructed and conducted.

"But a new canon of currency has of late been promulgated by persons of no mean authority. According to these authorities, it is not sufficient that the Bank notes should be at all times strictly convertible into coin, and that the banks, whether issuing or not issuing, should be solvent; they consider that a purely metallic circulation (excepting only as regards the convenience and economy of paper), is the type of a perfect currency, and contend that the only sound principle of a mixed currency is that by which the Bank notes in circulation should be made to conform to the gold, into which they are convertible, not only in value, but in amount; that is to say, that the Bank notes being supposed to be a substitute, and the only substitute, for so much coin, should vary exactly in amount as the coin would have done if the currency had been purely metallic; and that the test of good or bad management is not, as is considered under the mere banking principle, in the extent or proportion of reserve in treasure and in immediately convertible securities held by the banks; but in the degree of correspondence between variations in the amount of bullion and variations in the amount of Bank notes in circulation. A regulation of the issue of Bank notes, in conformity with this doctrine, is now understood to be designated as the ' Currency principle.'

"With a view to the application of this principle to practice, it has been suggested that either a national bank should be established under commissioners, whose duty and functions should be confined to the exchange of paper against gold and of gold against paper, for all beyond a fixed amount of paper issued against securities; or that the Bank of

England should be the sole source of issue, under the strictest rule of separation of the functions of issue from the merely banking department.

"The arguments urged in favour of such separation have, as it should seem, made considerable impression on the public mind, and schemes founded upon this principle have been strongly pressed on the attention of government, on the ground not only of guarding against the danger of suspension and insolvencies of the issuers, but of imparting more confidence and stability to credit and trade, and of securing greater steadiness in prices, and thus obviating or abating the alternations of feverish excitement and the extreme of depression, which have prevailed under the existing system, and which are imputed to *a neglect of the Currency principle*.

"The theory of the Currency principle numbers among its advocates many distinguished names. The fullest and most elaborate statements of it, however, are to be found in the publications of Mr. Norman, Mr. Loyd, and Colonel Torrens, and in the evidence of the two former gentlemen before the Committee of the House of Commons on Banks of Issue in 1840. I therefore avail myself mainly of their exposition of the doctrine, and their arguments in support of it, as affording the best grounds for an examination of the theory, and of the practice recommended as an application of it.

"The following extract from Mr. Norman's evidence conveys a concise statement of the theory, and of the proposed application of it, as the only sound rule for the paper portion of the currency, namely, Bank notes, which he limits to those notes which are in the hands of the public:—

" 'I consider a metallic currency to be the most perfect currency, except so far as respects inconvenience in some respects, and cost. In every thing else a metallic currency is the most perfect, and should be looked upon as the type of all other currencies; and as from their superior convenience and greater cheapness, bank notes are introduced to supply the place of a certain portion of metallic currency, I think that bank notes should be so managed, that they should possess all the other attributes of a metallic currency, and among those attributes, I conceive the most important to be that they should increase and decrease in the same way that a metallic currency would increase and decrease. I do not think it is possible to improve upon a metallic currency, except in the two points of convenience and cheapness.'[①]

"Mr. Norman afterwards explained that by convenience he meant the easier transfer, and by cheapness the economy of using the less costly material; so that the paper thus regulated, would be so far an improvement on a metallic currency.

"The following are the chief[②] evils which present themselves, according to Mr. Norman's view, in our existing paper circulation, from its not conforming to such rule: —

"1. A tendency to vary, both as to excess and deficiency, in an unnecessary degree, and at unsuitable periods.

"2. A liability to discredit, both mercantile and political, in a large portion of it, if not the whole.

"3. Temporary or permanent insolvency on the part of many of the issuers.

"Mr. Loyd in his evidence gives the following view of the inconvenience which he ascribes to the present system: —

---

① G. W. Norman, Esq. Evidence. Committee on Banks of Issue. Question No. 1749.

② *Remarks on Currency and Banking*, G. W. Norman, Esq., 1838.

"'*Q* 2748. Are there any other evils besides the danger of nonconvertibrlity that arise out of the present system?'— '*A*. There can be no doubt about it; the state of the circulation has a very direct effect upon the state of credit, of confidence, of prices, and of banking; and if the state of the circulation be allowed to become an unnatural one, unnatural and pernicious effects will be produced upon all those. If your circulation is subject either to depreciation from excess of its amount, or to violent fluctuations of amount, then undoubtedly that will be followed by corresponding effects upon confidence, upon credit, upon prices, upon banking, and so forth. Those things are also affected by other considerations. I do not see that it is possible to analyse the effects, and to attribute to each cause its respective share in producing those effects; all that can certainly be understood is, that if you regulate the paper circulation upon sound principles, you may be quite sure that you have then removed that portion of the evil effects which was attributable to the want of due regulation.'

"By an unnatural state of the circulation, and the want of due regulation, must be understood in the sense in which Mr. Loyd uses the term, a non-conformity of the amount of Bank notes to the amount of bullion." — (*Inquiry into the Currency Principle*, pp. 1-6.)

It will be observed, that in charging the system as it existed before the Act of 1844, with the evils here enumerated, and in imputing, as mismanagement on the part of the Bank of England and the country banks, their not so regulating the amount of the note circulation as to make it conform to the variations in the foreign exchanges, the propounders of the theory of the currency principle assume and affirm that it is in the power of the banks to act directly on their circulation; in other words, that they *can* and *do* exercise a direct control over the quantity of paper currency which they define to be Bank notes.

SECTION 4 *On the error of confounding paper credit with paper money*

In the assumption alluded to at the close of the last section, it is now quite clear that, in the currency theory, *paper credit*, that is Bank notes, resting on credit and payable on demand in coin, is confounded with *paper money*. The distinction between the two is thus pointed out by Mr. Huskisson.

"Of *paper currency* there are two sorts; the one resting upon *confidence*; the other upon *authority*. Paper resting upon confidence is what I have described *as circulating credit*, and consists in engagements for the payment on demand of any specific sums of *money*, which engagements, from *a general trust* in the issuers of such paper, they are enabled to substitute for *money* in the transactions of the community. Paper resting upon authority, is what, in common language, is called *paper money*; and consists in engagements issued and circulated under the sanction and by the immediate intervention of the public power of the state. ① Paper, such as alone used to be current in Great Britain before the restriction on the bank, was strictly *circulating credit*. The paper current in Austria, Russia, &c. is properly denominated *paper money*."

Professor Storch, in his very elaborate work "Cours d'Economie

① The confusion between paper credit and paper money seems to have given rise to the dogma of the currency theory, that the issue of promissory notes payable on demand, in coin, is a prerogative or function of the sovereign!

Politique," gives the following definition of paper money: —

"On reserve le nom de papier-monnaie à des billets que le souverain ordonne de reeevoir en payement à la place du numeraire metéllrque. Quelles que sorent la forme et l'origine de ces billets, qu'ils promettent un remboursement ou non, qu'ils soient émis par des particuliers ou par le gouvernement, dès que leur circulation n'est plus I'effet de la confiance, ils cessent d'être des billets de confiance et deviennent du papier-monnaie."

Billets de Banque he considers as *billets de confiance*, in other words, as paper credit, and therefore as differing essentially from paper money. Other authorities might be cited to the same effect.

Thus, for example, there is the following passage in Mr. Fullarton's treatise, already referred to: —

"Gold and silver coin pass current in exchange for all sorts of commodities, because gold and silver are themselves commodities of value, and furnish the buyer and seller with a convenient equivalent that is universally in demand. Inconvertible government notes, though valueless in themselves, acquire a value in exchange, as has been shown, from the conditions annexed to their emission, and by reason of that value are received in exchange for commodities precisely on the same principle as coin. These two descriptions of circulation, therefore, fall naturally under a common head, and the phrase 'money' may by a fair analogy be applied equally to the one as to the other. The operations performed by both, but more especially those performed by the coin, partake to a greater or less extent of the nature of barter. But when, in the progress of society, credit comes to perform an important part in all mutual dealings, and in the great majority of transactions supersedes the necessity for this interchange of equivalents, an entirely new principle is brought into play, and one governed by distinct laws. Credit becomes then the legitimate substitute for money, but, in all its modifications and phases, it is distinguished by a broad and impassable line from money itself. The real question then to be considered is, not whether this or that particular form of credit be entitled to the designation of 'money,' but whether, without a perversion of terms and an outrage of principle, that denomination can be applied to credit in any shape.

"Now, what are bank-notes but a form of credit? What are they but credit parcelled out into small and even sums, for greater convenience in circulation? Each note is simply a transferable acknowledgment of a debt due from the banker to the first recipient of the note, and which he (the banker) promises to pay on demand: the value of which it purports to convey is that which it enables the holder to command by sending it to the bank, from whence it issued, and no other; and it is a value which rises and falls with the value of the money it represents, whether that money be metallic or conventional; for a circulation of bank notes may have either indifferently for its basis."—(*Regulation of Currencies*, *2nd edition*, pp. 36, 37.)

The difference between the two descriptions of paper is highly important. In my tract of 1844, I noticed the error of confounding the two, and pointed out their distinctive features in practical operation. As my notice of that distinction, and of the practical consequences flowing from it, brought forth answers from some of the most prominent of the partisans of the currency theory, avowing their belief of the perfect identity of the two sorts of paper currency up to the point of convertibility, and denying any difference up to that point in their practical effect, it is essential to a clear view of the difference between us, to insert here the passages of my tract relating to it, and of the answers which it elicited.

"A great part of the examination of witnesses by the Committee of the House of Commons on Banks of Issue in 1840, was directed to the eliciting of opinions as to the terms by which the various kinds of instruments of exchange should be dcsignated and classified. The witnesses were severally called upon to define the sense in which they used the terms 'money, currency, and circulation,' and to say whether they included deposits in the Bank and bills of exchange under any or all of these terms.

"The importance which was attached to the attempt at settling those definitions seems to have arisen from an opinion which prevailed evidently among the members of the Committee①, that, by arriving at a conclusion as to what part of the various forms of paper credit should he considered exclusively as money or currency, conferring *a power of purchase*, some criterion or test might be found of the influence of one of the principal elements upon which not only the state of trade and credit, but also general prices depend; it being assumed that commodities, although liable in each particular instance to be influenced by circumstances affecting the supply and demand, are more or less under a direct influence from variations in the quantity of money or currency. And the same assumption of a direct

① From the tenour of the questions which were put to me and other witnesses by Mr. Hume, it might be inferred that he was of opinion that bank notes and deposits, as they conferred *a power of purchase*, were operative as a cause of variations of prices. And it is possible that such was *then* his opinion; but, not long before, he seems to have entertained a very different view. In the debate on Sir W. Clay's motion for a committee on Joint Stock Banks, May 12. 1836, Mr. Hume said, "With regard to the amount of paper issues, I think I could show that it would be impossible to issue too much paper money, if it were made convertible into gold in every part of the kingdom on demand. Indeed, I believe that great delusion exists in the country with regard to the effect on prices of the currency. My opinion is, that the quantity of money depends on the rise of prices; and that the rise of prices does not depend on the quantity of money. I hold the prevailing doctrine to be extremely erroneous on this point. The currency doctors I know differ from me; but there has never been a fair opportunity of demonstrating the truth of my propositions."

agency of the quantity of money, according to the assumed definition of it, on prices, will be found to be either expressed or implied in the vast majority of the numberless publications to which the currency question has given rise.

"An increase or diminution of the amount of Bank notes is evidently considered, not only by the professed adherents of the doctrine of the currency principle, but by a large proportion of the public who take an interest in the subject, to be analogous, in the effects on markets, to alterations in the quantity of a government compulsory paper; or, in other words, they consider that prices in such cases are under a direct influence from, and affected in the same manner by, variations in the amount of Bank notes in circulation, which they designate indiscriminately as paper money.

"I cannot help thinking that there is a lurking impression among the doctrinaires of the currency theory, arising mainly from their use of the term '*issue of paper money*,' which leads them to confound Bank notes, strictly convertible into coin, with a compulsory and inconvertible paper currency. It is true, no doubt, that they are aware that the liability to payment on demand in gold will eventually check any excess of issue in the one, and will thus distinguish it from the other. But it seems to me equally true, judging by all their expressions and the whole course of their arguments, that they are misled by a false analogy, and that although they admit in general terms that there must be a check to the power of issue by its being brought to the test of convertibility, they are of opinion that there is a power in each individual bank of issue, and in the banks of issue collectively, to operate at any given time in adding directly to the amount of Bank notes in circulation and in withdrawing them from it. The presumption that the advocates of the currency principle are under the influence of this mistaken analogy will be strengthened when we come to the consideration of the effects in trade, credit, and prices, which they ascribe to the influence of the quantity of money, meaning Bank notes and coin.

"This erroneous impression arises from a neglect of the consideration of the difference in the manner and purpose of the issue. I have not met with an instance in the inquiry by the committees, or in the numerous publications which have appeared on the subject of the currency, of any attention having been paid to this particular point. Indeed, the context in all of them seems to assume that there is no difference, and that therefore any attempt at explanation would be a work of supererogation. Thus, Mr. Porter, who, in the chapter on currency, in his highly valuable work 'On the Progress of the Nation,' attributes to the amount of the circulation great influence on prices, contents himself with observing, '*It is not necessary to explain*, at any length, *in what manner* excessive issues of currency tend to raise the general prices of goods.'[①] Now an explanation, however brief, of this point was exactly the thing wanted. And I cannot help thinking, that if he had suffered himself to pause and reflect upon it, he could hardly have failed to modify the opinion he has there expressed of the influence of the amount of the currency on prices, and he would possibly have been led to distrust the correctness of the view presented by the table which he has inserted in illustration of his opinion of that connection.

"A moment's consideration will serve to show the importance of the distinction to which I have here alluded.

---

① Progress of the Nation, vol. ii. p. 225. Mr. Porter, however, in a new edition, although he still retains the table and the general views alluded to above, has omitted the particular sentence given in the text.

" When a government issues paper money, inconvertible and compulsorily current, it is usually in payment for —

"1. The personal expenditure of the sovereign or the governing power.

"2. Public works and buildings.

"3. Salaries of civil servants.

"4. Maintenance of military and naval establishments.

" It is quite clear that paper created and so paid away by the government, not being returnable to the issuer, will constitute a fresh source of demand, and must be forced into and permeate all the channels of circulation. Accordingly, every fresh issue beyond the point at which former issues had settled in a certain rise of prices and of wages, and a fall of the exchanges, is soon followed by a further rise of commodities and wages, and a fall of the exchanges; the depreciation being in the ratio of the forcibly increased amount of the issues. ①

"It will hence appear that the difference between paper money so issued, and bank notes such as those of this country consists, not only in the limit prescribed by their convertibility to the amount of them, but in the mode of issue. The latter are issued to those only who, being entitled to demand

---

① Discredit is not an essential element in variations of the value of an inconvertible paper, nor is depreciation always a necessary consequence of inconvertibility. The notes of the Bank of England, and of the private banks of this country, were, for two years after the restriction, of the same value as if they had been convertible, and never experienced any discredit. There were great fluctuations in the credit of the paper money of the United States of America during the War of Independence, and also in the case of the French assignats, arising from fluctuating opinions as to the chances of redemption; and both descriptions became ultimately valueless by excess, when all prospect of redemption had ceased. But the Russian government paper, although, during the progress of its depreciation, by successively increasing issues, no certain or probable prospect of redemption had been held out, seems never to have suffered any discredit; and the variations of the exchanges beyond those produced by the mere excess of the paper, were such only as are incidental to variations in the state of trade.

gold, desire to have notes in preference; and it depends upon the particular purposes for which the notes are employed, whether a greater or less quantity is required. *The quantity*, therefore, *is an effect*, *and not a cause of demand.* A compulsory government paper, on the other hand, while it is in the course of augmentation, acts directly as an originating cause on prices and incomes, constituting a fresh source of demand in money, depreciated in value, as compared with gold, but of the same nominal value as before." — (*Inquiry into the Currency Principle*, pp. 68-70, 19, 20.)

Sir William Clay and Colonel Torrens, in pamphlets which appeared soon after mine, and professed to be refutations of my objections to their theory, each of them avowed that they could not see any difference between the two kinds of paper up to the point of convertibility.

The following is the passage of Sir William Clay's pamphlet[①], in which he makes that avowal: —

"I profess myself to partake of the blindness of the public in this matter, and to be wholly unable to perceive any other difference between the two issues of paper money here described than the point of convertibility, or in the phenomena which they are respectively capable of exhibiting. I cannot understand why paper money issued to defray the expenditure of the sovereign should be different in its effect when so issued, from paper money paid away for the expenditure of private individuals, why a five-pound note issued to the builder of a barrack should take a different course from a five-pound note paid to the builder of a shop or warehouse — why notes employed to defray the salaries of government clerks should be more

① *Remarks on the Expediency of Restricting the Issue of Promissory Notes to a Single Issuing Body*, by Sir W. Clay, Bart, M. P., 1844, pp. 38, 39.

disposed to 'permeate all the channels of circulation' than if used to pay clerks in merchants' counting-houses, or workmen in a factory? I myself am totally at a loss to conceive of any one circumstance or quality which might be predicated of the one, which might not with equal truth be predicated of the other. The one sole difference is convertibility — a most important one, no doubt."

This avowal of Sir W. Clay of his inability to perceive the difference which I had pointed out between the two issues is thus remarked upon by Mr. Fullarton: —

"Sir William Clay, however, cannot, it seems, understand this. 'He is wholly unable to perceive' any of that 'essential difference of character, independently of convertibility, between Bank notes and a government compulsory paper, which Mr. Tooke insists upon; he can see no point of distinction but in the convertibility of the notes; and, when Mr. Tooke points out, that the compulsory issues of Governments are usually in payment for the personal expenditure of the Sovereign, for public works and buildings, or for the maintenance of civil, naval, and military establishments, and that 'paper created and so paid away by the Government, *not being returnable to the issuer*, will constitute a fresh source of demand, and must be forced into and permeate all the channels of circulation,' Sir William Clay seems to think the proposition satisfactorily answered by a profession of his inability to discover 'why paper money issued to defray the expenditure of the Sovereign should be different in its effect, when issued, from paper money paid away for the expenditure of private individuals—why a 5*l.* note issued to the builder of a barrack should take a different course from a 5*l.* note paid to the builder of a shop or warehouse—why notes employed to defray the salaries of

Government clerks, or the pay of soldiers and sailors, should be more disposed to permeate all the channels of circulation, than if used to pay clerks in merchants' counting-houses or workmen in a factory.'①

"It is certainly not surprising that Sir William Clay should be unable to perceive the truth of a string of distinctions, which neither Mr. Tooke nor any other sane person has ever dreamt of maintaining, and which have no other existence than in his own imagination. But what does surprise one is, that Sir William Clay should not only have read, but should quote, and profess to criticise, Mr. Tooke's very plain proposition, and yet should pass wholly unnoticed the single and only point of distinction on which Mr. Tooke's argument turns, namely, that the Government paper is '*paid away*,' and is '*not returnable to the issuer*', whereas the bank notes are only *lent*, and *are returnable to the issuers*. If the truth of this distinction be not intelligible to Sir William Clay, nor its important bearing on the question under discussion obvious to him, I can have little hope of making the matter more apparent to him by any further illustrations. I shall, nevertheless, make one effort more to bring the argument home to his conviction. I shall take the liberty of supposing that, after the suspension of cash payments in 1797, by which the bank note circulation of this country was transformed from a convertible into a conventional currency, the Directors of the Bank of England, instead of exercising the privilege intrusted to them, in the discharge merely of their ordinary functions as bankers, according to the same system, and subject to the same rules by which in all times previously they had been governed,—that, instead of

① See Sir William Clay's "Remarks on the Expediency of Restricting the Issue of Promissory Notes," &c, pp. 38, 39.

making advances to individuals on the security of approved bills of exchange at short dates, and to Government on the security of the accruing produce of loans and revenues, they had chosen, and had been permitted to deal with, their issues of inconvertible notes as a private gentleman deals with his income,—to disburse them without stint or measure for objects of personal gratification, in building palaces, in laying out plantations and gardens, in the purchase of works of art, or in the pleasures of the table or the chace. Is Sir William Clay seriously of opinion that, in as far as respects the amount and value of the currency, this system of expenditure would have had no effect beyond that which would be produced by the same extent of issue in the ordinary course of banking operations? Should Sir William hesitate to reply in the affirmative, I may perhaps be permitted to observe, that the case which I have supposed is precisely that of every Government which attempts to defray the national expenditure by a compulsory issue of inconvertible paper. The paper so issued is expended in the purchase of naval and military stores, in building ships, in constructing public edifices, and in the payment of services performed to the state, and no precaution is usually taken to ensure its being ever returned again into the Exchequer. In the case of the Bank of England, on the other hand, the reflux of the notes was at no period interrupted. Perfect convertibility is no doubt one essential condition of every sound and efficient system of currency. It is the only effectual protection against internal discredit, and the best preventive of any violent aberrations of the exchange with foreign countries. But it is not so much by convertibility into gold, as by the regularity of the reflux, that in the ordinary course of things any redundance of the bank note issues is rendered impossible. When a greater number of Bank of England notes fall into the hands of any individval than he is likely to have any immediate call for, he does not, unless he wants specie to send abroad, present them to the Bank for gold. He merely lodges them with his own banker, who probably either places the sum to the credit of his own deposit account with the Bank of England, or throws them into the discount market, where they help to supply the vacancy left by the tide of notes continually setting back to the Bank. It is the *reflux* that is the great regulating principle of the internal currency; and it was by the preservation of the reflux, throughout all the perils and temptations of the period of the restriction, that the monetary system of these kingdoms was saved from the utter wreck and degradation which overwhelmed every paper-issuing state on the Continent, and which in all human probability must have been likewise our fate, had our currency at that epoch been administered by a Government Board instead of the Bank of England. I have adverted in a former page to *the deep debt which the nation owes to the Bank, for its services through that long and trying crisis.* I believe they cannot be too highly appreciated , and I believe, further, that the same services could not have been so beneficially performed by any mere bank of the state, or by any body whatever less intimately bound up in all its interests and relations with the commercial affairs and prosperity of the country. That will be an evil day for England, when the supreme executive authority of this country shall take the administration of a credit circulation into its own hands. I trust never to see it; and I hold the sort of levity with which the possibility of such an arrangement has sometimes of late been alluded to, and even hinted in the way of menace to the Bank of England, to be one of the worst indications of the existing state of public opinion on these all-important concerns."—(*On the Regulation of Currencies*, pp. 65,68.)

Colonel Torrens indulges himself in the following remarks on my description, which he quotes, of the difference between convertible and inconvertible paper: —

"Mr. Tooke's curious reasons for his curious conclusions, that an increase in the quantity of *inconvertible* paper money does, and that an increase in the quantity of *convertible* paper does not, cause an increase of prices, require to be noticed."

He then cites the passages from my pamphlet of 1844 (already given in the present volume), and proceeds in the following strain of comment: —

"Fallacies 'permeate all the channels' of the passages above quoted. In the first place, it is a fallacy that convertible paper is issued to those only who, being entitled to demand gold, desire to have notes in preference. In a large number, perhaps in a majority of cases, convertible paper is issued to persons who are not, at the time of issue, entitled to demand gold, and whose title to demand it is created by the paper they obtain. The merchant who discounts a bill of exchange at the Bank is entitled to demand gold, not because he was the holder of the bill, but because the Bank has advanced convertible notes upon it① An advance of convertible notes upon securities is a new creation of paper money, just in the same way in which an advance of inconvertible notes by Government is a new crcation of paper money.

---

① This does not follow; in a large proportion of cases no notes at all are issued when advances are made. Further, if the issue of convertible notes in discount of a bill of exchange be "a new creation of paper money," how is it to be denied that the increasing of a deposit account, to which a similar advance has been credited, is not also "a new creation," &c. In both cases there is created a new liability to pay in gold on demand; and if there be, in reference to the point here at issue, any essential difference between the enforcement of that liability through notes and through cheques, it remains for Colonel Torrens, and those who adopt the same line of reasoning, to make it apparent.

"There is no conceivable difference as regards the nature and character of the action upon prices between the action produced by convertible, and that produced by inconvertible paper. There is, however, a difference between the degree and extent of the action; the effect being, in the one case, unlimited, and in the other, limited by the speedy diminution in the quantity of the convertible paper money as soon as its value in relation to gold begins to decline. Sir. Tooke's argument, when fairly analysed, amounts to this—An increase in the quantity of convertible paper cannot reduce its value, because, when the increase of quantity has reduced its value, a diminution in its quantity will raise its value; therefore the quantity of convertible paper has no influence upon its value."—Q. E. D.—(*An Inquiry into the Practical Working*, &c., by Robert Torrens, Esq., F. R. S. London 1844, pp. 46,48.)

These distinct avowals, by leading authorities on the part of the currency theory, combined with the definition of the word "money" by Sir Robert Peel, and by Mr. Loyd and Mr. Norman, in their evidence and in their pamphlets, which designates Bank notes as, with coin, constituting money, are very important. I had before only suspected that such was their impression, because I could not in any other way account for that doctrine of the currency principle, which ascribes to the amount of Bank notes in circulation, to the exclusion of other forms of credit, an influence on prices, and, through prices, on the state of trade and credit. The illustrations adduced in their justification, and the explanation offered of the grounds for the opinion so confidently avowed, with a view to show that there is no difference up to the point of convertibility, between issues of paper money, properly so called, and the issues of banks whose advances are on loan for short periods

(advances for long periods, not usually coming within the legitimate province of banking) , afford a clue to the source of the error which I have endeavoured to point out as pervading all the reasoning, according to the currency theory, upon the state of the circulation from 1797 down to the present time.

During the restriction, there was a *primâ facie* ground for considering the promissory notes payable on demand as paper money, and the amount of them as being, therefore, under the direct control of the issuing banks.

But leaving, for the present, out of consideration how far the paper circulation of this country, during the restriction, might or might not be looked upon as similar in its general character and effects to inconvertible government paper, we have to examine what under the present constantly and perfectly convertible state of our note circulation are the salient points of difference between it and paper money.

SECTION 5 *On the circumstances which determine the outstanding amount, and the effect on prices, of a currency of convertible and of inconvertible paper*

In the assumption of a perfect similarity in the nature and character of a convertible, to those of an inconvertible paper, up to the point of convertibility (that is, up to the point at which, in an inconvertible state of the paper, the coin would be expelled through the medium of the exchanges), two conditions, which attach to the issue and circulation of convertible paper, and which essentially distinguish it from paper money, properly so called, are entirely overlooked.

These are — *the mode of issue* and *the reflux.*

1. *The mode of issue* for convertible notes is invariably through the medium of loans and discounts. But the amount of loans and discounts by the Bank of England, or other banks of issue, is no measure of the amount of their notes in circulation. And the loans and discounts, that is, the advances, are commonly made for short periods.

When the Bank of England, or a country banker, makes an advance, or discounts a bill, the borrower or discounter is asked how he wishes to have the amount. In the case of the Bank of England, the borrower, when the discount or loan is agreed upon, has the option of receiving notes or gold, or a book credit. In by far the larger proportion of instances, I believe the book credit is preferred; a cheque on the Bank is passed, and placed by the borrower to his account with his banker, who, as between himself and the Bank of England, sets off the amount against acceptances to bills, or cheques upon him, held by the Bank, or simply places it to the credit of his deposit account with the Bank. In these cases not a single note is created or issued, against several millions of securities upon which advances are made, whether to individuals or to Government. It depends entirely upon the purposes which the party, having received the loan, or discounted his bills, has in view, in which of the three modes he chooses to receive payment. Hence it is clear that the Bank of England cannot, by its advances, insure that the amount so advanced, or any part of it, shall add to the circulation of its notes in the hands of the public. Nor can it be *sure* that in reducing its securities, unless to a very extraordinary extent, it will diminish the amount of its outstanding notes.

In the case of the country bank circulation, if the banker consents to make an advance, it depends upon the sum and the purpose for which it is required, whether it is taken in his own notes, in notes of the Bank of England, or in a bill on London; or if the banker has correspondents at Liverpool, or other considerable places, the party receiving the advance may be accommodated with a bill drawn accordingly. The chief circulation of the country notes is in the agricultural districts; and the evidence of the bankers examined by the Committee of 1841, is full and complete to the effect that those notes are confined strictly to local purposes within a limited circuit; and are chiefly of the lower denomination, and for the expenditure of income in retail purchases.

But in the case both of the Bank of England and of the country banks, if it were conceivable, which it hardly is, that any addition, beyond the amount of notes required for specific purposes, could be forced into the hands of the public, there is an operation constantly going on which would almost instantaneously reduce the amount within the limits of these purposes.

The cause I allude to is,

2. The *law of reflux*.[①] This law operates in bringing back to the issuing banks the amount of their notes, whatever it may be, that is not wanted for the purposes which they are required to serve. The reflux takes place chiefly in two ways: by payment of the redundant amount to a banker on a deposit account, or by the return of notes in discharge of securities on which advances have been made. A third way is that of a return of the notes to the issuing bank by a demand for coin. The last seems, in the view of the currency theory, to be the *only* way by which a redundancy, arising from the unlimited power of issue, which they assume to exist,

---

① The passage from Mr. Fullarton, in reply to Sir William Clay, may be referred to as containing a very clear and full statement of the doctrine of reflux.

admits of being corrected in a convertible state of the paper. It is certainly the one least in use.

Let us now examine the nature and character of inconvertible notes, properly called *paper money*, and more generally known on the Continent as *bank assignations or assignats*.

The authority issuing such paper money, can determine exactly the quantity that shall remain permanently in the hands of the public. The power of issue is unlimited, because there is no reflux. A part, which is generally a small proportion, may, indeed, be returnable in payment of taxes; but the Government may immediately re-issue the amount so returned, and then keep up or extend the quantity, according to its own purposes.

Suppose, then, that the Government, having this unlimited power, should be so sparing and judicious in the exercise of it, as only to have issued its paper within such limits as should be consistent with the maintenance of the value of it strictly at par with the coin, concurrently with which it circulated. That such equality of value is consistent with experience in the case of paper money, I shall presently show. In the mean time, let us assume the amount of paper and coin, so circulating together at par, to be ten millions; and suppose then that the Government entering upon a war, or having to construct public works and make improvements, should, to meet the extra expenditure, instead of raising the amount by taxation or a loan, resort to an emission of paper money to the amount of one million.

Were this amount issued gradually, as required for the expenditure, the effect, in the general rise of prices and of wages, might be so gradual as to be almost imperceptible. The sums paid for the articles and services required by the Government would affect, first one set of commodities and then another, and gradually raise wages, till the whole extra quantity of paper money should be absorbed into the circulation. The rise of prices would render the balance of trade, supposing it to have been just before in equilibrio, adverse; and the exchanges would be depressed so as to induce an export of coin, if this existed in sufficient quantity, till the amount exported should make room for the addition caused by the introduction of so much paper. Thus, supposing the circulation to have consisted before of eight millions of paper, and two millions of gold coin, and that these ten millions were consistent with a maintenance of the value of the paper fully at par, then, upon the above hypothesis, one million of the coin would be expelled from the circulation by the additional million of paper introduced into it.

It would be through the medium of prices that the coin would be expelled. But there would be some, and, perhaps, no inconsiderable, interval before the rise of prices could operate sufficiently on the exchanges to induce an export of the coin. Now this is a state of things as nearly as possible analogous to that which Sir Robert Peel seems to have had in contemplation when he observed — (*Speech*, p. 27.)

"Unless the issuers of paper conform *to certain principles*, unless they vigilantly observe the causes which influence the influx or efflux of coin, and regulate their issues of paper accordingly, there is danger that the value of the paper will not correspond with the value of coin. The difference may not he immediately perceived; nay, the first effect of undue issue, by *increasing prices*, may be to encourage further issues and as each issuer when there is unlimited competition, feels the inutility of individual efforts of contraction, the evil proceeds until the *disparity between gold and paper* becomes *manifest*, confidence in the paper is shaken, and it becomes necessary to restore its value by sudden and violent reductions in its amount, spreading ruin among the issuers of paper, and deranging the whole monetary transactions of the country."

It is evident from the above passage—and others to the same effect might be cited—that Sir Robert Peel was under the impression that the country banks may, and do, exercise a power analogous to that of a Government issuing paper money; that in the progress of issue they raise prices①, and that the evil proceeds until the disparity between gold and paper becomes

---

① With reference to the effect of a strictly convertible paper on prices, I am happy to have the distinguished support of Mr. Mill. In the article in the *Westminster Review* already alluded to, he says —

"It seems to be thought by many people that the purchase of commodities implies the direct transfer of so much money from hand to hand in return for so much produce; and that the limit to the possible demand for a commodity at any moment, is the quantity of money then and there waiting to be exchanged for it. With this mode of thinking it is no wonder that any one should suppose that whenever you add to the money at that place physically present, you add as much to the demand, and consequently to the price But this is a very inadequate notion indeed of what constitutes purchasing power.

"The purchasing power of an individual at any moment is not measured by the money actually in his pocket, whether we mean by money, the metals, or include bank notes. It consists, first, of the money in his possession; secondly, of the money at his banker's, and all other money due to him and payable on demand; thirdly, of whatever credit he happens to possess. To the full measure of this three-fold amount he has the power of purchase. How much he will employ of this power, depends upon his necessities, or, in the present case, upon his expectations of profit. Whatever portion of it he does employ, constitutes his demand for commodities, and determines the extent to which he will act upon price.

"There is (as it seems to us) an almost whimsical exemplification of this common fallacy in Colonel Torrens's pamphlet, which we have not room to extract, but which those who wish to refer to it may find in pages 10-17. Having assumed, for the purposes of his argument, that Birmingham has a metallic currency composed of one million sovereigns, lie says, 'consequently the prices of commodities within the district would be governed by the power of effecting purchases to an amount not exceeding 1,000,000*l.*,' forgetting that the million sovereigns may serve, by successive payments, to represent and circulate incomes to the amount of many millions, and that it is this, and not the one million of sovereigns, which constitutes the purchasing power of the community. We admire the ingenuity and polemical acuteness of Colonel Torrens, which have never been more highly manifested than in this pamphlet, but we think in this particular instance he will find, on reconsideration, that he has built an elaborate superstructure upon a foundation of sand."

manifest. He does not say how, the paper being strictly convertible, there can be any disparity between that and coin. But he, of course, means that — as in the case of the inconvertible paper — the redundancy of the circulation is caused by excessive issues, and will depress the exchanges; and that then, and not till then, will the check upon the issuers operate by a return of their notes for gold, compelling them suddenly to contract their circulation, so violently as to cause revulsion and discredit. This very important point has been ably illustrated by Mr. Wilson, in the following passage, founded upon one of those instances of characteristic subtlety which abound so greatly in the writings of Colonel Torrens.

Mr. Wilson says —

"But the most subtle and truly curious argument is that used by Colonel Torrens. He admits that there is a difference between the liability to depreciation of an inconvertible and convertible paper, which he states thus: —

"'The increase in the quantity of convertible paper is limited by the power of the holder to exchange it for gold, as soon as from the increase of its quantity its value in relation to gold begins to decline. If the increase in the quantity of convertible paper had no effect in lowering its value in relation to gold, the holder could have no motive in exchanging it for gold.'

"Now, really this is a special case of magnificent refinement! Every case of an optional exchange of equivalents must be considered an evidence of depreciation! It is certainly an evidence of some preference, on greater applicability for the purposes immediately required. But let us ask this ingenious reasoner — Two men go the Bank counter on two successive days; one has received a remittance of a fifty pound note from the country, which is of no use to him till he has converted it into coin, and he presents it for payment; the other man has *fifty sovereigns*, but wishes to make a remittance to the country, and he receives a note in exchange for it. The one has a 'motive' for exchanging the note for gold, the other for exchanging gold for the note, the one had a preference for gold sufficient to take him to the Bank, the other had a preference for the note sufficient to take him there. Now, we ask, which was depreciated—the coin or the note for in one case there was more coin in circulation, and less paper, than the convenience of the public required for circulation, and there existed, therefore, a '*motive*' to convert coin into paper, an the other case, there was more paper and less coin in circulation than the public convenience required, and there existed a' motive' to convert it into coin. But enough. We will grant Colonel Torrens that bank paper may be depreciated in relation to coin to the extent of supplying a 'motive' to step to the Bank and exchange it; but he, too, must grant that sovereigns also may be depreciated to the extent of supplying a similar motive to exchange them. But when all the ingenuity of this most ingenious writer on these subjects has been able to give no better evidence of the liability of convertible bank paper to depreciation, *what are we to think of the minister who gravely affects to found a great bank measure on such a principle?*"—(*On Capital, Currency, Banking, &c.* pp. 58-59.)

The process in Sir Robert Peel's mind by which he ascribes to a convertible paper the effect of adding to the amount of the circulation at the will of the issuer, and thus raising prices, may be explained by the supposition of his following much the same train of reasoning on the similarity of the two kinds of issue, as is exhibited in the following passage by Colonel Torrens: —

"Mr. Tooke contends that the increase of an *inconvertible* currency would increase wages and prices, because it would be expended in the personal expenditure of the Sovereign or governing power, in salaries and in public works and buildings; and because, thus expended, it would permeate all the channels of circulation. *Now the increase of a convertible currency would produce the same identical effects, through the same identical process, which would be produced by the increase of an inconvertible currency.* "Were a nobleman to obtain from the Bank of England 100,000*l.* upon the mortgage of his estate, and were he to expend the amount thus obtained in enlarging his domestic establishment, in maintaining an additional retinue of servants, and in erecting a mansion and ornamental buildings, this convertible paper, thus expended, would, like an inconvertible paper expended by Government upon analogous objects, raise wages and prices, because it would permeate all the channels of circulation.' Were this nobleman to expend the loan advanced by the Bank of England in improving his estate, in draining, planting, and reclaiming wastes, exactly similar results, as regards wages and prices, would be produced, while results exactly similar, as far as regards wages and prices, would be produced were a master manufacturer to obtain discounts and other advances from the neighbouring banks of issue, and to expend the amount thus obtained in erecting new factories, in purchasing additional materials, and employing additional hands. In all these cases an increased quantity of convertible currency would 'permeate the channels of circulation', in the same way in which an increased quantity of inconvertible currency would permeate them. The nature and character of the effect would be the same, whether the increased quantity of currency should be convertible or inconvertible, though its extent and degree in the two cases would be different. In the case of the inconvertible paper, the effect would be unlimited; in the case of the convertible paper, the effect would be confined within narrow limits, because a slight action upon prices, and on the exchanges, would cause the increased quantity of convertible paper to be withdrawn from circulation, by being returned upon the banks in exchange for coin now demanded for exportation. But why should the coin be demanded for exportation? Simply because the increased quantity of convertible paper had reduced the value of the currency, or, in other words, had increased prices. The withdrawal of an increased issue of convertible paper from the channels of circulation, is the effect of the reduced value of the currency or increased range of prices, which, in the first instance, that increased issue had occasioned. Mr. Tooke's process of reasoning amounts to this, — that the existence of the effect proves the non-existence of the cause."— (*Inquiry*, &c. pp. 48, 50.)

On the illustrative case here given, I have to observe, that the Bank of England does not advance loans to noblemen and others for the improvement of their estates. But granting that it does so, and that, being on a security of landed property, bank notes might be required to pass in payment between the solicitors for the lender and borrower, there would be a hundred notes, of a thousand pounds each, handed over by the solicitor of the lender to the borrower, or his agent, on the delivery of the deed. The borrower would pay the notes in to his banker, who would have them placed to his deposit account at the Bank of England. The whole of a transaction like this would, with the requisite formalities, have been completed in less than three or four hours; and the probability is, that the notes taken out of the Bank in the forenoon, would find their way back to it by the afternoon of the same day, thus not having added a single note to the circulation.

But, even for such a purpose, bank notes are now usually dispensed with; a draft upon the Bank of England, or even upon other banks, being frequently substituted. The borrower having paid the amount in to his banker, would pass drafts on them for his expenditure; and the loan to him, therefore, would not, in the first instance, evidently, nor probably at all, entail any addition whatever to the circulation.

Here at once, *in the issue*, is a broad distinction. The advance by a bank issuing only convertible paper, does not, as we have seen, cause, necessarily, any increase of the circulation; and very rarely, if ever, to the same amount as the loan. Whereas, if the 100,000*l*. were expended by the Government, issuing its own inconvertible notes in payment, the whole sum so paid *would necessarily go into circulation, and form so much addition to the amount previously in the hands of the public.* And the same effect on the circulation would be produced if the Government advanced, in its own inconvertible notes, the 100,000*l*. as a loan to a nobleman, or other landed proprietor, to be expended in improvements.

If advances on mortgage to the same amount were obtained by a manufacturer from the neighbouring banks of issue, there would not, any more than in the case supposed of the advance by the Bank of England to the nobleman, be necessarily or probably any increase in the amount of the circulation, and certainly not to the whole amount of the advance. This would be made in the first instance by a book-credit, or by bills on London; and perhaps a portion by each mode. But no part of the purchases made by the manufacturer, or of the advances so received, would probably be made in Bank notes; or if so made, they would return immediately to the issuing bank.

So much as to the mode of issue: the difference being that the one does not, and the other does, add, necessarily, to the circulation, the full amount of the advance for the expenditure in question. But there is more in the difference of the conditions on which the issue is made.

It is of the very essence of the system on which banks of issue, of strictly convertible paper, can be conducted, so as to ensure the fulfilment of their obligations, that their advances, whether by loan or discount, should be for such short periods, and on securities so solid and convertible, as to insure the return of the money advanced in time to meet the utmost amount of their engagements. Advances on mortgage, for terms of years, are not proper banking securities; or, if at all, are so in a small proportion only, as for the investment of a part, and a small part, of their original and paid up capital, but in no case as an investment of any considerable part of the capital deposited with them, or held against their circulation. Accordingly, the Bank of England does not make advances of the kind in the case supposed. It has, in a few instances, made advances upon the debentures of joint stock companies, such as Dock debentures and the best description of Railway Companies' bonds (the London and Birmingham only, I believe), but these have been for periods much shorter than those for which mortgages on landed property arc usually made, and, in point of amount, for sums so small, compared with its capital and the mass of its securities, as not to be worth mentioning. And banks, whether joint stock or private — whether issuing or non-issuing — have almost invariably been observed to fail, if they have made advances on mortgage, or on indefinite credits, in any considerable proportion to their general liabilities. The limitation of the period for which the advance is made operates in two ways, each of which, independently of the mode of issue, distinguishes the effects of a convertible from an inconvertible paper: the one is the return of the notes, if any are issued; the other is the absence of any influence on prices.

If the loans or discounts are advanced on proper banking securities, for short periods, the reflux of the notes, if any have been issued, will be equal to the efflux, leaving the circulation unaltered. If, indeed, the transactions of the district, or the trade of the country generally, require more instruments of exchange, a larger amount of notes would remain out; but this increase of the outstanding circulation would *be the effect of increased transactions and prices, and not the cause of them*. Upon this point I am glad to have the concurrence of Mr. James Wilson, as expressed in the following passage of his late publication: —

"But in all these actions, which may be exercised on prices through the currency, there is nothing whatever in the least degree analogous to the action contemplated by the modern doctrine on which the New Bank Bill is founded, and involving the assumption "that, by an expansion or contraction of the issues of bank notes at pleasure, the prices of commodities can be increased or diminished." The increase or decrease of prices here alluded to is not *nominal*, but real, and in relation to the prices of other countries; an increase or decrease which shall constitute new motives for importing or exporting commodities, as the case may be.

"The assumption before us involves two questions — first, expansion and contraction of the currency at pleasure; and, second, as the consequence, a corresponding action on prices. Many authors, in treating of the latter, as a consequence, and even combating its truth, have laboured under great difficulties, by proceeding upon the admission of the former; but if the former be admitted, we confess we cannot understand how the latter can be denied as the legitimate consequence. If, in the language of Mr. Homer, there be any means by which "the quantity of circulating medium (being convertible paper and coin) can be permanently augmented, without a corresponding augmentation of internal trade, a rise will unavoidably take place in the price of exchangeable commodities." Such means, as we have already seen, do exist in the case of an inconvertible currency; but the rise in price, in consequence, is only nominal in that case, being immediately compensated to other countries by a fall in the exchange. But with a convertible currency, *if such means exist at all*, the rise in price would not be nominal, but real, as it would be expressed either in corn or notes convertible into coin, and therefore would not, as in the other ease, be compensated by any fall in the exchange. But this fact shows at once the impossibility of the "augmentation" alluded to in the premises, when the currency is *convertible*. A currency "augmented without any corresponding augmentation of internal trade," implies a quantity of notes retained in circulation, at the will of the issuers, which the public do not require. Now, the public do not receive notes from a banker without paying interest for their use; and, however low that may be, they will take no more than they absolutely require — nor do they retain notes in their possession beyond what the convenience of trade requires; and, therefore, if issued in excess of that quantity, and, if convertible, a portion would be instantly returned upon the issuers. Nor can we conceive any means whatever by which the circulation could be so augmented; and we have deeply to regret that, although such a power on the part of banks has been taken for granted by most of the writers during the last twelve years, no one has yet attempted to explain by what process it could be accomplished; and we are compelled to think that impressions, which gained ground many years since as applicable to an inconvertible currency, have been inadvertently associated also with a convertible currency.

"The impossibility of increasing the quantity of paper in circulation (when convertible), except as the effect of a corresponding increase of an internal trade, or of any depreciation in its value taking place, will be more evident when it is considered by what process an inconvertible currency becomes depreciated. On all hands it is admitted that as long as inconvertible paper is not issued in excess, as long as coin continues freely to circulate with it, the paper will not become depreciated; but as soon as the paper is issued in excess, and the coin is pressed out of circulation, it becomes depreciated, and the prices of commodities rise in consequence; though it is only a nominal rise, which would be better expressed by depreciation of the circulation. Now, how does this depreciation and rise of price take place? During the early issue of the French assignats, no depreciation or rise in price of commodities took place until the corn was pressed out of circulation, because, as the paper was issued, the tendency to a redundant currency was constantly corrected by the withdrawal of silver, which, being a commodity having a general value in the markets of the world, could be exported or taken for the general uses of the cambist or the silversmith. But as soon as silver was exhausted from the circulation, the issue of assignats still continuing, and the same quantity of internal exchanges only remaining, the currency became redundant, there being no means of absorption except in the existing quanties of commodities. Paper in the first place would accumulate in the hands of individuals, and as the issues of assignats continued for commodities for the use of the government, or of those receiving pay from the gevernment, the simple law of supply and demand would reduce the value of this paper, and increase the price of commodities expressed in paper. But it will be observed that this increase of price is only in reference to paper assignats, and not to the coin which they originally represented; for the coin or bullion at this stage rose in the same proportion as other things. During the high prices in this country from 1810 to 1816, as far as they were caused by a depreciation of the currency, they were *high* only in relation to paper, and not to gold, which rose equally, and at the same time, as other commodities, from this cause. Well, then, seeing that redundancy and consequent depreciation of paper can only commence when no part of the currency consists of coin which can be exported or taken for manufacturing purposes (the paper having no intrinsic use at home, or exchangeable value abroad), it follows, as a simple corollary of those principles which have been admitted by all winters worthy of mention, that as long as paper is at pleasure convertible into gold, no such redundancy can take place, no such difference can arise between the value of gold and the value of paper, and no such general increase of prices of commodities can be experienced.

"No doubt, if the internal transactions of the country increase, or if the prices of commodities use, a larger amount of circulating medium, whether purely metallic, or mixed of paper and com, will be required to conduct the exchanges; and thus, though an increased circulation could not be called into existence as a cause to produce higher prices, it would follow as the effect or consequence of higher prices. But in that case, " the circulation would not be augmented without a corresponding augmentation of trade." — (*Capital*, *Currency*, *and Banking*, by James Wilson, Esq., M. P. London, 1847, pp. 82-85.)

But while, as regards the effects on the *circulation*, there may be no perceptible difference between advances by the Bank of England and other banks of issue, whether the loans be on mortgage, for the purposes supposed in the two cases before referred to, or on discount of rapidly terminable securities, —each being an advance of capital, whether with or without the intervention of currency,— there may be a material difference in the effect on prices. It may be conceded to Colonel Torrens, that if the advances be on mortgage, or on open credit, for a long or indefinite term, and for the purposes supposed, they may, according to their extent, constitute a fresh source of demand, and cause a temporary rise of prices, or keep them at a higher level than they could otherwise reach or maintain. But the banks, when the local circulation is already full, can make such advances only out of the capital, of their depositors, or their own. If out of their own capital, it would in nearly all cases be only a change of investment, and so constitute no fresh demand. If advances for long terms are made out of the capital of depositors, the banker may be called upon for the deposits; which, being locked up in mortgages, will not be forthcoming; upon which the banker fails, and prices, in as far as they were raised by his misuse of the capital intrusted to him, must be depressed by his failure. Or if, in times of great abundance of capital, the country banker obtained credit from his London correspondent, and ventured, on the strength of it, to make such improvident advances, the same result would follow; while discounts of good commercial bills of usual and reasonable length of date, being merely calculated to enable parties to meet liabilities previously incurred — the loans thus running off—would be unattended with the effect of disturbing prices and credit.

SECTION 6 *On the effects of different modes of issue of a convertible and of an inconvertible paper. Mr. Ricardo's hypothesis of a gold mine in the bank*

The eminent writer of an article in the Westminster Review (Mr. Mill), for June 1844, after expressing his concurrence in my view of the purposes for which governments *usually* issue paper money, and thus cause a permanent increase of the circulation, makes the following remark: —

"We may add, with Mr. Tooke, that the issues of a *government* paper, even when not permanent, will raise prices; because governments usually issue their paper in purchases for consumption. If issued to pay off a portion of a national debt, we believe they would have no such effect."

This suggestion of the difference of effect, according to the purposes of the issue, opens a somewhat curious field for discussion. Suppose, for instance, that a government, having the power of creating paper money, should, with a view to raise the value of the public funds (the debt being, say one hundred millions), issue two, three, or more millions for the purchase of stock. The effect of such a fresh source of demand would be to raise the price, in other words, to reduce the rate of interest; while the purchases were in progress. All other securities would, for a time, rise in value. This rise in the value of securities, or fall in the rate of interest, would tend to force capital abroad for more profitable investment; and thus the coin might be expelled so as to make way for the addition of the paper money to the circulation, through the rate of interest, without having acted upon the prices of commodities.

The case here supposed is hardly within the range of reasonable probability, but it was worth a passing remark to follow out the idea started by Mr. Mill, and this more especially, because it will be found to bear upon one of the points of view suggested by the analogy which Mr. Ricardo assumed to exist between the effects of the issues of the notes of the Bank of England during the Restriction, and the issues from a gold mine supposed to be discovered within the premises of the Bank.

Mr. Ricardo, in his first pamphlet, introduced the hypothesis of such a discovery for the purpose of proving that the issues of the Bank of England would add to the amount of the currency in the same manner and degree as the issue of so much gold so discovered. On this assumed. analogy, Mr. C. Bosanquet makes the following observations: —

" Mr. Ricardo has assimilated the Bank of England during the Restriction, so far as relates to the effect of its issues, to a gold mine, the produce of which being thrown into circulation, in addition to a circulating medium already sufficient, is an excess; and has the acknowledged effect of depreciating the value of the existing medium, or, in other words, of raising the prices of commodities, for which it is usually exchanged. But Mr. Ricardo has not stated, what is essential to the comparison, *why* it is that the discovery of a gold mine would produce this effect. It would produce it because the proprietors would issue it (for whatever services) without any engagement to give an equal value for it again to the holders, or any wish or any means of calling back and annihilating that which they have issued. By degrees, as the issues increase, they exceed the wants of circulation gold produces no benefit to the holder as gold; he cannot eat it, nor clothe himself with it: to render it useful, he must exchange it either for such things as are immediately useful, or for such as produce revenue.

The demand, and consequently the prices of commodities and real properties, measured in gold, increases, and will continue to increase, so long as the mine continues to produce. And this effect will equally follow, whether, under the circumstances I have supposed, the issue be gold from a mine, or paper from a government bank.

"All this I distinctly admit; but in all this statement there is not one point of analogy to the issue of the Bank of England." —(*Practical Observations on the Report of the Bullion Committee*, by Charles Bosanquet, Esq., 1810, pp. 51, 52.)

To these observations of Mr. Bosanquet, Mr. Ricardo replied:—

"Now, supposing the gold mine to be actually the property of the Bank, even be situated on their own premises, and that they procured the gold which it produced to be coined into guineas, and in lieu of issuing their notes when they *discounted bills or lent money to government*, that they issued nothing but guineas, could there be any other limit to their issues but the want of the further productiveness in their mine? In what would the circumstances differ if the mine were the property of the king, of a company of merchants, or of a single individual? In that case, Mr. Bosanquet admits that the value of money would fall, and I suppose he would also admit that it would fall in exact proportion to its increase."

With reference to the questions put by Mr. Ricardo, which I have marked in italics, I should say that the effects would vary *widely* according as one or other of those modes of issue wore proposed. Supposing the issue of the gold to be on loan by the Bank: the effect of it, if confined to the discount of bills at short dates, or if extended to a loan to Government for a term of years, would be different. If confined to short-dated bona fide bills, it might take a great length of time before any considerable amount could be permanently added to the circulation, even supposing the Bank's rate of discount to be below the market rate.

The rules of the Bank at the time when Mr. Ricardo wrote were very strict, not only as to the bona fide character, and as to the term not exceeding sixty-one days, but as to various . technicalities of form of the bills, with various delays between the time of offering the bills for discount and of receiving the answer of acceptance or otherwise.

The reflux would be constantly opposing a counteracting force to the attempts of the Bank at rendering its treasure immediately available to any considerable extent in acquiring capital in any other form. But in whatever degree the Directors were able to surmount this counteracting force, by extending their advances, it would be slowly, by discounting at a rate decidedly below the market rate of interest. The market rate, however, although higher than the Bank rate, would, by this continued operation of the Bank, be kept lower than it otherwise would have been, and lower than its ordinary level abroad.

Nor would the daily transactions arising out of their immense connexion, as a Bank of *Deposit*, in any way add to the facilities at their command for the permanent emission of the treasure. It is clear that the efflux of gold which would take place in the payment of cheques would be balanced by the receipt of sums paid in to the credit of the several accounts. By one method, within the compass of possibility but scarcely a probable occurrence, the Bank might permanently emit a portion of the treasure through the private deposits. Assuming these deposits to be 5,000,000*l*.[①], if the Directors were

① It will simplify the hypothesis to leave out of view the public deposits, the character of which, and the obligation under which they are held by the Bank, distinguishing them in so many important points from the credit balances of individuals.

peremptorily to order that they should run off—in other words, if they were to liquidate every private deposit account, and give the recipients no option as to the mode of payment, except that every claim should be discharged in coin of full weight and purity, it seems plain that treasure to the extent of 5,000,000*l.* would be effectually placed in circulation. Under the terms of the supposition, a measure of this kind would be tantamount to so much positive improvement in the position of the Bank. For they would have discharged a liability of 5,000,000*l.* without at the same time, and in consequence, contracting their assets (*i. e.* the securities on which the deposits were invested) in any degree whatever. We may also conclude with some safety that the effect of such a compulsory liquidation would, in the first instance at least, be confined to a violent operation on the rate of interest. It would in point of fact be a virtual creation of five millions of extra capital, and an almost instantaneous addition of the whole mass to the quantity of immediately available funds, seeking employment through the medium of bankers and bill brokers.

The gold, therefore, to whatever extent it might ooze out in loans, would (supposing trade to be in equilibrio) in all probability be exported for the higher interest to be obtained by investments in foreign securities, or by extended credits to foreign merchants, or by outlay in mills, factories, &c. abroad. The issue of the gold through the medium of discounts of short paper only would ultimately, but very *slowly*, cause an export of it without necessarily affecting the prices of commodities. And if, instead of the slow process of discounting short bills, subject to the counteraction of the reflux, the Directors employed the gold directly in the purchase of government securities, the effect in forcing an export of the metals would be great and rapid, without perhaps, in the first instance, producing any effect on the prices of commodities; although the low rate of interest thus caused might, by inducing enterprize in the outlay of fixed capital, raise wages or extend employment of labour, and thus indirectly operate upon prices.

If the mine or treasure were possessed by the government, or, what would come to nearly the same thing, if the gold were advanced by the Bank in the way of loan for a term of years, and the government were to issue it in payments to that amount for extra expenditure in carrying on a war, or in extensive buildings, or public improvements of any kind, the effect would be exactly the same as in the outlay of so much *paper money* created for the purpose, while there remained coin in circulation, according to the hypothesis. Prices of commodities and the wages of labour would rise; but there could of course be no indication of depreciation by a difference between coin and bullion, there being no legal obstacle to the exportation of the former any more than of the latter. The rise of prices would (things being before in equilibrio) induce increased imports and diminished exports, in other words, would turn the balance of trade, and render the exchanges adverse in a degree sufficient to cause an export of the extra quantity of gold thus issued by the government. In this case the gold would go out of the country through the medium of prices.

But a case may readily be imagined in which, if the mine or treasure were suddenly discovered, and made available by the government, an immediate employment of the gold would not only not operate in raising prices, and thence depressing the exchanges, but would maintain the exchanges, and thus prevent the effect of depressed exchanges in enhancing the cost of production, and so raising prices.

For example, suppose that treasure, amounting to ten millions of gold, had been discovered and appropriated by the government at such a period as the close of 1808. There arose at that time, as I have elsewhere described, a sudden necessity for payments to be made abroad by this country to a very large amount. If, then, at that time, the government, in addition to about three millions of specie, which it brought from the Bank to send to the Peninsula, had, according to the hypothetical case, found a mine, the produce of which, to the amount, say of ten millions, would have enabled it to make all these extra payments by the direct transmission of the amount in the precious metals, there would have been no disturbance of the exchanges, or of so much of prices as depended on the exchanges. The exchanges and the price of bullion would have remained unaltered, and prices would have been lower by the difference which the fall of the exchanges did, in the actual case, add to the cost of production; while the rate of interest would have been somewhat lower by the government having so much less to borrow.

A recent financial operation of the Russian government supplies a case in point, illustrative of one of the modes in which, a surplus metallic treasure, analogous to Mr. Ricardo's gold mine, may be actually disbursed, without affecting prices. According to the exposition of the minister of finance, in a council① held in July last (1847), the government had determined, some months before, to employ the sum of 30,000,000 of roubles, equivalent at the exchange of 40*d* ② to 5,000,000*l*., (out of its reserve of 114,000,000*r*., or 19,000,000*l*. sterling held against the note circulation) in the purchase of the public stocks of Russia, France, and England; the principal part to be invested in the two latter.

---

① See in Appendix.

② The exact par, I believe, is as nearly as may be, 39*d*.

Without canvassing the merits of the operation, which seems, however, to have been a very judicious one, I have here to observe upon the effects of it only as exemplifying the point now under discussion. Its immediate effect was on the balance of payments between Russia on the one hand, and France and England on the other. In consequence of the extraordinary demand by the two latter countries for the productions of Russia, in the autumn of 1846 and the winter of 1847, the balance of payments became largely in its favour. The exchange on London rose to $40\frac{1}{2}d.$ and as this rate gave a profit on the importation, a transmission of bullion to Petersburg took placc to some extent.①

But as soon as the intended operation of the Russian government became known, namely, in February last, the exchanges gave way, and have since ranged at, from 39*d*. to 38*d*. In the mean time, so far as the mere outlay of the surplus treasure in question was concerned, it had not added, and could not add, to the amount of the circulation, or have any influence on prices in Russia.

This point may be further illustrated by reference to another operation of the same government. While it was, on the one hand, lending money to foreign states, it was, on the other, borrowing money on Treasury bills, bearing interest, in order to complete the railway from Petersburg to Moscow. Now, supposing that on that and other railways requiring an early

① An amount of about 600,000*l*, which the Bank of England held in Russian gold corn, was bought by merchants here and forwarded by land. I am not aware whether any silver went: if it did go, it must have been from Franco or Germany, for it did not answer to send it from hence. And as there was no mode of transmission except by land, the navigation being closed by frost, the expense of conveying so bulky a metal as silver (bulky, I mean, as compared with gold) would probably leave little margin for profit. The probability therefore is, that a small sum only, if any, went.

outlay of 30,000,000r. the government had determined to *expend* that sum out of its surplus treasure, instead of *lending* it, the effect would have been, in proportion as the expenditure went on, to raise prices and wages; and assuming that the amount of the currency had been before sufficient for the purposes of a circulating medium, the additional coin thus added to the circulation would have been expelled, through the medium of prices; causing an adverse balance of trade and a consequent depression of the exchanges. The case would be analogous to the issue of so much *paper money* in a currency consisting of paper and coin circulating at par. The coin would be gradually expelled, through the medium of prices, to make way for the paper: as will bc illustrated in the next section, in the case of the forty millions of roubles, in paper money, first issued by the empress Catherine. This is clearly the mode, and the only mode, in which, according to the theory of Mr. Ricardo and the Bullion report, the issues of Bank notes in this country were supposed to render the currency redundant, thus causing the adverse balance which depressed the exchanges. And, as I have endeavoured to show, a similar error, with less excuse for it, pervades the doctrines of the more modern theory of the Currency principle.

As the paper money of Russia, from its first issue till the notes were made convertible, by the Imperial edict of July, 1839, presents some curious phenomena, exemplifying several of the points now under discussion, I shall devote a section to the notice of it.

SECTION 7 *On the effects of an influx of gold, caused by a favourable exchange, as distinguished from an influx caused by increased productiveness of the mines*

The length of the foregoing disquisition will perhaps not be thought to have been carried beyond the importance of the topic discussed, when it is considered that the point involved in it lies at the very threshold of the whole question of the currency. The impression of the perfect similarity, up to a certain point, of *paper money* to Bank notes payable in coin on demand, is very common, and forms a striking feature in the questions now at issue between the Currency theorists and their opponents. The analogy of the gold mine, it will be observed, is no gratuitous or fanciful illustration of my own. It was broached by Mr. Ricardo; and raised an important point in the discussion between him and Mr. Bosanquet. I have merely suggested considerations which the former overlooked, and the latter has not sufficiently followed out.

In the more recent controversy to which the promulgation of the theory of the currency principle has given rise, the partisans of that theory, ascribing to the banks in this country the power of arbitrarily adding to the amount of the circulation, assume that the additional notes so issued have a partial effect on prices in this country, analogous to the general effect on prices in the markets of the world by an increased production of the precious metals, in consequence either of the discovery of new and more fertile mines, or of improved methods of working the existing ones.

Such seemed to be the impression of the members of the Committee on Banks of Issue in 1840, before whom I was examined. ①

The error of the assumed analogy is so important, that I am glad to avail myself of the effective aid of Mr. J. Wilson in the exposure of it, by

① In the Appendix will be found extracts from the minutes of my evidence on that occasion, and I may refer the reader to that examination, as containing a summary of the explanation I have just given of the distinction between convertible and inconvertible paper, and as to the effects on prices of the discovery of a gold mine.

inserting the following passage from his recent publication entitled "Capital, Currency, and Banking:" —

"Mr. Tooke expresses his view of the case thus: — 'That the prices of commodities do not depend upon the quantity of money indicated by the amount of Bank notes, nor upon the amount of the whole circulating medium; but that, on the contrary, the amount of the circulating medium is the consequence of prices.'

"To which Colonel Torrens replies: — 'The logical accuracy of this conclusion may be tested by affirming the analogous proposition, that the prices of commodities in Europe, after the discovery of the mines of South America, did not depend upon the quantity of money indicated by the amount of coin, nor by the amount of the whole of the supply of gold and silver; but that, on the contrary, the mines of South America, and the increased amount of gold and silver obtained therefrom, were the consequence of the subsequent rise of prices.'

"That this ingenious and accomplished economist should have stated these as two '*analogous propositions*,' is the most striking evidence with which we have yet met of the utter confusion which prevails in men's minds of the real nature of currency and capital — of coin as a circulating medium, and of the precious metals as a commodity of commerce; a confusion which must be so apparent to those who have followed our arguments thus far that we need not further refer to it. But some have an idea that in every case of an influx of bullion a similar effect should be experienced locally that is produced generally by an increase of metals from the mines. The difference is very essential. In the case of an ordinary influx of gold into this country, caused by a favourable state of the exchanges, the general quantity of gold is not changed, nor its relation in value to other commodities: a new distribution of it is all that takes place. To those who received larger quantities of metal from South America, in exchange for the commodities which they have shipped to that country, and in consequence of the increased productiveness of the mines, the additional quantity was, in the first place, so much increased profit, which not only enabled them to expend more money privately, but which also formed a powerful inducement to increase their purchases of goods and shipments to South America. Such additional demand for shipment to that country of woollens and cottons from England; of wine and silks from France; of flour and domestics from America, and the increased demand for articles of consumption, and for securities for investment by those who made the additional profit at fust, would soon increase prices generally in proportion to the new supplies of the metals.

"But in case of an influx of bullion, owing to a favourable exchange, the case is widely different. The very fact that merchants have recourse to bullion to bring home their capital from those countries where it is not produced, is usually an evidence that other commodities cannot be imported but at a loss. In consequence of the lessened imports the exchanges turn in our favour, and at length bullion is resorted to as the least advantageous medium of transferring capital from one place to another. But this neither infers a power for an increased private expenditure, nor an inducement for a repetition of purchases for shipment, and hence we find that in practice neither circulation nor prices increase under such circumstances, but that both diminish.

"In Article II. we fully considered the effect or an influx of bullion in consequence of a favourable exchange on a metallic currency, and the same precisely must take place with a mixed currency of coin and convertible notes.

"From the beginning of 1841 to 1843 we had an uninterrupted favourable exchange; the bullion in the Bank rapidly increased all the time from 3,965,000*l*. to upwards of 11,000,000*l*. ; every means were used, which properly could be, to increase the circulation, but it fell, during that time, from 35,660,000*l*. to 34,049,000*l*. , and dining the whole period, the prices of commodities generally were sinking lower , and in 1842, the year in which the largest import of gold took place, was the most depressed in prices, and the lowest in the circulation of any during the last thirty years. Nor were the stocks of commodities generally above an average, and the imports were much below an average , and, up to this time (April 19. 1845), though bullion has latterly increased to upwards of 16,000,000*l*, all the recent efforts of the Bank to increase the circulation have proved unavailing, and the prices of all kinds of commodities, even in the absence of any unusual stocks, with some few exceptions, continue unprecedently low. The events of the last four years must go far to convince even those who will not exercise the patience to investigate and understand the theory, that a great error has existed in regard to the connection between Bank circulation and prices of commodities." — (*On Capital*, *Currency*, *and Banking*, pp. 85,87.)

I quite agree with Mr. Wilson in his opinion, as here expressed, of the difference of the effects on prices between an influx of gold caused by an increase of metals from the mines, and the influx caused by a favourable exchange: supposing no alteration in the quantity of them, compared with the demand, in the general markets of the world.

SECTION 8 *Digression concerning Russian paper money*

The history of the Russian paper money, from its first issue, in the reign of the Empress Catherine II. , to its conversion into a convertible currency in the reign of the present sovereign, presents a more continuous record, and for a longer time, of variations in the quantity and value of a paper currency than any other that I am aware of. The variations of its value, as indicated by the foreign exchanges, are susceptible of being more accurately appreciated than those of any other nation, inasmuch as there are regular quotations of the rate at which bills were negotiated upon London, Amsterdam, and Hamburgh, in each week during the whole time, with an exception for the occasional suspension of the communication with the two latter places. It is, therefore, particularly fitted to illustrate some of the views which have here been sketched of the character and effects of a currency consisting of an inconvertible paper, as compared with a circulation of notes strictly convertible into coin.

It was at the close of 1768, in the reign of the Empress Catherine II. , that towards defraying the expenses of the war with Turkey, then entered upon, the *Bank of Assignats* was founded for the purpose of issuing notes payable to bearer. It was, from the first issue, doubtful in what money they would be payable. Professor Storch, from whom this account is taken, states that the tenor of these assignats does not clear up this doubt, for they were, from the beginning, nominally, and still, at the time he was writing, 1815, purported to be, payable in current money. The uncertainty, however, was, practically, cleared up within a few months after the opening of the Bank. For, though at first a few payments were made indifferently in silver or copper coin, they were soon made only in copper. Now, the copper coin was overvalued by 50 per cent, compared with the uncoined metal. The semblance of convertibility was therefore inoperative. It was only a great scarcity of copper coin for retail purposes that admitted of its circulating at a *nominal*, so much above its *intrinsic*, value. But as the notes were much more convenient in large payments, being in sums of 25 roubles, than the bulky metal, they circulated at the full nominal value of the copper coin. The whole issue was, in the first instance, limited to 40 millions of roubles; and no great depreciation attended the paper, as compared with the silver rouble, during the progress of the war. At the peace of Kaïnardji, in 1774, it rose fully to par, compared with silver. Professor Storch observes, that owing to the limitation of amount, which did not exceed the first issue of 40 millions for eighteen years, and to the circumstance that a certain amount of the taxes was required to be paid in assignats, this description of circulation was rendered so agreeable (as he says) to the public, that, until the year 1788, there was an agio, or premium, upon it of from 1 to 5 percent against copper; and that the difference between its value and that of silver never exceeded 3 per cent in favour of the latter.

Thenceforward war, and other causes, induced additional issues, until at the death of Catherine, in 1796, the mass of paper money amounted to 157 millions, being nearly four-fold of what it had been eight years before. The exchange on London, which had been as high as 41*d.* in 1787, was at 31*d.* in 1796. During the two subsequent reigns, the further issues increased rapidly, insomuch that in 1810 the paper money in circulation reached 577 millions, and the paper rouble was worth only $25\frac{2}{5}$ copeks, being only one fourth of its value in 1788. The exchange on London fell, in the autumn of 1810, to $11\frac{1}{2}$*d.*; on Amsterdam, to 8 stivers; and on Hamburgh, to 7 skillings banco, per rouble. And the prices of all produce and commodities rose, in a proportion, greater or less, to this fall of the exchanges.

The amount of notes in circulation had, according to a statement of Count Gurieff, reached, in 1817, 836 millions. I am not aware of the amounts at different periods between 1810 and 1817; but there is every reason to believe that the issues of paper were increased in 1811 and 1812; and, at any rate, it cannot be supposed that at such a time there could be any reduction of the amount.

Now, the following facts present an important view of the great influence of the circumstances of that period in causing enormous fluctuations in the exchange, perfectly irrespective of any alteration in the amount of the currency. Immediately after the close of 1810, the exchanges rose, with considerable oscillations, the lowest quotations, however, being above those of 1810; and they advanced rapidly when the invading armies of France approached the Russian frontier. In June, 1812, the exchange on London was 16*d.*; on Amsterdam, $11\frac{3}{4}$ stivers; and on Hamburgh $11\frac{1}{4}$ skillings; and, by the latter end of September, when Napoleon had entered Moscow, the paper rouble attained the enormously advanced rates of 25*d.*, $17\frac{1}{4}$ stivers, and $16\frac{1}{2}$ skillings banco. The silver rouble, and the Dutch ducat, which were respectively in 1810 at 400 copeks, and 1250 copeks, were, in different periods in August, 1812, as low respectively as 350 copeks, and 900 copeks.

This state of the Russian paper currency is not to be accounted for according to the doctrine of Mr. Ricardo, and Mr. Huskisson, and the Bullion report of 1810: for this would not allow for the violent disturbing causes then operating on the exchanges, irrespective of any alteration in the amount of the currency.

The truth is, that the circumstances operating in the great enhancement of the value of the Russian currency in 1810-1812 (without the possibility of assigning a contraction of the amount of it as a cause) were exactly the converse of those which were at the same period causing an apparent depreciation of the currency of this country, in so far as the foreign exchanges were an index of it.

The circumstances producing the extraordinary elevation of the exchanges in Russia were these.

The prices of hemp, flax, tallow, and other articles of Russian produce, had risen very considerably, in this country, in the autumn of 1811, and the commencement of 1812; partly from actual scarcity, and partly from apprehension that the invasion of that empire by the French armies would cut off future supplies. There were great inducements, therefore, to make purchases and shipments of produce from the ports of Petersburg and Riga, and other Russian ports, for British account, before the close of the navigation, by the setting in of winter. There were also similar purchases and shipments of produce, although on a limited scale (in consequence of the obstructions then prevailing to all commercial intercourse), made for Germany, France, and the United States. The immediate consequence was the drawing of an unusually large amount of bills upon these countries. But while there was this demand for articles of export from Russia, there was no sale whatever for imports. The native Russian merchants and shopkeepers could not be prevailed upon by any inducement of price to buy the goods which were imported into Petersburg from England, under the apprehension that, if the French succeeded in their invasion, they would proceed to the confiscation or burning of all British manufactures or produce, as they had done, not long before, in the ports of Prussia. The only remittances from Russia, therefore, were of sums collected from former sales, or as returns for gold and silver, of which some, although not large, quantities had been imported. There was, consequently, a vast disproportion, of drawers to takers of bills; and the inevitable effect was to raise the exchange, as we have seen.

Now an exactly opposite state of things was simultaneously existing in this country. There was an urgent want of the raw materials of our manufactures; cotton, especially, having become scarce and dear; and naval stores from abroad were required for our military marine. At the same time a great foreign expenditure for subsidies, and for the pay and maintenance of our armies in Spain, was going forward. Of extraordinary magnitude, therefore, were the payments to be made abroad; while as to nearly all articles of habitual export from this country there was an almost total absence of foreign demand, as has been shown by the extracts from Mr. J. D. Hume's Letters. It is no wonder that our exchanges were depressed; nor is there any need to assume a redundancy of our currency as the cause.

Here, then, is an illustration of the point which was at issue between Mr. Ricardo and Mr. Thornton, when the former controverted the position of the latter, viz. that, upon a sudden demand for corn, or for the payment, of troops or subsidies, there might be an *unwillingness* of the foreigner to receive goods from us in payment, and so the necessity might arise for sending gold, or making an enormous sacrifice in the exchange. The only answer given by Mr. Ricardo was, that we *ought not to indulge the foreigner in such unwillingness*!

Without, however, dwelling further on this point, which has been before discussed, I will proceed to observe upon the decline of the exchanges in Russia, after the extravagant rise of them in September, 1812. The fall began when it became manifest that the French army would be obliged to retreat from Russia without any attempt to reach Petersburg, and the quotations, by the end of the year, were respectively 16 $\frac{3}{8}$*d.* 11 $\frac{3}{4}$ stiv. and 11 $\frac{3}{4}$ sk. banco. Thenceforward the decline proceeded slowly, and with some oscillation, till October 1816; when it reached the lowest quotations of 9 $\frac{1}{2}$*d.*, 9 $\frac{15}{16}$ stiv. and 9 $\frac{3}{4}$ sk. banco, and the silver ruble was worth 400 to 410 copeks in paper. The Custom-house duties, and other taxes, had been calculated in silver rubles, and the bank notes were, after intermediate alteration, declared by the government to be receivable in the proportion of 4 to 1, thus avowing a depreciation of 75 per cent, being substantially a degradation of the standard to that extent. At this rate it continued for some time.

During the progress to this degree of depreciation, the prices of commodities experienced a corresponding advance, but subject to great fluctuation in the process.

Loans were subsequently raised, abroad, by the Russian government, in order to withdraw a portion of the notes from the circulation; and the amount of them was reported on the 1st of January, 1821, to have been reduced to 640 millions. The exchanges had, by that time, improved, so as to induce the government to admit the paper ruble in payment of taxes at 3 ro. 60, and eventually at 3 ro. 50 co. At which last-mentioned rate the conversion, from bank assignats to bank notes payable on demand in silver rubles, was ordained by an imperial ukase, dated 1st July, 1839.

My purpose in this digression has been —

1st. To exemplify the position that government paper money may be so issued that, as in the case of the first 40 millions of roubles, a very slight depreciation only may follow; just sufficient to displace so much coin; and that, by strictly limiting the quantity, it may be maintained in circulation at, or very near to, par with coin.

2nd. To show the prodigious range of variation in the exchanges to which an inconvertible paper currency is liable, while the amount of it may be either stationary, or tending in an opposite direction.

3rd. To direct attention to the extraordinary phenomenon of a currency of inconvertible government paper, largely extended in quantity, increasing in value by 100 per cent, as an invading victorious enemy was approaching; and the value falling as the enemy were retreating; and eventually sinking to a lower level than that from which it had risen.

4th. And finally, to point out the unaccountable misapprehension which has led persons, otherwise well informed, to allege, and reason upon, the assumption of a similarity between the circulation of bank notes in this country, during the suspension of cash payments, and the Russian paper money of the same period.

I have taken occasion in a former volume① to remark upon the error of Lord Ashburton, in referring, as he did in his evidence before the Agricultural Committee in 1836, to the adjustment by the Russian government of the value of its depreciated paper, as an example that ought to have been followed in this country upon the restoration of a metallic standard.

Mr. Hubbard②, in his pamphlet on the Currency, has the following passage: —

"When a paper currency is inconvertible, it may be depreciated by its quantity being increased; and the same consequences which attend the depreciation of the coin, attend the depreciation of the paper. The circulation of paper money in Russia was raised from two hundred millions of roubles in 1799 to six hundred millions in 1811: the food of rye flour rose in price from 70 to 200 copecs; the value of the silver rouble expressed in assignats rose from to four paper roubles; and the exchange on Hamburgh fell from twenty-six skillings to ten.

The Bank of England was restricted from paying its notes in gold; its circulation was enlarged from ten millions to thirty millions; the circulation of the private banks was similarly increased; coin was exported; and, if the general range of prices rose twenty-five per cent, the cause is to be found in the depreciation of the inconvertible currency of the country resulting from its increased quantity, and evidenced by the rise in the price

---

① Some, but a very small, part of the facts here introduced were then stated with reference to the opinion expressed by Lord Ashburton, that in 1819, if the feeling of parliament and the country had gone with him, he should have been inclined to propose a reduction of the standard "pound" to 15*s*.

② *The Currency and the Country*, 1843, p. 35.

of gold from 3*l*. 17*s*. 10 $\frac{1}{2}$*d*. to 5*l*. 5*s*. per oz,; and, by the fall of the exchange with Hamburgh, from thirty-seven to twenty-eight skilliugs for the pound sterling."

If the view which I have sketched of the state of the circulation of the Bank of England during the Restriction has any approach to correctness, there cannot be the shadow of a ground for the statement here so confidently made, of its having been similar in its principle and effects, to the Russian paper money during the same period. They agree only in the single fact of inconvertibility. The points of difference are so striking that I am quite content to leave it to my readers to draw their own conclusions.

But I cannot help remarking upon the circumstance which I have on more than one occasion had to notice as a very objectionable (and occasionally deceptive) practice of writers or speakers, who, when seeking to prove a depreciation of Bank of England notes, in consequence of excessive quantity, state the amount in circulation without reference to the distinction of the one-pound notes from those of a higher denomination.

If Mr. Hubbard had deducted the one-pound notes, as, according to every authority — Mr. Ricardo, Mr. Huskisson, and the Bullion Report — he ought to have done, he would have seen that the circulation in 1817, when it *nearly* reached the amount, he states, would, instead of being at the expiration of more than twenty years, enlarged from ten to thirty millions, be found to be increased to only twenty millions. And if he had taken the pains to examine a little further, he would have discovered that, when it reached this extreme amount, it was perfectly consistent with a state of the exchanges and of the price of bullion fully at par, or rather so much above it, as to have raised the treasure of the Bank to a higher amount than it had ever before attained. It is really surprising to find how many persons write and speak about the circulation. During the Restriction, and draw conclusion and institute comparisons regarding it, while they clearly have no knowledge of the real state of it at that time.

SECTION 9 *On a metallic circulation, as the type of a perfect currency*

It has been my purpose, in the preceding section, to show that the theory of the currency principle, according to the exposition of its promulgators, involves the error of confounding convertible with inconvertible paper; as regards its issue, and its effects in circulation up to the point of convertibility.

By the same authorities it is assumed, as an axiom, that a purely metallic circulation is the type or model of a perfect currency; and that, therefore, a mixed circulation of coin and paper ought to be made to conform in amount to the same variations as would be incidental to a purely metallic currency. I, and those who with me are opposed to the doctrine of the currency theory, as adopted by Sir Robert Peel and embodied in the act of 1844, readily admit so much of it as relates to this assumption. We are willing to consider a metallic currency as the type of that to which our mixed circulation of coin and paper ought to conform; but, further, we contend that it has so conformed, and must so conform, while the paper is strictly convertible.① And we deny the correctness of their view of the operation of a metallic circulation, according to their exposition of it, which I am about to quote.

Those who contended, prior to 1844, that such as is stated in the following extracts would be the operation of a metallic circulation, are naturally, *now that they have experience*, *so totally at variance with their anticipations* of the working of the system founded upon their model, disposed to explain away their former hypothesis. But it is right to record what *were* the opinions under the influence of which such great alterations were made in our system of banking. In my pamphlet of 1844 I cited

---

① Upon this point, nothing can be more forcible or more felicitously expressed than the following passage from Mr. Fullarton. "But we are told, now, that in order to preserve a mixed circulation of gold and Bank notes from depreciation, it is not sufficient that the Bank notes should at all times he convertible into coin; that, notwithstanding such convertibility, the notes may still be over-issued in such quantities as to raise the prices of all the commodities in the kingdom, and to cause the exportation of the gold, and that, to prevent such derangements, it is indispensable that the Bank note circulation should at all times be made to fluctuate exactly as a purely metallic circulation would have fluctuated. On these propositions I am content at once to join issue I deny that we have any evidence of such a redundance of circulating Bank notes having ever existed in coincidence with a really convertible state of the currency, as to raise prices or to cause an efflux of the precious metals, or that such a redundance under such circumstances is possible. And as to making a Bank note circulation fluctuate exactly as a pure metallic circulation would have fluctuated, I do not see how that can be constituted into a duty, until it be first shown that they ever fluctuate differently. As a general principle, indeed, I am quite free to admit that the increase or decrease of a circulation of Bank notes, from whatever cause it may proceed, ought to correspond with the increase or decrease which a currency of metallic coin would exhibit under the same circumstances. But I go further than this: I contend that there not only ought to be such correspondence, but that there always is , that, wherever the convertibility of the paper is perfect and secured from all delay or impediment, the coin of full standard value in weight and fineness, and the traffic in the metal, whether coined or uncoined, absolutely free and unrestricted, there the Bank issues, if left to themselves, must necessarily fluctuate in conformity with the principles which govern the supply of the standard metal, and it is only from the intervention of some such arbitrary and empirical system of restraint as is now projected that this conformity runs any risk of being disturbed" —(*Regulation of Currencies*, 2nd. edition, pp. 26, 27.)

passages from the principal authorities for the theory. These and my remarks, which they elicited, I here extract and insert: —

"Admitting, for the sake of argument, that a metallic circulation is the type of a perfect currency, it should seem that those who confidently pronounce it to he so, labour under a most egregious misconception of what the working of it would be.

"Upon the grounds which I have now to state, it will be evident that the operation of a perfectly metallic circulation would not be attended with the advantages which they contemplate; nor, on the other hand, with the disadvantages which might be apprehended if it were to work as they seem to imagine it would.

"According to the currency principle, every export of the precious metals under a metallic circulation would be attended with a contraction of the amount and value of the currency, causing a fall of prices until the degree of contraction and consequent fall of prices should be such as, by inducing a diminished import and increased export of commodities, to cause a reflux of the metals and a restoration of prices to their proper level. So, on the other hand, an influx of the precious metals would raise prices, till they reached a level at which the converse of the process would take place. This oscillating process of a rise and fall of prices with every influx or efflux of the precious metals, independently of circumstances connected with the cost of production of commodities, and the ordinary rate of consumption, would be perplexing enough, and any thing but convenient to the commercial, or the manufacturing, or the agricultural community.

"The advocates, however, of the doctrine contend that, although thus the oscillations might he more frequent, the scale of them would be more contracted, every divergence being more quickly checked. I firmly believe, however, that if every export and import of the precious metals were attended with the effects imputed to them by this theory, the inconvenience would be felt to be intolerable. and that some of what Mr. Norman calls economising expedients would be devised and applied as a remedy.

"But the operation would not be that which the theory, as it is stated in the following passages, supposes: —

" 'It is universally admitted by persons acquainted with monetary science, that paper money should be so regulated as to keep the medium of exchange, of which it may form a part, in the same state, with respect to amount and to value, in which the medium of exchange would exist were the circulating portion of it purely metallic. Now, it is self-evident, that if the circulation were purely metallic, an adverse exchange, causing an exportation of the metals to any given amount, would occasion a contraction of the circulating currency to the same amount; and that a favourable exchange, causing an importation of the metals to a given amount, would cause an expansion of the circulating currency to the same amount. If the currency of the metropolis consisted of gold, an adverse exchange, causing an exportation of gold to the amount of 1,000,000*l*., would withdraw from circulation one million of sovereigns.'—Torrens. (*Letter to Lord Melbourne*, pp. 29, 30.)

" 'The amount of the import or export of the precious metals is a pretty sure measure of what would have been the increase or decrease of the amount of a metallic currency.'— S. J. Loyd. (*Further Reflections on the Currency*, p. 34.)

" And Mr. Norman, after explaining the manner in which the exchanges, as between two countries, A. and B., may be rendered adverse to A., so as to cause an export of coin or bullion, goes on to say,—

"'The export of coin and bullion will cause general prices to fall in country A., and to rise in B., supposing the debt to B. not to be sooner discharged, until it becomes more advantageous to export goods than money.'"—(*Letter to C. Wood, Esq., M. P.* p. 17.)

"In these passages, and many more that might be cited, it is assumed that the precious metals, gold, and silver, and bullion, are synonymous with currency and money, and are convertible terms. And, accordingly, every export of the precious metals is not only considered, in the supposition of a metallic circulation, as a contraction of the currency of this country; but as so much added to the currency of the country to which it is exported. Such alteration in the relative quantity of the metals in the respective countries from which or to which they are transmitted being, according to this theory, an abstraction or addition of so much money; and prices, that is, the general prices of commodities, being considered as depending on the quantity of money, a corresponding rise or fall of them is assumed to be the consequence. In this view some very important considerations are overlooked.

"Before entering upon them, however, I must premise, that throughout this discussion the value of gold in the commercial world is assumed to be constant, *i. e.* that the cost of production and the general demand are unvaried; also that the tariffs of foreign countries are in *statu quo*, so as to confine the consideration to the effects of an influx or efflux of bullion on the currencies of the respective countries, divested of any reference to disturbing causes, beyond those incidental to the course of trade and international banking.

"There is, and must generally be, in a country like this or like France, a stock greater or less of gold and silver, beyond that which is in use as money or as plate, or which is in the mint, and in goldsmiths' and silversmiths' hands, in preparation for use as either. This surplus or floating stock may be considered as seeking a market, whether for internal purposes or for export; and, be the quantity greater or less, can it be said of it, if it is exported, that the amount is so much abstracted from the currency of the country, any more than if an equal value of tin or zinc, or lead or iron, were exported?

"Moreover, of that part of the stock existing in the shape of coin in this country it may be observed, that as the coinage is not subject to a seignorage, there may be, and frequently is, in that shape a considerable amount of the precious metals which may not be in the hands of the public, circulating as money, nor in the reserves of the different banks, the Bank of England excepted; but may, like the uncoined metals, be seeking a market at home or abroad. It may be in the coffers of the Bank of England; but held as bullion, being in the shape of coin equally convenient for every purpose, and more, convenient for some purposes, in that form, besides that of serving for currency, than in uncoined gold, that is, in bars or ingots.

"The idea of gold seeking a market, and not immediately finding one, may seem strange, and, by the firm believers in the currency-principle doctrine, may be set down as paradoxical and absurd.

"Gold is an object in such universal demand, or, in other words, so universally marketable, that its being supposed to be kept on hand at all, under the uncertainty of finding a suitable market for it, appears to be inconceivable, or almost a contradiction in terms.

"I am ready to admit that gold is a commodity in such general demand that it may always command a market, that it can always buy all other commodities; whereas other commodities cannot always buy gold. The markets of the world are open to it as merchandise at less sacrifice upon an emergency, than would attend an export of any other article, which might in quantity or kind be beyond the usual demand in the country to which it is sent. So far there can be, I presume, no difference of opinion.

"But there will be found to be no inconsiderable difference, if we distinguish as we ought to do, for the purpose whether of theory or practice, between gold considered as merchandise, *i. e.* as capital, and gold considered as currency circulating in the shape of coin among the public.

"Mr. Senior, in one of his lectures on the value of money, observes, 'The value of the precious metals as money must depend ultimately on their value as materials of jewellery and plate; since if they were not used as commodities, they could not circulate as money.' And he makes a remark to the same effect in an article in the 'Edinburgh Review,' for July, 1843, on Free Trade and Retaliation. 'The primary cause of the utility of gold is of course its use as the material of plate. The secondary cause is its use as money.' Of the truth of these propositions there can be no doubt.

"As this country is not only a large consumer of the precious metals for purposes other than money, but is also an entrepot for receiving from the mines, and distributing the greater portion of the quantity applicable to the consumption of other countries, the bullion trade, totally independently of supplying the currency, must of necessity be very considerable. In resorting to this entrepot the metals can only be considered as merchandise in transit, seeking a market for consumption either in this country or abroad.

"But beyond the stock which is requisite for this purpose, and which must always include more or less of surplus to meet occasional extra demand, there must be a very considerable amount of the precious metals applicable and applied as the convenient mode of adjustment of international balances, being a commodity more generally in demand, and less liable to fluctuations in its market value than any other. I will not venture, in the absence of any recognised grounds for computation, to hazard an estimate of the amount so required; but, bearing in mind the immense extent of international transactions, and the vicissitudes of the seasons, and other circumstances affecting the relative imports and exports of food, raw materials, and manufactures, besides the variations in the market value of national and private securities held interchangeably, the quantity of bullion required to be constantly available for this purpose must be very large; the principal deposits of it being in the Bank of England, the Bank of France, and the public banks of Hamburg and Amsterdam. These deposits may, moreover, in some of the public banks, be occasionally increased by coin which has become superfluous in the circulation.

"If, therefore, we take into account the magnitude of the stock necessarily imported, partly for the consumption of plate in this country, and partly for that abroad, and of the amount required as available funds for the adjustment of international balances, it may not be deemed an extravagant supposition that there might occasionally be under a perfectly metallic circulation fluctuations, within moderately short periods, to the extent of at least five or six millions sterling in the import and export of bullion, perfectly extrinsic of the amount or value of the coin circulating as money in the hands of the public, and perfectly without influence on the general prices of commodities, as equally without general prices having been a cause of such fluctuations.

"It may be objected that the quantity of bullion which I have supposed to bo in deposit among the principal public banks of the commercial world, applicable to the adjustment of international balances, should be looked upon as performing the functions of money, in restoring the level of the currencies, which the very fact of the necessity for the transmission of money from one country to another proves to have been disturbed. This objection is founded on the assumption that gold and silver are money or currency, and it is supposed that the transmissions of bullion for the purposes in question have a direct operation upon the amount of money or currency in actual circulation in the several countries. But in this objection the consideration is overlooked, that the coins only which enter into, that is, form part of, the internal circulation of the country, can be designated as currency, while bullion can only be viewed in the light of capital.①

"The distinction between bullion, as merchandise or capital, and coins, as money or currency, may be exemplified in the case of coins which are subject to a seignorage, and in cases such as that of Hamburg, where the

---

① With the exception of Mexican dollars, this being the form in which the produce of the silver mines of America is mainly distributed, and Imperials, the golden corn of Russia, being the form in winch the extraordinarily large and increasing produce of the Asiatic provinces of that empire is adding to the general supply of the precious metals , and further excepting the gold coins of this country, which, being issued without any charge whatever for manufacture, are found to be for some purposes of export more convenient than bars or ingots . with these exceptions, the instances are rare in which, unless depreciated at home by compulsory paper money, the coins usually circulating as money are withdrawal to supply foreign payments of any magnitude.

money current for all the ordinary expenditure of income consists chiefly of a variety of foreign coins, passing from hand to hand at a conventional value, while all mercantile payments are made by transfers of capital, deposited in the form of fine silver, and called bank money.

"In such a case as that of Hamburg there have been, and must often again be, very great fluctuations in the amount of silver in the bank, and, consequently, of bank money, without any obviously corresponding variations in the amount of money in circulation for current purposes of expenditure by the community, or any variation as arising from that cause in the general prices of their commodities. And if a seignorage were imposed on the gold coin of this country on correct principles (that is, accompanied by a limitation of tender, and by a power on the part of the holders to demand gold bullion at 3*l.* 17*s.* 10 $\frac{1}{2}$*d.* per ounce), there might be, and there would be, occasionally, supposing a purely metallic circulation, a very considerable variation in the amount of bullion in the coffers of the national bank, or in the hands of dealers in bullion, without necessarily in the slightest degree affecting the amount of the currency actually in circulation, in the ordinary daily transactions arising out of the expenditure of individuals composing the public, and without variation in general prices."—(*Inquiry into the Currency Principle*, pp. 6-15.)

SECTION 10 *On the distinction between currency and capital; and on the actual and imputed functions of country bank notes*

Totally unaware as the authors of our new system were of the distinction between currency and capital, when applied to the distinct functions of the precious metals, of serving, in the shape of coin, for internal purposes, and of capital when transmitted abroad in liquidation of an adverse balance of trade; still more striking, if possible, has been their disregard of that distinction in our internal exchanges.

I have before had occasion to notice the different uses of bank notes, with a view to point out the error of the currency theory which classes the two denominations together, as substitutes for coin. Dr. Adam Smith, in the following passage, has noticed the distinction between the two kinds of bank notes, and has, accordingly, in his views of our paper currency, steered clear of the confusion between currency and capital which pervades and disfigures most modern reasonings on the subject: —

"The circulation of every country," he observes, "may be considered as divided into two different branches — the circulation of the dealers with one another, and the circulation between the dealers and consumers. Though the same pieces of money, whether paper or metal, may be employed, sometimes in the one circulation and sometimes in the other, yet as both are constantly going on at the same time, each requires a certain stock of money of one kind or another to carry it on. The value of the goods circulated between the different dealers with one another never can exceed the value of those circulated between the dealers and the consumers, whatever is bought by the dealers being ultimately destined to be sold to the consumers. Paper money may be so regulated as either to confine itself very much to the circulation between the different dealers, or to extend itself likewise to a great part of that between the dealers and the consumers. When no bank notes are circulated under ten pounds value, as in London, paper money confines itself very much to the circulation between the dealers. When a ten pound bank note comes into the hands of a consumer he is generally obliged to change it at the first shop where he has occasion to purchase five shillings' worth of goods, so that it often returns into the hands of a dealer before the consumer has spent a fortieth part of the money."—(*Wealth of Nations*, M Culloch's edition, pp. 141, 142.)

Upon this passage there are the following remarks in my tract of 1844: —

"There can be no doubt that the distinction here made is substantially correct. Bearing in mind this distinction, the reason is obvious why, as far as relates to the interchange between dealers and consumers (including the payment of wages, which constitute the principal means of the consumers), coin, and the smaller denomination of notes serving as coin, are essential to such interchange, and why, consequently, if those smaller notes are withdrawn, their place must be supplied by coin; but not so as regards the interchange between dealers and dealers Bank notes are not only not essential to that interchange, but it must be manifest to any one having even a slight knowledge only of the manner in which such interchange is conducted, that, in point of fact, bank notes are rarely used in the larger dealings of sales and purchases.

"The great bulk of the wholesale trade of the country is carried on and adjusted by settlements or sets-off of debts and credits, the written evidences of which are in bills of exchange (including in that term all promissory notes payable to orders after date), while current payments, for what are called cash sales, are mostly discharged by cheques; the ultimate balance only arising out of the vast mass of such transactions requiring liquidation in a comparatively small amount of bank notes. The principal exceptions to this, I apprehend, are in the provision trade, and in the sheep and cattle and horse fairs, in which the payments are mostly made in coin and bank notes; but there can be no question that for amounts of 10*l*. and upwards, bills of exchange might be, as they formerly were, and, but for the increased stamp duty, would be substituted.

"Of the fact that, with the exception of these, and perhaps of some few other wholesale trades in which no credit is given, there is little or no intervention of bank notes in purchases or sales among wholesale dealers, no doubt can be entertained. And I have now to state the explanation, which I am not aware of having met with among the various lucubrations on the subject of the currency which it has been my lot to see, of the reason why, with the exceptions I have pointed out, such sales and purchases are effected without actual payment in money, which, by the currency theory, is defined to be coin or Bank notes.

"The reason is that all the transactions between dealers and dealers, by which are to be understood all sales from the producer or importer, through all the stages of intermediate processes of manufacture or otherwise to the retail dealer or the exporting merchant, are resolvable into movements or *transfers of capital*. Now, transfers of capital do not necessarily suppose, nor do actually, as a matter of fact, entail, in the great majority of transactions, a passing of money, that is, bank notes or coin — I mean bodily, and not by fiction — at the time of transfer. All the movements of capital may be, and the great majority are effected by the operations of banking and credit without the intervention of actual payment in coin or bank notes, that is, actual, visible, and tangible bank notes, not supposititious bank notes, issued with one hand and received back by the other, or, more properly speaking, entered on one side of the ledger with a counter entry on the other. And there is the further important consideration, that the total amount of the transactions between dealers and dealers must, in the last resort, be determined and limited by the amount of those between dealers and consumers.

"The business of bankers, setting aside the issue of promissory notes on demand, may be divided into two branches, corresponding with the distinction pointed out by Dr. Smith of the transactions between dealers and dealers, and between dealers and consumers. One branch of the banker's business is to collect capital from those who have not immediate employment for it, and to distribute or transfer it to those who have. The other branch is to receive deposits of the incomes of their customers, and to pay out the amount, as it is wanted for expenditure, by the latter in the objects of their consumption. The former may be considered as the business behind the counter, and the latter before or over the counter; the former being a circulation of capital, the latter of currency.

"The distinction or separation in reasoning of that branch of banking which relates to the concentration of capital on the one hand and the distribution of it on the other, from that branch which is employed in administering the circulation for local purposes of the district, is so important in its bearing on the question of regulating the circulation by the foreign exchanges, and on that of the connection between the currency and prices, that the fullest elucidation of the practical operation of that distinction may naturally be required. I have, therefore, as the best method of elucidating this point, drawn largely on the examinations by the Committee on Banks of Issue in 1841; and if it be objected that more than enough of the evidence is here adduced for the purpose, seeing that the point is so clear when simply stated, my answer to the objector is, that simple and clear as the distinction may appear to him, so imbued were the members of the Committee who took a prominent part in the examination, with the tenets of the currency theory, as to have remained apparently (judging at least by the reiteration of their questions to the same effect) unconvinced of the power-lessness of the banks of issue to influence directly the amount of the circulation of bank notes. And even to this day, with all the light of subsequent experience, it should seem, judging by speeches and publications, and the declamations against excessive paper issues, which still appear occasionally on the subject, that the dogma of the power of banks of issue to create paper money[①] *ad libitum* prevails to nearly as great an extent as ever.

"All the country bankers examined concur in stating that they have not the power by loans or discounts beyond the ordinary transactions of the neighbourhood to extend or contract the local circulation of notes, or to influence prices. They could, indeed, refuse to issue their own notes in answering the demands of their depositors, but such refusal must be accompanied by offering Bank of England notes or coin, and thus the local circulation would be equally filled up; they may curtail or call in their advances, and so diminish their engagements, and eventually render a smaller amount of circulation necessary; but the immediate demands for notes for local purposes must still be satisfied.

"It appears by that evidence, that their circulation is devoted and confined to local purposes, chiefly in small amounts, for the retail trade; and in the rural districts in advances to farmers for the purchase of stock

① *By paper money* being always understood, according to the doctrine under consideration, bank notes in the hands of the public.

and seed, and to cattle dealers and provision merchants; but that when called upon to make advances by way of loan or discount on a larger scale, it is always by a draft or order upon London, or upon such of their correspondents in other towns as happen to suit the borrowers—such loans or discounts being invariably made out of capital, or, in other words, out of the general resources of the bank.

"Among the country bankers of England, I have selected the evidence of Mr. Stuckey, the head of the admirably conducted banks of Somersetshire under his firm, because there is no one more conversant, both theoretically and practically, than he is with the subject of banking. By his position formerly he was in intimate communication with Lord Liverpool and Mr. Huskisson. He was examined by the Bullion Committee in 1819. He was an adherent to the principles of the late Mr. Ricardo; and he expressed opinions of the desirableness of having the circulation of bank notes regulated by a view to the foreign exchanges. But what is the result of his very large experience as a banker?"

"477. (*Chairman.*) Do you conceive that, generally speaking, there is an insuperable difficulty in country banks exercising such a control over their own issues, as to reduce them to some extent during a period of adverse foreign exchange?

"*I really do not see how that is to be done.*

"478. Then what is the practical effect of the regard to foreign exchanges, which you think all country bankers ought to pay?

"The practical effect is to make them more cautious and circumspect in the management of their money transactions; but I should not state, that in the agricultural districts, the circulation would be altered by the foreign exchanges.

"479. Do you conceive, that although the country bankers ought to pay regard to the state of the foreign exchanges, it is not in their power to bring that regard into practical effect by reducing the amount of their issues during the period of adverse exchange?

"*I do not see how it could be done.*

"480. Will, then, the regard which you recommend they should pay to the foreign exchanges produce any practical effect whatever upon their issues?

"Yes, it would produce effect in the management of their monied concerns.

"481. What practical effect would it produce on their *issues*?

"*Very little*: my own opinion is, that country issues have very little to do with exchanges.

"482. Would the regard which you recommend to the foreign exchanges produce any effect upon their issues?

"*Very little*: it would produce some effect upon the management of their monied concerns.

"483. (*Sir T. Fremantle.*) Upon their liabilities?

"Yes.

"484. *But comparatively little on their issues*?

"*Yes*: particularly in the agricultural parts of the country.

"485. Upon what do you think the issues of the country bankers depend?

"More on the state of agriculture than any thing else. When the landed interest is in a comfortable state, I consider the issues to be increased.

"491. (*Sir T. Fremantle.*) The advance which you make to the agriculturists is an advance of capital, whether it is paid to them in your own notes, or Bank of England notes, or gold?

"Yes; the advance is generally made to agriculturists in our own notes.

"492. But if the state of the country is such as not to require an increase of your own issues, you are quite sure that those notes will come back to you in the course of a short time?

"Exactly.

"493. Therefore the advance that you make in that case *is an advance of capital, and not an advance of mere issue*?

"*Exactly; it is made out of our resources.*

"501. (*Chairman.*) Will you state how you are affected by foreign exchanges?

"I think the London banker is affected by them, therefore I am affected; I naturally know that if my deposits are withdrawn, and any demand is made upon me, I must sell my securities; therefore I look to the foreign exchanges in order to ascertain how the money market is, that I may know what securities I shall dispose of.

"524. (*Chairman.*) Suppose the case of an adverse foreign exchange, when, according to your own opinion, the paper circulation of the country ought to be reduced, would you, on a depositor asking for the payment of a deposit in notes, be at all guided by the circumstance of the foreign exchanges, as to whether you paid that deposit in Bank of England notes, or in your own local notes?

"*I admit that I should not be guided by the foreign exchanges*, but I should be guided by knowing where the deposit money was to go to.

"525. (*Sir T. Fremantle.*) You have stated that when you have observed gold going out of the country, and money becoming tight in London, you have been in the habit of issuing directions to your different branches to be more circumspect in the advances they make; has the effect of that been practically to diminish the amount of your notes in circulation in those districts?

"*I do not think it has*; *I am not aware that it has.*

"526. What has the effect been?

"To make them *more cautious in their advances*, keeping our resources more within our own command; instead of discounting a bill, winch we should discount under some circumstances, we have refused it; and instead of advancing 1000*l*. or 2000*l*, we have desired the person to take 500*l*, therefore we keep our banking capital and banking resources more under our own command.

"527. But are you prepared to say that the circulation of your own notes has not been affected by that course of conduct?

"*I am not aware that it has.*

"537. Supposing, for instance, it should ultimately be thought that it is desirable that the country circulation should have a general conformity to the state of the foreign exchanges, do you conceive that this could be in any way effected by the country bankers?

"*I do not at present know how it could be accomplished*; and I may take the liberty of going further in that question, and saying that it appears to me that the country issues, as conducted in the west of England, have very little or nothing to do with the foreign exchanges.

"538. Do you conceive, then, that the only circulation which ought to have reference to the foreign exchanges is that of the Bank of England?

"I do conceive that it is the only thing which ought to have reference to them, being the circulation of London, and London being the spot where the foreign exchanges are generally effected.

"539. (*Mr. Grote.*) Do you mean to state that you think the circulation of the Bank of England ought to be made to vary in conformity with the foreign exchanges, but that the circulation of the country banks ought not to be affected by the foreign exchanges?

"No, I do not go so far as that; my opinion is that the country circulation does not affect the foreign exchanges, because it is a different kind of circulation; the foreign exchanges are, we all know, affected in various ways, but I do not think they are affected by the country circulation, and I have looked attentively at that question."

"The evidence of Mr. Gilbart, of the London and Westminster Bank, of Mr. Hobhouse, of a bank at Bath, and of Mr. Rod well, of a bank at Ipswich, is full of information as to the circumstances which influence and limit the country circulation without the possibility of reference to the exchanges. But as these gentlemen do not profess ever to have entertained an opinion of its being desirable, if it were practicable, to regulate the country circulation by the foreign exchanges, I have preferred a reference to Mr. Stuckey's evidence, he having entertained and professed an opinion that it was desirable, but had made the discovery, confirmed by long experience on a very extensive scale, of its utter impracticability.

"Mr. Gurney was examined on this point by the Committee on the Bank Charter in 1832. I have before had occasion to notice his evidence at some length, and will now only refer to the concluding part of it:—

"Does it not follow from what you have said, that an over-issue of notes of country bankers cannot easily be effected?

"*My belief is that it cannot be effected by any act of the country bankers.*"

"As far as this point is concerned, it might perhaps be deemed to be sufficiently proved by the evidence already adduced. But not the evidence only on this point is confirmed, but also much additional light is thrown on the distinction between capital and currency, by a view of the Scotch system of banking. The examinations of some of the managers of the Scotch banks by the Committee in 1841, are accordingly well worthy of attention as illustrative of that distinction.

"The evidence of Mr. Alexander Blair, treasurer and manager of the Bank of Scotland, which is the oldest of the chartered banks, having been established in 1695, and which appears to be conducted with great ability and prudence, is full of valuable information as to the machinery and working of the Scotch system of banking.

"He mentions a curious fact relating to the mode in which the balances resulting from the exchanges twice a week among the banks are adjusted by the means of Exchequer bills which, to the amount of 450,000*l.*, they hold for that express purpose. Here we have Exchequer bills answering all the purposes that Bank of England notes at the clearing-house in London do.

"Mr. Blair also states that seven millions in amount of notes is found to be requisite in order to keep up an *average* circulation of three millions — a very curious fact, as it appears that the stamp duty is paid upon the whole stock, whether in the hands of the public, or within the walls of the banks, and that the whole amount is out in circulation for a few days at two seasons of the year.

"It is stated, moreover, upon the same authority, that the total amount of deposits which, in 1826, was computed to be about twenty-one millions, had in 1841 reached to about twenty-seven millions.

"It is a remarkable circumstance that, while there has been a great extension of banking capital, and of banking accommodation, and of banking competition, in Scotland since 1826, the amount of the aggregate circulation has considerably diminished. What a commentary upon the received doctrine of the power of banks to increase their issues of paper money as suits their interests or convenience; and that it is the effect of the competition of banks of issue to create a vast mass of worthless paper.

"Mr. Blair gave the following statement of the increase of banking accommodation in Scotland:—

"There are about 380 bank offices in Scotland, of which 348 are branches. The population may be stated at 2,500,000; thus there is one bank for every 6600 individuals.

"There were in 1825, 167 offices, of which 133 were branch banks. The population being then 2,200,000, there was one bank to every 13,170 individuals.

"The amount of notes exchanged per annum by the banks of Scotland is believed to be not under 100,000,000*l.* delivered, and 100,000,000*l.* received. The Bank of Scotland alone delivers 10,000,000*l.*, and receives in exchange as much."

"But the immediate purpose of my reference to the evidence of Mr. Blair and other managers of the Scotch banks, is to show that they do not and cannot regulate their *circulation* by the foreign exchanges; and that, when they make advances, it is out of their capital or that of their depositors, without any direct influence on their circulation: that they attend to the conduct of the Bank of England in regulating their *advances*, which, however, have no immediate influence on their *circulation*.

"Mr. Blair was asked by the chairman,—

"Do you conceive that the amount of notes in circulation should be regulated in any way with reference to the state of the foreign exchanges? —I conceive that the loans and discounts of banks should be regulated with reference to the state of the foreign exchanges, *but I would not consider it necessary to regulate the circulation by the foreign exchanges*.

"1879. (*Mr. Grote.*) Then, is it your opinion that, at the same time when the Bank of England is contracting its circulation, for the purpose of correcting an unfavourable exchange, the provincial banks should proceed in the same track, and contract their circulation also?

"I think that they should consider the action of the Bank of England, at that time, with reference to their general rules of discount. *I would beg to leave the circulation out of the question*; I would say that the banks should look to the amount of their loans and discounts under such circumstances; and, at the same time, I would say, that the Bank (of England) should keep a large reserve, to be determined by their past experience and observation, for which, to the extent it is held for public account, they should receive compensation.

"1880. Then, is it your opinion, that at a period when the exchanges are unfavourable, and the Bank of England are contracting their circulation, the provincial banks ought to be more cautious in granting loans and discounts than they were before?

"Certainly.

"1881. (*Sir J. R. Reid.*) Does your bank act upon that principle?

"It does."

"The examinations, however, of Mr. Kennedy, manager of the Ayrshire

Bank, and of Mr. Anderson, of the Glasgow Union Banking Company, went more particularly to the question of the distinction between capital and currency; and their evidence is calculated to throw great light on this point.

Mr. Kennedy is asked—

"2092. (*Mr. Grote.*) You stated that the causes affecting the quantity of your notes which were out in circulation at any time, were, in your opinion, independent of the action of the foreign exchanges?

"I did.

"2093. But you also stated that at the time when the foreign exchanges were unfavourable, and when there was a pressure upon the money market, you thought it imperative, as a measure of prudence, to realise some of your reserves and to call in funds from Edinburgh or London?

"Yes, that is an accurate representation.

"2094. Then do you not think that that act of yours, in bringing into your country funds realised in Edinburgh or London is, in point of fact, tantamount to your acquiring for yourself a certain portion of the London currency or the Edinburgh currency, inasmuch as the local increase of your currency is not at that moment tantamount to the increase of the aggregate currency of the country?

"But we do not bring into our country the Edinburgh or London money. The diminution of our reserves takes place in this way: parties have payments to make in Edinburgh or London, or other places, and we draw upon our reserves there to meet those payments, *but we do not bring down gold or Bank of England* notes from the London market in order to pay them away in our country.

"2095. Though you may not actually bring down gold or Bank of

England notes, is not the effect of your diminishing the amount of your reserve in Edinburgh and London, and increasing by that means the advances to certain local borrowers, *tantamount to bringing down so much of the Edinburgh or London currency into your locality*?

"*I cannot see that I bring any currency down*; it is merely a payment made in London, or in Edinburgh, from one party to another.

"2096. Will you describe in what way your reserves are usually kept?

"In easy negociable securities, such as exchequer bills and short-dated bills of exchange, money lying in our bankers' hands in London, and in other parties' hands in London, and money lying in our agents' hands in Edinburgh and Glasgow, and other places.

"2097 Suppose you sell so many thousand exchequer bills either in London or in Edinburgh, of course the proceeds of those exchequer bills are placed to the credit of your agent, whether your Edinburgh agent or your London agent?

"Yes.

"2098. In that case, when you direct those funds to be paid out, *you do in point of fact dispose of an equal amount of London currency or of Edinburgh currency* for the purposes of your bank?

"Yes.

"2099. Then, in point of fact, do you not consider that you are enabled by means of *that portion of the London currency or the Edinburgh currency*, of which you thus acquire the disposal, to obtain a certain increase of the amount of notes in your own district, and does not that, in point of fact, occasion a certain *diminution in the London or the Edinburgh currency*, which may be set against the increase of your own local issues at the time?

"But when I give a draft upon the London agent I do not in consequence of the increased sum that I have put at his command give out notes for it. I give a draft upon London, payable to some party in London; the money is paid over in London, so that I do not make an issue upon that.

"2100. But *the quantity of currency* which is available to other parties in London or Edinburgh is diminished by that portion which you draw for your own use?

"*I do not see how it diminishes the quantity of currency in London, it merely transfers it from one party to another.*

"2101. If you were not to employ that portion of *the London currency which you acquire* by realising your exchequer bills, that portion would be at the disposal of some other person in London, for the purpose of granting accommodation to London borrowers?

"*But I do not take it out of London; it is still in the hands of some party in London.*

"2102. But if by means of that operation you are enabled to extend your accommodation to your local borrowers, you do make it serviceable to the wants of your district, and is it not tantamount, in point of fact, to a transfer of so much capital from employment in London to employment in Ayrshire? is not that the general effect of the operation?

"That may be the effect of it; *but it has no effect in diminishing the amount of the currency in the London market.* I do not bring out of London any currency; I merely take the currency from one party in London, and give it to another.

"2103. Do you not bring down from" London to Ayrshire a certain portion of capital which was before in London?

"I do not see that.

"2104. If the effect of this transaction be to enable you to supply the wants of borrowers in Ayrshire, which otherwise you could not supply, surely that does amount to a transfer of so much of your banking capital from London to the country?

"It is rather more the payment of a debt due by some parties in Ayrshire to some parties in London."

"Mr. Kennedy is right: the operation is the mere transfer of a debt. The Ayrshire bank is creditor of a bank in London to the amount of 1000*l.*, and passes its draft on London for that sum; the person or firm that takes and pays for the draft of the Ayrshire bank has a payment to make to his correspondent in London. The transactions balance each other. The ultimate balances, as between Scotland and England, must be adjusted by an increase or diminution of the funds possessed in England by the Scotch banks; and in some cases, although not frequent, nor to any considerable amount, there may be a transmission of Bank of England notes or coin.

"Notwithstanding the clearness of this evidence, the following questions, put by the Committee, as to the distinction between capital and currency, in the subsequent examination of Mr. Anderson, manager of the Glasgow Union Banking Company, will show the little impression produced by it on the examiners: —

"2323. (*Chairman.*) Do you at all attempt to regulate your circulation by the state of the foreign exchange?

"*Not the circulation*; we regulate our business by the state of the foreign exchanges, but we consider that the circulation does not require any regulation; *our advances and loans ice regulate, hut not the circulation of our notes*.

"2324. Do you conceive that the circulation is sufficiently regulated by your simply answering the demands of your customers?

"I think so.

"2335. Do you conceive that the consequence of restraining your loans and advances is to produce any effect upon the amount of your circulation?

"*No immediate effect upon the amount of our circulation.*

"2336. Does it eventually?

"The circulation is eventually affected by the langour that follows a pressure: when wages are low and people are out of employment, there is less money circulating among them, and our circulation is diminished, but the immediate effect of a pressure *is not to diminish the circulation.*

"2337. Does then any diminution of the circulation which takes place *arise from a less demand on the part of the public, and not as the result of any greater caution on the part of the Bank*?

"*Exactly.*

"2338. (*Mr. Grote.*) But the effects you have described imply an increased demand on the part of the public at such periods of your circulation?

"It is an increased demand for money①, but not for circulation.

"2339. When those demands are made, in what manner do you supply them? is it not by an increase of your own notes?

"In most cases an increased demand comes upon us in the shape of orders upon London, or orders upon Manchester or Liverpool: the pressure upon us is chiefly from the South, and extra demand from Loudon, Liverpool, and Manchester we feel as the first indication of pressure; it is not from our own immediate districts.

---

① It is quite clear that by money the witness means capital, as distinguished from circulation.

"2340. (*Chairman.*) Do you mean that your customers have demands upon them, which it is necessary for them to discharge in Manchester, London, and other places?

"Yes, that is to a considerable extent the case.

"2341. (*Mr. Grote.*) In what manner do you enable your customers to make those payments, which you have to make in Liverpool, or London, or Manchester?

"By giving them orders upon our agents and correspondents in those places.

"2342. You direct a certain portion of the funds which you have in London, or Liverpool, or Manchester to be applied to that purpose?

"We do.

"2343. Then, in point of fact, you make those advances not out of your own local currency, but out *of a certain portion of the London currency*, upon which you have a demand?

"*No*; *I think that does not precisely describe the operation. It is our capital*: it is capital which we have collected in Scotland, and placed in London for that purpose: *it is not London currency* lent to Scotland, *but it is capital* belonging to Scotland that has been placed in London, and is now applied to the purposes for which it is wanted.

"2344. But if you direct payment to be made in London, this payment must be made by means of the notes of the Bank of England, which alone circulate in London?

"Of course. ①

---

① The question and answer are both wrong. The former assumes that the payment must be made in Bank of England notes, and the latter acquiesces in the supposed necessity: they may be paid, and most commonly are, by set-off at the clearinghouse.

"2348. When increased demands are made upon you by your customers in Glasgow, do you not answer those demands by means of your own local notes, and not by orders upon London?

"Certainly: our circulation from Tuesday to Friday, and from Friday to Tuesday again, is increased upon this occasion; but *we do not reckon that circulation*, because we know that it is immediately to return upon us, and that it is an advance, not of circulation, but of capital; it becomes at the next exchange day *an advance of our capital.*

"2349. Yon feel satisfied that the increase of notes which you might make at that period would immediately come back upon you in the exchange, and that you would be required to pay them by orders on London?

"Yes; or by exchequer bills in Edinburgh.

"2361. Do you not, by means of this increased amount of advances in the extraordinary periods to which the questions have alluded, add to the means of purchasing goods possessed by the persons who borrowed from you?

"Yes, we do.

"2362. And is not that practically tantamount to *so much increase of circulation* in the local districts in which your loans take place?

"*I think not of circulation*; *I think it is capital*; because the notes we pay out are not retained for days or weeks to make the purchases; they are paid immediately to some other bank, and come back to us upon the exchange, and *they become an advance*, *of capital* by us to the party, to enable him to make his purchases. ①

---

① It is impossible to place in a clearer light the distinction between capital and currency, as applied to transactions between dealers and dealers.

"2363. But although ultimately it comes to be an advance out of your capital, yet for a certain time it is an advance made by means of your circulation only, without the aid of your capital?

"For two or three days it is.

"2364. For a certain time, longer or shorter, as the case may be?

"It cannot, I think, be longer than till the next exchange day with regard to those extra advances.

"2365. (*Mr. Gisborne.*) Practically, has it more effect *in giving power of purchasing* goods in London, than if you gave them a draft upon your banker in London?

"*No; I think not.*

"2366. (*Mr. Grote.*) But during the period which elapses between the time of your making the advance originally in your own notes, and the time when you give the order on London, in consequence of the notes coming back to you, during that interval, whether it be long, or whether it be short, must there not be an increase of the circulation of the country generally?

"I think that brings us back to the question which has been so much discussed here, viz. whether deposits form a part of the circulation. *Those notes which we pay out do not remain out*; they must be paid back either to us or to some other bank, in the shape of deposits, till they are to be used, and *they do not increase the permanent circulation of the country*, unless for a day or two, scarcely for even a day.

"2367. (*Sir James Graham*) What proportion of the people of Scotland receiving notes employ bankers?

"A very large proportion of the people of Scotland employ bankers; we have been inquiring into that since we came together. One of the gentlemen here, who is at the head of a bank with a large number of country branches, informs me that the number of creditors of his bank is 20,000. In our case, I have a return since I came to town, making the number in our bank 15,770; and one of the gentlemen who is here, and who is at the head of a bank without branches, says that he has 7000 people holding his obligations.

"2368. (*Mr. Grote.*) Deposit accounts?

"Yes; deposit accounts, or current accounts bearing interest.

"2369. (*Sir James Graham.*) Inasmuch as every payment into a bank, whether in the shape of a deposit, or to the credit of a current account, bears interest day by day, and inasmuch as no commission is charged upon operations on an account, and inasmuch as a great proportion of the people receiving money in Scotland employ bankers, does it not follow that every payment made in local notes finds its way almost immediately within the space of twenty-four hours into the hands of some banker?

"I think it does.

"2370. (*Mr. Grote.*) Would not the consequence of that proposition be, if followed out, that there should be no notes whatever in the hands of the public, but that all the notes issued by each bank should be in fact in the hands of other banks?

"That is the effect. There are three millions of notes out, which is a very small amount; *people must have a certain amount of money in their pockets and boxes at home*, *and shopkeepers must keep a certain amount of money in their tills*, the daily receipts of their business; *and manufacturers must keep notes to pay people's wages*, *and so on*; but that altogether forms but a small proportion compared to the circulation of England. Our three millions in Scotland amount to about 1*l*. per head of the whole population; in England, although you have a gold circulation for every thing below 5*l*., your paper circulation amounts to 2*l*. a head. I am taking about fifteen millions for the population, and thirty millions for the currency."

"The distinction between currency and capital, which is so clearly shown by these remarkably intelligent witnesses, is not a mere matter of classification or of verbal criticism. The confounding of one with the other is a prolific source of fallacy in reasoning, and of error in practical application, in questions relating to the management or regulation of banks.

"Of this a striking instance was exhibited in the reasons adduced by the advocates of the currency theory, in justification of the advances made by the Bank of England in 1835, against the deposits on the West India loan. The justification proceeded on the ground that, but for those advances *the currency would have been unduly contracted*. What the notion could be of undue contraction of the currency, that is, of an inconvenient want of bank notes in the hands of the public or of the bankers, as long as any amount might be obtained by discount at 4 per cent., passes all reasonable comprehension. The truth is, that it was wholly a question of disposable capital; and was it possible to imagine that there could be any danger of an insufficiency of it, at a time when the disposal of it was so recklessly going forward in credits to America? While as regards the circulation or currency, there is every reason to believe, on a view of the state of things at that time, that the amount would have been neither more nor less than it was, whether the advances had been made or withheld."—(*Inquiry into the Currency Principle*, pp. 34-54.)

If the questions which elicited these answers of the country bankers be examined, it will be observed that the only members who appeared to apprehend the point of view suggested by this evidence, although they did not follow it out to its consequences, were Sir James Graham and Sir

Thomas Fremantle. On the other members who took part in the examinations, the evidence seems to have made no impression whatever.

Sir Robert Peel, it appears, from an indifferent question or two that he asked, was present at these examinations. Whether he saw the comments upon them in my tract, which was published some weeks before the announcement of his measure, may be doubted. It is highly probable that under the overwhelming pressure of public business, he had not time, among the thousand-and-one pamphlets that solicited his attention, to notice mine; or, if he chanced to look at it, he may have been so prepossessed with his own views, founded on the doctrine of the currency theory, as not to consider my suggestion of the distinction in question, worthy of being attended to, and still less of being followed out to its practical bearing upon the measure which he had then in contemplation. To have admitted it would have unsettled the bundle of opinions① he had already made up, and in pursuance of which he had probably concocted his scheme, and already determined to carry it out.

The following passage of his speech exhibits in a striking point of view, how completely his mind was made up to acquiesce in the doctrine of the currency principle as an axiom, an ultimate truth; and how, consequently, it had become inaccessible to any idea that could call into doubt or question the infallibility of that truth: —

---

① I remember hearing of a gentleman who was so tenacious of his opinions, when once formed, that he would not entertain or listen to any question or doubt that was calculated in any way to disturb them. "When pressed, his answer used to be, that his opinions were like well-bound bundles of fagots; you could not take one out, nor put a fresh one in, without disturbing the rest, and loosening the whole bundle; and this would put him to the trouble, which he had no wish to encounter, of binding up his bundle afresh.

"I also attempted to show," he said, " from the admission of the representatives of issuing banks, that their practice was at variance with *the principle which ought to regulate a paper currency*; that there was no reference to the exchanges , that as it was once said by a private banker, 'there is no more regard to the exchange than to the snow on the mountains. ' "

He nowhere, however, attempts to prove the truth of the principle, according to which he assumed that they could, and that they ought, so to regulate their issues.

If there had been the smallest opening in his mind for the admission of an idea militating with the principle that the *circulation* ought to be regulated by the foreign exchanges, and that the country bank system was vicious because its issues were not so regulated, he could hardly have failed of perceiving, and drawing the fair inference from, the fact, that while the bankers, one and all, declared their inability so to regulate their issues, meaning their note circulation①, they took into consideration, in the regulation of their advances (being the only part of their business which they could control), the state of the money market in London, and the position of the Bank of England; this being, in substance, equivalent to a regulation by the exchanges. What more could be expected? — what more could be desired of them? The employment of their capital and credit they

---

① Mr. Goulburn, who was Chancellor of the Exchequer when the measure of 1844 was under discussion, and might be supposed, from having been one of the Committee on Banks of Issue in 1840-1841, to have obtained some insight into the nature of the country note circulation from the explanation given by the bankers of the circumstances that determined their issues, thus stated his view of it in the debate of the 13th of June—

"The country bankers said that they generally regulated their issues *by a consideration of prices* in their respective neighbourhoods; that when prices were high *they put out their issues*, and when they were low they contacted them."

did so regulate; and that only was within their power. Over the amount of notes which their advances or discounts would call forth they had no power, and still less could they limit or enlarge the amount which their depositors would require. ①

If a glimpse of this light had broken in upon Sir Robert Reel he would have seen that, in his parade of machinery to limit the amount of the note circulation of the country banks, he was dealing with a very small part of

---

① The following passage, from a very able article in the Quarterly Review for June last, will serve to show how very different is the country circulation from the currency notion of it: —

"The distribution of the greatest masses of the provincial circulation, so far from being coincident with the districts of greatest population, greatest trade, and greatest activity and enterprise, is in point of fact coincident with the districts where population and trade are alike of the most stationary character. Thus, the gross local circulation of Yorkshire is not more than 1,500,000*l*, and of this sum only one third finds employment in the manufacturing and mining districts, while two thirds are distributed among an agricultural population very nearly one-half less in numerical strength, and occupying a still lower comparative position with reference to all the elements of commercial activity and importance.

"The largeness of the circulation of the agricultural banks is every way as remarkable. So constant is this phenomenon, that in running the eye over the *Gazette* returns, published under the Act of 1844, whenever a sum extraordinary from its magnitude attracts attention, it will be found, with very rare exceptions (and those admitting of explanation), to belong to a rural locality. The maximum circulation for example of the oldest of the Boston banks is 75,000*l*., that of the oldest of the Birmingham banks is 23,000*l*.; the circulation of the Yarmouth hank is 53,000*l*., that of the hank at Hull is 29,000*l*., and the Bank at Saffron Walden has an issue very nearly as large as the oldest of the hanks at Leeds—the Saffron Walden figures being 47,000*l*., and those of the bank at Leeds 53,000*l*.

"It may perhaps be said that this line of argument does not. meet the real question—that it does not prove that banks of issue have not the power of emitting their notes *ad libitum*, but simply that the emission is larger in the regions of agriculture than in those of trade. But in truth that is the very point. According to the currency school, the amount of issue is regulated by the intensity of the demand for pecuniary accommodation on the one hand, and by the inclination to meet it on the other. But it will hardly be maintained that the bankers of Boston are exposed to solicitations more urgent than the hankers of Leeds, or that the atmosphere of competition is more intense in a country town of Lincolnshire or Norfolk, than in the busiest marts of the West Riding or of Warwickshire." — (*Quarterly Review*, July 1847, p. 240.)

their business①; the whole effect of his troublesome machinery being, not to prevent the enlargement of the entire amount of the circulating medium of the country districts under certain circumstances, when, according to the theory, it ought to be contracted, but to substitute Bank of England notes or coin for the country bankers' notes. This may be considered an advantage by that numerous class of persons who have a horror of the country circulation from what they have heard, and what they repeat by rote, of the excessive *issues* of the country banks: misusing, as they do, in this and in other instances, the term issues, so as to mean by it sometimes the mere note circulation, and at other times, the advances made by way of loans or discounts, whether these be attended with the passing of any notes or not.

The same want of perception of the distinction between currency and capital which led Sir R. Peel to attach such importance to the note circulation, as that part of the liabilities of the country banks which exclusively demanded legislative regulation, seems to have led him, in adherence to the currency principle, to consider the note circulation as that part of the liabilities of the Bank of England which required to be controlled in amount by the variations in the amount of its treasure: thus proving himself to be totally unaware that it was in the banking department, involving the receipt and distribution of capital, that lay the

① As one among other instances of the small proportion which the note circulation of country banks bears to their liabilities, it may be worth while here to notice the recent case of the North and South Wales Bank, which suspended its payments in October last. It appears by the statement laid before the creditors, that the total liabilities of the bank amounted to 491,073*l*. Of this amount the notes in circulation were only 35,710*l*. The deposits amounted to 326,798*l*., and other liabilities made up the larger sum The assets were shown to amount to 643,741*l*.; and it was arranged that the bank should be reopened with additional capital.

source of any inconvenience or danger arising from any want of prudence in the management; while the amount of the note circulation was not and could not be under the direct control or regulation of the directors, but depended upon the wants and convenience of the public.

It is impossible in my opinion to exhibit in a more striking manner the great error which pervaded Sir Robert Peel's views on this point, than by the following passage in his speech of the 6th of May, 1844.

"We think that the privilege of issue is one which may fairly and justly be controlled by the state, and that *the banking business*, as distinguished from issue, *is a matter in respect of which there cannot he too unlimited and unrestricted a competition.*"

Now I venture to affirm that this is *exactly the reverse* of the conclusion which can alone be legitimately derived from a correct view of the nature of the separate functions of, and of the distinction between, currency and capital. To the extent to which regulation is desirable or admissible, it is, fact, much more required to avert the dangers of excessive competition of banking than of issue.

But it seems that the great, the redeeming quality, whatever other objections there might be to the scheme, as regarding both the country banks and the Bank of England, was held out to be *the securing by it of the convertibility of the paper*, and consequently the maintenance of the metallic standard.

The question of convertibility of Bank of England notes I propose to examine when the operation of the act of 1844 comes under consideration.

In the ensuing section the discussion will be confined to a comparison of our country banks with the banks of the United States.

SECTION 11 *On the alleged insufficiency of convertibility to prevent excessive issues of bank notes, as asserted to be proved by the history of the American banks*

I have never yet met with a more lax use of terms, nor, consequently, greater confusion of ideas, than is to be found in the opinion of Sir Robert Peel (loudly echoed by his followers in the debates on the measure of 1844), that convertibility, while subject to competition in the issue of bank notes, was no security for the maintenance of the standard of 1819. After declaiming upon the enormity of the country bank system, which did not admit of its note circulation being regulated by the foreign exchanges, he goes on to say, —

"Thus it appears to me that the conclusions of reason against unlimited competition of issue are amply confirmed by the admissions of the advocates for it. Are the lessons of experience at variance with the conclusions we are entitled to draw from reason and from evidence? What has been the result of unlimited competition in the United States? In the United States the paper circulation was supplied, not by private bankers, but by joint stock banks established on principles apparently the most satisfactory. There was every precaution taken against insolvency; unlimited① responsibility of partners—*excellent regulations* for the publication and audit of accounts, *immediate convertibility into gold.* If the principles of unlimited competition, controlled by such checks, he safe,

① This may be a misprint, but it is repeated in the speech of the 20th of May 1844, as published by Mr. Murray. There is no doubt, I believe, that the liability of the banks in the United States is in all, or nearly all, cases *limited.*

why has it utterly failed in the United States? How can it be shown that the experiment was not *fairly* made in that country?"

Strange as it may seem, yet such is the fact, that a similar reference to the example of the banks of the United States, in proof that convertibility of bank notes is no safeguard for the standard, was made by each of the prominent supporters of Sir Robert Peel' s measure in the debate of the 20th of May. Thus Sir C. Wood: —

"We are not without experience as to the value even of convertibility as a safeguard for the preservation of the standard." —" In America the convertibility of bank notes is a fundamental article of the constitution; provisions more stringent than in this country are enacted *to enforce it in practice*; *every precaution is taken to render the banks safe and sound.* They are all joint stock banks, with *limited*① *liability and restrictions on issues*, paid up capital, and whatever other precaution can be devised for this purpose. What has been the result?"

Then follows the quotation of a statement of the number of banks, their capital and circulation, furnished by Sir W. Clay, with the remark: —

"In May of that year cash payments were suspended throughout every state of the Union."

"And," Sir Charles Wood adds.

"There was au end of course of any maintenance of the standard of value."

Sir William Clay made the same allusions to the instance of the banks of the United States, as proving the insufficiency of the principle of

① Here *limited* liability is included among the precautions calculated to render the banks safe and sound. And so far Sir C. Wood seems to agree with Sir W. Clay, who has strongly and perseveringly urged that the principle of limited responsibility should be extended to our banking system generally.

convertibility to maintain the standard.

But perhaps of all the changes thus rung upon the convertibility of bank notes in America, as proving that in England it was no safeguard for the standard, the most curious specimen is in the speech of Mr. Goulburn on that occasion.

"Was there not then in the United States," he asked, "a paper that was perfectly convertible? Was there not then a precise regulation that every note should be payable on demand in coin? Still, in consequence of competition, there was an excess of issues; and this, though there was a perfect publicity as to accounts, a rigid inspection by the government, and a rigorous control; and yet from the competition of issues they reduced the country to that state, that, as the honourable gentleman himself had said, they overlooked morality, and suspended cash payments. There was no want then of a convertibility of paper *enforced by law*; *but the competition of issues defied all law*, and made every man in the community anxious to increase the circulation in order that he might be able to promote his own wild speculations."

Before remarking upon these strange attempts of the several speakers to support and illustrate their position, that the convertibility of bank notes, as it was restored and is established in this country by the act of 1819, and has ever since been faithfully complied with, is no security for the maintenance of the standard, by a reference to the state of banking in the United States of America, I have to call the attention of my readers to the description given by Mr. M'Culloch and Mr. Fullarton of American banking.

In the edition of 1844 of bis great work, the "Commercial Dictionary," in the article on "Banks (foreign)," Mr. McCulloch has the following very emphatic passages: —

"Had a committee of clever men been selected to devise means by which the public might be tempted to engage in all manner of absurd projects, and be most easily duped and swindled, we do not know that they could have hit upon any thing half so likely to effect their object as the existing American banking system. It has no one redeeming quality about it, but is from beginning to end a compound of quackery and imposture. Our own banking system is bad enough certainly; but is as superior to the American as can well be imagined. A radical reform of the latter, or if that cannot be effected, its entire suppression, would be the greatest boon that can be conferred on the Union, and would be no small advantage to every nation with which the Americans have any intercourse."

With reference to the "excellent regulations" for the prevention of abuses and irregularity of which Sir Robert Peel, and his supporters in the debate, spoke in terms of such high approval, Mr. M'Cullocn has the following decisive statement: —

"But our readers need hardly be told that these elaborately contrived regulations are really good for nothing, unless it be to afford an easy mode of cheating and defrauding the public. Instances have occurred of banks having borrowed an amount of dollars equal to half their capital for a single day, and of such dollars having been examined by the inspectors appointed for that purpose, and reported by them, and sworn by a majority of the directors to be the first instalment paid by the stockholders of the bank, and intended to remain in it. — (*Gouge's Paper Money and Banking in the United States.*) We do not of course imagine that such disgraceful instances can be of common occurrence; but what is to be thought of a system which permits a company for the issue of paper money founded upon such an abominable fraud to enter on business with a sort of public attestation of its respectability? The publicity, too, to which the American banks are subject, is injurious rather than otherwise. Those who are so disposed may easily manufacture such returns as they think most suitable to their views, and the more respectable banks endeavour for a month or two previous to the period when they have to make their returns, to increase the amount of bullion in their coffers by temporary loans and all manner of devices. The whole system is in fact bottomed on the most vicious principles. But it is unnecessary, after what has recently occurred, to insist further upon the gross and glaring defects of American banking."

The passage from Mr. Fullarton is as follows:—

"Another topic which has also been much alluded to in the course of these discussions has been the disastrous results of the banking system of the United States of America; and no topic certainly could well be more unfortunate for the argument of those who desire to substitute a more diffused use of the precious metals in the circulation of this country in the place of the now existing system, which tends to the concentration of the reserves of gold in the hands of a single presiding body. I take it in the first place to be altogether a gratuitous assumption, that the hanks of the United States contributed to the commercial disasters of that country chiefly by the excesses of their circulation, instead of the more obvious and undeniable agency of their unlimited facilities of credit. But no person, who has given any attention to the evidence respecting the state of the American paper circulation, will venture to affirm, that, even previous to the universal and spontaneous suspension of cash payments in May 1837, that circulation was really and practically convertible. The system wanted, in the first place, two of the indispensable conditions of perfect convertibility, namely, a single and properly regulated national metallic standard, and, secondly, a limited subsidiary currency of small money issued by authority. In the United States, they possess in fact no metallic standard whatever, or at least they possessed none previous to their large recent coinages of gold. Almost every coin under heaven is a legal tender there, at a certain rate fixed by tariff; and, not very long ago, the quantity of foreign gold in circulation there was supposed to be as nine to one in proportion to the circulation of their own eagles. The effect was, that the bankers, when required to cash their notes, paid them in the coin which, for the time, was cheapest; and parties requiring a supply of Spanish dollars, the very money in which they keep their accounts, for transmission to India or China, could not procure them from the banks, but had to buy them in the market at a premium seldom under 1 or 2 per cent, and which has been known to rise even to 7 $\frac{1}{2}$ per cent. But, in fact, the banks of that country were, in a manner, virtually protected from demands for coin by the peculiar habits and ideas of the people. It was a point, we are told, so universally understood, that bankers ought not to be called upon for any payments in cash, which might have a tendency to cramp or limit their usual accommodations to the public, or might have any object beyond the mere convenience of fractional payments, that, however much a man might be in want of a sum in specie for exportation, he would be deterred from applying to a bank for the supply, from the fear of becoming a marked man in society. Then the wide-spread practice of issuing dollar notes, half-dollar notes, and even quarter-dollar notes, introduced another element of depreciation, somewhat similar to that which existed in Ireland in 1804, and which must have been still more pernicious in a thinly peopled country like America, where those small notes would so frequently be liable to be cut off altogether by distance from the places of their origin. To crown the whole,—for some time previous to the last suspension of cash payments in America, the banks there had fallen into the habit of advancing to the merchants in post-notes at four, six, and eight months' date; thus adding to the small-note abuses of the Irish, the evils of the optional-note system of the old Scotch bankers."—(*Regulation of Currencies*, pp. 184-186)

Loose and ambiguous as is the language, and confused as is the reasoning which marks the whole of the speeches from which the passages I am now commenting upon have been taken, there is no part of them to me more inexplicable than their confident allusion to the American banks. What possible meaning can the persons so using the word convertibility attach to it? By convertibility of the paper, according to the ordinary signification of the term, when applied to bank notes in this country, is meant that the holder of a promissory note, payable on demand, (and equally indeed of a bill of exchange, or any other written obligation, when due,) may require payment in coin① of a certain weight and fineness; and in the event of refusal or demur, such payment is enforced by law against the issuer to the utmost extent of his property. The issuer, whether a private or joint stock banker, is considered to have failed, the circulation of his notes is at an end, and he is subject to the process usual in cases of insolvency; while any thing like fraud on the part of the banker is visited with severe penalties.

---

① The legal tender clause, allowing Bank of England notes to serve as payment instead of coin, does not essentially affect the argument.

In this country, too, the strict regularity of the periodical exchange and liquidation of notes among all the issuing banks, whether private or joint stock, is well known. These exchanges take place once a week, at least, and in all the larger towns as often as twice or three times in the week. This regulation (which is not nominal, but rigidly acted upon) is most important, insuring a constant reflux, and thus operating as a limitation of the amount of outstanding notes. ①

Moreover, the banks in America are under limited responsibility; while in this country, with the exception of the Bank of England, the Bank of Ireland, and one or two of the chartered banks in Scotland, the issuing bankers are liable to the whole extent of their property. And while, in the United States, notes of as low a denomination as a dollar, and, in some instances, down to quarter dollar, that is, from *four shilling* down to *one shilling notes* were in circulation, the lowest denomination allowed to circulate in England and Wales is five pounds.

Now, I would ask, wherein is the similarity, as to any one of these particulars, between the convertibility of bank notes in this country, and

---

① It is a fact of much importance to the present argument that there was no regular system of note exchanges among the American banks. They were in the habit of retaining each others notes, and deferring indefinitely the period of settlement, by a payment of the balance in cash. It is from this cause that in all American banking statistics the columns of "Notes of other Banks," and "Claims on other solvent Banks," assume so imposing an appearance. For example; to select a case more than usually favourable to the system, the official Report of the Bank Commissioners for the State of New York for 1834, represents that among 76 banks, within their jurisdiction, this description of credits alone amounted to a *seventh part*, or 15 per cent. of the entire assets of the whole 76 establishments.

The figures will be found at length in the New York Almanack for 1835, at p. 212. With the aid of so many devices for securing the immunities of an *inconvertible* issue under the guise of *convertibility* on demand, it can excite little surprise that in seven years the number of banks in the Union was increased very nearly threefold in 1830, the number of banks was 330; in 1837, it was 829.

the asserted convertibility in America? Could the holder of a bank note in the United States, at the period alluded to, reckon on receiving payment in a welldefined standard, or could he reckon on receiving any payment at all, on demand, from banks professing to be solvent, excepting in their own depreciated notes, the circulation being, as it was, maintained in some parts of the Union, only by the notes of the failing banks passing from hand to hand at a discount?

In each of the speeches I have quoted, great stress is laid on the legal precautions and regulations adopted in America to preserve convertibility; but if, as is notoriously the fact, these regulations and precautions are, from the habits of the people, and the imperfect administration of the law, set at nought in practice, is there any resemblance to that, and that state of things in this country? As Mr. Goulburn, with great *naïveté*, expresses it, "There was no want of convertibility *enforced by law*, but the competition of issuers *defied all law*." This, indeed, is at the bottom of the whole of it. The law was ineffectual against the habits of the community.

I must confess myself amazed, when I reflect that persons of so much intelligence, and possessed of such attainments and reasoning powers as those whose speeches I have quoted, could bring themselves to adduce the banking sytem of the United States as affording cases in point, illustrative of, or by any possible similarity applicable to, the state of banking in this country. Such exemplifications as these are really monstrous—an outrage upon all that I have ever understood as recognized rules of reasoning from analogy.

It is just possible that, in the speeches I have quoted, "convertibility" may be confounded with "solvency." But here again is a difficulty. We have recently, under the existing law, had failures of issuing banks; but can it be said that such failures could, even if there had been more of them, be considered as proofs that convertibility is not a safeguard for the standard?

Upon the confusion between convertibility and solvency, as also upon the convertibility of Bank of England notes, I have already remarked.

SECTION 12 *Summary of the argument against the theory of the measure of 1844*

I have now to bring to a conclusion my examination of the arguments adduced by Sir Robert Peel, and his immediate followers, in support of the *principle* of so much of the measure of 1844 as provides for the limitation and regulation of that part of the business of banking which consists in the issues of promissory notes payable to bearer on demand.

In the course of my examination of Sir Robert Peel's exposition, I have endeavoured to show —

1. That the definition of money contended for is not sanctioned by any admitted authority, nor justified by any legitimate process of reasoning.

2. That bank notes, convertible as they are in this country, and forming a part of its paper credit, arc confounded with government paper money.

3. That, as a consequence of that confusion, the amount of the note circulation is assumed to be variable at the will of the issuers, this being controlled only by the necessity of conversion through the operation of an adverse exchange.

4. That, as a further consequence, the amount of bank notes, in our mixed currency of paper and coin, is erroneously supposed to have an

influence on prices different from that which would occur with a purely metallic currency.

5. That the properties and the operation of a purely metallic currency are wholly mistaken in the exposition of the theory of the Currency principle.

6. That the distinction so important in reasoning, and in practical application, between currency and capital has been wholly overlooked in that theory.

And, finally, that the theory so sought to be explained and established, as forming the grounds for the measure of 1844, is, in every point of view, erroneous, proceeding, as it does, on an ambiguous use of language, on unfounded assumptions of principles and facts, and on false analogies.

If any of my readers should be desirous of seeing a more complete exposure of the defectiveness of Sir Robert Peel's chain of arguments in support of his theory than is to be found in my examination of it, I would refer them to Mr. J. Wilson's work which I have before quoted; and they will find an elaborate, exhaustive, and admirably lucid argument in refutation of the assumptions which Sir Robert Peel advances in the support of the theory, according to which he considers that the paper circulation of this country should be regulated. The examination by Mr. Wilson of the assumptions on which Sir Robert Peel has proceeded is thus introduced: —

"These principles, and the course pursued by Sir Robert Peel, necessarily involve the following

"FIVE ASSUMPTIONS.

"*First*, That bank notes, though payable in coin, at the option of the holder, are still liable to be issued in excess, and are consequently subject to depreciation.

"*Second*, That convertibility is not alone a sufficient guarantee that a mixed currency of bank notes and coin shall conform, in its variations, to the same laws that would regulate a purely metallic currency.

"*Third*, That issuers of hank notes have power to increase or decrease the circulation at pleasure.

"*Fourth*, That, by an expansion or contraction of the issues of bank notes at pleasure, the prices of commodities can be increased or diminished.

"*Fifth*, That, by such increase or diminution of prices, the foreign exchanges will be corrected, and an undue influx or efflux of bullion, as the case may be, will be arrested.

"We think it will be admitted that these five propositions fairly represent the principles involved in Sir Robert Peel's measure, and maintained by those who advocate and support it. In the face of such an array of personal weight and authority, including the most expert and practised politicians of all parties, and men the most accomplished in economical science, it has not been without the most careful and diligent process of investigation and reflection that we have arrived at a conclusion that these propositions, which at first sight startle any thinking mind, as involving principles contradictory to those generally received as regulating ordinary mercantile pursuits, are not only *not true* and supportable by fact, but are, in every instance, nearly the *reverse of truth*.

I cannot easily imagine that any person (not a professed adherent of the currency theory, whose bundle of opinions is made up, for of such there is no hope), can rise from a careful perusal of Mr. Wilson's searching examination of these five assumptions without coming to the conclusion that the vaunted principles of the measure are *entirely destitute of any foundation in fact or reasoning.*

SECTION 13 *On the former monetary crises, asserted by Sir Robert Peel to prove the danger of over-issue of convertible notes*

Having concluded the examination of the theory on which Sir Robert Peel founded his measure, we have now to examine his statement of the reasons by which he was induced to put aside the entire system of banking, according to which the note circulation had been administered prior to 1844.

Towards the conclusion of his speech of 20th May, 1844, after assuming that he had made good all the links of his argument, he appeals to the experience of the twenty years preceding, as proving the necessity of interference by the legislature to *restrict the amount of the Bank note circulation.*

"Let us," he says, "review the several periods recurring within the last twenty years, when there has been a derangement in the monetary affairs of the country, — when, in order to maintain the convertibility into gold, there has been the necessity for a sudden contraction of issues. There have been, I think, four such periods, — in 1825, in 1832, in 1835-1836, and in 1838-1839. Now we all adhere, or profess to adhere, to the principles of a metallic standard, and convertibility of paper on demand; but it is said we have not sufficient grounds for interference with the existing system. Why, what warnings have we had during the last twenty years? (Hear, hear.) What we say is, that there have been in this country four great monetary crises. These crises took place in the years 1825,

1832, 1837, and 1839. In each it is *proved*[①] that there was *an over-issue of country bank-paper*; thus establishing the principle for which I am contending. But, says an honourable member, 'the Bank of England will have the power of saving itself.' The Bank may support the convertibility of its own notes, but at a great sacrifice. This is a result which I am anxious to avoid."

He then proceeds to notice the excessive issues in three of those years; in the two last, however, of which only are the actual issues known.

The question of the alleged excess of country issues has already been disposed of.

My purpose in referring to this passage of Sir Robert Peel's speech is, to show how loose is the statement of facts in this as in other instances which he has brought forward in support of his arguments. He here includes 1832, as one of the four periods when there has been a derangement in the monetary affairs of the country. This might at first be supposed to be a casual error; and, being an important one, he might be expected to have discovered and corrected it in a subsequent speech. So far from this, however, he repeats, with full emphasis, in his speech on the 13th of June, 1844, the same statement, *including* the year 1832.

I shall have something to say on each of the other three periods; but just now I confine myself to the year 1832. As regards that year, then, it so happens, and proof in abundance may be adduced of the fact, that there was not the slightest approach to any thing like what, by the utmost licence of exaggeration (so strongly marking the whole of the statements in the

① There is no authentic proof of the amount of the country issues in 1825—nothing but conjectural estimates. And as to 1832, there is no statement, that I have seen, conjectural or otherwise.

speeches of Sir Robert Peel on this occasion), can be called monetary derangement. Nor had there been any during the two preceding years in which the drain referred to was taking place. The early part of the drain was coincident with, if not in some measure caused by, the French and Belgian revolutions. Our political affairs, both foreign and internal, were in a very disturbed state; the funds had fallen very considerably; and there were also large importations of foreign corn. But notwithstanding this combination of untoward circumstances, there was no disturbance whatever of banking or mercantile credit. There was not the slightest derangement of monetary affairs— not the vestige of a commercial crisis. The statement of Sir Robert Peel therefore, including the year 1832 as one of those marked by monetary crisis, is in every sense of the word incorrect, or as nearly as possible the reverse of the actual state of facts.

Much, however, as this instance of incorrectness is calculated to damage his statement, I should not dwell further upon it, were it not that the circumstances of 1832 seem to form the *cheval de bataille* of the currency theory. Mr. Loyd, both in his evidence in 1840 (Ques. 2712 and 2713,) and in his writings, (and if I recollect, rightly, Mr. Norman likewise,) has instanced the drain ending in the year 1832 as one in which by early and steady *contraction* of the circulation on the part of the Bank a crisis was actually averted. In his latest publication①, soon after the bill of 1844 had passed, Mr. Loyd observes upon the fact that in the case of the drain ending in 1832, "*a decrease of bullion had been accompanied by a decrease of circulation corresponding steadily with the bullion in its progress.*" But the simple facts so stated would not have made much for the currency

① *Thoughts on the Separation of the Departments of the Bank of England.* 1844.

theory, because they amounted only to coincidence, without necessarily or obviously leading to an inference of the relation of cause and effect. In order therefore to make the case subservient to the theory, Mr. Loyd proceeds to observe —

"Enough has been stated to establish this very remarkable fact —

"That in three out of the four occasions on which the bullion has sustained a very heavy drain since the resumption of cash payments in 1819, the paper circulation has been increased rather than diminished; and these have all terminated in severe pressure upon credit and trade; viz. in 1825, 1837, 1839, whilst in the remaining case the drain was *met* from the commencement by a corresponding decrease of paper circulation, and this passed off *without discredit or distrust of any kind.*"

The words in italics are so in the original, with the exception of the word *met*, which I have so marked. In Mr. Loyd's evidence, the expression is, "the fourth drain, namely, that from 1830 to 1832, was *met* by a contraction on the part of the Bank of England." Of this the meaning clearly is, that the Bank took measures *designedly* (for if it did not mean this, it could not mean any thing to the purpose) out of the ordinary course of its routine, to contract, or, as the word implies, *forcibly* reduce its circulation. This it could only do by restricting accommodation in the way of loans and discounts, or by forced sales of securities. It is quite clear, however, by Mr. Palmer's evidence in 1840, that the Bank did neither, —*was perfectly passive.* And yet in 1844, Mr. Loyd recurs to the same illustration. And what is perhaps still more extraordinary, Sir Charles Wood, in his speech of the 20th May, 1844, after quoting Mr. Loyd's evidence as to the drain of 1832 having been "*met*" by a contraction of the circulation, adds, "I really do not see how proof in a matter of this kind can be pressed further." And this, after having heard, and of course having occasion, as Chairman of the Committee on Banks of Issue in 1840, to weigh, Mr. Palmer's evidence!

The inconsistency of the impression intended to be conveyed by Mr. Loyd's statement with the facts of the case is placed in a striking point of view by Mr. Fullarton: —

"I do not find in the publication of a second edition of Mr. Loyd's 'Thoughts on the Separation of the Bank of England into two departments' any addition of importance to his former arguments. I am glad, however, to take the opportunity of adverting to one of Mr Loyd's statements, which, from the manifest contradiction between its premises and its conclusions, I had always looked upon as carrying with it its own refutation, but which, from the favourable manner in which it has been noticed within these few days by an eminent and influential journal, would seem to be, neverthelees, calculated to produce some impression on the public mind. Mr. Loyd has thought fit, both in his pamphlet and in his evidence before the Committee of 1840, to contrast the history of the drain of bullion which the Bank sustained between May 1830 and May 1832, and the drains of 1825, 1833-1837, and 1838-1839, and to ascribe the facility with which the first-mentioned drain was brought to a termination, without any commercial distress or discredit, to its having been '*met*' on that occasion by a contraction of the Bank's circulation; whereas, in the other three cases, he says 'the paper circulation was rather increased than diminished.' Now it cannot, I presume, be unknown to Mr Loyd, that the drains of 1825, 1833-1837, and 1838-1839, were drains originating in commercial causes, whereas the demand for gold in 1830-1832 was a demand from panic It commenced in 1830 from abroad, in consequence of the political convulsions and worse forebodings on the Continent inducing merchants to countermand their orders and give money a preference to goods; and this was followed by an internal demand, originating in a like political discredit in this country, the result of the agitation produced by the Reform Bill, and which did not reach its acme till the spring of 1832, after the foreign exchange had not only been completely restored, but gold was flowing back again in large quantities. This drain was unpreceded and unaccompanied by any commercial excitement, by any speculation or rise of prices. On the contrary, the unexampled dulness of trade and stagnation of industry were the universal theme of complaint among merchants. The gold was withdrawn from the Bank, not to be launched out in foreign purchases, but to be locked up or buried in the earth. If no over-trading, then, nor undue augmentation of prices existed, how was it to be expected that there should have been any general embarrassment or distress from their recoil? If, by saying that this drain was '*met* by a contraction of the currency,' it be meant to imply that the Bank, on the occasion in question, adopted any positive measure of resistance at variance with its practice in the other three cases on which Mr. Loyd animadverts, the assertion is wholly unwarranted. The Bank was entirely passive on the occasion; and, if it did not re-issue all the notes which were sent in for gold, it was simply because the public did not call for them, because the very same circumstances, which at this time had been spreading distrust of all existing institutions, and inclined men to convert their property into specie, had also been paralysing trade, and restricting the frequency of transactions requiring the aid of specie. The Bank continued, throughout the whole crisis, to discount as freely as usual all the good bills which were brought to it for discount; and we have the express assurance of the Governor, Mr. Horsley Palmer, that, 'for eighteen months or two years previous to 1832, the Court had taken no measures for contracting the circulation.'—(See *Report of the Committee of 1832 on the Bank of England*, p. 22.) Whatever difference of opinion there may exist as to the proper method of treating a drain of specie, so long as there, may be the least colour for attributing it to a depreciation of the circulating medium from excessive issue, I am not aware that any one has ever presumed to contend, that a run for gold, caused by internal panic or distrust, would be likely to be stopped by the Bank suspending its discounts. And, while I quite agree with Mr. Loyd, that the circumstances connected with the crisis of 1832 furnish a most instructive lesson as to the right method of treating drains of the precious metals, I am bound to say, that the lesson which I draw from them is nearly the reverse of that inculcated by Mr. Loyd. I value it not, certainly, for any testimony which it affords of the advantage of meeting every drain of gold indiscriminately with a contraction of the Bank's issues, for it presents us with nothing to which I can consider the term 'contraction' applicable at all; but I value it as demonstrating, with how little shock to the even tenor of affairs a great crisis of this kind may, under certain circumstances, be surmounted, by the simple abstinence of the Bank from any officious or violent interference, or any attempt to withdraw its issues from the control of the public demand, and for the striking contrast which it suggests to our apprehensions, of the very different results which might have followed, had the Bank on this occasion administered its issues according to the principles advocated by Mr. Loyd."—(*Regulation of Currencies*, pp. 184-186.)

But whatever may be said or thought of the strange use made by Mr. Loyd, in the service of the currency theory, of the simple fact that in the drain of 1830-1882, a larger proportion than usual of the demand fell (in consequence of the peculiar state of public feeling connected with the Reform agitation)① upon the note circulation, it is quite clear that Sir Robert Peel could have had no accurate knowledge of the state of commerce and credit in 1832, when he characterised it, with reiteration, as a period of monetary derangement.

As to 1836-1837, it may be allowed to be designated as a period of monetary derangement; although it was but partially so. Sir Robert Peel seems to have known very little about it, and to have satisfied himself with the easy process of the currency theory, that of looking only at the amount of the note circulation; and if this did not vary with the variations in the

---

① Of the extent to which this feeling operated in a drain upon the Bank for gold, in exchange for notes, the following account is given among many agreeably told anecdotes by Mr. Francis, in his History of the Bank of England: —

"In 1832 occurred the last run upon the bullion of the Bank, occasioned by political causes. On every wall throughout the metropolis the significant words, 'Stop the Duke!' 'Go for gold!' were boldly placarded. For a week the corporation sustained a run upon its specie, which was reduced to 4,919,000*l*. In one day 307,000*l*. were paid. It soon became very questionable whether the run for gold would not clrain every banker in the kingdom. That the demand was political was proved from the trifling nature of the applications from the country bankers. 'I never saw the hall of the Bank,' said Mr. Richards, in his evidence in 1832, 'except in 1825, so crowded with applicants tendering their notes. They had not in general the appearance of being people from the country.' One person, who had money with Jones, Loyd, and Co. to the amount of 20,000*l*., drew it out from them in the form of notes, and then went to the Bank and demanded gold. The London bankers found that the claims extended to their establishments. Several refused to pay in gold; but on giving notes, said, 'You may go and get gold for them at the Bank.' The stockholders took alarm, sold their government securities, and demanded specie in return. The funds were low; and when the panic had subsided, and confidence reappeared, the same persons brought hack their sovereigns, and repurchased their stock at a heavy loss. *It is impossible to say how far the panic would have spread had the one pound notes been in existence*. But it is far from improbable, that out of the extensive organisation that then existed, some deeply-rooted scheme for a simultaneous demand might have arisen, and produced consequences as unforeseen as terrible. As it was, 1,500,000*l* were paid in a few days, but no further evil occurred to the Bank of England."

amount of bullion in the Bank of England, and still more, if it happened to vary in an opposite direction, setting it down as a sufficient cause of the crisis. I have in a former part of this work entered into a full explanation of the circumstances relating to the monetary derangement of that period; I therefore refer the reader to it; and I have no doubt that he will there find abundant proof that the amount of Bank notes in circulation had nothing to do with it. Both the Bank of England and the country banks were injudicious and indiscreet in their advances in 1835, and the early part of 1836; but of the excess of these advances the amount of Bank notes outstanding formed no indication.

But although I am willing to allow that 1836-1837 may be considered as a period of monetary derangement, I cannot consider it as coming within the category of memorable commercial crises. It was confined in a great measure to two branches of trade, the American and East Indian, including China. The trade with the Baltic, and with the continent of Europe generally, was perfectly undisturbed, both in prices and in credit. The Bank raised its rate of discount to 5 per cent., and laid some restriction upon the bills of the American houses, who were notoriously overtrading. But for purposes of trade, generally, there was no want of accommodation; and the utmost rate that was heard of was 6 and 7 per cent, for fair commercial bills of moderate length. And, with the exception above mentioned, there was no depression in the prices of produce.

Even Mr. Norman seems to have attached little importance to the derangement of 1836.

"The crisis," he says, "of 1836, was more partial than any that had preceded it; indeed it presented hut little more derangement than might be expected to occur every five or six years, excepting what the opening of the trade with China, and our relations with America, will fully explain" — (*Remarks upon some prevalent Errors with respect to Currency and Banking*: 1838, p. 74.)

Granting, however, to the utmost extent claimed, that 1836-1837 was a period of crisis, what are we to say to 1839, which is brought forward as a period of monetary derangement?[①] Why, surely, that there was never a greater misnomer. If Sir Robert Peel would give a definition of what he considers a crisis or monetary derangement, and the definition should be such as to bring fairly within its compass such a period as 1839, then I should say that we ought to amend our commercial vocabulary; and invent some other name to designate such a state of things as occurred in 1825 and in 1847. By common acceptation, monetary derangement supposes a fall of prices, commercial failures, and discredit. Now none of these happened in the year 1839. Markets for produce were remarkably firm; there were no forced sales for money to meet engagements; there was not a single failure of a commercial or banking firm of any eminence; nor was there any difficulty of getting accommodation by the Bank at 5 and eventually 6 per cent, for bills at ninety-five days' date, and in the discount market at a little higher rate for longer dated bills. The whole of the phenomena of that year are resolvable into a moderately increased rate of interest during a very short interval, and an uneasiness in the minds of the public at the unsafe position in which the Bank had, by want of foresight, suffered itself to be placed.

From this array, then, of four crises, we must wholly strike out two. The third is hardly worth mentioning. There remains but one—the solitary case of 1825, till we come to that of 1847, which I shall have occasion to

① Mr. Loyd employs the term *convulsion*, as applied to 1837 and 1839!

notice more distinctly hereafter. In the mean while I would observe, that there are only two other cases in the last sixty years that come within the same category as 1825 and 1847. They occurred in the years 1792-1793 and 1810-1811. In each of those instances the degree and extent of commercial distress and discredit are matter of historical record. They are not susceptible of exaggeration. In two of these cases the crisis was so urgent as to induce the interference of Government to mitigate it by the issue of exchequer bills. In 1825-1826, the Government, though it declined giving the aid of exchequer bills, prevailed on the Bank of England, against its rules and inclination, to make advances on goods in warehouses.

It is to be observed of these great occasional derangements of credit, which all resolve themselves into a previous abuse of credit, that no two of the instances are exactly alike. In the general features of overtrading, or overbanking, or both, they cannot but agree, because one or other, or both, involving transactions on credit, invariably precede the revulsion, which consists in a contraction or failure of credit. The circumstances which give rise to the disposition to overtrading and overbanking may vary infinitely; but, generally speaking, supposing the existence of motives to speculation and hazardous enterprize, there is one condition which seems most highly favourable, if not essential, to the development of them into extensive operation, and that is a low rate of interest of some continuance.

Thus in 1792, although the Bank rate of discount had not been reduced below 5 per cent. , the market rate had fallen to, or below, 3 per cent, per annum; and the 3 per cent, consols had reached 97 $\frac{1}{4}$ in the March of that year. This comparatively low rate of interest had been, in some degree, both a cause and an effect of the great extension of the country bank system which about that time took place. And in their competition for business, there could be no doubt, after the event, that their advances had been too large, and had been made on insufficient or inconvertible securities. Coincidently with this growth of banks and banking accommodation, there were several circumstances, both commercial and political, calculated to excite a spirit of mercantile enterprize. And it is observed, in contemporary accounts, that the low rate of interest and the high price of the public funds in this country had forced capital abroad in the shape of extended credits to foreign merchants, and of occasional investments in foreign government funds.

But the excitement, and the tendency to overbanking and overtrading, at that time, were not confined to this country. There was a vast chain of bill circulation extending over several of the principal trading towns of the continent of Europe, including London in the circle. One of the earliest instances of the giving way of the links in that chain of circulation, was the failure of the firm of Burton, Forbes, and Gregory, of London, who gave open credits to foreign houses. Several houses at Amsterdam formed part in that extensive circulation, and failed in the autumn of 1792, or early in the following year. In this country the number of failures, banking and mercantile, at that time, greatly surpassed those of any former period; and taking into consideration the relative magnitude of the trade, and the pecuniary transactions of the country, at the two periods, it would seem that the monetary derangement or crisis (either of which terms applies to the case of 1792-1793) was little, if at all, inferior in intensity to that of

1825. The circumstances connected with the pressure of 1792-1793 arc so important and instructive that I have thought it desirable to insert in the Appendix extracts from the Report of the Select Committee, (House of Commons) on Commercial Credit, in the session of 1793, and also from Macpherson's Annals of Commerce, descriptive of them.

The commercial distress and banking discredit of 1810-1811 nearly equalled, in point of intensity, those of 1792 and 1825; and the losses caused by the fall of prices in 1810 were, I am inclined to think, greater than they had been at any former period. In the still more violent fluctuation of prices which took place between 1812 and the close of 1815, it is possible that the losses were greater; but there was not then any such sudden and extensive revulsion of credit, and commercial distress, as occurred in 1810-1811. The spirit of enterprize and speculation which prevailed in 1808, and which led to this revulsion, had not been preceded, as in the other cases to which I have compared it, by a continuous low rate of interest. But it was a period in which banking accommodation was easy at about 5 per cent. The political events of the time, and the commercial contingencies depending upon them, were such as led irresistibly to the most sanguine speculations. These, and the reverses which attended them, I have elsewhere described. My reference to this period is chiefly for the purpose of observing that the revulsion by which it was marked had not been preceded by a low rate of interest, as was the case in 1792 and 1825; yet it is to be borne in mind, as I have before stated, that the speculations ending in the revulsion of 1810 had mostly their origin in 1808, when the circulation was relatively low, and the exchanges and the price of gold very near their par.

A careful reference to the great monetary derangements, or commercial crises, of 1792-1793 and 1810-1811, will show how imperfect was the knowledge, or how great the disposition to exaggerate, which could lead Sir Robert Peel to enumerate among his four instances of crises, such periods as those of 1832, 1836-1837, and 1839, when in truth there was only one of the four, namely, 1825, which could come fairly within that category, unless a name altogether new be given to designate such a state of things as occurred in 1825 and 1847.

Of the crisis or monetary derangement of 1825, the circumstances which led to it, and its termination, I have given an account at some length in a former part of this work; and I shall have occasion, when noticing the working of the act of 1844, to institute a comparison between the crisis of 1847 and that of 1825. In the mean time, before closing my review of Sir Robert Peel's exposition of the grounds for the measure of 1844, I have to notice the further proofs which he adduced of the necessity for restricting the circulation of banks of issue, by reference to the failures of country banks.

SECTION 14 *On Sir Robert Peel's statement relative to bankrupt banks*

Sir Robert Peel having, as he seems to have thought, established his position of the *four* monetary derangements or crises within twenty years, and having made a passing remark on the number of failures of country banks in the years 1814, 1815, and 1816, proceeded to observe: —

"With regard to the last few years, a return has recently been laid before the House. I hold in my hand a return of the number of private banks which became bankrupt in the years 1839, 1840, 1841, 1842, 1843, with the amount of dividends paid, so far as they can be ascertained." He then exhibited a tabular statement of eighty-two banks which had become bankrupt in those years; and he added, "in ten of the cases the amount of the assets; in others, the causes of failure were stated." Of these he gave some descriptive particulars; but in one instance, only, does his statement notice the amount of the note circulation; and in that single case it was 5,590*l*. Upon this very objectionable statement, Mr. C. Buller justly observed, —

"As to the appalling picture which had been presented by the Right Honourable Baronet of eighty-one banks insolvent in five years, the return given of them showed only twenty-nine had been banks of issue; but no information bad been given of the amount of notes issued; the rest of the number must either have been made up of London bankers (whose failure could not have resulted from issues, because they issued not at all), or, of those who, having failed in speculation, had been published as bankers, simply because they had held shares in joint stock banks. Such, at least, was the prevailing impression."

It was afterwards admitted that *six*, out of the number in this statement, were only persons who had held shares in joint stock banks. And of the twenty-nine that, were issuing banks, only a single instance is given, and that as having notes in circulation, amounting to less than 5,600*l*. The prime minister would surely have had no difficulty in obtaining returns of the circulation of the remaining twenty-eight. If the aggregate, or separate, amount had been exhibited, I feel very confident that it would not have borne out the impression intended to be conveyed. In this statement, as in the whole discussion, Sir Robert Peel seemed studious to blend the question of solvency of banks, with that of their possession, and alleged abuse, of the power of issue; two questions involving considerations so perfectly distinct, with reference to any legislative regulation applicable to them, that it is surprising how any person of common understanding could so confound them. He must either have had very confused notions on the subject, or have desired that the distinction should not be examined by those whom he was addressing.

I do not for a moment question the purity of the motives by which Sir Robert Peel was actuated, or believe that he had any other objects than the public interest and his own fame, in bringing forward this measure. But why, then, adopt a course of argument which so openly exposes him to the charge of confusion of ideas, or of disingenuousness? To the former charge he can hardly be thought liable, considering how capable he has, on various occasions, shown himself of lucid and luminous exposition, when he has to deal with a good case, of which he has made himself master. And it is still more difficult to entertain the latter charge, admitting, as I most fully do, the purity of his motives. The only way in which I can account for the difficulty is this: he appears to have suffered himself to be so captivated by the subtle reasoning of Colonel Torrens, as well as by the specious arguments adduced with so much eloquence by Mr. Loyd, and with so much earnestness by Mr. Norman, in favour of the currency principle, as to have become a warm proselyte of the school, and to have determined, with the sectarian zeal of a neophyte, to carry its doctrines into practice. But he does not seem to have made himself sufficiently master of these doctrines to expound them clearly. Nor is it, indeed, to be wondered at, that, amidst his pressing avocations, he had not time or attention to devote to the study requisite for attaining a comprehensive and accurate knowledge of the subject he was dealing with.

Accordingly, nothing can be more unsatisfactory, (as was well observed by the *Times*,) than his exposition of the principles on which he proposed to restrict the amount of the note circulation; nor more evident than that he must have had some misgivings as to the weak points in his argument. He seems to have endeavoured to make up for the defect by declaiming upon the evils of the banking system, as it had theretofore existed; and here, by way of showing the necessity of restraining the *competition of banks of issue*, he adds to the failures of *twenty-nine issuing bankers* a statement of *fifty-three non-issuing bankers*, six of these being admitted to be only shareholders in joint stock banks. ①

Lord Stanley, a few years ago, in a debate on a strongly contested railway bill (the Trent Valley, if I recollect rightly), observed, in answer to Sir

---

① A writer in the *Bankers'*, *Magazine*, for March, 1847, has been at the pains of examining the flies of the *Gazette* for the years included by Sir Robert Peel in his statement to the House, viz., 1839-1843, both inclusive. The result of this scrutiny differs most materially from the figures produced by Sir Robert Peel; and it is proper to add that the writer quotes at length the name, date, and description, of every one of the fiats, upon an enumeration of which his general conclusion is founded. The following is the form in which that conclusion is expressed: —

Private banks of *issue*—bankrupt, 1839-1843	–		27
Ditto non – issue, ditto	–		8
			—
Total of *bonaâ ,finde*, "Bankers"	– –		35
Duplicates of private bank fiats	– –	2	
Eiats issued against persons *merely* shareholders in joint stock banke	– – – – – –	34	—
			36
			—
Total	– – – – – –		71
			—

The circumstance here stated, that *one half* of the fiats were against persons who habitually had no connexion whatever with the profession of banking, very much diminishes, if it does not wholly take away the force of Sir Robert Peel's statement.

Robert Peel, to whom, although then united with him in party, he was on that occasion opposed, that no *one knew so well as the Right Honourable Baronet how to dress up a case for that House.* ① Now a case more palpably dressed up for that House cannot well be imagined. It was so far skilfully contrived, by blending convertibility with solvency, that however defective in argument, it was admirably adapted to the assembly he was addressing. Never was adroitness in parliamentary tactics more conspicuous, nor was there ever an appeal more successful than that which he made to the prejudices prevailing, in parliament and out of it, against *excessive issues*, and the consequent depreciation of Bank notes strictly convertible into coin. Accordingly, nothing could be more triumphant than the manner in which the measure, founded upon such reasoning, and such illustration as we have seen, was passed in parliament, and hailed by the public.

Mr. Hawes moved, in opposition to the second reading, "That no sufficient evidence has been laid before this House to justify the proposed interference with banks of issue in the management of their circulation." ②

---

① I am not sure of the exact words, because I cannot lay my hand on the volume of Hansard in which the debate is reported, but I have every reason to believe that the *point* of the remark is here correctly stated.

② The speech by which Mr. Hawes prefaced his motion showed accurate and extensive knowledge of the subject; and it was assuredly not adequately answered. When I say this, it may be objected to me that the opinions then expressed by Mr. Hawes agree in the main with mine, and that I, therefore, judge partially. I should be quite willing, however, to refer on this point to the judgment of any one who takes a sufficient interest in the subject, and whose bundle of opinions, consisting of the tenets of either the currency principle or the Birmingham School, is not already made up, to say, after being at the trouble, as I have recently been, of looking over the speeches in that debate, whether anything like an answer was given to Mr. Hawes's objections to the bill. Mr. Goulburn, as Chancellor of the Exchequer, was foremost in reply; and I have given specimens of the knowledge he displayed on two of the points he made; the rest of his speech being well represented by those samples. Sir Robert Peel seemed to think it quite sufficient to taunt Mr. Hawes with the heresy of denying the depreciation of bank notes during the

This motion, worded, as I think, most correctly, was negatived by 185 to 30; and of this small minority there were only four members,—Mr. Hawes, the mover, Mr. Hastie, the seconder, Mr. C. Duller and Mr. Gisborne, who were adherents to the principle of a metallic standard, and who, consistently with that adhesion, declared themselves opposed to the bill in all that related to the amount of the circulation, that is, to the whole *principle* of the bill; the rest of it being mere matter of regulation, not affecting the principle. Nearly all of the minority, excepting the four above mentioned, whose objections, however forcibly urged, seemed to have been utterly disregarded, were considered to be either adverse, or of doubtful adhesion, to the act of 1819. Mr. Hume objected to some of the provisions of the bill, but voted for the second reading.

In the House of Lords the bill passed without a division, and almost without the form even of a debate. Lord Ashburton was, if I recollect rightly, the only peer who objected to the principle of the bill. So that it may be said to have been carried, as nearly as might be, unanimously, by those who approved of the principle of convertibility. By the public

---

restriction. Mr. Hawes, however, in his acceptation of the term depreciation, has the sanction of authorities so high as Mr. Blake (Observations on the Effects produced by the Expenditure of Government during the Restriction of Cash Payments, by Wm. Blake, Esq. F. R. S. 1823.) and the late Mr. James D. Hume. These have due regard to the prices of commodities; but they also allow for the peculiar circumstances of the time; and they give due weight to the fact that the fluctuations in the amount of the circulation and the concurrent variations of prices in no instance afforded ground for a fair inference that the latter were the effects of the former. In that point of view, they have a specious ground of argument for asserting that there was no depreciation, in the ordinary sense of the term; and I perfectly understand them. At the same time I have always used, and still adhere to the use of, the term depreciation, to signify the difference at that period between paper and gold. If the promise to pay is not performed according to the terms of it, I hold it to be depreciated in the exact degree in which it falls short of the value of the specific thing promised.

generally, by the press, and even by merchants and bankers, with the exception of some hardly audible expression of misgiving, the act of 1844 was hailed as establishing the currency on a sound and solid footing; which would not only preserve the convertibility of bank notes beyond all possibility of danger, but would prevent all those derangements and revulsions which were ascribed to the mismanagement of the *circulation* by banks of issue: the charge against the management being that the amount of their outstanding notes did not vary as it ought, and as it thenceforth would be made to do, with the variations in the amount of bullion in the Bank. So much for the state of public information on the question at that time!

SECTION 15 *On the anticipations respecting the success of the act of 1844, as expressed by its advocates and opponents*

If I have succeeded in my endeavours to show that the theory on which the Act of 1844 has been made to rest, is incorrect, and that the statements brought forward to prove the tendency to *excessive issues* by the country banks, do not bear out the conclusion sought to be established, the natural presumption is, that a measure founded on such mistaken views could not answer the expectations held out by the framers of it. And such is the fact.

The advantages which, by the framers of the Act, and by the propounders of the theory on which that Act was founded, were held out as being likely to be the result of the change thus introduced into the banking system of this country may be collected from the following extracts.

The subjoined passages are from the pamphlet published by Mr. Loyd, immediately after the passing of the Bill in 1844.

"The consequence of this system (the system previous to 1844) has been an abrupt and violent action upon credit and prices at an advanced period of the drain, and the ultimate evil, exhaustion of the bullion, obviated, not without great difficulty, and at the expense of severe pressure upon the public. The bill now under consideration proposes to substitute a system of early, steady, and continuous contraction, in the place of that which has been late in its commencement, sudden and violent in its operation, and irregularly carried out. By this means it seems almost a matter of demonstration that the occurrence of many circumstances by which the intensity and extent of former drains have been increased will be prevented, and that the correction of those causes of drain which cannot be altogether obviated, will be brought into operation in an earlier stage of the drain, and will, therefore, be effected with less contraction of the *circulation*, and, consequently, with less inconvenience to the public. (*Thoughts*, *&c.*, 1844, p. 8.)

"It is now proposed to adopt a different course. The difficulty is henceforth to be met at the very moment of its commencement, and the corrective measures, founded upon intelligible and well ascertained principles, are to be applied, without interruption, until the evil has been subdued. Contraction of *Circulation* is to be *made precisely coincident*, *as regards both time and amount*, *with diminution of the bullion*; and thus it is conceived that the danger of total exhaustion, which could not befal a metallic circulation, will be rendered equally impossible with respect to a mixed circulation of gold and paper. The result remains to be ascertained; but all reasoning confirms the soundness of the grounds upon which this experiment is founded, and justifies a sanguine expectation that by a close and steady adherence to principle, the safety of our monetary system will be more effectually secured. Whatever may be the inconvenience to the public involved in the measures necessary for this purpose, it would be unwise in the extreme not to submit to it There is fair ground, however, to anticipate that many adventitious difficulties, which have arisen out of the working of the present system, will be obviated, and that the essential object of the bill will be accomplished without subjecting the public to any increase of the inconveniences which they have hitherto experienced during a drain of bullion." — (*Ibid.* p. 12.)

Colonel Torrens ventured to speak in terms still more confident, and specifically prophetic. A few examples will suffice.

"Under the proposed system for the regulation of the currency, an adverse exchange, originating in the currency itself, will be a rare occurrence, and any considerable or permanent deviation from the par-of-exchange equilibrium an impossible event. *Practically considered, fluctuations in the rate of interest and in the state of commercial credit, so far as they can result from alterations in the value of the currency, may, under the operation of the proposed system, be taken at nihil.*" — (*An Inquiry*, &c., 1844, p. 97.)

"I believe that it will fully accomplish this object (*i. e.*, the perfect assimilation of our currency to the metallic model), and that it will effectually prevent the recurrence of those cycles of commercial excitement and depression of which our ill-regulated currency has been the primary and exciting cause; and so believing, I continue to retain, after an attentive and patient consideration of all the objections urged by the able and scientific Reviewer, the opinion which I formerly expressed, that the adoption of Sir Robert Peel's plan for the renewal of the charter of the

Rank of England will be the most important improvement in our monetary system which has been effected since the passing of the act of 1819 for the resumption of Cash payments. "—(*Ibid.* p. 100.)

The following question has been asked ①:—"If under the proposed plan, 14,000,000*l.* had been issued on securities, and if 8,000,000*l.* was the amount in which notes had been issued on gold, making the present circulation of the Bank 22,000,000*l.*, and if a time should again occur when so large a sum as 7,000,000 should be taken from the Bank in the short space of nine months, what would be the effect of such a violent collapse?" The proper answer to this question is, that when the Government plan shall have been carried into effect, the abstraction of 7,000,000*l.* of treasure from the coffers of the Bank in a period of nine months will be morally impossible. ② The violent fluctuation which occurred between December, 1838, and September, 1839, was the result of the system which the querist would desire to uphold. Had the Bank of England in 1838 and 1839 been limited to the issue of 14, 000, 000*l.* upon securities; had there been functional separation; had the department of banking been denied all aid from the department of issue; and had a gradual contraction of the circulation consequently commenced with the first efflux of bullion, it would have been utterly impossible that the drain should have extended to 7,000,000*l.*; utterly impossible that the pressure

---

① By Mr. Hastie. Speech of 13th of June, 1844.

② The following figures, from the actual returns of the Bank, under the Act, afford a striking illustration of the correctness of this "answer": —

		Bullion.		Circulation.
12th Sept. 1846	···	£ 16,350,000	···	£ 20,920.000
24th April, 1847	···	9,210,000	···	20,690,000
Decrease	···	7,140,000	···	230,000

upon the money market, consequent on the suspension of confidence and the stagnation of trade, should have been so severe and so protracted as they unfortunately became. The proofs of these positions I have detailed in the preceding pages, and need not here repeat. — (*Ibid.* pp. 99. &103.)

Sir Robert Peel, towards the close of his speech of the 20th of May, 1844, observed: —

"Some apprehend that the proposed restriction upon issue will diminish the power of the Bank to act with energy at a period of monetary crisis, and commercial alarm and derangement, But the object of the measure is to prevent (so far as legislation can prevent) the recurrence of those evils from which we suffered in 1825, 1836, and 1839. It is better to prevent the paroxysm than to excite it, and trust to desperate remedies for the means of recovery."

Sir William Clay, in remarking, in 1844, upon my pamphlet of that, year, observed, with reference to the proposed separation of the functions of the Bank of England —

"That serious difficulties or dangers would attend the working of such a plan, when once carried into effect, *I see no reason to apprehend.* At least, if there be, they must be something very different from those stated by Mr. Tooke; for any thing more thoroughly gratuitous than the difficulties he has stated — any stronger manifestation of a disposition to create the giants, he afterwards means to slay, I must be permitted to say I never witnessed."

He then cites the passage of my pamphlet, wherein, commenting on a hypothetical case, I concluded with the remark that in the event of a drain, it was a possible event that the banking department might be obliged to stop payment while the issuing department had 6,000,000*l*. of bullion, "unless

Government should step in to prevent so ridiculous, however lamentable a catastrophe," upon which Sir William Clay observes — "Ridiculous, indeed, but one the occurrence of which I cannot see the slightest reason for anticipating." And further on, after describing the phenomena which under both systems would attend an adverse balance of trade, be observes —

"Under both systems these phenomena will be exhibited; but under the system of which I advocate the adoption, it appears to me certain that they will be less in degree, gentler in their transition, more gradual in their succession. The necessary contraction would begin at the right time; it would never be delayed too long; it would be precisely to the extent required, because it would not have been prcceded by a previous factitious expansion."

Let us now see, on the other hand, what were the opinions entertained and expressed by the opponents of the measure, and of the theory on which it was founded. Mine happened to be the first in the order of time, the pamphlet in which the opinions are stated having been published in March, 1844.

"Without attaching such exaggerated importance as Mr. Bosanquet and Mr. Gilbart, and some others who oppose the currency principle do, to the effects of great variations in the rate of interest, I am inclined to think that, excepting the convertibility of the paper and the solvency of banks, which are and ought to be within the province of the legislature most carefully to preserve, the main difference between one system of banking and another is the greater or less liability to abrupt changes in the rate of interest, as compared with the other. And a careful consideration of the various plans which have been submitted to the public for carrying out the currency principle, has led to a confirmation of the opinion which I have before expressed, that under a complete separation of the functions of issue and banking, the transitions would be more abrupt and violent than under the existing system; unless, and upon this, in my opinion, the question hinges, the deposit or banking department were bound to hold a much larger reserve than seems to be contemplated by any of the plans which I have seen.

"The difference between the two systems cannot be placed in a more striking point of view than in the following passages of a printed letter which Colonel Torrens addressed to me on the occasion of the opinions which I had expressed on the subject in a former work.

"'The difference,' Colonel Torrens says, 'between us is this, you contend that the proposed separation of the business of the Bank into two distinct departments would check over-trading in the department of issue, but would not check over-trading in the department of deposit; while I maintain, on the contrary, that the proposed separation would cheek over-trading in both departments. The manner in which the separation would have this twofold effect will be seen by the following example.

'Let us assume that the Bank holds 18,000,000*l*. of securities and 9,000,000*l* of bullion, against 18,000,000*l*. of outstanding notes and 9,000,000*l*. of deposits, and let an adverse exchange require that the depositors should draw out their deposits in bullion to the amount of 3,000,000*l*.

'In this case, if the business of issue were mixed up with that of deposit, the drawing out of the 3,000,000*l*. of deposits in bullion would have no other effect than that, of reducing both deposits and bullion by the amount of 3,000,000*l*., while the amount of the circulation, and of the securities, and the power of the bank, as its securities fell due, to continue the discount business to the same extent as before, would suffer no diminution. But let the department of issue be wholly separated from that of deposit, and the result would be widely different.

'As soon as the separation was effected the deposit department holding

9,000,000*l*. of deposits with 9,000,000*l*. of securities would be obliged to sell some part of its securities, say one-third, in order to be prepared to meet the demands of its depositors. The state of the two departments would then stand thus: —

Circulating Department.

Circulation		– –	18,000,000*l*.
Securities	–	– –	9,000,000
Bullion	–	– –	9,000,000

Deposit Department.

Deposits	–	– –	9,000,000*l*.
Securities	–	– –	6,000,000
Reserve in bank notes		–	3,000,000

'This being the previous state of things, the demand of the depositors for 3, 000, 000*l*. in gold would produce the following changes. The 3,000,000*l*. of bank notes held by the deposit department as reserve, would be drawn out by the depositors and paid into the circulating department in exchange for gold while the directors of the deposit department, in order to recover a reserve equal to one-third of their deposits would be obliged to sell 2,000,000*l*. out of the 6,000,000*l*. held in securities. The results would be, that in the circulating department the bullion would be reduced from 9,000,000*l*. to 6,000,000*l*., and the circulation from 18, 000, 000*l*. to 15,000,000*l*., and that, in the deposit department, the deposits would be reduced from 9,000,000*l*. to 6,000,000*l*., the securities from 6,000,000*l*., to 4,000,000*l*., and the reserve from 3,000,000*l*. to 2,000,000*l*. It is self-evident that the effect of these changes would be not only a contraction of the circulation but a limitation to the power to over-trade in discount and loans. '

"I am willing to admit this statement as exhibiting in substance the difference between us. According to my view, as there may be variations of international payments, in other words, of a balance of trade, without any grounds for inference of alterations in the value of the currencies of the countries from which or to which such balance may be due, the presumption is, that an occasional efflux of four or five or six millions would be followed, at no distant period, by a fully equal reflux. Such was the case in 1828-1829 and 1831-1832, when the treasure of the Bank having been reduced by five or six millions, was replenished without the slightest operation of the Bank on the amount of its securities or its rate of interest. And such efflux and reflux might again take place under a continuance of the present system, provided that the Bank habitually held a large reserve, without any disturbance of the money market, and without any influence on the amount of bank notes in the hands of the public. Now, under a system of separation, and in the position of the two departments in the case supposed by Colonel Torrens, what would be the operation of a demand for export to the extent of three millions of gold? In all probability, this demand would almost exclusively fall upon the deposit department.

"This being the case, the directors would not have a moment to lose upon the first manifestation of such demand, without taking measures for retaining or restoring the proportion of their reserve. They must sell securities, or allow the existing ones, if short-dated, to run off, and they must inexorably shut their doors to all applications for advances or discounts. This would, as Colonel Torrens justly observes, operate as a limitation of the power to over-trade in discount and loans. Most effectual, indeed, would it be, and, under certain circumstances of the trade, it would operate with a degree of violence on the state of credit, of which, as it appears to me, Colonel Torrens has no adequate idea. This is not to be wondered at in a writer not practically conversant with trade or banking; but that other advocates for the measure of separation, who number among them merchants and bankers, should be so unaware of it as they seem to be, does indeed surprise me. Before two or three millions of bank notes could be forcibly abstracted from the amount in circulation among the public the pressure upon the reserves of the London bankers must be extreme. They would, of course, to the utmost extent practicable, call in their loans, and resolutely refuse further accommodation.

"Although there is no modern experience of such a state of things, if any merchant, banker, or money dealer were to have the case laid distinctly before them, could any of them for a moment have a doubt as to the extremity of pressure which it would cause? I am most intimately persuaded that it would be within the mark to suppose that a rate of discount (assuming that the doors of the Bank and the ears of the Directors were inexorably closed against all applications) of 20 per cent, and upwards, would, in many cases, be submitted to, and sacrifices of goods, if any large proportion were held on credit, would be made at a still greater loss. And, after all, it might be a question, whether even this effort of the Bank on its securities would be effectual in restoring its reserve *in sufficient time* to meet the exigency. This would depend entirely upon the character of its deposits. If these were strictly payable on demand, while the circumstances determining the efflux were strong and urgent, the payment of 3,000,000*l*., accompanied by forced sales of securities, might prove insufficient in point of time to arrest the demand; and, in this case, while the circulating department would still have 6,000,000*l*. of bullion, the deposit department would have no alternative but to stop payment. A most absurd, however disastrous state of things. But it would be too disastrous and too absurd to be allowed to take its course. If such a crisis were to happen, as most probably it would, at the time when the dividends on the public funds became due, the Government would be imperatively called upon to interfere and prevent so ridiculous, however lamentable, a catastrophe. And the only interference that could meet the emergency would be to authorise a temporary transfer of coin from the issuing to the banking department." — (*An Inquiry into the Currency Question*, pp. 105-110.)

Mr. Hawes, in his speech of the 13th of June, 1844, which I have already alluded to, among the other arguments which he urged against the bill, observed: —

"I cannot doubt that while the proposed restrictions are unnecessary, they will be productive of evils greater than those sought to be remedied. That in the attempt to secure ourselves against commercial pressure, we shall only aggravate their evils when they do, as they will, occur. If it be supposed, that under the plan now proposed, the. Bank will be enabled, as she has hitherto done, to use any such discretion in meeting a commercial pressure, it is a great error. By adopting the present plan we may obtain a fancied additional security for the maintenance of our currency on a par with the value of gold; we may make an effort to cheek speculation, over which we have no control; but whenever serious commercial pressure shall occur, and the proposed system is enforced, the reaction upon public credit will be violent and unmitigated. And whoever has been accustomed to watch the proceedings of the Bank of England and of the London bankers at such times, will readily anticipate that what we saw in 1825 or 1839, will be trifling in comparison with what may then take place."

And Mr. Hastie, in seconding Mr. Hawes's motion, stated his views concisely in the passage which Colonel Torrens undertook to answer, by saying that, under the new system, an export of 7,000,000*l*. of bullion within nine months would be *impossible*.

Mr. Fullarton stated his misgivings with his usual force and felicity of expression: —

"What may be the practical working of such a scheme no man can absolutely foretell, and past experience gives us no clue to discover. It remains to be tried. For this, it must be admitted, the times are sufficiently propitious; and, while exchanges continue favourable, interest low, and the stock of bullion overflowing, all will no doubt proceed smoothly, and the unruffled aspect of monetary affairs will be cited and allowed as a proof of the beneficial operation of the government plan. But if it is to be something more than a mere fair-weather pageant, if its principle is really and literally to be carried out, at all seasons and in all circumstances, with stern and unflinching pertinacity, it may happen that, at no very distant period, (at all events, long before the ten years of the new charter shall have expired,) contingencies may present themselves, which will put the virtues of the panacea to the test, may possibly even shake a little the general confidence in their efficacy, and rouse a fresh spirit of inquiry into the nature of those periodical hurricanes which visit from time to time the great marts of industry throughout the world, and the real extent of the means (much more insignificant, it is to be feared, than seems to be commonly imagined) by which we can hope to divert or moderate them."— (*Regulation of Currencies*, 1844, p. 4)

And again, thus: —

"It is certainly within the chapter of possibilities that the restrictive clauses of the Bank Act may, even before they are called into effective action, be reduced to a mere nullity, by some happy development of those remedial resources, which credit, judiciously administered, can always bring into play under the pressure of any strong necessity, or that their worst consequences may be avoided by a resort to the safety-valve of the bank-post-bills, or some other similar measure of evasion. In that case, there will be no undue contraction of the circulation, no refusal of the accustomed supply of capital; the great purpose of the authors of the restriction will have been simply defeated or abandoned; and the event will be at once an infinite relief to the public, and the *euthanasia* of this first attempt to legislate on the principles of the currency theory. The law, nevertheless, may still remain unrepealed; and it is even possible that there may be found persons to cry up this failure as only a new proof of its 'admirable working!' The course of events, however, which, if the spirit in which the restrictive clauses of the Bank Act are framed, is to be consistently acted up to, must be considered, I fear, as by far the most probable, would lead to a very different termination. And although that termination also might, no doubt, be liable to manifold modification from circumstances, a state of circumstances can well be imagined, in which the catastrophe would be as tremendous as it would in all likelihood be sudden and irretrievable, shaking even to its foundations the entire financial fabric of the realm." — (*Ibid.* p. 252.)

Mr. Mill, in his very able article in the *Westminster Review*, for June, 1844, on "The Currency Question," pointed out, the dangerous character of the innovations introduced by the bill, in the following admirable passage: —

"It is a fact, attested by experience, that a drain of gold upon the Bank for exportation takes place in most cases mainly by drawing out deposits. As, in the proposed system, there is nothing to cause any change in this respect, we must suppose that this would still be the case, and that the demand for gold would be first felt by the deposit department.

"Now, under the present arrangements, in case of a run upon the deposits, the Bank has to rely, not only on the portion of reserve which it retains, like other bankers, against the deposits themselves, but also on the gold in reserve on account of its notes. Until all the gold in the possession of the Bank is exhausted, it is in no danger of stopping payment. But under the proposed system the department of deposit must rest upon its own resources. The reserve in the deposit department could derive no aid from the issue department, while it would have to hear the first brunt of the whole action intended to be exercised through it upon the latter. As it would he prohibited from meeting this demand by creating more notes, or even by having the notes which it paid out, and which then went to the issue department for gold, returned to it; either the reserve of the deposit department alone will require to be as great as is now requisite for the deposits and issues together, or it will be obliged to suspend its discounts and sell its securities much earlier and more abruptly than is necessary under the present mixed system.

"While the circulating department was still abundantly supplied with gold, the deposit department might have no alternative but to stop payment."

Mr. James Wilson, also, did not omit to give very clear and forcible warnings of the perils to which the country would be exposed by the practical enforcement of the new theory. In the *Economist* of the 26th of April, 1845, after an elaborate exposure of the tendency of the act of 1844 to aggravate the evils of a drain of bullion, he concluded by saying:—

"Under this action of the new currency bill we look forward with no small alarm to the increased and aggravated consequences which a failure in the harvest, and a continuance of high prices, must exercise over the manufacturing industry of the country — not, as it is pretended, subjecting it to an earlier but less intense depression, but, as we have shown, to an earlier, it is true, but also to a more intense and protracted suffering."—(*Capital*, *Currency*, *and Banking*, p. 95.)

And again, on the 3d of May, 1845, in discussing the measures then before parliament for the regulation of Banking in Scotland and Ireland, Mr. Wilson has the following able and lucid passage on the real effect of the ministerial plan: —

"Sir Robert Peel says, take the average of the last thirteen months — fix your circulation at that; if you exceed it, increase your bullion to the same extent. Now one great fallacy of the averages of circulation is, that the average of a week, taken at the close of business, is no criterion of the actual quantity of notes which must, during the week, be issued at particular times to represent exchanges, the greatest part of which return to the issuers before the amount in circulation is taken at the end of the week; but when notes are issued, it is always uncertain what precise portion will return within a given time. A banker dealing with his notes, therefore, keeps a reserve by him for such momentary purposes, and to sustain a circulation of 100,000*l*., as shown by the returns, he will have 150,000*l*. or 200,000*l* of notes, more or less, and occasionally in use. But under such restrictions as proposed, he will not be able to venture the issue of such notes, being uncertain as to their return, without holding bullion to avoid the penalty in the event they do not return. The system of averages is, therefore, extremely fallacious; and we cannot understand how it is to improve the condition of the Bank of England, if for the limited stock of gold in the world it is to have the fresh competition of all the Scotch and Irish banks, in order that they may hold uniformly larger quantities than they do. But this is the least of the evil.

"Let us suppose a period of pressure. The bullion of the Bank is reduced to seven or eight millions (no very small amount compared with some periods), so that the circulation of notes is nearly equal to the securities of 14,000,000*l.* and the bullion together. What will take place in Scotland and Ireland under the new bill then? The Scotch banks have to protect 3,000,000*l.* of circulation and 30,000,000*l.* of deposits. Pressure is felt and is further expected. The Scotch banks feel that it is necessary to increase their reserves; that their deposits may be required by their customers to assist their friends to pay up railway calls, or any other purpose for which money becomes so much required at a time of pressure. They see they cannot move without increasing their amount of coin; they are the largest holders of securities and stock in London of any class of bankers; they order them to be sold in the market, draw bullion from the Bank, and increase the drain already rapidly going forward.

"It does appear the most extraordinary idea for a minister to entertain, that he can relieve the bank at a period of pressure by bringing a new, and powerful, and irresistible class of competitors into the market, in the sale of securities and the struggle for bullion. *If his object were to increase the intensity of such a crisis, he could not adopt a more certain plan.*"—(*Capital, Currency, and Banking*, pp. 103-104.)

Looking at these opposite opinions, expressed before or soon after the passing of the act of 1844, I am quite content that my readers should judge for themselves, without any further comment from me, whether the advocates for the measure, or its opponents, had formed the more correct view of its probable operation.

I shall now proceed to a view of the actual working of the law, from its taking effect in September, 1844, to the close of 1847.

SECTION 16 *On the operation of the act of 1844, from September, 1844 to January, 1847*

Let us now, with the benefit of the experience of upwards of three years, since the passing of the Act of 1844, see what has been its actual operation.

I have already stated, that immediately on the act taking effect, the Bank of England reduced its public rate of discount from 4 per cent. for all classes of bills, to $2\frac{1}{2}$ per cent. for first-class bills, and 3 per cent. for notes. And, in March, 1845, the rate was reduced to $2\frac{1}{2}$ per cent. for notes also. The Directors thus entered into direct competition with the bankers and money dealers; and in so doing, they acted strictly in the spirit of the bill. Sir . Robert Peel had said: —

"The *principle of competition*, though unsafe, in our opinion, when applied to issue, *ought, we think, to govern the business of banking.* After the issue of paper currency has once taken place, it is then important that the public should be enabled to *obtain the use of that* issue on as favourable terms as possible."

The obtaining of that issue, on as favourable terms as possible *meant*, *for it could mean nothing else, as low a rate of interest as possible*; and the Directors, in adopting the course they did, were, clearly only acting upon this exhortation of Sir Robert Peel.

This active competition by the Bank of England with the private bankers, and the money dealers, had the effect, if not of reducing, of, at least, continuing, longer than it otherwise would have been continued, the very low rate of interest which then prevailed. As a proof that the Bank, by this reduction of its rate of interest, was successful in obtaining a larger share of the discount business, it may be observed that the securities, other than public, were thenceforward larger in amount than they had been for some time previously. And there can, I imagine, be no question but that this low rate of interest, and the consequent abundance of banking accommodation, tended to facilitate and promote the railway speculations which were then (September, 1844) in progress, and which reached their culminating point in the summer of 1845. And it is no less clear that the same low rate of interest and abundance of banking accommodation tended to promote the spirit of adventure which was then abroad for other undertakings involving the outlay of borrowed capital.

The railway speculation went at that time to such an extent as to occupy the attention of the public almost exclusively. But it is evident, from the disclosures to which the late commercial failures have led, that a good deal of what now appears to have been improvident outlay in fixed capital abroad, including foreign railways, was also then in progress, and was, no doubt, encouraged by the advances which were so liberally and so largely afforded upon distant forthcoming returns. Investments, too, in mills and mines, and various projects of internal improvement, besides railways, entailing the conversion of circulating into fixed capital, were going forward on a scale sufficiently extensive to have attracted public notice, but for the all-absorbing topic of the railway mania. This was surely not a time during which it was desirable, or (looking to probable, if not inevitable results) safe, to aid the continuance of so low a rate of interest

But though the conduct of the Bank of England, in so greatly reducing its public rate of discount, may be considered to have prolonged the facility of banking accommodation which marked that period, no blame whatever can attach to the Directors for that reduction; or, at all events, they are not open to reproach for it from the promoters and admirers of the act of 1844, and, least of all, from Sir Robert Peel. They would not, I think, have ventured upon that step if they had continued under the responsibility which was previously considered to rest upon them in the "regulation of the Currency," as it was termed; and for which, under the former system, they were considered accountable. But from such responsibility they were entirely, and even ostentatiously, released; the great merit of the new system having been repeatedly declared by its authors to consist in its confiding the regulation of the Currency to a self-adjusting principle, totally independent of the Bank management. In acting as they did, the Directors were, as I have before observed, fairly carrying out the spirit of the measure, as expounded by Sir Robert Peel. That they had his approval cannot be doubted, if we look at the manner in which he expressed himself in his speech of the 25th of April, 1845, (the House being in committee, on Banking in Ireland and Scotland), with reference to the working of the act of 1844.

"I am," he said, "quite as well aware as, I believe, any one can be, of the necessity of great caution in drawing inferences as to the effect of measures of this nature on the circulation and on the public credit of the country. I draw my inferences from the closest observation of the subject, and of the working of those measures which the shortness of the interval would permit me to give them; and I must say, that so far as we can judge from experience, we have a perfect light to be satisfied with the operation of the measures which were then adopted. Admitting our experience of these measures to be short, so far as it has gone, I contend that *it has been decidedly in favour of the policy and justice of the measures sanctioned by this House in the course of the last session of Parliament.* Since these measures were adopted, we have had in this country a period of extraordinary commercial activity: we have had a great demand for the application of new capital to manufactures, and other branches of the public industry; and we have had a very unusual degree of speculation connected with the internal improvement of the country. I refer particularly to the projects for the extension of locomotion by means of railways. But I cannot find that the restrictions imposed last year have, in the slightest degree, cramped or fettered the commercial energies of the country. I cannot find that there has been the slightest ground of complaint, either that prices have been unduly affected, or that the increased demands of the country cannot be met on account of a restricted circulation"

Here was Sir Robert Peel taking credit for the favourable operation of his measure, and defending it by reference to the speculations then afloat, from the charge to which he seemed to think it might have been liable, of cramping and fettering the commercial energies of the country by a too *restricted circulation.* He seems to have been totally unaware that the charge to which his measure might properly be considered obnoxious, was, that in the state of things as it then existed, it did not only not restrain, but greatly favoured the speculations in railways, and the commercial enterprises which were then assuming a dangerous character. Blinded by his exclusive view of the note circulation, he failed to perceive that it was the employment and direction of capital, or, in other words, the amount of banking accommodation, and not the amount of notes in circulation, that was in question, in judging of the working of his act. If, while engaged, as he stated, in closely observing the working of his new measure, he had been aware of its real operation, or if, in the course of his observation, he had conceived any doubts of the propriety or prudence of the conduct of the Directors of the Bank, in acting as they did, he would naturally, feeling the strongest interest in the proper working of the act, have given some hint or caution to the governors, with whom he, or at least the Chancellor of the Exchequer, were necessarily in occasional communication. But it does not appear that any such hint or caution was ever given to them; nor, indeed, is it likely that it should have been, seeing how little of inconvenience or eventual danger Sir Robert Peel seems to have apprehended.

While Sir Robert Peel was thus unconscious of the immediate and principal effect of that portion of the act of 1844, which had divided the Bank of England into two separate departments, he seems to have been equally unaware of the bearing of the state of things then existing upon the arguments by which the legislature had been led to impose a restriction on the amount of the note circulation of the country banks. Those arguments went distinctly on the ground that the power of issue afforded the means, and that the competition of banks of issue supplied motives, to the bankers, to favour speculations by increased issues of notes; and that consequently, by restricting their power of adding to the note circulation, the tendency to speculation in the provinces would be repressed; and that this restriction, whatever inconvenience to bankers and speculators might attend it, would operate most beneficially to the public. Sir Robert Peel, however, in the spring of 1845, took credit, as we have seen, to the act of 1844, for *not having restrained* the speculations, or (to use his expression), cramped or fettered the commercial energies of the country, which were then evidently tending to excessive action. If the close observation which he was giving to the working of his measure had drawn his attention, concurrently, to the extent of the speculations *then* going forward in railways, besides those in mills and mines, &c., he might possibly have been led to doubt whether the *amount of the note circulation* had, or could have, any necessary or accessary influence in promoting or checking a tendency to speculation.

As a large part of the public still, apparently, participate the opinion on which the act of 1844 proceeded, that excessive issues of notes, whether by the Bank of England, or by the country banks, are essential, or materially accessary to the originating or extending of speculation, it is worth while here to show to what an enormous extent, both as to extravagance of prices, and of the nominal amount of capital involved in the transactions, speculations may be carried on, without influencing, or being influenced, by variations in the amount of the outstanding circulation. With this view, I have to solicit attention to the following extracts from a paper drawn up by Mr. Danson, with admirable conciseness and clearness, and read by him before a meeting of the Statistical Society in January 1847.

"Between March and September 1845, joint stock speculations, for the immediate investment of capital, were set on foot, involving a larger aggregate amount than had ever before been so involved in this country. The amount to raise which, for railways alone, the sanction of Parliament was actually applied for in the following session, exceeded 340,000,000*l*.

sterling. And if we include all the new schemes in which scrip, or letters of allotment, were actually selling in the market at a premium in July, August, and September, 1845, the amount cannot be estimated at less than 500,000,000*l*.

"Many of the schemes of 1845 reached a high premium within a few weeks after their issue; and all those first in the market, and having any substantial merit, were raised considerably above their true value. For instance, the Leeds and Thirsk Railway—50*l*. shares, with only a deposit of 2*l*. 10*s*. paid — were selling, in March, at 3*l*. 10*s*.; in September, at 23*l*. 15*s*.; and in November at 4*l*. 15*s*, per share. Again, the Bolton, Wigan, and Liverpool—40*l*. shares, with 4*l*. paid—were selling in January 1845, at 4*l*. 10*s*.; in September, at 42*l*. 15*s*.; and in December, when 9*l*. had been paid, at 20*l*. per share. If we assume an average premium of 10*l*. per cent. upon the schemes then in the market, the property temporarily created by these speculations (and the repeated purchase and sale of which, on commission, furnished profitable employment to some thousands of brokers,) must have been, at least,50,000,000*l*.

"And to this there is to he added an increased value, during the same period, of the shares in the established lines of railway. For instance —

"The Midland Stock,—amount 4,180,000*l*., — was selling in January 1845, at 114 per cent.; and in July at 188 per cent; showing a rise of 74 per cent, and an increase in the aggregate value of the stock of 3,098,000*l*.

"The Great Western — share capital issued, 8,160,000*l*. — 100*l*. shares selling in January 1845, at 156*l*.; and in July, at 228*l*.; and (allowing for a call at 5*l*. per share in the interim), showing a rise of 67 per cent, and an increase in the aggregate value of the shares of 5,467,000*l*.

"The Manchester and Leeds — share capital 4,660,000*l*. — 100*l*.

shares selling in January 1845, at 126*l*.; and in August at 215*l*.; showing a rise of 89 per cent, and an increased value in the aggregate of 4,147,000*l*.

"The average increase in the value of 100*l*. shares in these three lines was 76*l*.; and the total increase of value in August and September was upwards of 12,000,000*l*.

"It will be seen, on reference to the tables, that during those months in which the purchases and sales of railway property were most numerous and extensive, while every body was buying and selling shares, and the current rate of interest was only $2\frac{1}{2}$ per cent, that portion of the circulating medium, which consisted of Bank of England notes, was but very slightly, if at all, increased; and that it reached its greatest amount when the prices of shares were lowest — when every body had ceased to speculate — when the number and amount of current transactions were reduced to the lowest point by descredit, and when the current rate of interest for fist class bills bad risen from $2\frac{1}{2}$ to $4\frac{1}{2}$ per cent."

And yet, notwithstanding the evidence afforded by the facts here stated, of the absence of any connection, whether as cause or effect, between the amount of the note circulation and the enormous extent of the speculations described in the foregoing statement, there were persons then, and there have been others more recently who, when pressed to account for these phenomena, consistently with the expectation held out by the advocates of the act of 1844, that it would operate as a salutary preventative of the recurrence of such extravagance of speculation as had been witnessed under the former system, have answered — Oh! the speculations would have gone much further if the issues of the country banks had not been restricted.[1] I have myself met with persons who have given that answer; but when further asked why they thought so, and how they could, by the utmost force of imagination, conceive the possibility of folly, and recklessness of pecuniary engagements, going further than they then did, no attempt at explanation was made; nor indeed was it likely that a satisfactory reason could be given for so extraordinary a supposition.

It is further to be observed, with reference to the railway mania, that from the date of Sir Robert Peel's speech in April 1845, to the culminating point of that speculation, namely, in the September following, there is no reason to suppose that either he or the Chancellor of the Exchequer hinted to the Governors of the Bank any doubt of the expediency of their keeping their rate of discount so low as it then was.

I have to refer to the account given in a former chapter of the variations in the Bank rate of interest, from the period here noticed, till April 1847.

Until after Jan. 1847, there cannot, on the part of the currency

---

① In a letter, which appeared in the *Times*, of the 15th of April last, signed "Mercator," and commonly ascribed to a high authority, in favour of the Act of 1844, is the following passage: —

"The bill of Sir R. Peel was passed in 1844, and from that time till the end of August 1846, there was an almost uninterrupted influx of bullion into this country; so that, at that time, the amount in the cellars of the Bank reached, I believe, the unprecedented sum of sixteen millions. I will not now stop to discuss the effect of Peel's Bill in preventing that undue expansion of the country circulation, which has usually occurred during a state of favourable exchanges and influx of bullion. *Without this salutary restraint, the speculative mania, with respect to railroad investments, would undoubtedly have been carried to a far more dangerous extent than it has actually reached*; and to the same cause we are probably, in a great degree, indebted for the comparatively sound state of trade and commercial transactions generally at the present moment. Our present condition, in this respect, presents a most satisfactory contrast, as regards both the state of the money market and of trade, with that which has usually existed at the commencement of monetary pressure, following, in close succession, upon a prolonged period of favourable exchanges and uninterrupted growth of confidence and credit."

theorists, be the shadow of a ground for impugning, in the slightest degree, the management of the Bank. The rate of discount was reduced from 3 $\frac{1}{2}$ per cent to 3 per cent in August 1846: a step which appeared to me at the time, and which I still think was injudicious; but according to the doctrine that the currency should be expanded or diminished with the increase or diminution of the bullion, there was every reason for that reduction; seeing (as I presume the partisans of that theory begin now to see) that it is only through the rate of interest that the Directors could act at all. The amount of bullion in the Bank had been steadily increasing for several months, and had, on the 29th of August, reached 16,366,068*l*., being within a trifle of the highest amount it had ever attained. According to that doctrine, therefore, there can be no question that the reduction of the rate of discount was a proper measure. Or even regarding them simply as bankers, and looking only at their reserve, it amounted to 10,000,000*l*., being more than it had been for a considerable time. There is, therefore, no ground on which the partisans of the act of 1844 can, consistently with their doctrines, call in question the management of the Bank until January 1847. The whole of the criticism which has, with so much severity, been lavished upon the conduct of the Directors, must therefore, in justice, be considered as confined to the period following January 1847.

According to the view thus far taken (that is, from September 1844, to January 1847) of the operation of the act of 1844, it may be held to be demonstrable that it did not, and indeed could not, work, in any way that, by the most zealous of the admirers of it, could be construed as being beneficial. While, as I have shown, there is every reason, on reference to the facts of the case, to believe that it operated prejudicially.

SECTION 17 *On the operation of the act of 1844 in the year 1847*

In the interval between the 21st of January, 1847, when the Bank rate of discount was raised to 4 per cent, and the 8th of April, when it was further advanced to 5 per cent, the bullion, in the two departments of the Bank, experienced a considerable reduction; the reserve in the banking department sustaining by much the greatest relative diminution.① A decrease of reserve to such an extent, and apparently still in progress, clearly indicated the expediency of a further advance in the Bank rate; and the Directors were much blamed (and not altogether without reason) for not having advanced the rate sooner.

But, in extenuation of whatever want of foresight may be charged to them, in not having raised the rate of interest between January and April, they have to plead that the Chancellor of the Exchequer (who has not been backward in blaming them, and who, from his position had superior means of ascertaining and observing the circumstances leading to the prospect of a further drain on the treasure of the Bank) made the following admission in his speech of the 14th of May last, on the Loan Discount Bill.

"*Even so late as February or March, no one anticipated the severity of*

---

① The following were the exact figures —

Dates.		Total Bullion.		Banking Reserve.
1847.		£		£
23d January	–	13,440,000	–	6,840,000
10th April	–	9,870,000	–	3,460,000
17th April	–	9,330,000	–	3,080,000

The *Reserve* of the 17th April shows the lowest point to which it fell at that time.

pressure which has since taken place, arising, I believe, in no inconsiderable degree from the alarm which was excited in the minds of the public by their observing, in the published account of the Bank of England the small amount of notes in reserve which appeared on the 17th of April."

The first part of the above sentence goes far to exonerate the Bank Directors from having been more wanting in foresight than they would have been under the guidance of a government officer, down to the end of March at least; so that, as the rate of interest was actually raised on the 8th of April, any blame at the hands of the Government can apply only to the delay of a single week.

This extent of delay would have been insignificant under the former system, with upwards of nine millions of bullion. But the urgency of the case, and the severity of the pressure arose, as the Chancellor of the Exchequer truly observed, in no inconsiderable degree (I would add *wholly*) "from the alarm which was excited in the minds of the public, by their observing *the small amount of notes in reserve which appeared on the 17th of April.*"①

There was enough, certainly, to alarm both the public and the Directors; and the cause of alarm, thus candidly admitted by the Chancellor of the Exchequer, constitutes, of itself, sufficient ground for the condemnation of the bill. The small amount of the reserve having alarmed both the Directors and the public, it became imperative, with a view of preventing an entire exhaustion of it, to have recourse to measures of extreme severity.

On the 15th of April, in announcing that 5 per cent per annum was the

---

① If the Bank Directors had exercised more foresight than the Chancellor of the Exchequer seems to have done, and had raised their minimum rate in the early part of February to 5 per cent, and by the middle of that month to $5\frac{1}{2}$ per cent, what would have been his own position with reference to the Irish loan of eight millions?

minimum rate, the mention of the term of ninety-five days was omitted; and this omission was found to mean that the minimum rate applied to bills having only a very few days to run; while much higher rates were charged for bills having more than ten days or a fortnight to elapse before maturity; and, what was felt as a still more severe restriction of accommodation, a limit was applied to the *amount* of bills admitted for discount, however unexceptionable they might be, and however high the credit of the parties offering them. At the same time, merchants who had received advances at the usual quarterly period, were peremptorily called upon to repay the loans without the accommodation of renewal, which had usually been granted, if desired; the bills lodged being, of course, unexceptionable. There is no question of the expediency of the decisive steps thus taken by the Directors, under the urgency of the case; and they were so effectual, that an immediate stop was put to the efflux of bullion; and a sum of about 100,000*l*. in sovereigns, that had actually been shipped for America, was relanded.

No measure of so extreme a character had, I believe, been resorted to by the Bank since December 31, 1795, when public notice was given of a similar restriction. ①

The effect of this severe contraction of accommodation was to paralyse nearly all transactions on credit throughout the country. No merchant or manufacturer, however well stocked his portfolio might be with the most

---

① The following were the terms of the notice of 1795: —

31*st December*, 1795.

"That in future, whenever bills sent in for discount shall, on any day, amount to a larger sum than it shall be resolved to discount on that day, a *pro rata* proportion of such bills in each parcel as are not otherwise objectionable, will he returned to the person sending in the same without regard to the respectability of the party sending in the bills, or the solidity of the bills themselves."

solid bills, could be sure of their being available to meet his immediate engagements, unless at most exorbitant rates of discount. There were instances of rates as high as 12 and 13 per cent per annum being paid for unexceptionable six months' paper; and of similar bills beyond that date not being discountable at all.

To apply the term "panic" to the state of things as it existed during the last three weeks of April, and the first four days of May, would convey a very inadequate idea of the suffering of that period, seeing how indiscriminately that expression, as also the term "crisis," has been applied to comparatively slight cases of pressure. Nothing approaching to the same degree of intensity, not only of immediate pressure, but of alarm for the future, had been experienced since 1825. This alarm, which aggravated all the other causes of distress arose, as the Chancellor of the Exchequer observed, from the narrow margin of the reserve, which the published accounts of the Bank exhibited, week by week, and which led to the apprehension that any further reduction would be attended with a still more forcible restriction, if not a total denial of further accommodation. Lord Ashburton justly remarks upon this state of things,—

"Now this fright of the Bank, with ten millions in her coffers, of violating this parliamentary restraint, has driven her into proceedings which have depreciated, to a very great extent every description of property, food only for evident reasons excepted. It would not be easy to estimate this depreciation, extending over all merchandize, stocks, railroad shares, &c.; it probably would not have been overstated at from 10 to 20 per cent: but what is worse, it has paralysed this property in the hands of the possessors, rendered it unavailable towards meeting their engagements, and thus produced, in many cases, pecuniary sacrifices, much beyond the mere depreciation of the value of property itself. It has further occasioned the suspension of the execution of orders from our customers in every quarter, thus distressing manufacturers, and impeding those very operations which would have corrected the tendency to an unfavourable balance of trade, and given safety to the circulation of the Bank."—(*Financial or Commercial Crisis Considered*, pp. 18, 19.)

It was the fright of the Bank, perfectly justifiable as regarded the defensive measures adopted by the Directors under the operation of the act of 1844, which converted what, in the undivided state of the Bank treasure, need not, and, in all probability, would not have been more than a moderate and sustained pressure on the money market, into panic amounting to agony. And this is the charge against that provision of the bill which, while it appropriated an amount of bullion, much larger than was found to be required, to the issue department, left the deposits and dividends without any security at all.

There was one circumstance attending the pressure, when, at its, greatest height, in April, that puzzled the supporters of the currency theory, and of the act founded upon it, more than any other; and that was, that although the pressure was so severe that it had turned the exchanges, and was bringing back the gold, it had not reduced the amount of the circulation. This perplexing fact was thus noticed by Mr. F. Baring, in the debate of the 3d of December last: —

"So far, therefore, my expectations of the Bill have not been falsified. I wish I could say the same with regard to that third anticipation which I formed. *Amongst other expectations was this, that the Bank would commence their operations earlier; and, by withdrawing their notes gradually from circulation as the gold was withdrawn from the country, the effect upon commercial people would be gradual and cautious.* Under the old system the Bank neglected the signs of the times, and did not take their precautions early enough; the consequence of which was, that when a time of difficulty and danger came, the Bank sought to save itself at the expense of whatever interest it might he which happened to be affected by its acts. My expectation was, that by compelling the Bank to take earlier precautionary steps, and by making that precaution gradual, the country would have been saved from those convulsive efforts which the Bank was accustomed to make, and crises such as these, although they might still occur, would yet be more limited in their operation. *I admit that the expectation has entirely failed.* (Heat, hear.) But still I cannot help feeling that the principle upon which that expectation was founded was correct and true; and the more so, when I look at the operations of the Bank itself. I have avoided troubling the House with statistics; but for the purpose of making myself clear upon this point, I will trespass upon them with an extract, merely requesting the House to observe that I take the figures under the old system. I find, then, that the amount of *bullion* in the Bank, on September 12, 1840, was 16,354,000*l.*, and that on April 17, 1847, it was reduced to 9,330,000*l.*, being a *diminution* of 7,024,000*l.* Now, I take the same dates with respect to the *circulation* of notes, and I find that on September 12, 1846, the amount was 20,982,000*l.*, and on April 17, 1847, it was 21,228,000*l.*, being an increase of 246,000*l.* (Hear, hear.) *Now I do not know what might have been the expectation of my right hon. friend, or of those gentlemen on the opposite benches, who are more acquainted with this subject than I am; but for myself, I must say, that I never entertained the idea that it would have been possible, under the operation of this bill, to have shown such a set of figures as that.* (Hear.) If we could have supposed this possible, when we were in committee in 1840, collecting the evidence upon which the bill was founded — if a case had been brought before us in which, when the bullion had run off 7,000,000*l*., the notes had increased 250,000*l*.—then I should have said not only that that was impossible, but that it was the strongest argument for the alteration of your system, and the strongest reason for a bill founded upon the principles of the right hon. baronet. I know I am told in answer to this that it is all the fault of the Bank. *I believe, if we look back, we shall find that the operation of that question of the reserve was not sufficiently considered, either by those who were favourable, or those who were opposed to the bill. I cannot find in the discussion of the period two sentences leading me to suppose that danger arising from such a cause was contemplated or referred to*, and, in my opinion, the Bank was enabled to do that which it ought not to have done—when gold was running out not to reduce their circulation by a single pound. I do not think that the system works satisfactorily in this respect, and, in fact, the point did not receive anything like a sufficient consideration. Perhaps it was impossible, before the bill was in practical operation, to see how the reserve of notes would operate, *but it certainly never entered into the contemplation of any one then considering the subject, that 7,000,000l. in gold should run off, and yet that the notes in the hands of the public would rather increase than diminish.*"

The admissions contained in this extract, from the speech of Mr Baring, are as important as they are candid; and they fully explain the deep anxiety which was manifested by the supporters of the measure in the early part of 1847, to explain away, by most unsparing animadversions on the Bank management, its palpable failure, as regards any control over the circulation. It is hardly conceivable that the wide difference between the actual working of the measure, and their anticipations of it, should not have struck them all as it did Mr. Baring. The almost inevitable presumption is that they were so struck; but have wanted either the courage or the candour to admit it. Before alluding further, however, to the character of these animadversions, I must be permitted to point out that Mr. Baring is in error in stating that "neither by those who were favourable, nor those who were opposed to the bill," was any expectation entertained or expressed that it would fail to regulate the amount of the outstanding circulation; and that the question of the reserve was not sufficiently considered. I would beg to refer to the work of Mr. Fullarton, and to my own pamphlet of 1844, in proof of the fact, that both these topics received a very full share of attention on the part, at least, of those who were opposed to the measure of that year. It was, in truth, the utter unconsciousness of the currency party of the vital importance of these precise points of the question which excited most astonishment among their opponents.

One of the earliest expressions of disapprobation of the conduct of the Bank was contained in a letter, under the signature of "Mercator," which occupied a very conspicuous place in the *Times* newspaper of the 15th April (1847). Lord John Russell alluded to this letter in the debate of the 3d of December, in the following terms: —

"I do not at present consider whether the Bank should have taken precautions before the month of April last; but in the month of April, a very remarkable letter having appeared in *The Times* newspaper, showing the continued drain of gold that was going on, and that it all operated on the reserve of the Bank, and in no way on the discounts or circulation, the Bank Directors immediately began to change their course. To a great extent they limited their discounts, and the circulation was diminished from the month of April to the beginning of June by about 1,500,000*l.*"

In consequence of the allusion thus made to that letter by Lord John Russell, and the important effect on the Bank management which he attributed to it, I was induced to refer to a file of the "Times," and have made the following extract from it. This extract contains all that is material of the letter, pointing out, as it does, *the three courses that were open to* the Bank, and animadverting on the management for not having adopted that which was most suited to the occasion.

"From the beginning of January the drain of bullion assumed a more serious aspect; and, of course, as the bullion was drawn from the Bank the notes at the command of the Bank would be diminished to an equal amount. It became incumbent upon the Bank, therefore, to look seriously at its position, and to form a determinate judgment as to the principle upon which it would regulate its banking operations. *Three courses were open to it*: —

"1. It might determine to meet the drain of bullion by a diminution of the notes in the hands of the public to the same amount, and thus retain its banking reserve undiminished. But the banking reserve was at this time at a high amount, such as would safely admit of some reasonable reduction. This course, therefore, would have caused more, sudden and severe pressure on the money market and the state of credit than was necessary; and the Bank was entitled so to conduct its banking operations as to throw a portion of the contraction of notes rendered imperative by the decrease of bullion upon its banking reserve.

"2. It might make the necessary contraction of notes fall partly upon that portion of the notes which were in the hands of the public and partly upon its banking reserve. This is the course which the Bank, acting in obedience to the rules of ordinary prudence in the management of banking operations, ought to have pursued. Had it done so, a pressure upon the money market and upon credit would have been produced, commencing simultaneously with the drain of bullion, acting steadily and equably, and necessarily increasing in power as the drain of bullion progressed. By this means it can hardly be doubted that the drain of bullion would have been gradually restrained and regulated, and the adverse state of the exchanges corrected, without the necessity for any sudden or violent action by which alarm may be created or the regular course of transactions be seriously disturbed.

"3. It might determine that the necessary contraction should fall entirely upon its banking reserve, thus keeping the notes in the hands of the public undiminished during a heavy drain of bullion. This is the course which the Bank has pursued up to the present time. It has permitted an enormous reduction of its banking reserve to take place, whilst its deposits and its notes in the hands of the public — that is to say, its liabilities — have remained undiminished This has occurred, moreover, during a heavy drain of bullion, and in a period of enormous imports, accompanied with every indication of a prolonged continuance of the adverse balance of trade. It is needless to observe that this course of procedure is in opposition to all ordinary rules of prudence in the conduct of banking operations. This mismanagement of its banking business by a concern of immense magnitude has been productive of its natural results — inconvenience and injury to the public interest. The natural tendency of money to rise in value during a drain of bullion has been checked, and from this circumstance, as also from the absence of any decrease of notes in the hands of the public, the full benefit which might have arisen from a more early and gradual correction of the drain of bullion has not been secured. This is the result of inconsiderate measures in its banking department by a concern whose resources and operations are of such disproportionate magnitude to those of any other concern, as to render them formidably powerful for good or for evil in their effects upon the general state of credit and of commercial transactions. The provisions, however, of Peel's bill for securing the convertibility of the Bank note still remain in unimpaired force. The conduct of the Bank in its banking department cannot invalidate the efficiency of those provisions, although it may to some considerable extent affect the degree of inconvenience and pressure which will arise under their operation."

In stating that there were *three courses open to the Bank*, the writer must mean that the Directors had not only the *option* but the *power* to act upon any one of them, *directly and exclusively*, according as it might suit their views. Believing, therefore, according to the currency doctrine, that it was, under the circumstances, incumbent on the Bank to contract its *circulation*, he blames the Directors for having pursued the course No. 3, instead of No. 2, which alone, he contends, was adapted to the occasion.

The assumption of *these three courses* being open to the Bank, offers an excellent opportunity of rediscussing the currency theory. As, however, I have already, in the preceding pages, gone through this task, I shall not weary my readers with a repetition of it, but leave it to the committees of the Lords and Commons already appointed, to inquire, if they think fit, into the grounds for the opinions thus confidently expressed.

After the first week of May there was a sensible abatement of the pressure. The Bank reserve was increased, and some addition, though small, was made to the stock of bullion in the two departments; and the directors became more liberal in their accommodation. The announcement too, which had been recently received, of the intention of the Russian government to invest a portion of its treasure, to the extent of thirty millions of silver rubles, (4,750,000*l*.,)[①] chiefly in the public funds of France and England, removed the apprehension that the large forthcoming supplies of corn from Russia might create an adverse balance of payments, and a consequent renewed export of bullion from this country. And although the prices of corn were still advancing, as they had been through the greater part of the period of pressure, the season was favourable for the growing crops, and there was therefore less alarm than there had been about the prospect of the ensuing harvest. Towards the end of May, in consequence of large importations, the prices of corn gave way considerably.

These circumstances tended to restore confidence to some extent. By the close of May, the period of great pressure and derangement of the money market, in as far as alarm was an operative cause of it, might be considered to have terminated. And with reference to this period, it may be remarked, as a curious fact, that intensely severe as the pressure was, it was not attended with any commercial discredit. There were no failures; or none that attracted any public attention. This absence of failures gave an appearance of soundness to the state of credit at that time, which the events of a few months later proved to have been deceptive; and it is certainly somewhat difficult to understand how so many of the houses, which fell in September and October, stood their ground through the shock in April. As to some of them, it is not improbable that the very high rate of interest they had to pay, and the immense losses incurred by forced sales of produce, and other property, in order to meet their engagements during the period here alluded to, weakened them so much, as to render them unable to stand a second

① It is supposed that this sum includes about 1,500,000*l*., invested in French rentes, in March previous.

shock. I would be understood, however, merely to notice the circumstance of the absence of failures during the period in question, as a singular fact, without pretending to have the means of satisfactorily accounting for it.

Although, at the end of May all, or nearly all, the immediate causes of the monetary derangement which had characterized the period in question had ceased, the rate of interest, both at the Bank of England, and in Lombard Street, did not fall to the level from which it had risen in the two preceding months. The continued demand for capital by the railway companies, in the shape of calls and loans was, of itself, a sufficient cause for a higher rate①.

① Considering the prominence which has been given to the subject of the railway expenditure, it may be worth while to reduce to a tabular form the official statement of the amount of that expenditure, given by the Chancellor of the Exchequer on introducing the bill for regulating railway companies, on the 26th November, 1847. It is necessary to say in explanation of the last column of the following table, that it represents the gross expenditure diminished by *one-fifth*, that being the estimated proportion of the *gross* expenditure which is absorbed by the purchase of land, and the parliamentary expenses. The remaining fourfifths may be taken to represent the *bonâ fide* outlay on labour and materials.

Years.	Capital authorised to be raised.	Capital expended.	Expenditure less one-fifth, leaving as actual outlay on labour and materials.
	£	£	£
1840 – –	4,000,000	—	—
1841 – –	3,500,000	1,470,000	1,176,000
1842 – –	6,000,000	2,980,000	2,384,000
1843 – –	4,500,000	4,435,000	3,548,000
1844 – –	18,000,000	6,100,000	4,880,000
1845 1st half year	59,000,000	3,500,000	2,800,000
2d —		10,600,000	8,480,000
1846 1st —	124,000,000	9,800,000	7,840,000
2d —		26,685,000	21,348,000
1847 1st —	38,000,000	25,700,000	20,560,000
2d —		—	—
	257,000,000	91,270,000	73,016,000

There was, moreover, as connected with the railways, an uneasy feeling prevalent, arising from the enormous extent to which the prospective outlay on them was proceeding. And, in other directions, there were no clear grounds of confidence in looking to the future. As the period of the payment of the July dividends approached, apprehensions began again to prevail with reference to the effect which that payment would have upon the Bank reserve. And when, at the end of July, it was found that a very decided reduction of it[①] had taken place, while the exchanges were wavering about par, there were strong indications of a tendency to renewed pressure. In order to repress the rising demand for advances, the Bank, somewhat out of its usual course, gave, on Monday, the 2nd of August, a semi-official intimation that, in future, the rates would be 5 per cent on bills having one month or less to run, $5\frac{1}{2}$ per cent on two months' bills, and 6 per cent for longer dated paper, not exceeding 95 days. On the following Thursday, the 5th of August, these measures were confirmed, and a formal notice issued that the *minimum* rate was advanced from 5 to $5\frac{1}{2}$ per cent per annum. This movement of the Bank had a considerable effect in raising the general terms of accommodation.

The next alteration of the Bank rate of interest was on the 2nd of September, when the directors announced that they would make the usual quarterly advances till the 14th of October, at 5 per cent per annum. This was followed on the 23rd of September, by a notice, of some stringency, raising the *minimum* rate on two months' bills to $5\frac{1}{2}$, and on three months bills to 6 per cent. This alteration produced a very decisive effect, and may

① 19th June, Bank notes and coin – £ 6,540,000
31st July, Bank notes and coin – 4,440,000

be described as the virtual commencement of the pressure of October. Consols, which had stood at 86 $\frac{1}{2}$, fell very rapidly to 85, and there was a palpable rise in the market rate of interest. On the 25th of September, the banking reserve had fallen to 4,704,000*l*.; and on the 1st of October, the directors adopted very stringent means for the protection of this fund. They intimated that 5 $\frac{1}{2}$ per cent would be the *minimum* rate on all bills falling due before the 15th of October; and further, that they declined *altogether* to make advances on Stock or Exchequer bills. The latter clause of the intimation produced violent excitement on the Stock Exchange.

"The effect of the announcement," says the *Economist*, of Saturday, the 9th of October, "made by the Bank on Friday last, viz., that no further advances would be made on public securities, produced a severe panic on the Stock Exchange, on Monday and Tuesday (4th and 5th Oct.). Large orders were received, both from town and country bankers, to sell consols and exchequer bills in order to convert them into money. On Tuesday the pressure became so great, that while the price of consols was 84 $\frac{1}{2}$ for the account, due on the 14th October, that for present money was only 83 $\frac{1}{2}$, which difference indicated a rate of interest of 50 per cent per annum, for the nine days; while exchequer bills were currently sold at 30*s*. discount, and in some cases at 35*s*., indicating a rate of interest of 7 $\frac{1}{2}$ per cent, per annum, for the six months which they have yet to run. The rate of depreciation continued even greater on Wednesday morning at the opening of business, exchequer bills having been sold at 37*s*. discount, when the Bank intimated their willingness to advance on these securities to a limited amount, which immediately gave ease to the market, so that at the close of that day they left off at 23*s*. to 17*s*. discount."

During the occurrence of these events a new and very important cause of monetary derangement came into operation, namely, commercial discredit. This began with failures in the corn trade, following each other, in rapid succession, from the 6th of August to the end of that month, and exceeding, in amount, any thing of the kind that had ever been experienced before in Mark Lane. It was still, however, considered that, with the exception of this branch of trade, (the losses in which, by the enormous fall in the prices of corn, accounted for the failures,) the general commerce of the country was in a sound state. But this impression was doomed to be lamentably dispelled by the events of the two months following. On the 10th of September, the stoppage of the house of Gower, Nephews, and Co. was announced; and this was followed by the successive fall of several other firms, of great importance from the extent of their connections and the vast amount of their liabilities, during the remainder of September and part of October. These *mercantile* failures, in number, and in the amount of property involved in them, were beyond all precedent in the commercial history of this country.

There was no failure of a bank (except the unimportant firm of Cockburns and Co., of Whitehall,) till the 13th of October, when the suspension of the Abingdon Old Bank (Knapp and Co.) was announced. This, however, was speedily followed by others. Much alarm was excited on Monday, the 18th, by the stoppage of the Royal Bank of Liverpool; a concern having a paid up capital of 800,000*l*., and standing in the first rank among the banking institutions of the kingdom. The immediate consequence of this event was to send down the price of consols 2 per cent, or from $79\frac{7}{8}$ to $77\frac{3}{4}$, which was the lowest point to which they fell. In the course of the following five days, other important bank failures took place at Liverpool,

Manchester, Newcastle, and in the West of England. At Newcastle, the banking discredit was exceedingly severe, and the most important bank of the district had a very narrow escape from a suspension of payments.

The course of commercial events, from the beginning of August to the week ending the 23rd of October, thus proceeded in an uninterrupted progression of disaster, discredit, and dismay. At the close of that week, all circumstances tended to what is termed a crisis; not such a crisis as, by profanation of the term, has been applied to comparatively slight cases, but to so critical a state of things as threatened to involve a total suspension of all business and of all payments.

The reserve of the Bank of England had been reduced below two millions, being less by one million than its lowest point in April, against more than thirteen millions of liabilities. ① It was then quite upon the cards that a few days more of the prevailing alarm, which was causing a general hoarding of bank notes and coin, might exhaust it altogether; thus realizing the predictions of those who, with myself, had pointed out, as a not

① The following figures will show the amount of banking reserve and deposits on the days indicated. —

Dates.				Reserve.		Deposits.
1847.				£		£
16th Oct.	–	–	–	3,070,000	–	14,160,000
23rd Oct.	–	–	–	1,990,000	–	13,340,000
30th Oct.	–	–	–	1,600,000	–	13,600,000

Consols were at something above 79; exchequer bills at between 20*s*. and 30*s*. discount; bank stock at 178 to 180; and the difficulty of obtaining discounts in Lombard Street so great, that rates of interest of almost incredible extravagance were readily given upon first-rate paper having only a few days to run. In confirmation of this latter statement, I may mention a circumstance which fell under my own immediate observation. On Thursday, the 21st October, I happen to know that for the discount of about 10,000*l*. of City bankers' acceptances, having not more than seven days before maturity, a rate of interest and commission was paid equal to 13 per cent per annum.

improbable effect of the act, *if strictly enforced*, as it was intended to be, that the ridiculous, although lamentable catastrophe, might be witnessed, of the banking department being compelled to stop payment, while there were more than six millions of bullion in the issue department. Any further reduction, it was then manifest, must drive the directors to still more desperate measures, even to a denial of all discounts and advances whatever, and further, possibly, to making forced sales of government securities.

During the progress of things to this critical state, representations and remonstrances, whether by deputations, or memorials, or petitions, were in vain urged upon the Chancellor of the Exchequer, to induce some relaxation of the obnoxious law. He was inexorable. The very important deputation of merchants from Liverpool, which waited upon *ministers* on Tuesday, the 19th, was dismissed without the least indication of any intention on the part of government to interfere. *So perfect a measure as the act of 1844 could not be in fault*, and no alteration of it, therefore, was to be thought of. It was not until Friday, the 22nd, or Saturday, the 23rd of October, that, at an interview of some of the leading City bankers with the head of the government, such a picture was drawn by them of the fearful consequences to be apprehended from further persistence in maintaining the existing restriction; and these statements were so forcibly corroborated by the alarming intelligence from Newcastle, that the desired relaxation was at length conceded.

Early on Monday, the 25th of October, a letter was addressed, by the First Lord of the Treasury and the Chancellor of the Exchequer, to the Governor and Deputy Governor of the Bank, recommending to the directors to enlarge the amount of their discounts and advances upon approved security, but suggesting that the rate of interest should not be less than 8 per cent. ; and undertaking to obtain an indemnity from Parliament should this course lead to any infringement of the existing law.

Injudiciously conceived, and ungraciously expressed, as were the terms in which this relaxation was granted by the government, it was effectual for its main purpose. The barrier which had cut off the resource of the bullion in the issue department from the banking department, having thus been removed, all that part of the pressure and distress, which had prevailed for some weeks, arising from alarm at the smallness of the Bank reserve, ceased immediately. Hoards of Bank notes and coin came forth, and although the rate of interest continued high, there was an end of the extravagant rates which had, in some instances, been charged; and merchants had an assurance, which they had not before, that what good bills they were in possession of would, although beyond Bank time, be available to meet their engagements. The immediate relief, thus produced, while it fully justifies the government in having sanctioned a contingent infringement of the law, is the crowning proof of the impolicy of the act of 1844.

Were the occasion less grave, it would be calculated to excite a smile to observe the great anxiety of ministers to justify their sanction of a contingent infringement of the law, when the real, and, as I conceive, the unanswerable charge against them, was that of having withheld it too long. The justification urged by the Chancellor of the Exchequer, in his speech in the debate of the 30th of November, affords grounds for the severest condemnation, not only of the act of 1844, but also of the delay of government in affording the only relief from its operation that could be effectual. The description given in that speech of the state of things from the 2nd to the 23rd of October, and of the immediate consequences of the letter of the 25th, is so graphic, and, at the same time, has so much of the stamp of authority for the facts, while it fully bears out my view of them, that I am induced here to extract the following passages from it.

"When I came to London on the 2nd of October, I found the whole city in a state of the greatest excitement and alarm. For one day, the continuation was at the rate of 60 per cent per annum. I certainly never passed through so painful and anxious a period as the three weeks which succeeded that day. My time was occupied in seeing persons of all descriptions from the moment I came down in the morning until I went to bed at night. Parties came to me, and represented that it was perfectly impossible that the loans could be repaid to the Bank; that if the Bank relied upon such repayment for the payment of the dividends, they would be disappointed; that the Bank dared not sell the securities on which the advances had been made, and consequently, that it was impossible that the public credit could be maintained during the next week. What, however, was the fact? The next week came, and the loans were repaid almost without an exception. ① During the whole of this period, the Governor and Deputy-Governor of the Bank acted with extreme prudence and discretion, in dealing with these loans, and it is satisfactory to know that, on the whole, they were very punctually paid; it is also a most remarkable thing, that at this period to which I am alluding, the Bank notes taken out of the Bank in the first four days of the payment of the dividends, exceeded only by 300,000*l*. the amount taken out in the four corresponding days of the preceding year. It is an extraordinary fact, that in such a crisis, when the

① If it is meant by this remark of the Chancellor of the Exchequer that the representations were exaggerated, the simple answer is, that alarm is prone to exaggeration; and the very alarm here described formed a very important symptom of the disease for which the remedy was then sought.

need of additional *Bank notes is represented to have been so extreme*, *parties who might have claimed* 7,000,000*l*. *from the Bank during these four days*, *drew only* 300,000*l*. more than had been drawn in the four corresponding days in 1846.[①] Thus ended the week of the dividends. On the following Monday the failure of the Royal Bank of Liverpool took place, and the intelligence reached London just at the moment when a better state of feeling was beginning to exhibit itself. The failure of that bank is obviously attributable to gross mismanagement. With a paid up capital of little more than 600,000*l*., they lent, if I remember correctly, no less than 500,000*l*. to one house. Great apprehension was entertained also respecting an eminent broker at Liverpool, who, however, succeeded in obtaining assistance from the Bank of England. On the Thursday of this week, so far as London alone was concerned, there was every appearance of a somewhat better state of things, but there was a very great change in the character of the accounts from the country. The country had always been the greatest cause of apprehension, and on the Thursday, Friday, and Saturday, the accounts were very alarming. Another bank at Liverpool, called, I think, the North and South Wales Bank, failed, and much anxiety was felt respecting others, more especially those in commercial districts; for, except in one or two instances, the banks in agricultural districts were comparatively easy. A bank at Abingdon, and another in the West of England, however, failed, the latter of which it appears will be unable to pay more than a small dividend. Other failures also occurred elsewhere. Intelligence of the failure of a large bank, the

① Is it possible to give a more striking instance of the fallacy of all the reasonings of the currency theorists on the importance attached to the *amount* of the note circulation as an efficient cause of any of the phenomena of trade, and credit, and prices?

Union bank at Newcastle, was received on the Thursday, and this caused a severe run on the District Bank in that town.

"Allusion was made on a former evening to the manner in which it is supposed that this bank obtained assistance, in consequence of the interference of the government; but I can only state that Mr. Richardson, the manager of that bank, came up to London to solicit assistance from the Bank of England, and returned *without having obtained it.* That in itself is sufficient to satisfy any person that the case of that establishment was not recommended to the favourable consideration of the Bank of England by the government. It is true that the bank was assisted to a large amount by the branch Bank of England at Newcastle, the manager of which was Mr. Grote, the brother of the gentleman of that name whom many gentlemen remember with pleasure as a member of this house. Mr. Grote, fearful of *the ruin* which the possible suspension of the District Bank might cause in the neighbourhood, *took on himself the responsibility of affording it*[①], *to a very large extent, by advances on the securities which they placed in his hands, the means of meeting a formidable run which was made upon it on Friday and the early part of Saturday.* The measure was quite successful, and in the afternoon of Saturday many of the parties who had drawn out their money came to the bank and tendered it again in deposit, and the credit of the bank, of whose ultimate solvency there never could be a

① What a reflection is this upon the Act of 1844, and upon the reluctance of government to interfere! Sir Charles Wood takes credit for the fact that the government did not recommend the case of the District Bank of Newcastle to the favourable consideration of the Bank of England; and he admits that but for the boldness of Mr. Grote, the manager of the branch of the Bank of England at Newcastle, the District Bank would probably have failed—a failure which at that critical moment would have caused ruin and confusion in that populous and important neighbourhood.

doubt, was re-established. About this time the sense of danger was seriously aggravated by *an application for assistance to the Bank of England from some Scotch banks.* It has always been supposed that the banks in that country rested upon so safe a footing that they were able to take care of themselves, and that, consequently, it would never be necessary for them to seek for assistance from the Bank of England; but on this occasion the application was made, and certainly the statement laid before the Bank was of a nature to excite alarm; because, looking to the enormous amount of the deposits in the Scotch banks, however solid and sure may be the ultimate security of those establishments, the temporary embarrassment of any portion of them could not have failed seriously to aggravate the existing pressure in this country. The Bank of England was pressed directly for assistance from all parts of the country, and indirectly through the London bankers, who were called upon to support their country correspondents. The country banks required a large amount of notes to render them secure against possible demands, not so much for payment of their notes, as of their deposits. Houses in London were applying constantly to the Bank for aid. Two bill-brokers had stopped, and the operations of two others were nearly paralysed. The whole demand for discount was thrown upon the hands of the Bank of England. Notwithstanding this, the Bank, as I before said, never refused a bill which it would have discounted at another time, but still the large mass of bills which under ordinary circumstances are discounted by bill-brokers, could not be negotiated.

" During this period we were daily, I may say almost hourly, in possession of the state of the Bank. The Governor and Deputy-Governor at last said that they could no longer continue their advances to support the various parties who applied to them, that they could save themselves, that is, they could comply with the law, but that they could not do so without pressing more stringently upon the commercial world.

"At this crisis a feeling as to the necessity of the interposition of government appeared to be generally entertained, and those conversant with commercial affairs, and least likely to decide in favour of the course which we ultimately adopted, unanimously expressed an opinion, that if some measures were not taken by the government to arrest the evil, the most disastrous consequences must inevitably ensue. Evidence was laid before the government which proved not only the existence of severe pressure from the causes which I have stated, but also that it was aggravated in a very great degree by the hoarding on the part of many persons of gold and Bank notes to a very large extent, in consequence of which an amount of circulation, which under ordinary circumstances would have been adequate, became insufficient for the wants of the country.

"It was difficult to establish this beforehand; but the best proof of the fact is in what occurred after we interfered. As soon as the letter of the 25th of October appeared, and the panic ceased, thousands and tens of thousands of pounds were taken from the hoards, some from boxes deposited with bankers, although the parties would not leave the notes in their bankers' hands. Large parcels of notes were returned to the Bank of England cut into halves, as they had been sent down into the country, and so small was the real demand for an additional quantity of notes, that the whole amount taken from the Bank, when the unlimited power of issue was given, was under 400,000*l*. The restoration of confidence released notes from their hoards, and no more was wanted, for this trifling quantity of additional notes is hardly worth notice. I think, therefore, that I am fully borne out in the assertion, that the notes in the hands of the public were amply sufficient for the purposes of trade, but that their circulation was paralysed by panic; and this was the general purport of the representation which we received. Parties of every description made application to us for assistance, with the observation, 'We do not want notes, but give us confidence.' They said, 'We have notes enough, but we have not confidence to use them; say you will stand by us, and we shall have all that we want; do anything, in short, that will give us confidence. If we think that we can get Bank notes, we shall not want them. Charge any rate of interest you please, ask what you like.'

"Mr. Spooner: 'No, no.'

"The Chancellor of the Exchequer: I beg pardon of the honourable gentleman, but I may be permitted to know what was actually said to me. I say that what I have stated was the tenor of the applications made to me. Parties said, 'Let us have notes, charge ten, twelve per cent. for them — we don't care what the rate of interest is —*we don't mean indeed to take the notes, because we shall not want them — only tell us that we can get them, and this will at once restore confidence.*'

"We have been asked, what was the change of circumstances which induced us to act on Saturday, when we declined acting a day or two before. I reply, that the accounts which we received on Thursday, Friday, and Saturday, were of a totally different description from those which had been previously brought to us, and we were convinced that at length the time had arrived when, in the words of Mr. Huskisson, in the pamphlet to which I have already referred, 'the stagnant and straitened circulation of the country wanted life and aid, and became every day more embarrassed, whilst each new calamity, produced by such a state of things, contributed to spread and increase the general apprehension.' It was on Saturday, and not before, that this conviction was forced upon us, and it was not till then that we felt it necessary to sanction a violation of the law. I took the greatest pains to sift the accuracy of the statements which were made to me. *I do riot wish to deny that I was most unwilling and reluctant to interfere, but I felt that I* should be utterly unworthy of the office which I have the honour to hold, if when the conviction was forced upon me that interference was for the public good, I had hesitated for one instant to do what I believed to be right in consequence of any opinions which I might have formerly expressed.

"Having determined to act, there was, of course, the question in what mode we should carry our intentions into effect. I do not mean that this question had to be considered after we had determined to act, for very soon after my arrival in town it became my duty to consider the matter, and we — that is my noble fiend and myself—had made up our minds as to the best course of action. I should have been glad if we could have taken any course which would have been equally efficacious *without running the risk of infringing the Act of* 1844."

The description thus given by Sir Charles Wood of the imminent perils which awaited any further delay, and of the relief which so immediately attended the application of the remedy, was evidently intended to reconcile the more fanatical of the adherents of the Act of 1844 to the necessity of a conditional suspension of its provisions. And their acquiescence was very reluctantly granted. During the height of the pressure, their language had been that of exhortation to the government to be firm in its resistance to all application for relaxation. They contended that, as the existing distress arose from the extraordinary expenditure upon railways, followed by the failure of the potato crop, entailing a great loss of the national capital, no interference of government could immediately supply that loss by the creation of fresh capital; that it might, indeed, authorise the Bank to create more notes, but that the effect of thus creating and issuing more "paper money" would only be to reanimate speculation in railways, and to raise prices, and by withdrawing gold from the issue department, to endanger the convertibility of Bank notes. And that as to the existing discredit, the numerous failures which had occurred were the legitimate consequences of overtrading; and that to invoke a cessation or abatement of the hurricane then raging in the commercial world, would, if the prayer were granted, only delay the fall of houses which, for the common good, ought to fall.

The late Mr. Windham, who was secretary at war many years ago, is reported to have exclaimed — I forget the precise occasion — "Perish Commerce, live the Constitution!" The language held by some of the currency theorists on this occasion, might not unfairly be construed into "Perish Commerce, live the Act of 1844!"

To the first, of these objections to interference, the simple answer was, that though the government could not create capital, it might release that which was withheld from use by the Act of 1844, in the issue department. And the event proves that none of the evils predicted followed the temporary removal of the restriction.

With regard to the second objection, it may be observed that the letter of the 25th of October, which stilled the storm, did not save weak, or even preserve from failure, or difficulty, some solvent, houses: — witness the failures and difficulties which unfortunately marked the month following the 25th of October. On the other hand, there cannot, I imagine, be the shadow of a doubt that, if that relaxation had been withheld, there would have been, during the week commencing on that day, a state of things exceeding in the intensity of mercantile and banking derangement and distress even that which was felt during the memorable week following the 12th of December, 1825, of which I shall have to give an account in the following section.

Sir Charles Wood, in his speech of the 30th of November, entered into an elaborate statement of the causes which had led to the extensive failures which so disastrously marked the period from the beginning of August to the end of November.① In the main part of his exposition of those causes I am disposed to concur. There can be no doubt that the previous facilities of the money market, or, in other words, of banking accommodation, led to an unsound state of credit; and in no branch of the commerce of the country has the extension and abuse of credit been more signally exhibited, or attended with more disastrous results, than in the East India trade. There appeared in the *Manchester Guardian* of the 24th of November a very striking account of the manner in which that trade had, of late, been conducted. The whole of the article is too long for insertion, but the following extract from it will suffice for a general view.

"The India trade has been one huge system of credit. If goods were bought in Manchester, by a house in London, they were paid for by bills at six months' date; and, as soon as shipped, an advance was obtained again by a bill at six months for a large part of the first cost, by the consignee, who, again, in his turn, not unfrequently drew upon the house in India, against the bills of lading when transmitted. The shipper and the consignee

① In the November number of the *Bankers' Magazine*, page 587, it is estimated that from the commencement of the month of August last, the total amount of liabilities which would have to be liquidated under the inspection of creditors, amounted to 17,000,000*l*. Other computations have been made, which raise the estimate above 20 millions.

were thus both put in possession of funds, months before they actually paid for the goods; and, very commonly, these bills were renewed at maturity, on pretence of affording time for the returns in a 'long trade.' Moreover, losses by such a trade, instead of leading to its contraction, led directly to its increase. The poorer men became, the greater need they had to purchase, in order to make up, by new advances, the capital they had lost on the past adventures. Purchases thus became, not a question of supply and demand, but the most important part of the finance operations of a firm labouring under difficulties.

"But this is only one side of the picture. What took place in reference to the export of goods at home, was taking place in the purchase and shipment of produce abroad. Houses in India, who had credit to pass their bills, were purchasers of sugar, indigo, silk, or cotton,— not because the prices advised from London by the last overland mail promised a profit on the prices current in India, but because former drafts upon the London house would soon fall due, and must be provided for. What way so simple as to purchase a cargo of sugar, pay for it in bills upon the London house at ten months' date, transmit, the shipping documents by the overland mail; and, in less than two months, the goods on the high seas, or perhaps not yet passed the mouth of the Hoogly, were pawned in Lombard Street, — putting the London house in funds *eight* months before the drafts against those goods fell due. And all this went on without interruption or difficulty, as long as bill brokers had abundance of money 'at call,' to advance on bills of lading and dock warrants, and to discount, without limit, the bills of India houses drawn upon the eminent firms in Mincing Lane. But the first breath of discredit, the first great scarcity of money, has thrown the entire system into eonfusion. The first link that broke shattered the whole chain to pieces. But we fear, that in the fall, many houses deserving a better fate, actuated by more legitimate and *bonâ fide* motives, have been carried away in the common wreck."

That there has also been a great deal of recklessness in other branches of trade, has been made but too manifest by the painful disclosures to which so many of the late failures have led; and that business, so conducted, must inevitably have a ruinous result cannot but be admitted. Accordingly, Sir Charles Wood is quite triumphant in replying to the persons whom he considers as asserting "that those failures were occasioned *solely* by the stringent operation of the Act of 1844." But I have never heard any one having the slightest acquaintance with commercial affairs allege *that* as the sole, or originating, cause of the extensive failures which have recently occurred. He is, therefore, when rebutting that charge, fighting with a shadow, — a very convenient mode, according to approved parliamentary tactics, of diverting attention from a weak point. The charge against the act is not that it was the originating cause, but that it greatly *aggravated* the operation of all the other existing causes of commercial failures and distress. And it would pass my comprehension to conceive how any person of competent understanding and knowledge could doubt that such must have been its effect, were it not that I am fully aware of the operation of a sectarian feeling for a theory, in blinding those who are under its influence to the most palpable evidence of reasoning and facts, if these are found to militate with the doctrines of the sect.

According to the view which I have endeavoured to present, and which, I believe, to be perfectly correct, the operation of the Act has been to convert what would have been a moderate rise in the rate of interest, in April last, into an intense degree of panic, entailing most ruinous sacrifices of property. These sacrifices must have fallen with peculiar weight on the houses which stood most in need of credit at that critical period, and cannot have failed to deepen the insolvency of those which were then insolvent, and also to weaken many which were solvent at that time, in such a degree, as to insure their fall in the second, and still more violent shock in the autumn; so that, in that second shock, which was distinctly attributable to the absurd provisions of the Act, several houses fell which otherwise would have stood.

Without, however, dwelling more upon these points at present, I propose to institute a comparison between the monetary derangement which has so fatally characterized the year 1847, with the ever memorable one of 1825. Lord Ashburton, writing in May last, when the phenomena of the shock just then subsiding were alone under observation, expressed his opinion that there were strong traits of resemblance between 1825 and 1847. Whatever may then have been the points of similarity, they are much more numerous, and strongly marked, now that we have the lamentable features of the commercial distress of last autumn to add to the picture.

SECTION 18 *Comparison of the crises of 1825 and 1847*

In 1825 there was only one period of panic.

In 1847 there were two such periods, broadly distinguished.

In 1825 the Bank of England did not vary its rate of discount from 4 per cent per annum (for all admissible paper), nor the term of the bills, during the whole progress of the drain upon its treasure, till the 13th of December, when the rate was raised to 5 per cent per annum; but this advance was accompanied by an extraordinary extension of the amount of accommodation.

In 1847 the Bank of England varied its rate of discount thirteen times①;

① The following is a statement of the alterations of the Bank rate of interest in the course of 1847. On the 1st of January, 1847, the notice of the 27th August, 1846, fixing the minimum rate at 3 per cent per annum on 95 days' bills was still in force: —

	1847.	Per cent. per ann.	
1.	14th Jan.	$3\frac{1}{2}$	minimum on 95 days' bills.
2.	21st Jan.	4	……
3.	8th Apr.	5	……
4.	15th Apr.	5	omitting all stipulation as to the term of the paper.
5.	2nd Aug.	5	on 1 month bills; $5\frac{1}{2}$ on 2 months; 6 per cent above 2 months.
6.	5th Aug.	$5\frac{1}{2}$	minimum rate.
7.	2nd Sep.	5	on loans till 14th Oct.
8.	23rd Sep.	$5\frac{1}{2}$	on 2 months' bills; 6 per cent on 3 months.
9.	1st Oct.	$5\frac{1}{2}$	on every thing falling due before 14th Oct.; and total refusal to advance on public securities.
10.	25th Oct.	8	minimum rate under authority of the government letter of this date.
11.	22nd Nov.	7	minimum rate.
12.	2nd Dec.	6	……
13.	23rd Dec.	5	……

And on the 27th of Jan., 1848, the minimum rate was reduced to *four* per cent.

but the published rate was only a minimum, and the variations of the actual rate charged, according to the number of days the bills had to run, (in no case exceeding ninety-five,) and their quality, were doubtless much more numerous; and, at one time, the total amount of paper, admissible for discount, was limited. And in several of the instances, the rise of rate was accompanied by restrictive conditions.

In 1825 the speculations were for the most part in loans and mining adventures, and other investments *abroad.*

In 1847 the speculations were chiefly directed to railways and other projected improvements at *home*.

In 1825 there was no importation, or none worth mentioning, of foreign corn; but notwithstanding the absence of this, which has been the frequent cause of a demand for gold for exportation, the foreign exchanges were so much depressed as to be the cause of a nearly continuous drain on the bullion of the Bank till near the end of the summer of that year.

In 1847 the importations of corn, flour, and meal were of unprecedented magnitude and value, and were the immediate cause of the depression of the exchanges, which led to a sudden and great demand for gold for exportation. This ceased by the end of April, and was slightly renewed in July and August, but thenceforth ceased altogether.

In 1825 the foreign drain was not counteracted by any operation of the Bank Directors①, which I am ready to admit that it ought to have been. It was suffered to run its course; and might therefore be said to have ceased of its own accord; that is, by simple efflux, towards the close of the summer.

① Unless the sale of about one million in exchequer bills in September be considered in that light.

See Mr. Harman's evidence, Bank Charter Report, 1832.

In 1847 the foreign drain was counteracted by the most violent efforts of the Bank of England; and ceased after the early part of August.

The two periods agree in the circumstance that, after the demand for gold for exportation had ceased, there supervened a drain upon the bullion in the Bank by an internal demand for gold.

In 1825 banking failures, and a state of commercial discredit, preceded and formed the earlier stage of the panic. ①

In 1847 the panic of April was not preceded, or accompanied, or immediately followed by mercantile or banking failures, or by any appearance of commercial discredit. It arose from a rapid contraction of banking accommodation; and was aggravated by the fear of still greater restriction from seeing the narrow margin of the Bank reserve.

The panic of October 1847 had more features of resemblance to that of 1825; having been accompanied and much aggravated by commercial discredit and distress.

When the two panics of 1847 were at their height, the bullion in the Bank of England amounted to about nine millions; whereas in the crisis of 1825 it was reduced to about one million.

Both in 1825 and in 1847 the tendency to speculation, and to an undue extension of credit, was preceded, and probably caused, and most certainly was favoured and promoted, by the low rate of interest which had existed for some time previously; and this low rate of interest was apparently prolonged, in each case, by the operations of the Bank of England.

---

① Here, however, it is requisite to bear in mind an important difference between the state of the bank-note circulation as it was in 1825 and in 1847. At the former period, the small notes of the country banks were still in circulation in England and Wales; and it was through this medium that the severest part of the run was brought to bear upon the country bankers.

The greatest variation, on each occasion, in the price of 3 per cent consols was, from the highest, 28th of April, 1824, 97 $\frac{1}{4}$, to the lowest, 14th February, 1826, 73 $\frac{7}{8}$; and from the highest, 2nd of December, 1844. 101 $\frac{5}{8}$ (with div.) to the lowest, October 1847, 77 $\frac{3}{4}$

In the autumn and winter of 1824-1825, the Bank, when its stock of bullion was declining, when already the spirit of wild speculation which reached its acmc a few months afterwards, was showing itself, and when assuredly no increase of banking accommodation could be really wanting, extended its securities from 20,904,530*l*. on the 31st of August, 1824, to 24,951,330*l*. on the 28th of February, 1825.

It is true that the engagements between the Bank and Government, which led to the greater part of that increase, had been entered into[①] while (January, 1824) the stock of bullion was very large, viz. 14,200,000*l*.; but still the fact remains that those operations prevented, or, at least, retarded a rise in the market rate of interest. If the Bank had not taken the dead weight, the Government must have resorted to a loan. And if the Bank had declined to engage to pay off the dissentients on the reduction of the 4 per cent to 3 $\frac{1}{2}$ per cent, either that measure must have been postponed, or some equivalent must have been resorted to. In either case there would have been less facility in the money market; in other words,

① The purchase of the dead weight annuity had been agreed for by the Bank in 1823; and the undertaking to pay off the dissentients from the reduction of the 4 per cent stock to 3 $\frac{1}{2}$ per cent had been entered into in January, 1824.

some rise in the rate of interest; which, at that time, could not but have had a salutary effect in checking, in some degree, the then rising spirit of speculation.

The reduction by the Bank of its rate of interest, immediately on the Act of 1844 coming into operation, and in accordance with what was then understood to be the spirit of that act, had, as I have before observed, the effect of extending the railway speculations then manifesting themselves. And there can be no doubt that the same facility of banking accommodation favoured the undue extension of credit, in other undertakings, both at home and abroad. Both in 1825 and in 1847 the expansion of credit, the abuse of which caused the commercial embarrassments of those periods, had, in some degree, been promoted by the conversion, in the two or three years preceding, of a large portion of the government stocks into lower denominations of the interest payable on them.[1] In such cases, a feverish anxiety is apt to prevail among those who, rather than submit to the reduced rate of interest, have consented to be paid off; and having been thus, in a manner, forced out of government securities, they seek investments which, while promising a larger income, involve more hazard.

In 1825 there had been extensive speculations in produce other than corn, both by purchases on the spot, and, to a greater extent abroad for importation.

In 1847 there were not, and had not recently been, any speculations in commodities or produce other than corn. There had been some speculation on the short cotton crop of the United States in 1846, but it had ceased

① The reduction of the new $3\frac{1}{2}$ per cents was effected in 1844.

soon after the close of that year. Corn speculations had been engaged in to an enormous extent.

In 1825 the market rate of interest was lower, exclusively of the period of panic, than in 1847: the higher rate in the latter year being mainly attributable to the extraordinary absorption of capital in railways.

In 1847 *each* of the two panics of April and October was of longer duration than the single panic of 1825.

In 1825 the great severity of the pressure can hardly be said to have been of longer duration than about three weeks. It may be considered to have begun with the announcement of the failure of the Bank of Sir William Elford and Co. at Plymouth; but the greatest alarm and discredit occurred in the interval of about a fortnight, ending the 19th of December. During that interval the intensity of suffering was greater than in the equal interval, ending the 23rd of October, 1847. The following extracts from the file of the *Times* newspaper in 1825, afford striking specimens of the intensity of the panic, and the prodigious sacrifices of property which were made, chiefly, it was understood, by bankers, in order to sustain themselves against the suddenness of the demands then made upon some of them.

"*Friday*, 9*th Dec.*, 1823.— (City article.) The failure of the banking house of Wentworth, Chaloner, and Co., of 23 Threadneedle Street, was announced yesterday. The firm is identical, we believe, with two banks in the country — one at Wakefield, and the other at York — which will of course stop payment also, as soon as the intelligence shall reach them. As a London house, their business seems to have been chiefly confined to the agency of the banks in Yorkshire, so that as far as the city is concerned, its failure is considered an event of no great importance In the country, however, the calamity cannot fail to prove a very serious one, as their local notes were in very general circulation among the small manufacturers.

"*Saturday*, *10th Dec.*, 1825.—(City article.) — Yesterday Was a day of comparative tranquillity in the city, no commercial disasters of importance having transpired, and men in general finding consolation, as is usually the case, from the absence of any thing detrimental.

"It is understood that the panic produced by the failure of Wentworth and Co. caused a run yesterday on several of the London bankers, but they were all perfectly well prepared to meet it, and no inconvenience whatever followed.

"On the Stock Exchange the natural consequences of a quieter state of things out of doors was produced. The market was steady throughout the day, and whatever variation occurred, both in the foreign and English funds, was chiefly in favour of improvement. The only exception was in exchequer bills, large amounts of which were sold by the London bankers.

"*Monday*, *12th Dec.*, 1825. — (City article.)— Consols for the January account closed on Saturday at about one half per cent lower than on the preceding day, having left off at 83 $\frac{1}{2}$. The market had been particularly buoyant in the early part of the day, when the same stock reached 84. It appears that the extreme difficulty in procuring accommodation on commercial bills (indeed, the scarcity of money was so great, that discount was refused, in some cases even on Navy bills,) had compelled many merchants and bankers to resort to the stock market, where 3 per cent. Reduced, and Exchequer bills to a very large amount were sold. The stock maintained its value, notwithstanding the large amount poured in, but Exchequer bills fell to a discount of 35*s*.

"*Tuesday*, *13th Dec*, 1825.— (City article.) — An indescribable gloom was diffused through the city yesterday morning, by the knowledge of the fact, previously suspected, that the house of Sir Peter Pole, Thornton, and Co., of Bartholomew Lane, bankers, did not open for business. The house was among the most considerable in London, the firm being agents for no less than forty-seven provincial banks. It ought to be observed, since the declaration can no longer be injurious, that this is the house adverted to on a former occasion as having received assistance from the Bank, on laying before the directors such a statement of their affairs as was admitted at the time to be satisfactory. The amount advanced by the Bank is said to have been near 300,000*l*., and that sum, it was alleged, would be sufficient to secure the house against any further danger. In a week from that time, however, the firm has suspended its payments. The letters from the country brought intelligence of the failure of two provincial banks, one at Huddersfield, the other at Maidstone; the latter was one of the agency banks of Pole and Co. An extraordinary number of country bankers from all parts of England were in town yesterday, either for the purpose of procuring specie and bank notes as a protection against a run upon them, or to ascertain by their own observations the state of affairs among their London friends. Several of them were to be seen in most of the leading banking houses, anxiously waiting their turn for an interview with the principals. The gloom without doors, and the events which produced it, were sensibly felt at the Stock Exchange. Such was the pressure to effect sales of exchequer bills, that those securities not only fell to an enormous discount, but the brokers who deal in them, and who are few in number, became so much alarmed, that they closed their books, and actually refused for a short time to engage in any transactions whatever. At that period the current quotations were 50*s*. discount, but some purchasers at that price having appeared in the market, the brokers took courage, and business went on as usual. The discount afterwards fell to 60*s*., and even on those for which money may be obtained at the Exchequer at a day's notice the discount was 25*s*, in other words, a holder preferred receiving his 100*l* *minus* 25*s*. today, rather than wait till tomorrow to receive his 100*l*. in full. India Bonds were at 45*s*. discount; 3 per cent. Reduced fell to 79, and 3 $\frac{1}{2}$ per cent, to 84 $\frac{1}{2}$; sales being particularly pressed in those stocks, the books of which are still open for transfers. The same facility, however, was given at the Bank as was done on Saturday in making transfers of 3 per cent. Consols; and such transfers were effected to a large amount, though at a sacrifice of 1 per cent. or more, as compared with prices for the opening in January.

"*Wednesday*, *14th Dec.*, 1825.—(City article.)—The agitation and alarm in the City have as yet experienced no abatement. At an early hour yesterday morning it was announced that another London banking house had suspended its payments. Some of the houses in Lombard Street and its immediate neighbourhood were also besieged with crowds of people on some false alarm given — a manoeuvre, which appears to have been adopted for the purpose of picking pockets. In one instance, as we have heard, on Monday evening, a house which had closed its shutters on account of the fog and lighted candles, was actually for no other reason reported to have stopped payment. The difficulty of raising money on stock, bills, or any species of security, whether private or public, is entirely without example in the City of London. The rate of interest, wherever any species of accommodation is afforded, cannot be estimated in some cases at less than

50 per cent. As the usury laws form a bar to ordinary transactions of this nature, various plans are said to be adopted to evade their operation. For example, the current price of Consols for the January account being 83, any person wishing to convert that stock into ready money would not obtain offers for it at more than 79. At that rate the money for it is paid, and as soon as the transaction is completed the purchaser can sell the same stock for the January account at 4 per cent. advance. He will receive his money for it in the middle of January, and thus gain more than 50 per cent per annum for its use in the intermediate period. In the foreign exchanges an advance was produced by the scarcity of money.

"*Thursday*, *15th Dec.*, 1825.—(City article.) — Another day of agitation and alarm has passed over the city. As early as nine o'clock in the morning, the hour at which business commences in the London banking houses, it was ascertained that two of them had suspended their payments. The Bank directors assembled again yesterday, and displayed much energy in administering to the relief of the persons who made applications in various forms for assistance. Among the first of them was an eminent country banker, who had been in town the whole of Tuesday, vainly endeavouring to raise 50,000*l.* on securities worth double that sum. The Bank directors have also given way on a point respecting which they have hitherto resisted all applications, viz., in lending money on the security of Government or of Bank Stock, and large sums were yesterday advanced on such securities, particularly to country bankers, who had to state that they were wholly unable to convert them into money in the open market, except at enormous sacrifices. The Stock Exchange exhibited the same scene yesterday as on the two preceding days. The interest of money, as derived for the 'continuation' in stock, or the difference between the price for immediate transfer and for the account, was greater than in any former instance. A sale of Consols for money was made at 76 $\frac{1}{2}$①, when the price for the opening was 82 $\frac{1}{2}$, which would yield interest at the rate of 70 per cent per annum.

"*Friday, 16th Dec.*, 1825. —At the Stock Exchange yesterday afternoon a large amount of 4 per cent. stock, the books of which are now closed for the dividends, was offered for sale. The condition was, that it should be *paid for immediately in Bank notes, and a large sacrifice in the price would be made for that accommodation. The bargain was struck at* 93; *but all the money in notes the jobbers in that stock could raise was* 50,000*l.*, *though it had been intended to sell a much larger amount.* No doubt can be entertained, from the nature of this transaction, that it was effected for a country banker, to whom immediate supplies were indispensable: *but the extraordinary sacrifice made may be estimated when it is remarked that the party could have sold the same stock for the next day at* 97, *and probably at* 102 $\frac{1}{2}$ *for the opening of the books in January.* The Bank, as usual, allowed the private transfer, the necessity of which accommodation is now so fully established that it is granted as a matter of course.

"*Monday, 19th Dec.*, 1825. —(City article.)—It was reported in the city, late on Saturday afternoon, that at the Cabinet Council held on Friday evening, and which sat till near two o'clock on the following morning, the determination was adopted of suspending for a short time payments in

① As this price included the dividend due in January, it would be about 75 ex. div.

specie at the Bank. We cannot pretend to state that such was absolutely the case; and the false alarms which are circulated at this period require that every piece of information should be very cautiously weighed before it is given to the public; but we receive this from a quarter in which we are so accustomed, from long experience, to place reliance, that we feel fully justified at least in mentioning it. Rumour adds that the measure is not only to be temporary, but that the power of acting under the suspension of legal payments is not to rest solely with the court of directors, a board of control being to be appointed to regulate the issues of Bank notes.

"The sacrifices made on sales of Consols for money continue to be enormous, and prove that there has been no abatement hitherto of the unexampled scarcity of money in the City. Late on Saturday afternoon a sale of Consols for money was made at 77, the purchaser of which immediately sold them for the opening in January at 81 $\frac{1}{2}$, thus gaining 4 $\frac{1}{2}$ per cent per *mensem* for the use of his capital.

"*Tuesday*, *20th Dec.*, 1825.—(City article.)—Yesterday morning, at 10 o'clock, a letter from J. C. Herrics, Esq., dated Treasury Chambers, Dec. 17th, was read at the Bank, in which notice was given that Government has raised the interest of all exchequer bills outstanding to 2*d*. per cent, *per diem*, and that the increase is to take place from yesterday. It will be recollected that the exchequer bills of a particular description, viz., those dated in October, November, and December, 1824, have been called in, the holders having the option of money, or new bills at 2*d*. per cent *per diem*. The advance of interest, therefore, becomes general over all the issue. It is evident, however, that in the present state of the money market such an advance must be perfectly nugatory, as was sufficiently proved yesterday on the circulation of this notice, after which exchequer bills fell to a discount of 80*s*. Indeed, had the interest been advanced to 3*d*. it is obvious that the bills could have found few purchasers in a market where, owing to the exigency of the moment, capitalists are enabled to make a profit of 50 per cent, and, consequently, must have been at a discount. It had been far better, therefore, to leave those securities in their present state, than to betray weakness by thus altering the interest on them without effect.

" *Wednesday*, *21st Dec.* , 1825. — (City article.)—The improvement was pretty general yesterday in every description of Government security. Consols for January opened at 79 $\frac{1}{2}$, and declined to 79 $\frac{1}{4}$, but experienced shortly afterwards a rapid advance to 80$\frac{1}{4}$, and after declining to 80, left off with a firm appearance at 80 $\frac{5}{8}$ buyers. In the 3 $\frac{1}{2}$ per cents, a very rapid advance occurred, that stock having opened at 81 $\frac{3}{4}$; then, with scarcely any intermediate price, it rose to 85, and closed at 87. The 3 per cents. Reduced left off at 79. Exchequer bills after having been at 85*s*., closed at 25*s*. discount; and India Bonds, which opened at 75*s*., closed at 25*s*. discount. "

On the state of things in 1825, the following remarks by Lord Ashburton, who was called into counsel with the government on occasion of the extreme pressure felt in December of that year, cannot but be allowed to be of great interest.

"The withdrawing of the metals from the coffers of the Bank will be determined by one of two causes: —

"1st. Either by a panic and distrust, commercial or political, within the country, or,

"2nd. A demand to send them abroad, in consequence of an unfavourable state of the foreign exchanges.

"In 1825 the drain was entirely of the former description.① The exchanges were favourable; there was no demand upon us from abroad; but the Bank was exposed, not to a partial drain, but to being completely exhausted and run dry; and as I was on that occasion called in to counsel with the late Lord Liverpool, Mr. Huskisson, and the Governor of the Bank, the symptoms and their treatment are very distinctly in my recollection. The case was this. Adventures of the most wild and hazardous description, assisted, though it can hardly be said that they were created, by facilities given by the Bank, were followed by an entire prostration of the credit of all parties, with the single exception of the Bank of England. Private bankers in town and country fell in numbers, and the panic naturally consequent on such a state of things produced a rush upon the most wealthy and solid establishments by all who had claims upon them, either by holding their notes or as depositors; and it is worthy of remark that the claims of the depositors were always the most formidable. They called for their hundreds, while the holders of notes, though more numerous, came for single pounds. This sudden alarm, stopping in the first instance all circulation of credit, obliged every country banker to draw from London all the sovereigns out of the Bank; and the extent of their

① This is not quite correct. The exchanges were adverse, and the demand was from abroad, till after July.

demand will be best explained by the statement of one of the most wealthy and respectable of those bankers to me, that he could not sleep till he had gold in his house for every note he had out. It may well be supposed that this was not accomplished without great sacrifices; but to a banker no price is too dear for the maintenance of the purest credit, and even at this moment the public will never know the individual losses occasioned by the present pressure: these are secrets which few are able to make public with impunity.

"The gold of the Bank was drained to within a very few thousand pounds; for although the public returns showed a result rather less scandalous, a certain Saturday night closed with nothing worth mentioning remaining. The application made to Lord Liverpool was for an Order in Council to do that which necessity seemed about to accomplish — the suspension of cash payments; and this gave rise to the conference I have mentioned between Lord Liverpool, Mr. Huskisson, the Governor of the Bank, and myself.

"We recognised at once the following facts in this case — for, as has been already observed, the position of things in cases of alarm and pressure are seldom or never exactly similar.

"The credit of the Bank for all domestic purposes was perfect. There was no man in the country who was not ready to take its paper as a means of circulation, and to give even his gold for it, the moment he was assured that his neighbour would take it from him again. The gold was not wanted to send abroad; the state of the foreign exchanges forbade it; there was, therefore, no fear of depreciation of paper. The necessity and pressure were purely domestic: what was wanted was something which everybody was disposed to trust as a substitute for what everybody distrusted; and the paper of the Bank of England answered in such a state of things the purpose as well as gold—it may be said to have done so even better, as being more transmissible, and reaching more readily and rapidly the points where it was wanted.

"In this state of things the remedy for the difficulty was obvious, and unanimously agreed to by us. Although the Bank had no specie left, a large additional issue of notes was made, and about 1,500,000*l*., of those of 1*l*.[①], which were accidentally found to be in existence, were circulated: the relief was immediate, the country received a circulating currency in which everybody had entire confidence, and the useless gold was returned to the Bank. The notes by this proceeding were increased from 19,748,000*l*. in December, 1825, to 24,479,000*l*. in March, 1826; and having served to relieve the pressure, they gradually subsided before the end of that year to their ordinary amount again of 19,951,000*l*., while the bullion in the Bank was successively increased by this increase of paper in opposition to the theory of 1844, which presumes from such cause a necessary diminution.

"It is hardly necessary that I should guard myself from being supposed to maintain that an increased issue of paper is an invariable remedy against a drain of specie; but what I do maintain is, that it was the fit remedy for that particular case, and that it was undeniably proved to be so by the result, while a contrary treatment might have suited a drain caused by adverse exchanges. But the Act of 1844 says that all cases of drain shall be

---

① The amount of 1*l*. notes *immediately* applicable did not exceed the sum of 700,000*l*. to 800,000*l*. There had been an amount of near 400,000*l*. long outstanding, and apparently not in circulation; and further sums were prepared and issued in the spring of 1826, making the amount altogether between 1,500,000*l*. and 1,600,000*l*.

treated in the same manner; that there shall be no discretion or judgment allowed as to causes; and my reason for dwelling so long on the case of 1825-1826 is to substitute for speculative reasoning a clear proof that the Act of 1844 not only would not have suited that case, but would have aggravated all the difficulties; that it consequently is not of universal application, and therefore cannot, without danger, be suffered to govern indiscriminately our circulation.

"I think I might stop here, and hold that I had proved enough by positive facts and results, and not by mere brainspinning, the fallacies on which this Act is founded. Its machinery does not suit the case of pressure on the Bank from domestic distrust and panic, and these must always be a large and formidable portion of our monetary visitations. It may also be shown, though perhaps not by the same pregnant proof from past facts, that it is not always suited as a remedy for the other causes of a drain of the Bank's coin. It must be admitted that the difficulties under which we are now labouring have no reference, to the causes I have before mentioned of domestic discredit existing in 1825; on the contrary, the commercial credit of the country is truly said to be more than usually sound①, but the circulation of that commerce never was more severely distressed, and that mainly by the operations of the Bank, acting under the terrors of the law by which it is fettered."—(*Financial and Commercial Crisis Considered*, pp. 11-15.)

From this statement by Lord Ashburton, it might seem that the measure carried into effect by the Bank of England, on the 13th of December, of granting an enormous and almost indefinite extension of accommodation in

① This was written early in May, 1847.

the way of discounts and advances, was not only sanctioned but suggested by the Government. According to the evidence of Mr. Harman and Mr. Palmer, however, the Government took no responsibility, but threw the whole of it on the directors. But whether the design of the measure originated with Government or with the Bank directors, the merit of it was very great. It was as judicious as it was bold; and it proved to be eminently successful. There cannot, I think, be a doubt, but that it averted the necessity of a suspension of cash payments.

The lowest amount of the Bank treasure was, on the 24th of December, viz.

Coin	– –	426,000*l.*
Bullion	– – –	601,000*l.*
		1,027,000*l.*

But according to the evidence of the governor of the Bank[1], the demand had so far ceased by the seventeenth of that month, that the directors thenceforward felt easy.

The accidental discovery (for such it was said by Mr. Harman, in his evidence in 1832, to have been) of an amount of 1*l.* notes, which had been put away in the Bank, was, doubtless, a fortunate circumstance; for although the sum was not large (between 7 and 800,000*l.*), it served to meet the peculiar difficulty of that time, which consisted in an extensive discredit of the small note country circulation. And it is probable that it had an immediate, and very great effect in stopping the demand from the

① *Bank Charter Report*, 1832, p. 405.

provinces for gold. Alone, however, it would have availed but little towards relieving the intensity of discredit and distress which prevailed in London, and in the great trading and manufacturing towns of the kingdom. The measures of the Bank for relieving these were on the largest scale. Discounts, loans, and advances were made upon all descriptions of securities that had any pretension to solidity. Upon this point I may cite the evidence of Mr. Harman①, who was a director at that time.

"2217. Will you describe the manner in which the Bank lent its assistance at that time? — We lent it by every possible means, and in modes that we never had adopted before; we took in stock as security; we purchased exchequer bills; we made advances on exchequer bills; we not only discounted outright, but we made advances on deposit of bills of exchange to an immense amount; in short, by every possible means consistent with the safety of the Bank; and we were not upon some occasions over-nice; seeing the dreadful state in which the public were we rendered every assistance in our power."

And of Mr. Horsley Palmer, who was also then in the direction: —

"583. You have stated, generally, that you conceive that under circumstances of particular pressure in London, a Bank, composed as the Bank of England is, of commercial men, could afford facilities which a government bank could not afford — do you think that in the year 1825, at the period of the panic, if there had been a government bank in existence, managed by commissioners, they could have afforded the same facilities, and would have been willing to have run the same risks to relieve the credit of the commercial body in London that was done by the Bank of England at

---

① Bank Charter Report of 1832.

that period? — I do not think it could have been readily managed by commissioners, when I see the magnitude of the aid which was given on that occasion. *I see from the paper in my hand, that upon one occasion, on the* 8*th Dec.*, 1825, *the discounts of the Bank were seven millions and a half; on the* 15*th they were eleven millions and a half; on the* 22*nd, the next week, they were fourteen millions and a half; and on the* 29*th they were fifteen millions. The number of bills discounted in one day were* 4200.

"584. Can you state how low the amount of commercial discounts was before it rose to that emergency? — On the 3rd of November they were 5,000,000*l*.

"585. So that they rose from 5,000,000*l*. to 15,000,000*l*.? — Yes.

"596. Did not the Bank in 1825 and 1826 run considerable risks with regard to the securities they took, looking rather to the relief of the money market, than examining very closely into the securities they received? — From the magnitude of the advance some considerable risk must necessarily have been incurred, but I cannot state what the actual loss was.

"597. Do you believe that it runs a risk greater than was likely to have been undertaken by private individuals in discounting? — *Certainly; inasmuch as advances were made upon the simple deposit of title-deeds, without having the power of examining them, relying upon the credit of the parties to whom the property was stated to belong.*"

The effect of this seasonable aid was soon felt in the removal of the more urgent symptoms of the distress and discredit, which were, at that time, felt chiefly among the bankers, both in town and country, and which entailed such enormous sacrifices as we have seen in the sales of Government stocks and exchequer bills.

The vast extent of accommodation thus afforded by the Bank,

accompanied with an additional increase to its circulation of more than eight millions①, had not only no depressing effect on the foreign exchanges, but was attended with a great rise of them. ②

While, however, this intervention of the Bank of England was so effectual for its object of filling the chasm in the circulating medium caused by so extensive a failure of credit, it did not operate as a preventive of mercantile failures. These were numerous and extensive in January 1826, and continued into February. Urgent applications were made to Government to relieve the mercantile distress by loans of Exchequer Bills. This they steadily refused to do. But as some compensation for their refusal, they induced the Bank, with considerable difficulty, to consent to make advances, to the extent of three millions, on goods in warehouses at Manchester, Glasgow, and some other considerable towns. The amount,

---

①

Dec. 3rd	– – – – – – –	£ 17,477,290
Dec. 10th	– – – – – – –	18,037,960
Dec. 17th	– – – – – – –	23,942,810
Dec. 24th	– – – – – – –	25,611,800
Dec. 31st	– – – – – – –	25,709,410

② The following were the exact quotations: —

Dates.		Hamburgh.			Lisbon.		Paris.	
1825.							3 days, at	
Nov. 29.	– –	37	1	– –	0	– –	25	25
Dec. 13.	– –	37	9	– –	$50\frac{1}{2}$	– –	25	40
Dec. 20.	– –	38	1	– –	50	– –	25	50
1826.								
Feb. 21.	– –	37	10	– –	51	– –	25	70
March 28.	– –	38	10	– –	51	– –	25	80

The sudden improvement of the Exchange in December is fully accounted for by the difficulty of negotiating bills at almost any price. The same thing occurred, but in a more marked degree, in October, 1847.

however, advanced in this way was less than 400,000*l*.

I have been induced to dwell, at some length, on the circumstances attending the great monetary derangement of 1825, not only because a comparison between that period and 1847 is frequently drawn, but because it affords me an opportunity of observing, that I am ready to confess that in the view which I took, in some former publications of mine, of the conduct of the Bank on that occasion, I hardly did justice to it. I admitted, indeed, that it was successful. That of course, could not be denied. But I expressed myself with hesitation as to its wisdom, considering it to have been empirical, hazardous, of doubtful precedent, and justified only by the event. Looking back to the period, now twenty-two years ago, when I first commented upon that measure, in a rather disparaging tone, and to a more recent period, now more than ten years since, when I had again occasion to remark upon it, less disparagingly, but not fully approving, I consider myself entitled to plead the lapse of time, and the experience derived in the interval, as my justification for the more unqualified approbation which I now give to it. And if I had been more doubtful than I was, down to the year 1847, of the soundness of the grounds on which the Bank had proceeded in December 1825, the events of October last would have been sufficient to remove from my mind whatever doubts I might, till then, have retained.

At the time the measure was adopted, it might fairly be said to be empirical, because there had been no experience that could be considered as being in point; and it was in contravention of the sound general principle of banking which prescribes a reduction of advances and discounts, in other words a contraction of liabilities, as the means of meeting increased demands for cash, by depositors or note holders. But when the experience of 1825 was found to have answered completely the exigencies of the case, and to have borne out so fully the reasoning of Mr. Henry Thornton, who had argued, both in his evidence before the Select Committee in 1797, and in his Treatise published in 1802, that if the Directors of the Bank had extended their accommodation at the close of 1796, instead of contracting it as they did, the drain would have abated, and the suspension been averted; a principle might be considered as established, which, under analogous circumstances, should be admitted as modifying or superseding the more general rule. Mr. Thornton's argument, and the precedent of 1825, of course proceed upon the assumption that the foreign exchanges happen to be such as to preclude a demand for export of gold; and that there exists a state of general discredit from which the Bank of England is wholly exempt; thus distinguishing an internal demand for Bank of England notes or gold from an external demand for gold only.

If the Bank Directors in 1825, having committed the errors which led to the too great reduction of their treasure by the foreign drain, down to the autumn of that year, had, when the foreign demand for gold was found to be at an end, and when it had become manifest that the demand for gold was for the purpose of meeting the effects of discredit of the country banks, determined to extend their accommodation two or three weeks earlier, it is not improbable that the severity of the subsequent pressure might have been materially mitigated.

In the case, in many respects parallel, of October 1847, the indication was, if possible, still more clear, in favour of extended accommodation by the Bank of England, more especially as having in its vaults upwards of eight millions of bullion. There was no external demand for gold. The exchanges had, for some time, been so favourable, that the Bank had been enabled to buy, since April, about two millions of gold, which had all been withdrawn from it for purposes of internal circulation. But the gold was not wanted in exchange for Bank of England notes. These were equally in demand to supply the vacuum caused by the discredit, greater or less, of all other paper. But precisely in proportion as the demand for its notes proved that its intervention was necessary, the restrictive operation of the act of 1844 diminished the power of the Bank to supply the deficiency of the circulating medium. If the Bank, *at the beginning of October*, when the legitimate and pressing wants of the internal circulation became manifest, had extended its accommodation (as but for that act it probably would have done), there can be no doubt that, with an increased circulation of its notes, it would have had an accession to its treasure. And great, indeed, would have been the mitigation of the suffering which prevailed through the whole of October, had the Bank been in its former position, and consequently, with such an amount of treasure, enabled to grant the utmost assistance that the nature of the case required.

SECTION 19 *On the defence of the act of 1844, by Sir R. Peel, in his speech of the 3rd of December, 1847*

Having passed under review the working of the Act of 1844, and having stated the grounds on which I consider it to have operated injuriously, in favouring an undue extension of credit during the first two years after its enactment, and in greatly aggravating the causes of the monetary pressure, and the collapse of credit which have so disastrously characterised the year

1847, I deem it right to lay before my readers Sir Robert Peel's vindication of his part in originating that measure, and his view of its effects, now that the cycle of events is so far completed as to throw the full light of experience upon its operation. I shall, with this view, give extracts of so much of his speech of the 3rd of December last (as reported in the *Times*) as related to these points, with my remarks upon them.

The considerations which led Sir Robert Peel to propose to Parliament, in 1844, the measure which he so triumphantly carried, are thus stated by him: —

"I now come to the Act of 1844, and to the doctrines held by the right honourable gentleman who most ably presided over the committee which then inquired into and reported to the House on the subject which now engages our attention. The Bank Charter was then about to expire; some proposition it was necessary to make as to the renewal of that charter, and it was then perfectly competent to us to relieve ourselves from any direct responsibility respecting that and the other measures which were then necessary for the regulation of the currency. I need scarcely remind the House, that in the year 1844 it became necessary to propose to Parliament a specific measure, and I now want to call the attention of the House to this, that in the five preceding years five committees sat for the purpose of investigating this subject, of collecting information and reporting their opinions thereupon to the House. Those committees sat in 1836, in 1837, in 1838, in 1840, and in 1841; still, notwithstanding their minute and protracted inquiries, I have heard it said that the subject has not been exhausted, and that the measure of 1844 was not based upon a sufficient inquiry. Yet antecedent to the measure of 1844 there was an amount of inquiry on the subjects of currency and banking which it is difficult to look at without surprise. I find that by the first of these committees as many as 3000 questions were put; thus we have in the year 1836, 3000 questions and 3000 answers; in the next year, 1837, the committee which then sat, put 4570 questions and received as many answers; but that did not seem to be sufficient, for we have in the year 1838 a further supply of questions and answers to the extent of 1700 of each, and yet with no practical result from those apparently endless investigations; then, in the year 1840, as the period at which the Bank Charter must expire drew near, a committee was appointed, over which the right honourable gentleman the Chancellor of the Exchequer presided with great ability. In 1840 the committee, as I have said, to consider the subject of banks of issue was re-appointed, and up to that time as many as 9000 questions were put, and then in 1841 we had 3859 questions, to each of which long and reasoning answers were received, and which at length reached a total of not less than 14,000 questions, and at that time we had the labours of another committee closing without any practical amendment having been effected or proposed. It might then at all events have been expected that the theory of this subject would have been clearly established. The committees had examined Mr. Tooke, Mr. Jones Loyd, Mr. Horsley Palmer, and Mr. Page.

"It was then decided to apply to Her Majesty's servants to submit to Parliament measures for the regulation of the currency and for the renewal of the Bank Charter: they invited the House of Commons to come to some practical decision on the subject, and I must be allowed to say, with respect to the measures then proposed to Parliament, there was not within my recollection any question of importance carried by a larger majority — on no occasion did more than thirty oppose the progress of that measure, and in the House of Lords it was carried unanimously. I, therefore, affirm that the House of Commons — after the means of information placed within its reach — after looking at the control which it might have exercised — cannot now say, that for light and inconsiderable reasons it was induced to give its consent to the bill which the advisers of the Crown then thought it their duty to introduce."

The remark that most naturally occurs on this statement is suggested by the obvious disposition of the speaker *to dress up the case.* The chief purpose is evidently to show that the course of proceeding which had been usual when any legislative measure was to be proposed affecting the Bank of England and the banking institutions of the country—that of first seeking the aid of a Committee of Inquiry, appointed with special reference to the object in view — was, in this instance, superfluous.

There is a very elaborate statement of the number of years in which committees on banking sat, and of the number of questions asked, and the long answers received by them. But as to the committees of 1836, 1837, and 1838, they were appointed solely to inquire into the *joint stock* banking system, and their proceedings have scarcely any reference to the general subject. They undoubtedly elicited a great deal of valuable information on that branch of the subject to which their attention was particularly directed; but I am not aware that they either sought, or obtained, any as to the propriety or expediency of a measure calculated to affect the paramount interests involved in the great change introduced by the bill of 1844, or that any thing they did, or failed to do, affords any valid excuse for the introduction of such a measure, without a previous inquiry by a committee, not only into the working of the existing system, but into the probable operation of that which was to supersede it.

The Committee of 1840 and 1841 was appointed simply "to inquire into the effects produced on the circulation by the various banking establishments issuing notes payable on demand." The grounds assigned for its appointment were, the allegations contained in a petition from the *Manchester Chamber of Commerce*, relating to the state of the currency. Nothing could well be more vague than the object here proposed for the inquiries of the Committee, and seeing the vagueness of the object, and the mode in which the inquiry was conducted, it is not to be wondered at that the results were unsatisfactory.

A great part of the time and attention of the Committee in 1840 were taken up with examinations as to mere verbal definitions and distinctions, and their supposed consequences. A more tiresome exhibition of mere logomachy cannot easily be imagined; and I will venture to say it cannot be equalled in the instance of any other parliamentary inquiry. The committee became a mere arena for conflicting theories, based chiefly upon arbitrary verbal distinctions; such, for instance, as whether deposits, payable on demand, were, or were not, money, or whether they were, or were not, capable of performing the functions, and of thus superseding the use, of metallic money; or whether, if they possessed the properties of money, it was not *in an inferior degree.* Mr. Hume was intent on showing the error of the currency theory on this point, and some days were occupied in disputation upon it. In my examination a great deal of time, and a multitude of questions, were expended in repeated efforts by the members of the committee, professing the creed of the currency principle, to obtain from me an admission that it was upon the circulation, and not upon the securities, that the Bank ought to act in its endeavours to counteract a drain; and whatever may be the merits of my answers, the event proves that they made not the slightest impression on those who used so much time and pains in obtaining them. It is a striking circumstance, that the committee of 1840 elicited hardly any facts, or any information of value, on the practice of banking, either in the metropolis, or in the provinces. And it may be observed, incidentally, of the avowed adherents of the currency theory, that their views, whether enunciated in their evidence before this committee, or in their writings, or in their speeches in parliament, betray an extraordinary paucity of illustration by reference to facts, or to occurrences in the actual course of banking or mercantile business.

The examinations in 1841, although not occupying half the time, or marked by half the number of questions, or length of answers, distinguishing those of 1840, are pregnant with useful information. But it seems to have been thrown away upon Sir Robert Peel. The only quotations he made from that evidence were those in which the country bankers stated that they did not, and could not, regulate their issues, that is, their notes in circulation, by the foreign exchanges; which might have led him to the inference that neither could any regulation by government make them so conform. And the opinion which he gave in his expository speeches in May 1844, of the influence of the competition of issue among the country bankers in raising prices, is directly opposed to the whole of that evidence. Sir Robert Peel says of this committee of 1840 and 1841, that having reached the extent of 14,000 questions, it *closed* "without any practical amendment having been effected or proposed." But he does not say *why it so closed*. The fact was that the labours of the committee were terminated abruptly by the dissolution of parliament, in June 1841, without their having had the opportunity of discussing, and concluding upon, the terms of a report founded upon the evidence they had received. The committee, upon its functions being thus abruptly and prematurely abridged, made the following brief report, under date of 15th June, 1841: —

"With respect to the great questions involved in their inquiry, they feel that before the probable period of the *termination of this session of Parliament it will be impossible for them to give that consideration* to the many and important points suggested in the evidence already before them *which would enable them to report any well-grounded opinion to the House.* They are aware that some disappointment may be caused by the circumstance of no final report being made after so protracted an inquiry; *but on points of such importance to the whole country, and involving so many and such complicated interests, they cannot allow this feeling to weigh against the necessity of due caution, and the fullest deliberation in arriving at any conclusion.*

"It will be for the House in the next session to determine whether *any committee shall be appointed, to whom the evidence taken in this and the last session of Parliament shall be referred* for the purpose of framing a report either on that evidence *or after such further examination of witnesses as they may think necessary; but in existing circumstances* your committee consider that the only course which they can pursue, is to report the evidence which they have taken without further observation to the House."

Hence it appears that it rested with Sir Robert Peel on his coming into power—he having it in contemplation to propose an important legislative measure upon the very subject the consideration of which had thus been left incomplete — to reappoint such a committee, with instructions to take into consideration the evidence of 1840 and 1841, and upon that, and such other evidence as they might receive, to report their opinion of the existing system, and of any improvements of which it might be susceptible, by a separation of departments, or by any other means. Such a report, although it might have proved to be more or less dictated by the currency theory, seeing that the chairman had become a proselyte to that doctrine, could hardly have thrown overboard, (as Sir Robert Peel did,) every part of the evidence which in any way militated with it.

By these remarks, I mean only that the reasons assigned in the passage which I have quoted from the speech of Sir R. Peel do not bear out the objections stated in it to the usual course of proceeding, on the occasion in question. It is quite true, as Sir Robert Peel says, and as I had occasion to observe before his recent speech was delivered, that the measure was passed by a triumphant majority in the House of Commons, and unanimously in the House of Lords, and that, therefore, it is not competent to parliament to hold him accountable for any disappointment that may have been felt from the working of the measure. It is beyond question, that if any responsibility attaches, it is to the legislature which passed the measure, as it were, by acclamation. Viewing it then simply as an act of the defunct parliament, I am entitled to express myself freely upon it, and I therefore venture to say that it is, in my opinion, *one of the most wanton, ill-advised, pedantic, and rash* pieces of legislation that has ever come within my observation, upon a matter which I had taken some pains to make myself acquainted with.

In the following passage of his speech, Sir Robert Peel avows his disappointment in the failure of one of the three purposes of the Act of 1844, and throws the blame of its failure on the Bank Directors.

"There seems to have been some misapprehension as to the object contemplated by that Act: that which we contemplated was that its future effect would be to prevent the recurrence of those convulsions which had heretofore frequently taken place. It had previously been thought, and might afterwards have been expected, that the Bank of England would have taken precautions against the ill-regulated issue of its treasure, and, therefore, the bill contained no imperative regulation affecting the banking department. We did hope that after the panic of 1826, after that of 1836, after that also of 1839, we did hope that the Bank of England would have confined itself to those principles of banking which their own directors admitted to be just, but from which they had admitted their own departure, though prescribed in part by their own regulations. In that hope I am bound to acknowledge that we have been disappointed. Seeing commercial difficulty coming, seeing the approach of a panic, they still did not conform to those regulations; commercial houses were swept away which had long been insolvent; other houses, which under different circumstances might have proved perfectly solvent, suffered from the failures of those whose inability to meet the demands against them was previously well known. The Bill has not sufficed to prevent these results, and so far, also, I admit that we have been disappointed; for the bill was intended to impose, if not a legal, at least a moral restraint on the Bank, and we hoped that it would prevent the necessity of having recourse to measures of extreme stringency. In that hope, likewise, I admit that we have been disappointed; for this I must contend, that it was in the power of the Bank, had it taken early precautions, if not to prevent all the evils that have arisen, at least greatly to diminish their force. If the Bank had possessed the resolution to meet the difficulty of a contraction of its issues by raising the rate of discount, by refusing much of the accommodation which they granted between the years 1844 and 1846 — if they had only been firm and persevering in those precautions, the necessity for any extensive interference with their operations might have been prevented; it might not then have been necessary for the Government to authorise that violation of the provision, the sole end and object of which was to constrain the Bank of England and prevent a recurrence of the panics of 1836 and 1839. Here I think I may be permitted to refer to what I said on the second reading of the Bill of 1844: at the close of the speech which I then made I thus expressed my opinions: —

"The ministers were not wild enough to suppose that this measure would prevent all undue speculation, or insure an invariable paper currency; but there was a species of speculation dependent on an undue issue of paper which they hoped the measure would check. Speculation could not be prevented in a commercial community, but it might be aggravated by a species of paper credit within the control of Parliament; and though ministers did not aim at checking legitimate speculation — though they admitted they could not prevent illegitimate speculation — which was, perhaps, necessarily incident to mercantile enterprise, particularly in a country like this, — still they asked Parliament, by assenting to this measure, not to aggravate evils which it could not control, nor refuse to check those which came properly within its jurisdiction."

Upon this avowal of the failure of the act, in one of its professed objects, I have only to remark that there having been no reasonable ground for any one, not misled by the currency theory, to entertain the expectation that any of the provisions of the bill would secure that object, it ought not to be matter of surprise or disappointment that it has failed. But the attempt by Sir Robert Peel, who held out that expectation, to transfer the blame of the disappointment from his own Bill to the Bank Directors has, indeed, excited my suprise, and is, perhaps, calculated to excite a still stronger feeling on the part of the public; at least among that part of it which takes an interest in the present subject, and is not bigoted in its adherence to what is called the principle of the Act of 1844.

Sir Robert Peel is, of all persons whatever, the one least entitled to condemn the Bank Directors for the course they pursued between 1844 and 1846.

I have already, some pages back, which were written before the debate of the 3rd of December, noticed the satisfaction expressed by Sir R. Peel, in 1845, at the state of things then existing, and especially at what he then considered the favourable working of the Act of 1844; and there I observed upon the impossibility of his being otherwise than well informed, not only at that time, but down to the summer of 1846, of all the proceedings of the Bank. Now surely, interested as he was, in every point of view, in having the act properly administered, it was to be expected that he would warn the governors, if he thought that they were keeping the rate of interest too low, or in any other manner contravening the admitted "principles of banking."

But, in truth, as I have before had occasion to observe, until the flagrant failure of the Act became manifest, nothing ever fell from its authors or partisans, indicative of their attaching any blame whatever to the conduct of the Bank Directors; either as to the rates of interest or discount charged by them, down to the close of 1846, or as to any other portion of their management.① And I have already shown how little aware, even the

---

① The following extracts from the City article of *The Times* of the 31st of December, 1846, afford a fair specimen of the tone held by the supporters of the Act, even after the setting in of the drain which ultimately brought about its suspension:—

"From the remarks which have been made every Thursday during the past few months, it might he imagined that our monetary system had of late years undergone no change, and that the regulation of the currency still rested with the Bank of England. Upon the breaking up of each court the question if the rate of interest has teen raised is asked with no less anxiety than formerly, and the funds are affected, and speculators become bold or timid, according to the answer. Opinions also abound as to what would be the proper 'policy' for the Bank to pursue as varied and conflicting as those which used to prevail before the Act of 1844. Everything, in short, tends to show that the public, who when the Bank possessed the power of controlling the currency never ceased to clamour for its removal and to complain of the want of a fixed principle, prefer, now that the removal has been effected, to recognise that establishment as their guide, instead of watching the principle which has been set up, and which is daily in unmistakeable operation before their eyes.

"In this state of things it may be well to call attention to the fact that the Bank can now exercise no influence over the value of money, save such as, in their degree, may be exercised by all other capitalists. If the current rate be 3 per cent, a resolution of the Court of Directors declaring that it shall be $3\frac{1}{2}$ or 4 could have no effect in fixing it at that point. The only result would be that those who now go for discounts to the Bank would then take their bills into the market; and the Bank, instead of letting out their funds in the usual way, would have to seek other channels, or would find them disappear by a reduction in their deposits It will easily be seen that such a course is not likely to be adopted by a body whose only duty is to make as much as they can of the commodity in which they deal

"One great cause of the prevailing misconception is in *the fancy that the Bank still have duties to perform by 'acting on the circulation.' But they have no duties of the kind. Their only responsibilities are such as they share in common with their brother traders throughout the kingdom*, and Messrs Jones Loyd, or Glyn, or any other bankers, might as well deem themselves called upon to attempt an interference with the natural movements of money as the Bank of England. *All that any of these parties have to do is to take care of their own interests, and to leave the currency, under Sir Robert Peel's Act, to take care of itself.*

"The Bank lives by lending, and it is its business at all times to be satisfied with the market rate, and to look to nothing but good security. Anything beyond this would be to attempt to meddle with processes which it has been the great success of modern statesmanship to place beyond its power of interference.

"Taking this view, it will be expedient, when parties assert that the Bank of England should have raised the rate of interest at such a time, or lowered it at another, to ask why, when they could only get 3 per cent. for their commodity, they should have insisted upon having 4; and also the grounds on which, when they could get 4, they should refuse it, and content themselves with 3. These would be speculative rather than present Chancellor of the Exchequer was, of the impending pressure, till the end of March 1847.

It is now, for the first time, that we hear of "the *ill-regulated issue of its treasure by the Bank*," and though perfectly new, it is any thing but a clear description of what appears to be meant. The only function of the Bank which had ever before been regarded by the currency theorists as of any importance to the public, was that of regulating *the amount of the circulation.* It may be seen in the questions put to me by those who were on the committee in 1840, how strongly prepossessed they were with the idea that it was by operating upon the *circulation* alone, that the directors could, or ought to, influence the exchanges. It was upon this ground that they maintained, that if the circulation were duly regulated by the issue department, the public could not suffer from any want of judgment in the regulation of the banking department. Proofs that their opinions were precisely to this effect might be collected from their evidence, and subsequently from their speeches and their pamphlets, so as to fill a volume. Upon this topic, however, though tempting, I cannot now afford time or space to dilate; and shall only add that I consider the charges brought against the Bank by Sir R. Peel to be most unfair, and the reasoning by which it is attempted to support those charges, extremely inconsistent, and wholly inconclusive.

---

sound business proceedings, and it would be interesting to learn the principles on which they could be defended.

"Meanwhile, the advice, look to the foreign exchanges and to the course of trade, cannot be too often reiterated. The Bank, with a lingering dream of their old power, may still announce their rates to the world as matters of importance, but the announcement cannot alter the real state of things, and those who look to it and watch for it as a great sign will inevitably find that they have been wasting their time, and that shrewder observers have outstripped them."

After thus avowing that one of the objects of the bill which, at the time it was brought forward, was dwelt upon as of the greatest importance, had entirely failed, Sir Robert Peel proceeded to observe,—

"I say then that the Bill of 1844 had a triple object. Its first object was that in which I admit it has proved a failure, namely, to prevent a panic and a confusion such as that which has been obviated by the intervention of the Government; but there were two other objects of as great importance; *the one being to maintain and guarantee the convertibility of a paper currency into gold, and the other to prevent the aggravation of those difficulties which arise at all times from undue speculation, encouraged by an abuse, of paper credit. In these two objects* my belief is that *the Bill has completely succeeded.* (Hear.) My belief is that you have had a guarantee for the maintenance of the principle of convertibility such as you never had before; and my belief also is, *that whatever difficulties you are now suffering from a combination of various causes, those difficulties would have been infinitely aggravated if you had not wisely taken the precaution of checking the abuse of paper credit by an unlimited issue of the notes of joint-stoch banks and private banks, such as the abuse which existed antecedent to the year* 1844."

Two of the objects of the bill are here affirmed to have *completely succeeded*:—the one being to maintain and guarantee the convertibility of a paper currency into gold, the other to prevent the aggravation of those difficulties which arise from undue speculation, and the abuse of paper credit; and the speaker goes on to say, that if it had not been for the restriction of the bill on the issue of notes, the difficulties which have arisen would have been *infinitely aggravated.*

With regard to the second of the two objects, the affirmation is entirely unsustained by proof. On the contrary, as all the subsequent declamatory statements of the speaker tend to show, there was, at the period referred to, an extent of speculation, and an abuse of credit, such as it would require an almost inconceivable stretch of the imagination to suppose exceeded. And I have, in the preceding pages, adduced reasons for believing that the bill, according to the exposition of the spirit of it by Sir Robert Peel, led to increased facilities of banking accommodation, and thus favoured, instead of checking, the spirit of speculation already afloat. As to the assertion that the difficulties which have arisen would have been infinitely aggravated but for the Act, it is so astounding—so much the very reverse of the inference which reasoning *à priori on the tendency* of the bill under such circumstances, would lead to, and of the *evidence which experience and observation afford of its actual operation*, that I must decline to meet it otherwise than by referring to the description which I have given of the state of things in April and October last. I confess that I shall be infinitely surprised if, in the inquiry by the present committees, there can be obtained any thing approaching to a confirmation of Sir Robert Peel's views on this point.

I must here, however, guard myself against misconstruction. In as far as the provisions of the act of 1844 may be found to afford greater security against the insolvency of banks, whether issuing or non-issuing, they have my approbation. The provisions of it to which I specifically object, (besides those which divide the Bank of England into two departments,) are those that *limit the amount of Bank notes* which shall be in the hands of the public. The grounds assigned for such limitation of amount are, in my opinion, entirely unsound in principle, and the operation of the restriction has been, as I believe, productive of great inconvenience, both to bankers and to the public, without in the slightest degree adding to the security of the banks.

But waving further discussion of this part of Sir Robert Peel's defence of his bill, I shall proceed to remark upon his allegation of the success of the first, and only remaining object, out of the three which he had contemplated in the framing of it. It seems, in fact, to be the only one now relied upon by the partisans of the bill; the other two having been gradually given up. I now never hear any other answer, when they are asked what they think of the operation of the Act, than that it is calculated to prevent the suspension of cash payments. Some, indeed, go so far as to add that, but for the Act, the Bank treasure would have been exhausted, and cash payments suspended in the course of 1847!

With regard then to the allegation by Sir Robert Peel, that the Act of 1844 has afforded a better guarantee for the maintenance of the principle of convertibility than we ever before had, I have to observe, that as it is unsupported, either by reasoning or by facts, the opponents of the measure would be perfectly justified in meeting it, simply by a counter assertion, which cannot be better expressed than in the powerful language of the writer of the article in the *Quarterly Review* for June 1847.

"By no contrivance could the great purposes of that Bill (of 1819) be so effectually brought into discredit, or the permanence of the measure itself so seriously endangered as by identifying it in any way with the Bill of 1844."—

It is my sincere belief that the principle of convertibility is seriously endangered by the Act of 1844. The opponents of that principle have unquestionably gained ground in numbers, and in plausibility of argument, by being enabled to refer to the two tremendous shocks which the commerce and industry of the country have sustained by the endeavour, as they contend, (by the act of 1819, as well as that of 1844,) to maintain a system which involves, and necessarily entails, the liability to such convulsions. Now I hold that neither of those shocks would, in all probability, have occurred, but for the restrictions imposed by the Act of 1844.

My reasons for this opinion may be collected from what I have already had occasion to say on the working of that Act; and I shall presently endeavour to show, particularly, how, if the Bank had not been divided into two departments, those shocks might have been avoided.

In the mean time, let us revert to the assertion of our having a better guarantee than we ever before had for the maintenance of the principle of convertibility; meaning, of course, specifically, the convertibility of Bank notes into coin on demand. I will grant, for argument sake, that the guarantee afforded by the Act is sufficient; (which I deny it to be under all circumstances,) but it can only be so on the supposition that the separation of departments should be considered inviolable. So it was evidently intended to be; for it will be recollected that Sir Charles Wood, in his speech, stated how much alarmed he had been at an intimation that a power of relaxation was to be confided to the government. ① Supposing *perfect inflexibility* in the law, such as the currency theory clearly contemplated, then I think it is

① Any admission of flexibility on the part of the new law would have been fatal to the vaunted principle of it. And so far Sir Charles Wood was right when he expressed alarm about the introduction into the Bill of an *expansive clause*, as it was called. It was to be either flexible by an expansive clause, or strictly inflexible. If flexible, it was only having a political governor set over the Governors of the Bank. And in this there would be a liability to the same fallibility of judgment as was complained of under the former system, with the disadvantage that the establishment would be so much the more subservient to the purposes of the administration.

demonstrable that cases might occur, within reasonable probability, entailing the suspension of payment by the deposit department of the Bank of England. Nor is it clear that such might not have been the case recently; indeed it is rather probable that it would have been, had not the government letter of the 25th of October been issued.

Has it ever occurred to Sir R. Peel or Sir C. Wood to consider whether a suspension of payment by the Bank of England of its deposits, including the dividends due to the public, would be attended with less of inconvenience, or with less of national discredit and disgrace, than a suspension of payment

---

If inflexible, the payment of the depositors in the Bank, including the dividends on the public funds and deposits in the savings' banks, might readily be compromised under circumstances such as we have been very near witnessing.

A certain degree of misgiving on this dilemma seems to have come across the mind of Mr. Loyd. Accordingly, on the supposition of a contingency, in his view *barely possible*, (that under the operation of the self-adjusting principle applied to the circulation a case of danger may arise,) he contends that the emergency should be met by the interposition of Parliament, but not by anything short of it.

In support of his view of the propriety of such an interposition under the supposed circumstances, he quotes a passage from Mr. Huskisson, who, when referring (in 1810) to the possibility of such a combination of circumstances (when the restriction should be removed) as to drive the Bank to part with its last guinea, not only without having checked the drain, but, with the certainty of increasing it in proportion as the amount of their notes was diminished, said, "At such a moment the preservation of the Bank from actual failure, though an important, is but a secondary consideration, — that of the country is the first. The possible cases, however, which may call for such an intervention of power, are not capable of being foreseen or defined by law. The necessity may not occur again: if it should, the application of the remedy must be left to those at the head of affairs, subject to their own responsibility, and to the judgment of Parliament."

It is clear from this passage that Mr. Huskisson had in view the possible occurrence of such an extraordinary combination of circumstances as might again place the Bank of England under the necessity of suspending its payments in coin. But I am convinced that if Mr. Huskisson had lived to contemplate the scheme of 1844 he would have revolted from the idea of the possible necessity under that scheme of resorting to such interposition, and would have considered such a contingency as being of itself an insurmountable objection to it. He would hardly have failed to apply the rule of Horace, —

"Nec Deus intersit, nisi dignus vindice nodus."

of Bank notes in coin on demand? I am convinced that it would be attended with very much *more* of inconvenience and national discredit; and I think that the onus of showing that it would not, rests upon those whose favourite measure obviously renders it the more imminent danger of the two.

As regards the public convenience, or the national faith, there is no apparent ground for the preference of *an exclusive guarantee for the notes. They are not, nor ought they to be, as the dividends are, a debt of the state.* During the Bank restriction they were, I believe, distinctly under the guarantee of the state; but it was upon the special ground that the restriction was imposed for state purposes. Upon what principle is it, then, that, with so much inconvenience, we secure the notes, while we leave the dividends without any security, or with one which is plainly assumed to be inferior in value?

There is the same, mistake in the assumption of a necessity for this exclusive guarantee of the notes, as pervades the whole of the reasoning of the currency party. They confound notes, such as those of the Bank of England, with Government notes.

The notes of the Bank of England are, independently of other points of dissimilarity, so far unlike Government notes, that if any demur or delay, from inability to meet the demands of the holders, should occur, the law can at once be appealed to and enforced against the corporation; which it could not be against a government, in the ordinary sense of a government paper money. The law in this country, unlike the law in the United States, may be enforced against that as against any other corporation; or as the law is enforced against other banks. The only difference is in the magnitude of the transactions of the Bank of England. But this magnitude, it may be said, makes a great difference. Granted. I am not disposed to underrate that difference. But it does not justify Sir Robert Peel, and Sir C. Wood, and the supporters of the Act of 1844 generally, in having made such a bugbear of the possibility of a suspension of cash payments by the Bank of England, as to "fright the isle from its propriety." And as the risk of encountering that catastrophe is now apparently the only remaining ground put forth for the maintenance of the Act, it may be desirable to reduce the apparently giant evil to its proper shape and dimensions.

The great terror prevailing at the mention of it, seems to have had its rise in the expression of Mr. Huskisson, that in December 1825, we were within twenty-four hours of a state of barter: meaning, of course, that a suspension of cash payments by the Bank of England would have brought us to that state. At the time when the expression was used, hyperbolical as it appeared to me, I had no objection to it, because it was desirable to impress upon the directors of the Bank, and upon those who were in favour of a lax management, a salutary apprehension of the consequences of it. But as the exaggerated apprehension of those consequences has now become the main ground relied upon for reconciling parliament and the public to the quackery of a new, unnecessary, and mischievous measure—one, certainly, never contemplated by Mr. Huskisson,—it is right to inquire what this "state of barter" amounts to.

I will venture to assure such of my readers as may have been so frightened by the expression as to be induced to acquiesce in the Act of 1844, as a guarantee against the possible occurrence of a state of barter, that they need not apprehend any thing of the kind in the event of a suspension of cash payments. There would not, without the Act of 1844, have been, in 1847, any reasonable ground of apprehension of such a suspension. But supposing that such an event (which I deprecate as much as the most zealous of the currency theorists) had occurred, what would have been the ensuing state of things, as regarded the general transactions of the country? Why, there would not have been a single transaction more in the way of barter than now occurs. There would have been no instance, more than now, of a load of wheat bartered against a horse or an ox; nor of silver spoons bartered for millinery or groceries.

There is a most apt precedent for the course things would take. Government and parliament would interfere, somewhat as the Court of Bankruptcy now does, to protect the defaulting persons, namely, the Directors, till the state of their affairs could be looked into, and the causes of the failure of engagement ascertained; and the concern being, beyond all question solvent, to determine whether it should be wound up, and another bank or banks be established in its stead, or whether it should go on under some guarantee for more prudent management. In the mean time, the material fact of solvency being placed beyond all possibility of doubt, there would be meetings of merchants and bankers entering into resolutions expressive of their confidence, in some such terms as those used in 1797.

And the consequence would be, now as it was then, that there would be no single instance of a shopkeeper refusing a 5*l*. Bank of England note, either for goods to that amount, or to give change out of it. The example would be followed in the provinces, as to those banks which enjoyed the confidence of the neighbourhood; and the circulation would go on very much in its accustomed train.

There would, however, necessarily be a contraction of accommodation. This, if trade were in an unsound state, as it has recently been, would hasten, and, perhaps, extend the range of, commercial failures. Otherwise, for instance, under circumstances like those of 1839, little if any inconvenience of the kind would be felt. But the contraction of accommodation, or in other words, the scarcity of lendable capital, would soon bring it in from abroad, in the only available form, that of gold, —as was the case in 1825-1826, in 1836-1837, and in 1839. And it may be assumed, as a certainty, that if the law of 1819 should remain unrepealed and unrelaxed, as I hope and trust it will, there would be a very short interval, if any, in which the paper would be depreciated in value, that is, by a further fall of the exchanges or rise in the price of gold. Under such circumstances it could not be said that *the principle of convertibility* would be compromised. The sole difficulty would be one of friction in the operation, from the vast magnitude of the subject involved. No one would be more grieved than myself that the principle should be so sorely tried, but I am convinced that it would come out of the trial with much less damage than is generally apprehended.

But whether the extreme alarm felt (or at least expressed) by the currency theorists, at the idea of a suspension of cash payments, and the consequent sacrifice of the principle of convertibility, or my more moderate estimate of the consequences of such an event, be the more rational, I am quite convinced that there would not have been in 1847 any real danger of suspension without the mischievous aid of the Act of 1844.

SECTION 20 *On the arguments advanced to prove that the act of 1844 has already averted or diminished the risk of a suspension of cash payments*

It is for those who maintain the affirmative of the danger of a suspension of cash payments, in the absence of the restrictions imposed by the Act of

1844, and of the fatal consequences of the event, should it occur, to prove their grounds for such apprehension.

The only attempt to show that there would have been a suspension of cash payments had it not been for the Act of 1844, which I have seen, from a quarter entitled to any attention, is in the speech of the Chancellor of the Exchequer, in the debate of the 30th of November. From deference to the authority of one who holds so eminent a station, and whose opinions, on all other grounds, claim the most respectful consideration, I should have been induced to notice Sir C. Wood's argument at some length, were it not that I have already devoted as much time and space to this topic as I can well afford. Indeed, to do justice to the objections to which I consider his views to be open, I should have to write as much as would be equivalent to a moderate-sized pamphlet, there being hardly a point, in the whole of his argument, in favour of the bill, which it is not my misfortune to see reason to dissent from.

Two points, however, I cannot resist noticing.

After describing the inevitable tendency of the drain on the Bank in April to have proceeded indefinitely, had it not been checked by the violent measures of the Bank in April, Sir C. Wood asks —

"If the drain of bullion had gone on, if the amount in the coffers of the Bank had been diminished, as has been the case heretofore, to two or three millions, the publications of the state of the Bank, stating accurately the facts, week by week①, does any body suppose that under those circumstances the alarm would not have taken the course of a run upon the

---

① Under the former system, here supposed, there would *not have been* these weekly publications of the state of the Bank.

Bank of England for gold?"

In answer to this question, I cannot but express my surprise and regret at its having been asked. I should hardly otherwise have imagined that any ordinarily well-informed person could, for a moment, have supposed the possibility, much more the probability of a run upon the Bank of England for gold. The only meaning to be attached to the expression "a run for gold," is, that the holders of the notes entertain, or affect to entertain, doubts of the value of the notes, and therefore hasten to exchange them for gold, without having any specific use for the latter. Now such doubts, or in other words, such discredit of Bank of England notes cannot be said to have existed as a cause of *extensive* demand by the holders of its notes for coin since 1745; when, according to an amusing account by Mr. Francis, in his history of the Bank of England, the directors were obliged to resort to very ingenious, though not very creditable devices, to eke out their resources. In 1796-1797, there was a great deal of political disaffection prevailing, and it might have been the policy of our enemy to promote it; but it does not appear that it entered much, if at all, into the demands upon the Bank at that time. The only clear instance for more than a century, of a "run" upon the Bank of England for gold, was in 1832; but that partook of the ridiculous; and has acquired importance only from the extraordinary use made of it by the partisans of the currency theory. In 1825, when it was notorious, without any publication of accounts, that the Bank had not the means of maintaining its payments in gold, if the demand should continue for a week, there is no well-authenticated instance of a holder of its notes requiring gold from distrust of the paper. Nor was any such distrust manifested when the bullion in the Bank in 1839 was reduced to 2,500,000*l*. No stronger proof of the weakness of an argument can well be imagined than the necessity, here so plainly implied, of aiding it with so miserable a make-weight—so utterly unfounded an apprehension as this.

The only other point which I have to notice in the speech of the Chancellor of the Exchequer is that of his remarking, as a triumphant argument in favour of the Act of 1844, that it secured to the Bank a minimum treasure of eight millions. He says, "we owe much to that eight millions," and asks, "to what are we indebted for the possession of that eight millions, but to the operation of the Act of 1844?" I should hardly trust myself to give, in fitting terms, an answer to such a question, but I luckily find, ready to my hand, some remarks upon it in the current number of the *Quarterly* Review, which express truly, but in language more lively and effective than my own, all that I should wish to say with reference to the extraordinary claim thus set up by the Chancellor of the Exchequer in behalf of the Act of 1844.

"Since the foregoing hints were penned, we have read the debate on the appointment of the Banking Committee. We are gratified to find in it in the aggregate clearer views than we have been used to in such parliamentary discussions. The defence of the Bill of 1844 was exactly what everybody anticipated. 'Tis true that the Bill did not prevent wild speculation and panic, though we said it would. We said there would be no more 1825's, but we never thought so, and you must not find fault with us; that was only allowable parliamentary exaggeration. This, however, we tell you, that but for the Bill of 1844 the speculation and the panic would have been a great deal worse than they have been.' As this defence requires neither knowledge nor talent, nor any qualities but a bold face and great confidence in the timidity and ignorance of your audience, we have nothing to say to it. *But one assumption was made by two or three speakers in the debate so extremely barefaced that we cannot wholly pass it by. It was assumed that but for the Bill of* 1844 *more than seven millions of gold would not have remained in the Bank of England during the worst of the pressure. The reason seven millions odd remained, was that there were sixteen millions odd to begin with, and that the export of nine millions sufficed to turn the exchanges.* About the same sum turned them in 1825, and a very much less sum on every other occasion. *Does any one suppose that if the Bank had begun with eight millions of gold, and tie famine, and the Bill of* 1844, *that a single sovereign would have been left at the end of the pressure?* In 1797 we exported not only all the gold in the Bank of England, but every guinea out of our circulation to carry on a foreign war; and do you suppose that the men of 1847 would have let the two sides of their stomach grow together for want of food, because we had put some stupid quackery into an act of Parliament, and had divided the Bank into a banking department and into an issue department? We send gold abroad when we want something for it, and we keep it at home when we don't, without in either case consulting the fancies of Sir William Clay or Sir Charles Wood. Now, we do not send abroad because we want nothing; we do not want food nor tea, nor sugar, nor coffee, nor indigo. Neither, it appears, do we owe money abroad, because people from all quarters are sending bullion to pay their debts to us."— (*Quarterly Review*, No. 163. Dec. 1847, p. 230.)

It seems quite certain that the original propounders of the currency theory never contemplated an amount of treasure in the Bank materially exceeding, if often reaching, nine or ten millions. Thus Mr. Norman, writing in 1838, when the stock of bullion in the Bank, after having, in the spring of 1837, been reduced to between three and four millions, had increased to about ten millions, observed, "It is probable that an increase will be found in the treasure of the Bank, between its lowest amount last spring, and the highest just previous to the next turn of the exchanges of from seven to eight millions. Now such an influx of treasure is quite unnatural, and could never occur with a metallic circulation." And Colonel Torrens in his illustration of the supposed working of the system he recommended, assumed nine millions as the amount of bullion that might be required in the two departments. Neither in Mr. Loyd's writings, nor in his evidence, do I recollect any thing indicative of an opinion that an amount of treasure larger than that which had been held by the Bank, on an average, between 1832 and 1839, would be at all necessary under the system which he advocated. Nor was any stress laid upon this point by Sir Robert Peel, or his supporters when the bill of 1844 was under discussion.

If it had so happened, that in the autumn of 1846, the bullion in the two departments had been nine instead of sixteen millions, there can hardly be the shadow of a doubt that the Act of 1844 could not have survived the month of March last, in its immaculate state; and any effort to maintain its restrictions would certainly have been attended with imminent danger, or rather the certainty, of a suspension of cash payments.

Having expressed my firm persuasion that, with an undivided power over the whole amount of bullion which the Bank possessed, at the commencement of the drain in the autumn of 1846, the directors might (and as I believe would) have so managed as, without producing such convulsions as those which were sustained in the course of 1847, perfectly to have preserved the convertibility of their notes,—I propose, in order to illustrate my view of what would probably have been the state of things throughout 1847, in an undivided position of the Bank, as contrasted with that which actually existed, to compare the course which Sir Robert Peel adopted in 1844, in his arrangements with the Governors of the Bank with that which I venture to think would have been the wiser and safer course for him to have taken.

It does not appear by the correspondence between the Chancellor of the Exchequer and the Governors respecting the separation of the Bank into two departments, with which of the parties the suggestion of having that separation established *by law* originated; but the presumption is that Sir Robert Peel first, proposed it: that the governors cordially acquiesced in it is well known.

The directors of the Bank had, it seems, for some time previous to 1844 adopted, by way of experiment, the plan of a separation of the two departments, in the mode of keeping their accounts. Mr. Hubbard, one of the directors, in a pamphlet published in 1843, took occasion to illustrate some of his views by tabular statements of the position of the Bank on the footing of keeping a distinct reserve of bullion for all the notes issued beyond the fixed amount of fifteen millions, which was to be distinctly considered as issued against securities. The directors had, it seems, of their own accord, substituted this mode of regulating their issues for that which they had been understood to be guided by, under the mode of management recommended by Mr. Palmer—namely, that of keeping their securities at a nearly even amount, and leaving the bullion to be acted upon by the public; but from which the committee of 1841 recommended them to consider themselves released. The governors, in their interview with Sir Robert Peel in 1844 gave, it is supposed, as the result of their experience of the working of this new guide for their issues, a favourable opinion of it; and concurring, as this did, with whatever other information he had received, and, with the principles of the currency theory (to which, as is evident from his speeches, he had become a proselyte), he determined, it would appear, to found the measure about to be laid before Parliament for the renewal of the Bank Charter on that plan, reducing the fixed amount of issues against securities to fourteen millions; and excluding the post bills.

The proposal of a novel measure, involving a great change, and affecting vast interests, without the sanction of the recommendation of a committee, strikes me to be a parallel case to one which might be imagined, in reference to a similar occasion in the past—as thus: — Suppose that, in 1832, Lord Althorp, having been greatly struck with Mr. Horsley Palmer's evidence and his exposition of the plan by which, while governor of the Bank, he bad successfully regulated its issues, (namely, that of keeping the securities at a nearly uniform amount,) and, being so prepossessed with the scheme, had brought into Parliament, and succeeded in carrying, a bill founded upon it, what would have been said of the prudence of the proceeding, when the measure was found, as it would have been, to fail within three or four years after its enactment, and to require legislative interference for its suspension or repeal? And was the proceeding of Sir Robert Peel very unlike this, or much less rash, in proposing and passing into a law, a scheme which the Bank directors had been induced, in pursuance of a plausible theory, to make trial of as a *mere experiment*: this experiment having been continued only for two or three years without any circumstance having occurred in that short interval likely to bring its efficacy to the test?

The course which I should have thought that so experienced and prudent a statesman would have adopted, (especially entertaining, as he did, the opinion that an enlarged basis of gold was necessary for our enormous superstructure of credit, in which opinion I entirely agree with him,) instead of risking such vast interests, on so novel a scheme, might have been something of this kind.

He would have apprized the governors of the Bank, when treating for the renewal of the charter, that the management had not been so prudently and vigilantly conducted as to avoid giving grounds of alarm to the government and the public for the safety and credit of the establishment, on more than one occasion since the renewal of the charter; that unfortunately they had professed, upon principle, not to exercise foresight in anticipating a drain, but to wait for its operation on their treasure[①]: that they had, accordingly, from want of exercising sufficient foresight in anticipating a drain, and from not taking effective measures for counteracting it when it had strongly set in, given just occasion for questioning the propriety of their management, — instancing the years 1835 and 1836, and also 1838 and 1839, in the last of which years they had suffered themselves to be reduced to the necessity of resorting to a very questionable expedient to save their treasure from complete exhaustion: that they had evidently attempted to conduct the vast business of their establishment upon too small a scale of reserve; thus placing themselves in the alternative, on the occurrence of a drain, of allowing it to proceed to a dangerous extent, or of abruptly contracting their usual scale of banking accommodation, and producing what, in the language of the money market, is called a panic: that in his view, therefore, the most important consideration in the question of the renewal of the charter, was to ascertain whether it was in the power of the governors and directors, and if so, whether they would undertake, on their responsibility, so to conduct the

① See Mr. Palmer's evidence, Bank Charter Report, 1832.

business of the company, as to retain habitually a much larger reserve than they had hitherto thought it necessary or consistent with the interests of their proprietors to maintain.

What the answer of the governors to such an appeal would have been, I do not, of course, take upon me to say. But with respect to the power of maintaining a much larger *average reserve* of bullion than had hitherto been thought necessary, Mr. Horsley Palmer had already given it as his opinion that there would be no difficulty on the part of the Bank, in regulating its business *on a larger basis of bullion*, and that it was mainly a question of expense.① I presume, therefore, that the answer of the governors would

---

① This is a most important point; and Mr. Palmer' s opinion upon it is of the highest authority. I therefore give the following extracts from his evidence before the Committee of 1840: —

"1595. With the experience of the last few years, since the renewal of the Charter, and taking a review of the various circumstances which occurred at the time, can you now suggest any other course which it would be advisable for the Bank to pursue as to the principle of its management? — I know of no other course which could be taken *beyond holding a larger amount of bullion*, but which I and not prepared to say the Bank could do without means being devised to remunerate that establishment for the expense and charges that would attend such a measure.

"1596. Do you think that the principle of management, as laid down in 1832, *with a larger proportion of bullion, and a smaller proportion of securities, with reference to their liabilities*, would be the best rule for the management of the Bank? — *With reference to the whole circulation of the country, I think it would.*

"1597. Under those circumstances, if notes were issued on securities, as in the summer of 1839, notwithstanding the drain of bullion, might not the currency even then be maintained in excess; — would this rule be any preservative against an excess of Bank notes? — It would be no preservative against events which require special action on the part of the Bank. *The increased amount of bullion would afford increased means for meeting foreign payments of such a character as existed in* 1839, *without the necessity of resorting to those means which were taken to supply the dificiency.*

"1598. *Would its operation be to preserve the convertibility of paper without resorting to means which it may not at all times be in the power of the Bank to take?* — *Certainly.*

"1599. Do you conceive that it would be always in the power of the Bank to take such measures as they did adopt in the summer of 1839 for the protection of their bullion? — *I think it would be very undesirable to resort to those measures except in extreme cases.*

have been to the same effect; and that the condition of the maintenance of a *much larger reserve of bullion* would have had to be considered in the general terms of the arrangement. ①

Supposing the governors, upon reference to and consultation with the Court of Directors, to have expressed their acquiescence in the practicability of maintaining an average reserve, larger by five or six millions than that which the Bank had possessed since the last renewal of the charter, and their consent (with the understanding that the additional expense should be a consideration in the arrangement) had been obtained, pledging their responsibility so to regulate their business as to accomplish, as far as possible, the object in view,—what would, in all probability, have been the course of management adopted, and what the probable state of monetary affairs, compared with that which has existed since the change of system in 1844?

It is of course not possible to show to demonstration what, under these circumstances, would have been, instead of what has been, the state of things. But as Sir Charles Wood undertook to prove how much *worse* the state of things *would have been* but for the Act of 1844, I will

---

"1622. *A* larger proportion of bullion could not be kept without some diminution of the profits of the Bank of England? — No.

"1623. But supposing the Bank consent to that, you see no difficulty in their keeping such a reserve as to be a security against all ordinary danger? — No."

① The governors might probably have added, that although the condition of holding so large a reserve might be compensated in the general terms agreed upon on the renewal of the Charter, the Court of Directors would be placed in a disagreeable position; because the proprietors, seeing in the periodical returns so large an amount of bullion, would remonstrate and express displeasure at the unproductive state of so large a proportion of their assets. To this objection Sir Robert Peel might have replied, that if such was likely to be the ease, the proprietors should be apprised that it would be a condition of the Charter that they should have no voice in the declaration of a dividend.

endeavour to show how much *better* they might have been (by a very simple precaution, which it was quite open to the Government to take,) than they have proved to be under the complicated and hazardous machinery of that act.

As Sir Charles Wood has assumed, in his view, the advantage of the circumstances which existed in 1844, and from that time till the autumn of 1846, and which determined a large influx of the precious metals into this country (most assuredly *not caused by that measure*), I must claim the same advantage for my view.

Assuming such to have been the state of things on the renewal of the Charter, and such as I have stated, the implied engagement entered into by the directors, and the responsibility thus thrown upon them, it is perfectly impossible to suppose for a moment that they would have ventured to take such a step as they did — that of reducing their rate of discount from 4 per cent, to 2 $\frac{1}{2}$ per cent — immediately upon the Act of 1844 coming into operation. Nor is it at all likely that they would have thought it right or safe to reduce their public rate of discount at any part of the period in question below 4 per cent. And as to their quarterly advances, the same motives would have deterred them from reducing the terms below those which they had required before the passing of the Act of 1844.

I am not disposed to exaggerate the influence of the reduction of its rates by the Bank between 1844 and 1847. Some influence it cannot but have had, as I have before observed, in facilitating the speculations which were then in progress. But, waiving the consideration of its influence in that way, it is to its influence, small though it may have been, upon the state of the Bank treasure, that I would now direct attention. In whatever degree the management of the Bank in 1844 may have tended to reduce or keep down the general rate of interest[①], it must have favoured the efflux of capital for foreign investment, and consequently must have somewhat abated the tendency to influx, or to the maintenance of the then existing amount of bullion. I cannot, therefore, but think that if the Bank in 1844-1845-1846 had kept up its rates, and thus kept down or reduced its securities, there would have been an increase of its treasure beyond the utmost amount that it actually did reach. One million additional of treasure is, I conceive, the lowest computation of what must have been the effect of the Bank allowing its securities to run down to so low an amount as they must have reached if the rate of its discounts and loans had been kept up as I have supposed, and that the directors had not made purchases, as I take for granted they would not, of public securities at the high prices then prevailing. The treasure would thus, I presume, have amounted, in the summer of 1846, to nearly 18 millions; assuming all other things to have been the same as regards the reserves of gold held by other banks subsequent to the Banking Acts of 1844 and 1845. The provisions of those acts, however, rendered it in some degree incumbent upon all issuing banks to hold larger reserves of gold than they had previously been accustomed to hold. The extra amount of gold thus reserved beyond the amount previously held, or that would, but for those acts, have been held by the provincial banks, can hardly be computed at

---

① Allowance should be made, with reference to the reduction of the Bank rate of interest, for the circumstance that after March, 1845, it was a *minimum* rate, — a new practice of the Bank, which has aggravated all the other inconveniences of a variation of its rate, rendering the real rate somewhat higher than the declared rate, but also preventing the former from being publicly known.

less than two millions.[①] If, therefore, the amount of these extra reserves had been added, as in the absence of the acts in question they would have been, to the Bank treasure, the amount of bullion in the Bank in August, 1846, would have been between 19 and 20 millions, viz. :—

Amount as it stood 29th Aug., 1846 -	£ 16,366,000
Addition supposed from diminished securities of the Bank - - -	1,000,000
Addition of what, but for the extra reserves of provincial banks, would have flowed into the Bank - -	2,000,000
	£ 19,366,000

① I believe that I am considerably within the mark in confining myself to an estimate of two millions as the amount of the gold coin absorbed by the *extra* reserves which the legislation of 1845 compelled the Scotch, and Irish bankers habitually to retain; and it is fortunate that so important a point can be placed on a more certain foundation than a mere statement of individual opinion. Confining, in the first instance, my observations to Scotland and Ireland, I may observe that the acts of 1845 rendered it imperative on the bankers of those countries to retain *in coin a sum equal* to the excess of their outstanding circulation above a given maximum. The legal maximum of circulation for Scotland was 3,087,209*l.*, and for Ireland, 6,354,294*l.*; and the following table represents the state of the Scotch and Irish note issues in December, 1845: —

	Date.	Actual circulation.	Excess of actual circulation above the maximum.
		£	£
Scotland -	5 Dec. 1845 -	3,804,000 -	717,000
Ireland -	5 Dec. 1845 -	7,715,000 -	1,361,000
			2,078,000

As the whole of this excess of actual circulation beyond the statutory limit was represented by coin in the safes of the several banks, it is plain, that leaving England entirely out of view, an extra internal demand of more than two millions was caused by the acts of 1845 in Scotland and Ireland alone. The maximum of the English country circulation was fixed at 8,478,893*l.*, an amount considerably less than that usually in circulation in past years of ordinary prosperity. The vacuum has been filled to a certain extent by the paper of the Bank of England. But a very large proportion of the new medium has been in the shape of coin; and whether this proportion may be one half, three fourths, or the whole of a million, according to the periods of the year, it is certain that it constitutes an important addition to the extra demands from Scotland and Ireland, and more than justifies the assumption made in the text.

Here, then, would have been the Bank with a treasure of upwards of 19 millions at the first manifestation of a drain in the autumn of 1846. I may also take credit for the probability that the drain would have been somewhat less by the difference of the rate of discount between 3 per cent as it was, and 4 per cent as it would, upon my hypothesis, have been in the interval from August, 1846, to January, 1847. The directors might safely have looked on without altering their rate till the end of January, 1847. By that time having lost (say) $3\frac{1}{2}$ millions of their treasure, and being under the responsibility of keeping up a large reserve, and exercising foresight with that view, which would have led them to thc conviction that the causes of drain were of a formidable character, they would, as I imagine, have raised their rate to 5 per cent.

It is not improbable that the directors, having raised the rate to 5 per cent at the end of January, and having still so large an amount of bullion, would have waited till the 8th of April to judge of the progress and character of the drain; when, seeing a further loss of 3 millions, they might have thought it necessary to raise the rate to 6 per cent per annum. If this advance had not had the effect of visibly checking the drain, and if by the 17th of April there were to have been, as there was, a further loss of treasure, the directors might have reduced the dates of bills admissible for discount to 60 days, instead of 95 days. This would have operated as a considerable restriction of accommodation, but would not have been attended with any thing like the shock to credit that attended the violent measures which were actually adopted by the Bank at that period, and which I have elsewhere described.

Every merchant, or manufacturer, or banker, possessing good bills not exceeding the Bank time, would still have been secure of converting them, so as to enable him to meet his engagements; but this he could not be sure of under the restrictions which were actually imposed.

The effect of the shock of the 17th of April was almost immediately to turn the exchanges; and, in a few days after, to stop the drain.

The mere increase of the rate of interest to 6 per cent, and a restriction of bills to 60 days, would not have had the same effect in turning the exchanges; and there would consequently have been some longer continuance of the drain.

I will suppose, therefore, on account of this difference, that two millions more of bullion would have been exported before the foreign demand ceased. This, I am convinced, is a large allowance.

The drain, then, which was surmounted in the beginning of May by the payment, of seven millions, and by the violent restriction of credit by the Bank in the middle of April, would, in my hypothetical case, have been surmounted a few weeks later with the loss of nine millions.

Under the existing system, the bullion remaining when the drain was stopped by the violent shock that has been described, amounted (24th April, 1847) to 9,210,000*l*.

According to the system which I have supposed, by the simple pressure of a high, but uniform rate of interest, and moderately restricted accommodation, the drain would equally have been surmounted, although a few weeks later, and with the loss of two millions more of bullion; but the amount of bullion held by the Bank would, at the end of the drain, have been 10,300,000*l*., or one million more than actually remained after the convulsion in April last.

Such, I conceive, is, as nearly as may be estimated, the

difference between what *actually occurred* in the first six months of 1847, under the Act of 1844, and *what might, and in all probability would, have occurred* without it; and with only the precaution which, according to the view I have suggested, a wise minister might be supposed to have taken in agreeing to the renewal of the Bank Charter: — a stipulation that the directors should hold, habitually, a much larger reserve of bullion.

The case is still clearer as regards the last six months of 1847.

The great, immediate, and most formidable causes of the drain having been overcome before the end of June, the policy of the Bank would have been, in pursuance of the same system, not to have relaxed from whatever rate of interest, or restriction of accommodation, it might have imposed, till the whole of the disturbing causes had subsided, and the influx of bullion had so far set in as to afford ample assurance of the reinstatement of the proper amount of its treasure.

Under this policy, the feverish state of the money market, commencing at the end of July, and the convulsion of it terminating in the crisis of the week ending on the 23rd of October might, as I think, have been avoided.

I have already supposed that the drain of the first six months, which carried away seven millions of the Bank treasure under the present system, would have taken two millions more under the system which I have suggested. The amount of the treasure would, therefore, have been, on the 26th of June, 1847,10,300,000*l*. Or, in other words, allowing for an addition of three millions to the amount of bullion held by the Bank at the commencement of the drain, and for the drain having lasted two months longer, and carried away two millions more than it did—the amount of the bullion, at the end of June 1847, would have been one million greater than it was when at its lowest point in the last week of April. The balance of trade was, at that time, as nearly as possible, adjusted. A few hundred thousand pounds (not exceeding half a million) formed the utmost extent of any foreign demand within the four or five weeks following; and there is no reason to suppose that the demand would have been greater in my hypothetical case than that which actually occurred under the present system.

Thenceforward, that is from the commencement of August, there was not any foreign demand for gold, and there would not, as I believe, have been any, supposing the Bank rate of interest to have then been 5 per cent, or, at the utmost, 6 per cent as a uniform rate, for all such bills as were admissible under the former system, and for the description of accommodation usually granted. In the early part of August, the great fall in the price of all descriptions of food had removed all apprehension of further large importations; and the extensive failures in the corn trade, followed by the still more important and extensive failures in other branches of commerce, these being, moreover, accompanied by failures of banks, caused such a degree and extent of discredit as left an immense vacuum in the ordinary channels of circulation. The whole of the increased demand, therefore, on the Bank of England, for accommodation, thenceforward was clearly for purposes purely internal, and with the amount of bullion which it then possessed, and still more with the amount which it would have possessed in my hypothetical case, there was not, and could not have been the shadow of any ground for apprehending a further inconvenient reduction of its treasure.

The directors therefore, instead of resorting to violent measures of restriction, as they were bound to do under the Act of 1844, from the latter part of September to the 23rd of October, in order to protect the narrow margin of their reserve, might, with perfect safety, have extended their accommodation to all legitimate claims upon them within their ordinary rules. Thus some of the enormous sacrifices of property, and much of the intense suffering of a large part of the commercial community might have been spared. And I verily believe that, under the management here supposed, there would have been a larger amount of bullion in the Bank than there proved to be at the end of October last — namely, about eight millions.

I have thus sketched an outline of the grounds on which I consider it beyond question, that if, instead of the pedantic scheme of dividing the Bank into two departments, and restricting the *amount* of the circulation of the country banks, the simpler plan had been adopted of requiring the Bank of England to possess habitually a much larger reserve than it had before held, the two tremendous shocks, of April and October last, might have been avoided, without the possibility of danger to the convertibility of the paper, and consistently with leaving a larger amount of treasure in the Bank, not only through all the earlier and more rapid stages of the drain, but also at the final termination of it.

But I will put a still stronger case in illustration of my opinion, that, without the Act of 1844, there would have been no real danger to the convertibility of Bank notes.

Let us suppose that, in 1844, seeing no reason for a change of system in the Bank management, Sir Robert Peel had confined his arrangements, for the renewal of the charter, to a merely pecuniary consideration of the terms; or, what is, perhaps, a still more simple hypothesis, that the charter had been renewed in 1832, as on former occasions, for an uninterrupted term of twenty-one years. We will also suppose, that whatever regulations might have been thought necessary or expedient with a view to greater security for the solvency of the country banks, there would have been no restriction imposed on the amount of their circulation, as by the acts of 1844-1845. What then would, probably, have been the management of the Bank, and what the results, as compared with those which we have experienced?

The presumption I think is, that in September, 1844, the directors not considering themselves, as they did, in obedience to the spirit of the new act, released from their former rules or practice, would not have reduced their rate of discount. If they had kept to their routine line of policy in that respect, the probability is (on the grounds which I have suggested in the former part of this section), that the influx of bullion would have been increased by about a million at least; and of the whole stock of bullion then in the country, there would, as in my former hypothetical case, have been two millions more in the coffers of the Bank of England, by the release of so much required, by the acts of 1844-1845, to be held by the country banks. With the addition, then, of these three millions to the stock of bullion in the Bank, in August 1846, the amount would, as I have supposed in the former case, have been somewhat more than nineteen millions to meet the drain then setting in. The only difference between the former hypothetical case and this is, that in the first, the directors might be supposed (being bound by an implied engagement entered into for the maintenance of a larger habitual reserve of bullion), to have taken earlier measures to counteract the drain; whereas, under the second supposition, having no such engagement, they might be supposed to have allowed the drain to proceed much further before they raised the rate of interest above 4 per cent.

Granting that the directors, in the case last assumed, had suffered the drain to proceed till the 8th of April without any advance of their rate; by that time the loss of bullion would have been so striking, that whatever might be the stupidity, perverseness, or ignorance, so liberally ascribed to them by Sir Robert Peel and Sir Charles Wood, they could not fail to have advanced the rate to 5 per cent per annum. Thus far, then, they would have been *pari passu* with the state of things that actually occurred.

In each case, namely, the actual one, and that which I have last supposed, the rate on the 8th of April would have been raised to 5 per cent. But while, under the new act, the amount of bullion in the two departments was ten and a quarter millions, not more than one-third of it was applicable to the most variable, and consequently most hazardous branch of the liabilities.① Under the former system, according to my hypothesis, there would have been thirteen and a quarter millions applicable to the whole of the liabilities②, and the question now is, how, under those circumstances, it is likely that the directors would have acted.

It can only be on the presumption that they were perfectly uncorrected and incorrigible by experience, and had, therefore, not profited at all by the lesson of 1839, that they can be supposed, after having raised their

① Bullion in the Bank on 17th April, 1847.

Issue department - - - - - - -	£ 6,250,000
Banking department- - - - - - -	3,080,000
Total - - - - - - - - - - -	9,330,000

② But probably somewhat more, as before observed, in consequence of the higher rate of interest between August, 1846, and January, 1847.

rate of discount, on the 8th of April, to 5 per cent, to have remained perfectly passive under the further progress of the drain. I should rather believe that, seeing the strength of the tendency to a further efflux of bullion during the remainder of that month, they would, before the close of it, have taken a further step, by either raising the rate of discount, or reducing the number of days for bills, or by the sale of securities, or by adopting all these means of checking the drain. But I will allow to the currency party the full benefit of the assumption, that the directors would have been imprudent enough to have taken no step whatever for the reduction of their securities; and thus to have allowed the drain to have taken its course unchecked, as far as the Bank of England was concerned. What then would have been the further course which the drain would have taken, thus unchecked by the Bank, except by an advance of one per cent. in the rate of discount?

According to the currency theory, the drain, unless the Bank *contracted its circulation*, would proceed, uninterruptedly, to the utter exhaustion of its treasure.

This doctrine of the *interminable* nature of drains, like every other peculiar to the currency theory, I consider to be utterly untenable upon any, general ground of reasoning, and at variance with all experience and evidence of facts.

I cannot better convey my opinion of the nature, and causes, and limits, of a drain of gold, for export, than by quoting the following passages from a writer in whose views of the subject, expressed with admirable clearness, I perfectly concur:—

"Considering how great, and almost exclusive, a stress has been laid upon the extraordinary security said to be furnished for the convertibility of

Bank notes by the Act of 1844, there is perhaps no point of more importance than to define as far as possible the nature of the only danger to convertibility against which that act can be imagined to contain a safeguard. Danger from internal panic, we have seen, it does not prevent. On the contrary, it tends to produce such danger when it does not exist, and to aggravate it when it does. But the danger of having the whole of the Bank bullion drained out for exportation is that against which we are assured that the Act of 1844 is an effectual remedy. How is it, then, that we ever come to be exposed to this danger, and what are the means of averting it?

"The general law under which drains of gold for export take place is extremely simple, and if the whole of the circumstances naturally attending its operation were investigated, it would probably be found much less alarming than it has been generally represented. The debts and credits of two countries trading together generally balance each other, or are brought to an equality by the aid of sonic third country, which is a creditor to one of the two, and a debtor to the other. Thus, directly or indirectly, goods are paid for in goods. But it happens, from time to time, that payments requiring to be made out of the ordinary course of trade are most easily effected by a transmission of the precious metals, and when this happens, gold or silver, as the case may be, will flow out of the debtor country. The chief cause of such payments in time of peace is a sudden and unusual import, which, from the nature of the case cannot be met by a sudden and equally large export; and imports of corn to supply a defficient harvest have been hitherto, in the anomalous state of our corn trade, almost always of this kind. When such an event occurs, however, it is evident that a certain definite payment has to be made, and that when gold enough has gone out for the purpose, the exchanges will revert to their ordinary state, and the general movement of trade will be the same as before. It would be clearly an absurdity to infer from the fact that a set of London merchants had incurred a debt of five millions sterling for corn to a set of New York merchants, and were discharging it by sending out gold, that therefore there would be no end of the transmission of gold, unless active measures were taken to stop it. The debt would be paid by the individual merchants, let the law or the Bank say what it might; but it is equally certain that the payment would not exceed the debt. We have had some considerable drains of gold which came to an end without any effort being made for the purpose. The definite extent, and the natural course and termination of drains, resulting from a variety of causes, have been explained in the most lucid and instructive manner, by Mr. Fullarton, in his able work on the currency. *In almost all cases, if we had a sufficient stock of gold in hand at the outset, the drain might safely go on until the foreign demand was satisfied, without disturbance to commerce.* If, therefore, our stock of bullion were adequate, and our commerce generally in a sound state, the infliction of pressure to check so harmless a movement would be gratuitous folly.

"Our stock of bullion, however, may not be, large enough to bear much diminution, or, though large, the probable drain may be great enough to threaten a dangerous reduction of it. In either case something must be done to keep up an adequate stock of treasure. There are but two things that can be done. One is to force goods abroad in payment of the debt, instead of gold. The other is to induce foreigners to send gold for investment in our interest-bearing securities. In the latter case we pay the debt by the export of stocks and shares. In all cases the debt is discharged. The principle upon which the Act of 1844 was founded was that of counteracting a drain by forcing the export of goods. This, however, even when it is practicable, can only be done by a most violent and destructive operation upon the value of all kinds of mercantile property dependent upon credit. The arrangements of the act are such as to ensure practically that when the bullion in the Bank is no more than about eight millions discounts shall be stopped and merchants thrown for the means of meeting their engagements entirely upon their own resources. By this means goods held upon credit may be forced upon the market, and the reduction of price so brought about may facilitate exportation. It must be admitted that this, if it be a remedy, is a truly desperate one. It is, in fact, a kind of quackery, which may possibly be admissible when all else fails, but which certainly ought not to be called in except in the last extremity.

"The only other mode of counteracting the effects of a drain of bullion is by establishing, if possible, such an advance in the current rate of interest as may attract capital from foreign countries. The application of this remedy need not of necessity be attended either with serious commercial disturbance or with discredit. It would make discounts dear, but neither unattainable nor uncertain; and supposing trade to be upon the whole in a sound state, the greatest evil arising from it would be a temporary diminution of commercial profits. It is by this remedy only that the drain of gold has been counteracted in the present year, and it is only in so far as it operated upon the rate of interest that the Act of 1844 has had any real influence in preventing the exhaustion of the Bank bullion. If the act had had no other operation, the country would have been spared the distress and mischief of the two panics, and yet have been just as well supplied with gold as it is at present. But even this remedy, though the most effectual and least objectionable, cannot in all cases be relied upon, for the gold will at all events flow out to discharge the foreign debt, and it is not always certain that the gap can be filled up from some other quarter. Hence we may conclude, that not only the ease and security of our commerce, but the steadiness of our whole monetary and financial system, require the maintenance in this country of a stock of bullion large enough to meet such demands upon it as may occasionally arise from an unfavourable exchange; or what, with a paper convertible into gold, is the same thing, from an adverse balance of foreign payments. The practicability of keeping up a great stock of gold is sufficiently proved by the fact, that in the ordinary course of trade the precious metals have a stronger tendency to flow into England than into any other country; but the objection hitherto made to such a measure has always been its expense. It is of course natural to expect that the Bank of England should be unwilling to hold an excessive proportion of its capital in a form generally unprofitable, and its readiness, if not impatience, to get rid of its gold on some remarkable occasions, however injurious to the public, cannot be considered surprising in a commercial corporation. But if the management of this vast central hoard of bullion, being as it is a national reserve for certain great emergencies, were viewed in its true light, as an object of primary national importance, we do not believe that there would be any serious difficulty about the cost of keeping it up."—(*Morning Chronicle*, 29th Dec., 1847.)

My belief, then, is, that the stock of bullion in the Bank, at the beginning of April, namely, twelve and a half millions, would have been *ample* to have satisfied the drain, without resort, by the Bank, to any measure more violent than an advance to 6 per cent and, possibly, a reduction of the *echéance* to sixty days. But I am inclined to think that it would have been *sufficient* if the rate had been simply advanced to 5 per cent.

I have already supposed that, with an advance to 6 per cent and 60 days' *echéance*, the drain would have carried off two millions more of gold than actually went in April and May. Granting, then, that in consequence of not advancing the rate above 5 per cent, and retaining the *echéance* at ninety-five days, one or two millions more had gone, making the reduction of treasure altogether greater by three or four millions than that which actually occurred; and taking the reduction at four millions; this, added to the seven millions, by which the treasure had been diminished between August 1846 and May 1847, would make eleven millions to have gone towards redressing the adverse balance of trade: leaving, still, eight millions in reserve.

Now that the whole cycle of events, from the commencement to the termination of the drain, is completed, it would be well worthy of the consideration of those who have better means of judging than I have, how far the circumstances affecting the trade of the country, and the value of securities, including railway investments, would justify the supposition that a much larger sum than that which I have here assumed, would have been required, without any violent contraction of accommodation by the Bank.

There are two reasons that weigh with me in coming to the conclusion that the sums I have set down would have been more than sufficient to satisfy the demand for export.

One reason is derived from a reference to the drain of 1824-1825. It appears that from the 31st of August, 1824, to the 31st of August, 1825, the loss of treasure by the Bank was about eight millions, namely, from 11,727,430*l.* to 3,634,320*l.* But, as the exchanges had turned before the end of July, 1825, the probability is that some part of these eight millions had been taken for internal purposes; especially as there were already premonitory symptoms of discredit among the country banks. At any rate, these eight millions had fully satisfied the foreign demand, and the drain had run out without the smallest effort on the part of the Bank to resist it; there having been no advance in its rate of discount above 4 per cent. Here, then, was the case of a perfectly spontaneous termination of a drain, which was of a very formidable character, by an export of eight millions of gold.

The other reason, on which, indeed, I lay more stress, is derived from a reference to the Bank of France. That establishment was, in December 1846, very critically situated, so much so, as to be compelled to have recourse to a measure very similar to that which had been resorted to by the Bank of England in the autumn of 1839. It borrowed a sum of 800, 000*l.* from parties in London; and its prospects, at that time, were full of peril. In proportion to the magnitude of the commerce of the two countries, the balance of trade seemed *relatively* to be more adverse to France than to this country, the former requiring an enormous importation of food, while its resources for the payment of it, by exports of commodities, were much less; and yet the Bank of France took no other measure for the counteraction of the effects of that adverse balance, than a very late and reluctant advance in its rate of discount from 4 to 5 per cent. The purchase from it of fifty millions of rentes by the Russian government no doubt operated as a relief. But it operated also, though indirectly, as a relief to the Bank of England, because, if the Bank of France had not been so relieved, its difficulties and necessities would have caused a further depression in our exchanges on Paris, and would have required more effort on the part of the Bank of England to turn them. I mention the instance of the Bank of France, because the doctrine of the currency theory that drains cannot be surmounted without a contraction of the circulation, would apply to it, in an eminent degree; and yet the drain there did terminate without any contraction worth mentioning of the circulation, and with only a rise in the rate of discount, from 4 to 5 per cent. And, further, because the example of the Bank of France has, on some former occasions, been held up in disparagement of the Bank of England. ①

But, recurring to the comparison between what has taken place, under the Act of 1844, and what would have taken place, if the only precaution taken by the Bank of England, in April last, had been confined to an advance of its rate of discount from 4 to 5 per cent, according to my supposition, I think there might have been an export of bullion, in all, between August 1846 and August 1847, of about eleven millions; thus

---

① In proof of the pertinence of my allusion to the experience of the Bank of France, and as a further instance of the occurrence of a serious drain of treasure in the face of an almost undiminished outstanding circulation, I may refer to the official returns of that establishment. I would particularly direct the attention of the partisans of the currency theory to this striking addition to the catalogue of anomalies which they find it so difficult to explain in accordance with their peculiar doctrines. For here in France is the same discrepancy as in England between the variations of the notes and of the bullion. The following were the average results of the quarters ended, —

Quarters ended.			Outstanding circulation. Francs.			Coin and bullion. Francs
25 March, 1845	–	–	256,000.000	–	–	266,000,000
26 Dec., 1845	–	–	269,498,000	–	–	187,334,000
26 Dec., 1846	–	–	259,459,000	–	–	72,734,792
25 March, 1847	–	–	249,404,000	–	–	79,535,000

leaving, after the full satisfaction of the drain, at the latter date, eight and a half millions, which, inasmuch as all further demand, if any, for gold, must have been for internal purposes, would, unquestionably, have been quite sufficient.

The hypotheses I have ventured to introduce in the preceding pages, will of course be contested, and I readily admit that I have no means of proving them: they are mere conjectures; but they are better entitled to attention, presenting, as they do, some tangible grounds for computation, than the confident assumption, without any details whatever, by the advocates of the Act of 1844, that, but for that measure, we should have had a suspension of cash payments.

I will, however, bring the matter to a still closer test. Let us take the supposition by Sir Charles Wood, in his speech of the 30th of November, that, but for that act, the bullion in the coffers of the Bank might have been reduced to between two and three millions. The reduction of the bullion to this low amount, supposes that the drain from August 1846, to October or November 1847, would, in the absence of the act, have gone to the extent of sixteen millions.

Granting, for the sake of argument, that the amount of bullion had been so reduced; but not, for a moment admitting the remotest probability of such a run for gold, subsequently, as Sir C. Wood proposes, I would ask whether, after having parted with nine millions of gold more than actually was exported, amounting in all to sixteen millions, from the commencement of the drain, and therefore satisfied so much of the foreign debt, the directors would have found more difficulty in rectifying the exchanges than they did in April 1847? Is it possible that any competent person can, for a moment, doubt that there would, under such circumstances, have been less difficulty, if any difficulty at all; —and, if not, what becomes of the bugbear of our being reduced to suspend cash payments?

SECTION 21 *The conclusion of the argument on the act of 1844*

The view which has been sketched in the preceding section of *what might have been* compared with *what was*, is not only of importance in showing how much in error Sir Robert Peel and Sir Charles Wood were, and probably still are, in their estimate of the operation of the Act of 1844: it also suggests the consideration of the immense advantage which a large treasure is calculated to afford to the Bank in an undivided state, in greatly mitigating the pressure which is inevitably incidental to the occasional occurrence of casualties entailing, suddenly, an adverse balance of trade.

The advantage which I thus ascribe to the possession by the Bank of a large treasure, consists in its enabling the directors to regulate their management with fewer and less abrupt changes in the rate of interest, and in the degree and kind of accommodation, than would be necessary with a comparatively small reserve. The difference, in this respect could not, by possibility, be more strikingly exemplified than by the experience of the present law.

I have shown, on the strongest grounds of hypothetical reasoning, with how few changes, in the rate of interest, the Bank might have surmounted the recent pressure, if it had had the *undivided possession and use of the bullion in its vaults*; and more especially, if it had had the possession and use of the two millions or thereabouts, which were, and are, absorbed very uselessly, as a consequence of the restriction on the circulation of the country banks.

Under the present law, according to the experience which we have had of it in the memorable year which has just closed, the changes in the rate of interest, and still more in the extent and kind of accommodation, have been at least as frequent, as abrupt, and as violent, as might have been found to be necessary if the Bank had been on its former footing, with little more than half the amount of bullion which was in its vaults in August and September 1846. With a stock of bullion of ten millions at that time, on its former footing it might have counteracted the drain so as to have saved itself (that is, it might have rectified the exchanges, notwithstanding the formidable extent of the adverse balance of trade,) by measures not more violent than those which the directors were, in self-defence, obliged to resort to in April last (1847).

We will suppose that, having a treasure of only ten millions in August and September, 1846, they had been as supine in the interval between that time and April, as they were in 1839, and that, by the middle of April, the bullion, after the payment of seven millions towards satisfying the adverse balance of trade, had been reduced to the same amount as the banking reserve was at that time, namely, about three millions.[①] If, then, having no resource such as was resorted to, in 1839, by a loan from France, the directors were determined, at any sacrifice, to save themselves from the necessity of suspending cash payments, as resolutely as the directors were last April to protect the reserve in the banking department, there is no

① There were eight weekly returns in 1839 (six of them consecutive, in August and September) in which the bullion was only 2,400,000*l*.

reason whatever to suppose that they would not have been equally successful in turning the exchanges, and consequently stopping the drain. ①

The fair inference to be deduced from this view is, that by the mistake—and a gross mistake it is, or, to use a more emphatic, and therefore more appropriate term, the great and grievous blunder②, committed in the separation of the Bank into two departments; the six millions of capital in the shape of bullion in the issue department were perfectly inert, cut off, and inapplicable to the purpose of relieving the intense pressure which was felt from the want of available capital; and that consequently no advantage whatever was derived by the country from possessing, accidentally, (*for it was by no merit of the act*,) so very large an amount of bullion as existed at the commencement of the late drain.

It is hardly possible to imagine confirmation more complete than that which is thus afforded by experience and the evidence of facts, of the correctness of the anticipations which were entertained and expressed of the

---

① Sir Robert Peel seems to have had a glimpse of the power of the Bank to save itself under most circumstances, and of its being only a question of the effects on the commercial community, whether it is expedient to resort to measures so violent as in some cases might be necessary. In the following passage of his speech in the debate of April 25th, 1845, he admits that under the former system there might be a *guarantee for the permanent convertibility*; but there would be a liability, he supposes, to a violent contraction of the circulation deranging the monetary transactions of the country. How much less, might it be asked, has there been of derangement than was contemplated in the following remarks?

After repeating some of the assumptions on which the House had proceeded, Sir Robert Peel added, "There was another assumption on which the House also acted — that with a perfectly unregulated competition in the issue of paper there was no necessary guarantee for the permanence of the convertibility of that paper, or rather, I should say, that *though there might be the guarantee of permanent convertibility*, yet there was no guarantee, where competition was perfectly unrestricted and unlimited, *against the occasional necessity of sudden and violent contractions* of the circulation, *leaving, indeed, the notes convertible into gold, but deranging the monetary transactions of the country, and shaking all confidence, even in public credit.*"

② According to Dr. Johnson, the meaning of the word "blunder" is "a gross mistake."

probable operation of the act by those who had originally opposed the measure. With a larger stock of bullion than was ever before accumulated in the vaults of the Bank, the commerce of the country has been visited with shocks which could not have been exceeded in violence, if the total amount of treasure at the commencement of the drain had been only one half of that which it actually reached.

With upwards of 16,000,000*l*. of bullion in hand, the Bank, when called upon to meet a drain for foreign payment, the actual extent of which did not reach nearly half that amount, and which, in all probability, would not, under the least vigilant management conceivable, have reached 10,000,000*l*., found itself so crippled by the arbitrary separation of its departments, that the directors were under the necessity of resorting to measures more severely restrictive of commercial credit than any that had been known since 1796-1797. The variations, in the rate of interest, during the year 1847, have exceeded in frequency and extent any of winch there is to be found an example in the commercial history of this country. The number of the variations of the Bank minimum rate of discount has already been noticed. The *range* of variation of the Bank rate, since Sept. 1844, has been from $2\frac{1}{2}$ per cent up to 9 per cent, and recently down to 4 per cent. But within little more than nine months, namely, from the beginning of April, 1847, to the end of January, 1848, the range has been from 4 per cent up to 9 per cent, and back to 4 per cent. While the market rate has varied, in this latter interval, from 4 per cent to 12, 15 and 20 per cent, and fallen back to less than 4 per cent.

The three concluding propositions with which I terminated my view in 1844, of the plan then in contemplation, pursuant to the currency theory of dividing the Bank into two departments, will perhaps form the most fitting conclusion of my argument on the act by which the scheme, then in contemplation, was carried into effect.

"15. That it is only through the rate of interest and the state of credit, that the Bank of England can exercise a direct influence on the foreign exchanges.

"16. That the greater or less liability to variation in the rate of interest constitutes, in the next degree only to the preservation of the convertibility of the paper and the solvency of banks, the most important consideration in the regulation of our banking system.

"17. *That a total separation of the business of issue from that of banking is calculated to produce greater and more abrupt transitions in the rate of interest, and in the state of credit, than the present system of union of the departments.*"

Sir Robert Peel, in the peroration of his speech of the 6th of May, 1844, thus described the importance of the measure he then brought forward, and the beneficial effects it was calculated to produce: —

"Considering the part which I tools in the year 1819 in terminating the system of inconvertible paper currency, and in reestablishing the ancient standard of value, it will no doubt be a great source of pleasure to me, if I shall now succeed, after the lapse of a quarter of a century since those measures were adopted, in obtaining the assent of the House to proposals which are, in fact, *the complement of them, and which are calculated to guarantee their permanence, and to facilitate their practical operation.*"

A greater contrast cannot well be conceived between the expectations thus held out by the framer of the Act of 1844, and the results which have attended its operation. So far from there being any just ground for the claim set up for it to be considered in the light of a complement of the measures of 1819, calculated to guarantee its permanence, or to facilitate its practical operation, it may with more truth be said that *it is an ugly excrescence, calculated to endanger the permanence, and to impede and derange the operation of the measures of* 1819.

As the result of a careful examination of the principle① on which the Act of 1844 was founded, and of the experience of its working since the time when it came into operation, I have no hesitation in giving it as my opinion that it is a *total*, *unmitigated*, *uncompensated*, and, in its consequences, *a lamentable failure.*

In conclusion, I am wholly unable to suggest any scheme of regulation by which the occasional recurrence of periods of commercial discredit and distress can be prevented. But whatever may, hereafter, be the causes of such disasters, their effects cannot, in my opinion, fail to be greatly aggravated by restrictions, such as those of the present law, upon the amount of the Bank note circulation; and, more especially, by the division of the Bank of England into two departments, (as one of the methods of imposing a limit on its issues.)

All that I have to recommend is —

---

① I have here to repeat, what, I cannot too strongly impress upon my readers, that it must be distinctly understood, that throughout the whole of my argument on the principle and operation of the Act of 1844, I have in view only those provisions of it which divide the Bank of England into two separate departments, and which *limit the amount* of the country circulation As to those provisions of the Act which relate to better securing the solvency of the country banks, whether issuing or non-issuing, whether joint stock or private, I have not entered upon them at all. I have no objection to any measures calculated to improve the *quality* of the notes, that is, the solvency of the issuers. My objections are confined to inter ference with their *quantity*.

1. A total abrogation of those provisions of the Acts of 1844 and 1845, which limit the amount of the note circulation, and separate the function of issue from that of banking in the business of the Bank of England.

2. Such an arrangement with the Bank of England as will insure that its business shall be conducted upon a much larger average amount of bullion than that which, from the renewal of the charter in 1832 down to 1843, the Directors seem to have considered it incumbent upon them to maintain.

APPENDIX

SUPPLEMENT TO PART I

It would appear that the yield of the harvest of 1847 was, in the first instance, in some degree over-rated. This was a natural result of the appearance of bulk on the ground, and in the gathering, which seems to have distinguished the wheat crops throughout the greater part of the kingdom. The average quality of the grain yet brought to market leads to the inference that, though the produce per acre was larger than in most previous seasons, this is materially counterbalanced, in effect, by a comparative deficiency in the yield of flour.

From the week ending the 18th of September, when the average price of wheat fell to 49*s*. 6*d*. to the end of January (1848) the price has been remarkably even, varying little from an average of about 53*s*. per quarter.

The importations of foreign grain continued to be unusually large till near the middle of November; but the quality, particularly of the wheat, being found, generally, very inferior, these supplies had a much less effect upon the market, during the remainder of the year, than might be anticipated from a mere statement of their extent. It is understood that a large portion of the foreign wheat of low quality, previously in store, was, in December and January, disposed of, at reduced prices, as a substitute for inferior descriptions of grain.

The corn-markets during the last three months of the year were dull and quiet. Wheat of good quality, home or foreign, being apparently not abundant, or likely to be so, has been firmly held for the highest current price; and had the demand not been checked by the depressed state of the manufacturing districts, or had the prospects of trade during the ensuing six months been less gloomy, the prices of grain would probably have ranged somewhat higher after the cessation of the imports in November; the yield of the last harvest being still variously estimated, and the reported condition of the stocks in the corn-growing countries, rendering it unlikely that we shall receive any considerable supplies from abroad, unless at very high prices, before the next harvest.

Average prices of corn in England and Wales

It is generally known that the average prices of the six principal descriptions of grain and pulse, published weekly in the "London Gazette", are founded upon returns made by inspectors stationed in a large number of the towns of England and Wales, in which corn-markets are held. During a part of the period embraced in the present volume — that is to say, from its commencement to about June, 1842, — the number of towns from which returns were received, was 150. At about the last mentioned date the number was extended (under 5 & 6 Viet. c. 14.) to 290. This change would appear to have increased the quantity of corn brought under inspection in the process of sale, in the proportion of about four to three. ① The effect on the apparent average price, if we may rely upon a comparison of the weekly averages, as calculated separately under

① Sec Parliamentary Paper, Commons, Session 1843, No. 23.

the Act above mentioned, and that (9 Geo. 4. c. 60.) previously in operation, during the 57 weeks immediately following the 28th of January, 1843[①], was, generally, to raise the apparent average price (of six weeks) by which the duty was regulated, (which then ranged at about 50*s*.,) by an amount varying from 1*d*. to 5*d*. per quarter. The weekly variation must, of course, have been greater. In other respects, the method of computing the averages appears to have been the same throughout.

In using these averages, it is requisite to bear in mind one or two circumstances connected with their origin. The particular purpose for which they have hitherto been taken — that of regulating the importation of foreign com — seems to justify their cxclusive reference to sales of home grown corn. But in applying them to any other purpose this should not be forgotten. The foreign grain which passes into consumption in this country is usually inferior in quality to our own. If included with that of home growth it would, therefore, tend to lower the general average. The quantity of foreign and colonial wheat, and of other grain, annually taken into consumption, varies from a few thousand quarters to one-sixth or one-fifth of the whole quantity supposed to be consumed; and the importance of the element of foreign supply, in a comparison of different years, has, of course, a similarly wide variation. It is also to be considered that the average *quality* of the grain consumed, home and foreign, varies annually, as well as the quantity of each of these taken to make up the aggregate consumption. It need hardly be observed that a quarter of wheat does not always yield the same quantity of flour; and so has not always the same effect upon the ultimate demand; which has reference as well to the

① Papers, Commons, Session 1844, No. 122.

nutritive value as to the money price of the article.

The annual average prices, as made up by the inspector of corn returns, arc not required for the purposes of the law regulating the importation of corn; nor can they, as at present obtained, be deemed particularly valuable with reference to the more general purposes of statistical inquiry. In computing the weekly averages, regard is had both to the *price and the quantity* included in each contract of sale. But the yearly average is obtained simply by adding together the weekly averages for a year, and dividing the sum by 52. The accuracy of the result therefore depends upon the contingency — that the inequalities of the quantities sold weekly, at different periods of the year, shall so balance each other as to render immaterial an entire exclusion of the element of quantity. In most years, the home supply is so regularly distributed over the whole period that the error would probably be very small. In others, however, it is not so.

The average price for the year 1847, as made up in the usual way, is 69*s*. 9*d*. ; or 11*d*. less than that of the year 1839. But if regard be had to the quantities sold at each weekly average price, the average for the year is only about 68*s*. per quarter.

Again, the average price for the 52 weeks immediately following the first week in September, 1846, (during which the British crop of that year may be supposed to have been in the market,) if taken in the usual way, is 68*s*. 9*d*. But so irregular was the actual distribution (as shown by the inspected sales) of the produce of the harvest of 1846, over this period, that, were strict regard had to the element of quantity, the average price at which it was really sold, would probably be found not much to exceed 60*s*. per quarter. The following were the aggregate quantities of wheat returned, as sold m each of the four periods of thutecn weeks, each following the

28th of August, 1847, with the average price for each such period, obtained *Table of the Weekly Average Prices of Wheat in England and the Nineteen Years.*

	1829.	1830.	1831.	1832.	1833.	1834.	1835.	1836.
	s. d.	*s. d.*	*s. d.*	*s. d.*	*s. d.*	*s. d.*	*s. d.*	*s. d.*
First week	75.11	55.5	68.3	59.1	52.6	49.2	40.1	36.0
Second week	75.2	56.1	69.8	59.2	52.7	49.2	40.5	36.6
Third week	74.10	56.3	70.6	59.5	52.8	49.1	40.7	37.0
Fourth week	74.7	56.2	71.8	60.0	53.1	48.10	41.3	37.10
Fifth week	74.7	56.6	73.3	59.11	53.3	48.7	41.7	39.3
Sixth week	74.6	56.6	74.8	59.9	53.0	48.11	41.5	39.7
Seventh week	73.11	57.2	75.1	59.2	52.3	48.9	40.10	39.7
Eighth week	72.11	58.4	73.10	58.10	52.1	48.8	40.4	40.7
Ninth week	68.11	59.1	72.4	58.2	52.2	48.4	40.4	42.6
Tenth week	66.6	59.11	71.9	58.8	52.2	48.0	39.10	44.7
Eleventh week	66.2	60.8	71.8	59.5	52.3	47.8	39.8	45.0
Twelfth week	67.1	61.2	72.2	59.5	52.10	47.2	39.11	44.2
Thirteenth week	69.4	62.9	72.4	59.9	53.4	47.4	40.0	44.7
Fourteenth week	70.3	65.1	71.7	59.6	53.10	47.3	39.9	46.5
Fifteenth week	70.3	66.3	70.8	60.0	53.8	47.2	39.3	47.7
Sixteenth week	70.7	66.1	70.10	60.11	53.5	47.6	38.10	48.8
Seventeenth week	69.8	66.5	70.5	61.8	53.0	48.3	38.7	48.10
Eighteenth week	69.0	65.11	70.3	62.1	53.5	48.4	38.6	48.3
Nineteenth week	69.2	66.6	68.11	62.1	53.6	48.7	38.9	47.11
Twentieth week	69.9	65.4	68.4	61.11	54.1	47.11	39.8	49.3

Continued

	1829.	1830.	1831.	1832.	1833.	1834.	1835.	1836.
	s. d.	s. d.	s. d.	s. d.	s. d.	s. d.	s. d.	s. d.
Twenty-first week	69.6	65.2	65.5	61.9	53.6	47.2	40.0	50.4
Twenty-second week	70.7	65.10	66.4	61.9	53.7	46.8	39.10	49.10
Twenty-third week	71.5	65.11	66.10	61.9	52.10	46.10	39.8	49.5
Twenty-fourth week	71.3	65.8	67.9	62.4	52.9	47.10	40.1	51.0
Twenty-fifth week	70.7	66.5	68.1	62.4	53.1	48.10	40.4	51.1
Twenty-sixth week	69.4	67.5	66.7	63.1	54.4	49.6	40.0	50.6
Twenty-seventh week	68.2	68.6	65.9	63.2	54.7	48.11	40.5	50.8
Twenty-eighth week	66.3	69.6	64.11	63.5	54.1	48.4	41.6	50.7
Twenty-ninth week	65.10	70.3	64.3	63.7	54.8	48.1	42.1	49.4
Thirtieth week	66.2	72.8	64.6	63.7	55.4	48.5	43.6	49.2
Thirty-first week	66.11	74.11	65.3	63.5	56.5	48.4	44.0	49.6

Wales, as computed by the Inspector of Corn Returns, during ending 1847.

1837.	1838.	1839.	1840.	1841.	1842.	1843.	1844.	1345.	1846.	1847.
s. d.	s. d.	s. d.	s. d.	s. d.	s. d.	s. d.	s. d.	s. d.	s. d.	s. d.
58.9	52.9	80.2	66.1	61.8	63.1	47.1	49.10	45.8	55.1	66.10
59.0	52.4	81.6	65.10	61.9	63.0	47.1	50.9	45.10	56.3	70.3
59.6	52.11	81.4	66.0	61.7	62.5	47.10	51.8	45.7	56.2	73.5
59.1	53.7	79.3	65.4	60.9	61.5	49.1	52.3	45.7	55.7	74.11
58.9	54.10	77.0	65.2	60.9	60.7	49.3	52.6	45.5	54.8	73.10
57.5	55.4	74.1	64.11	60.7	60.6	48.1	52.7	45.5	54.3	71.7
56.5	55.4	71.6	65.3	61.1	59.11	47.5	53.6	45.4	54.9	71.7

Continued

1837.	1838.	1839.	1840.	1841.	1842.	1843.	1844.	1345.	1846.	1847.
s. d.	*s. d.*	*s. d.*	*s. d.*	*s. d.*	*s. d.*	*s. d.*	*s. d.*	*s. d.*	*s. d.*	*s. d.*
56. 2	55. 3	71. 10	65. 11	61. 10	60. 0	47. 11	55. 1	45. 2	55. 0	74. 7
55. 9	55. 2	72. 10	66. 4	62. 5	60. 10	48. 6	56. 2	45. 0	54. 6	74. 4
55. 11	55. 3	73. 8	66. 11	63. 6	60. 9	48. 3	56. 0	45. 0	54. 10	74. 2
56. 7	55. 4	74. 1	68. 2	63. 11	59. 11	47. 5	56. 3	45. 1	54. 3	75. 10
56. 9	6. 3	71. 3	69. 3	63. 9	59. 9	47. 6	56. 5	45. 5	55. 1	77. 0
56. 8	10	68. 11	69. 1	64. 4	58. 4	47. 2	56. 5	45. 10	55. 5	77. 1
56. 2	57. 9	68. 8	68. 7	64. 1	57. 8	46. 2	55. 5	46. 5	55. 9	74. 5
55. 11	58. 8	68. 3	68. 11	64. 0	58. 2	45. 5	55. 1	46. 3	56. 0	74. 1
55. 5	58. 10	71. 0	69. 6	63. 8	59. 10	45. 9	55. 4	45. 11	55. 10	75. 10
55. 6	58. 9	72. 7	68. 7	63. 8	60. 7①	46. 7	55. 6	45. 11	55. 6	79. 6
55. 9	59. 0	71. 0	68. 5	63. 8	61. 0	47. 0	55. 3	46. 0	56. 5	81. 10
55. 10	60. 0	70. 6	68. 1	63. 2	60. 8	46. 4	55. 1	45. 10	56. 8	85. 2
54. 7	60. 10	71. 2	68. 7	62. 5	59. 9	46. 2	55. 10	45. 9	57. 0	94. 10
53. 4	62. 2	70. 8	68. 0	61. 6	60. 9	47. 2	55. 10	45. 9	65. 5	102. 5
54. 4	62. 4	70. 5	67. 10	61. 6	61. 10	47. 9	55. 6	46. 3	53. 4	99. 10
56. 2	63. 1	69. 7	67. 1	62. 4	63. 6	47. 11	55. 6	47. 7	52. 10	88. 10
56. 4	64. 3	69. 2	67. 7	62. 2	64. 0	48. 4	55. 9	48. 2	52. 0	91. 7
56. 5	64. 11	68. 1	67. 4	62. 5	63. 10	48. 11	55. 8	47. 10	51. 5	91. 4
56. 11	65. 6	68. 1	67. 8	63. 5	63. 11	49. 8	55. 9	47. 11	52. 2	87. 1
57. 0	67. 3	67. 10	67. 8	63. 11	64. 3	49. 8	55. 8	47. 11	52. 10	82. 3
56. 4	68. 0	69. 0	68. 6	64. 3	64. 10	49. 10	54. 10	48. 10	52. 3	74. 0
56. 1	68. 0	69. 2	69. 6	64. 11	65. 8	51. 2	54. 1	50. 0	50. 10	75. 6

① The Act 5 & 6 Viet. c. 14. came into operation; but the averages mere not affected by it for some weeks afterwards.

Continued

1837.	1838.	1839.	1840.	1841.	1842.	1843.	1844.	1345.	1846.	1847.
s. d.	s. d.	s. d.	s. d.	s. d.	s. d.	s. d.	s. d.	s. d.	s. d.	s. d.
50.11	68.2	69.8	71.4	66.3	65.4	54.2	52.9	51.7	49.11	77.3
59.2	69.1	71.3	71.11	68.3	63.9	57.7	51.0	53.3	47.5	75.5

Table of the Weekly Average Prices of Wheat in England and the Nineteen Years.

	1829.	1830.	1831.	1832.	1833.	1834.	1835.	1836.
	s. d.	s. d.	s. d.	s. d.	s. d.	s. d.	s. d.	s. d.
Thirty-second week	66.10	74.11	64.6	63.2	56.1	48.6	43.2	50.8
Thirty-third week	66.7	73.4	64.3	63.2	54.2	49.6	42.6	50.4
Thirty-fourth week	60.1	71.4	61.9	62.0	54.8	48.9	41.1	48.10
Thirty-fifth week	66.4	70.5	64.2	59.7	54.7	46.5	40.4	46.11
Thirty-sixth week	68.3	66.7	63.4	58.0	58.1	44.3	39.5	48.1
Thirty-seventh week	67.1	62.4	63.7	58.0	55.0	43.4	38.10	47.9
Thirty-eighth week	61.1	60.2	62.9	57.9	53.10	43.2	38.0	47.10
Thirty-ninth week	60.3	60.8	61.7	56.6	53.0	43.7	37.7	48.5
Fortieth week	60.0	62.0	61.0	54.7	52.10	42.9	37.1	48.2
Forty-first week	59.4	62.8	59.11	52.4	52.4	41.10	37.0	47.2
Forty-second week	58.3	62.6	59.2	51.3	51.7	41.1	36.11	47.0
Forty-third week	56.4	61.6	60.10	52.7	51.4	40.8	37.0	47.7
Forty-fourth week	55.4	61.3	61.3	53.3	51.7	41.6	36.5	49.7
Forty-fifth week	55.7	62.3	62.7	52.7	51.6	42.4	36.7	51.8
Forty-sixth week	56.4	63.9	62.5	52.6	51.4	42.6	36.7	55.6

Continued

	1829.	1830.	1831.	1832.	1833.	1834.	1835.	1836.
	s. d.	*s. d.*	*s. d.*	*s. d.*	*s. d.*	*s. d.*	*s. d.*	*s. d.*
Forty-seventh week	57.1	64.8	62.4	53.3	50.11	42.4	36.10	60.4
Forty-eighth week	56.10	64.8	61.8	53.11	50.8	41.11	36.11	61.9
Forty-ninth week	57.2	65.7	60.9	54.7	49.8	41.11	36.9	59.7
Fiftieth week	57.2	66.1	59.6	54.9	49.5	41.1	36.8	60.4
Fifty-first week	57.3	67.2	59.3	54.5	49.5	40.11	36.6	60.6
Fifty-second week	56.5	67.7 68.1	59.2	53.2	49.2	40.6	36.0	59.2
Annual average	66.3	64.3	66.4	58.8	52.11	46.2	39.4	48.6
Highest weekly average	75.11	74.11	73.1	63.7	56.5	49.6	44.0	61.9
Lowest weekly average	55.4	55.5	59.2	51.3	49.2	40.6	36.0	36.0
Difference	20.7	19.6	15.11	12.4	7.3	9.0	8.0	25.9

obtained from the weekly averages, without regard to quantity:—

	Quantity returned or sold in the inspected Markets.	Average Price. s.	d.
1st quarter to 28th Nov. 1846, -	1,891,561 -	56	10
2nd quarter to 27th Feb. 1847, -	1,618,773 -	67	10
3rd quarter to 29th May, 1847, -	1,258,383 -	80	6
4th quarter to 28th Aug. 1847, -	594,479 -	79	5
	Apparent average	7	12

Wales, as computed by the Inspector of Corn Returns, during ending 1847—(*continued*).

1837.	1838.	1839.	1840.	1841.	1842-	1843.	1844.	1845.	1846.	1847
s. d.	*s. d.*	*s. d.*	*s. d.*	*s. d.*	*s. d.*	*s. d.*	*s. d.*	*s. d.*	*s. d.*	*s. d.*
60. 1	69. 11	72. 0	72. 10	70. 5	61. 3	60. 9	48. 10	55. 3	45. 2	66. 10
59. 5	71. 8	72. 3	72. 4	72. 5	58. 11	61. 2	49. 1	57. 0	45. 1	62. 6
59. 6	75. 7	71. 1	72. 7	74. 7	56. 5	59. 9	50. 4	57. 0	45. 11	60. 4
58. 2	77. 0	71. 10	72. 4	76. 1	55. 0	56. 8	60. 11	56. 6	47. 10	56. 8
56. 5	74. 5	71. 9	68. 11	74. 1	53. 3	54. 2	48. 6	55. 10	49. 0	51. 4
56. 6	70. 2	70. 9	65. 4	71. 2	51. 6	53. 0	43. 11	54. 1	50. 0	49. 6
57. 8	64. 2	69. 8	64. 2	64. 8	52. 8	50. 10	45. 3	52. 6	51. 3	53. 6
56. 7	61. 10	70. 1	64. 1	63. 4	54. 0	49. 3	45. 9	53. 2	53. 1	56. 9
56. 6	62. 11	70. 4	64. 7	61. 9	53. 2	49. 5	46. 1	56. 0	54. 0	54. 2
55. 9	64. 9	67. 2	64. 0	61. 6	51. 6	50. 6	46. 3	57. 9	56. 10	54. 3
53. 6	66. 0	65. 6	63. 3	62. 3	51. 1	50. 8	46. 3	58. 2	59. 10	55. 2
51. 8	65. 7	66. 5	62. 5	63. 6	50. 9	50. 1	46. 0	59. 5	60. 10	53. 6
51. 0	66. 4	68. 5	61. 7	64. 5	49. 5	50. 5	46. 0	60. 1	61. 9	52. 4
51. 7	69. 5	67. 4	62. 1	65. 5	48. 7	51. 8	46. 3	59. 7	62. 3	53. 8
52. 11	72. 11	68. 6	62. 2	66. 4	48. 8	52. 1	46. 4	58. 6	61. 5	54. 3
54. 4	73. 10	69. 0	61. 8	65. 11	49. 8	51. 7	45. 10	57. 11	59. 8	52. 11
53. 7	73. 4	67. 1	60. 0	64. 9	49. 6	51. 0	45. 4	58. 2	59. 0	52. 1
52. 6	73. 1	66. 3	59. 7	63. 6	48. 6	51. 1	45. 2	59. 0	59. 7	51. 11
52. 8	75. 6	65. 8	58. 10	62. 7	47. 3	50. 9	45. 1	59. 4	60. 3	52. 2
53. 5	78. 4	66. 8	59. 1	62. 9	46. 10	50. 3	45. 3	57. 11	59. 10	53. 0
53. 2	78. 4 78. 2	66. 5	60. 1	62. 10	47. 2	49. 9	45. 6	55. 4	61. 6 64. 4	53. 11

Continued

1837.	1838.	1839.	1840.	1841.	1842-	1843.	1844.	1845.	1846.	1847.
s. d.	*s. d.*	*s. d.*	*s. d.*	*s. d.*	*s. d.*	*s. d.*	*s. d.*	*s. d.*	*s. d.*	*s. d.*
55.10	64.7	70.8	66.4	64.4	57.3	50.1	51.3	50.10	54.8	69.9
60.1	78.4	81.6	72.10	76.1	65.8	61.2	56.5	60.1	64.4	102.5
51.0	52.4	65.6	58.10	60.7	46.10	45.5	45.1	45,0	45.1	49.6
9.1	26.0	16.0	14.0	15.6	18.10	15.9	11.4	15.1	19.3	52.11

If the annual average price be computed with regard to the element of quantity only, as here exhibited, for the quarters, and without descending to the (greater) weekly variations, it will be found to be, instead of 71*s*. 2*d*. only 64*s*. 6*d*.

There is another objection to the present method of making up the annual averages, in their exclusive relation to the astronomical year, beginning the 1st of January. They are thus based, usually, upon about 35 weeks' sales of the produce of one harvest, and about 17 of the produce of another; and so afford no satisfactory indication of the character of either. The period at which the produce of each harvest begins to rule the current price varies, in some degree, with the seasons; but it would obviously not be difficult to fix a date for the commencement of the harvest year, (as, for instance, as the first week in August,) which would cause the annual average price to indicate, with tolerable accuracy, at once the comparative yield of successive harvests, and the annual variations of the cost to the consumer.

Home supplies of wheat, in harvest years, as indicated by the official returns for England and Wales: 1839-1847

The quantities of wheat of home growth returned as sold in England and

Wales in the markets inspected for the formation of the official averages, in each harvest year, are stated in the following table. The harvest year is here computed from the first week in *September* forward. *It will be borne in mind that about June*, 1842, *the returns were extended from* 150 *to* 290 *markets*, *under the Act* 5 & 6 *Vict. c.* 14.

Harvest Years.	First Quarter.	Second Quarter.	Third Quarter.	Fourth Quarter.	Total.
	Qrs.	Qrs.	Qrs.	Qrs.	Qrs.
1839-1840	1,051,352	988,671	925,669	1,056,308	4,022,000
1840-1841	904,807	953,934	862,456	1,149,451	3,870,648
1841-1842	924,939	766,445	806,925	1,127,864	3,626,173
1842-1843	1,318,543	1,226,329	1,254,724	1,279,393	5,078,989
1843-1844	1,489,025	1,400,627	1,216,621	1,107,181	5,213,454
1844-1845	1,617,608	1,751,637	1,630,058	1,665,065	6,664,363
1845-1846	1,708,018	1,414,866	1,398,264	1,178,821	5,699,969
1846-1847	1,891,561	1,618,773	1,258,383	594,479	5,363,196

Prices and foreign supplies of wheat, in harvest years, since 1828

If it be assumed that each year's crop of wheat rules the weekly average price from the first week in August forward, and that all wheat and wheat flour of foreign production entered for home consumption after the 5th of August in each year goes into consumption with the crop of the current year, the following may be received as an accurate statement of the prices of the harvest year since 1828, and of the foreign supply added, in each year, to that of home growth.

In the Harvest Year.	Annual Average Price.		Quantity of Wheat and Wheat Flour (stated as Wheat) entered for consumption.
	s.	*d.*	Qrs.
1828-1829	70	4	1,954,457
1829-1830	63	9	548,859
1830-1831	67	10	2,857,403
1831-1832	61	3	157,107
1832-1833	54	5	329,962
1833-1834	49	9	77,774
1834-1835	41	5	45,084
1835-1836	42	8	27,707
1836-1837	55	0	35,386
1837-1838	57	10	246,994
1838-1839	71	8	3,560,957①
1839-1840	68	0	1,762,482
1840-1841	63	6	1,925,241
1841-1842	63	4	2,985,422
1842-1843	49	4	2,405,217
1843-1844	53	9	1,606,912
1844-1845	46	7	476,190
1845-1846	54	8	2,732,134
1846-1847	68	9	2,458,000

① It would appear from the official accounts whence these figures are taken, that upwards of 500,000 quarters of the wheat entered for consumption in the autumn of 1838, had lain in bond for five or six years.

The following is a more complete statement of the foreign supplies of grain, and similar food, imported into the United Kingdom, during the harvest years, 1845-1846 and 1846-1847: —

				1845- 1846.		1846-1847.
Wheat	–	–	qrs.	1,669,026	–	1,571,433
Barleyt	–	–	qrs.	203,865	–	870,444
Oats	–	–	qrs.	656,273	–	1,294,207
Rye	–	–	qrs.	324	–	28,885
Peas	–	–	qrs.	111,623	–	241,791
Beans	–	–	qrs.	235,689	–	390,454
Maize	–	–	qrs.	363,111	–	2,906,248
Wheatmeal or flour, cwts.				2,655,201	–	4,463,724
Oatmeal	–	–	qrs.	3,622	–	24,329
Ryemeal	–	–	qrs.	1	–	200,729
Indian meal	–	–	qrs.	95,064	–	1,007,160

The following Table, exhibiting the operation of the three different scales of import duty in use since 1828, at intervals of 5*s*. in the price, may serve to indicate, nearly, the conditions under which the foreign supplies above stated were received, prior to the suspension of the corn laws in January, 1847:

When the Price of British Wheat per Imperial Quarter was —	Import Duties by					
	9 Geo. 4. c. 60 (1828.)		5 & 6 Vict. c. 14. (1842.)		9 10 Vict. c. 22. (1846.)	
s.	*s.*	*d.*	*s.*	*d.*	*s.*	*d.*
50	36	8	20	0	7	0

Continued

When the Price of British Wheat per Imperial Quarter was —	Import Duties by					
	9 Geo. 4. c. 60 (1828.)		5 & 6 Vict. c. 14. (1842.)		9 10 Vict. c. 22. (1846.)	
s.	*s.*	*d.*	*s.*	*d.*	*s.*	*d.*
55	31	8	17	0	4	0
60	26	8	12	0	4	0
65	21	8	7	0	4	0
70	10	8	4	0	4	0
75	1	0	1	0	4	0
80	1	0	1	0	4	0

SUPPLEMENT TO PART II

The state of the markets for produce other than corn, have already been observed upon, down to about the middle of September, 1847. To complete the review of the year, it remains to notice the fluctuations of prices during the last three or four months. This period, though short, derives some importance from its embracing considerable variations as well in the prices of some descriptions of produce, as in the rate of interest, and in the amount of Bank notes in circulation. It seems proper, therefore, in treating it, to enter somewhat into detail.

The Table on the next page exhibits the prices of the most important articles of general consumption in this country, in the last week of December, as compared with their prices at the same period in each of the two years immediately preceding; and if taken in conjunction with the similar Table given in the same articles in the second week of September, in each of the same years, it affords a tolerably complete view of the state of prices at the beginning and end of the period now to be considered, during three consecutive years.

If the prices of December 1847 be compared with those of December 1846, a fall will be observed upon about one half, in number, of the articles quoted; but in many of these instances the price of December 1847 will be found, notwithstanding, to be higher than that of December 1845. If the prices of September 1847 be compared with those of the end of December, here given, a fall will also be observed, as to about the same number of articles.

In considering what may have been the causes of this fall of prices, particularly after September 1847, it is desirable to take first into account those which are most obvious, and which appear to have operated most widely. There is not, then, it would appear, a single article among those, the prices of which appear to have fallen during the last four months, or indeed during the whole of the year 1847, the *demand* for which was not materially reduced during that period. Not only was the actual consumption diminished, in consequence of a diminution of the means of purchase of a large proportion of the consumers — by high prices of food in the earlier part of the year, and by want of employment and reduced incomes towards its close — but, as is apparent from all the reports of the state of the markets for produce, dealers also very generally refrained, as far as was practicable, from renewing their stocks, either from scarcity of pecuniary means (present or apprehended), or from a natural tendency to await the condition of markets as they should he affected by the restriction of credit, either already felt or anticipated.

	1845. December.	1846. December.	1847. December.
Timber, for, Dantzic and Memel *load*	4*l*@4*l*. 10*s*.	4*l*. @4*l*. 10*s*.	4*l*. @4*l*. 10*s*.
— Qnebee yellow pine – *load*	3*l*. 10*s*. @4*l*.	3*l*. 10*s*. @4*l*.	3*l*. 10*s*. @4*l*.
Hemp, St. Petersburg, elean – *ton*.	30*l*. @30*l*. 5*s*.	37*l*. 15*s*. @38*l*.	36*l*. @36*l*. 5*s*.
Flax, Riga, P. T. R. – – *ton*.	46*t*. @52*l*.	46*l*. @54*l*.	41*l*. @52*l*.
Tar, Stockhalm – – *barrel*	15*s*. 6*d*. @16*s*.	17*s*. 3*d*. @17*s*. 6*d*.	17*s*. 3*d*. @17*s*. 6*d*.
Tallow, St. Petersb., New Y. C. *cwt*.	42*s*. 3*d*. @42*s*. 6*d*.	50*s*. 3*d*. @51*s*. 6*d*.	44*s*. 6*d*. @45*s*. 6*d*.
Ashes, Canadian, pearl – – *cwt*.	24*s*. @24*s*. 6*d*.	28*s*. @28*s*. 6*d*.	36*s*. 6*d*. @37*s*.
Iron, British, bars – – – *ton*.	9*l*. 15*s*. @10*l*.	10*l*.	8*l*. @8*l*. 5*s*.
— Swedish. in bond – – *ton*.	12*l*.	11*l*. 10*s*. @12*l*.	11*l*. 5*s*. @11*l*. 10*s*.
Copper, tough cake – – – *ton*.	93*l*.	88*l*. 10*s*.	98*l*.
Lead, British, in pigs – – *ton*.	19*l*. 10*s*.	18*l*. 10*s*.	18*l*.
Tin, English, bars – – – *ton*.	104*l*. 10*s*.	99*l*. 10*s*.	83*l*. 10*s*.
Cotton, bowed Georgia – – *lb*.	$3\frac{5}{8}$*d*. @5*d*.	$5\frac{3}{4}$*d*. @$7\frac{1}{2}$*d*.	$4\frac{1}{9}$*d*. @6*d*.
— Surat – – – – *lb*.	$2\frac{1}{2}$*d*. @$3\frac{3}{4}$*d*.	4*d*. @$5\frac{3}{4}$*d*.	$2\frac{3}{4}$*d*. @$3\frac{3}{4}$*d*.
Wool, English – – – *fleece*	12*s*. @16*s*. 10*d*.	11*s*. @15*s*. 10*d*.	9*s*. @13*s*.
— Spanisb, Leonesa – – *lb*.	2*s*. @2*s*. 4*d*.	1*s*. 8*d*. @2*s*.	1*s*. 8*d*. @2*s*.
Silk, East India – – – *lb*.	8*s*. 6*d*. @19*s*.	8*s*. @17*s*.	7*s*. @14*s*.
— Italian – – – – *lb*.	21*s*. @30*s*.	18*s*. @25*s*.	14*s*. @20*s*.
Coffce. St. Domingo – – *cwt*.	31*s*. @35*s*.	28. @32*s*.	27*s*. @30*s*. 6*d*.
— Jamaica – – – *lb*.	30*s*. @130*s*.	25*s*. @115*s*.	25*s*. @128*s*.
Tea, Congou – – – – *lb*.	$8\frac{1}{2}$*d*. @2*s*. $3\frac{1}{2}$*d*.	9*d* @2*s*.	8*d*. @1*s*. 6*d*.
Tobacco, Virginia, in bond – *lb*.	$3\frac{1}{2}$*d*. @$5\frac{1}{2}$*d*.	$2\frac{1}{4}$*d*. $5\frac{1}{2}$*d*.	$2\frac{1}{4}$*d*. @$5\frac{1}{2}$*d*.
Indigo, East India – – – *lb*.	1*s*. 10*d*. @6*s*. 8*d*.	1*s*. 8*d*. @6*s*. 4*d*.	1*s*. @5*s*. 6*d*.
Cochineal – – – – *lb*.	5*s*. 1*d*. @7*s*. 2*d*.	4*s*. 6*d*. @6*s*. 9*d*.	4*s*. 4*d*. @6*s*. 9*d*.
Logwood, Jamaica – – – *ton*.	4*l*. 15*s*. @5*l*. 7*s*.	4*l*. 5*s* @4*l*. 10*s*.	4*l* @4*l*. 5*s*.
Saltpetrd, East India – – *cwt*.	25*s*. @28*s*. 6*d*.	23*s*. 6*d*. @27*s*. 6*d*.	30*s*. @32*s*.
Sugar, Muscovatlo, Gaz aver. *cwt*.	37*s*. 3*d*.	32*s*. $2\frac{1}{4}$*d*.	26*s*. $1\frac{1}{2}$*d*.
Rum, Jamaica – – – *gull*.	3*s*. @3*s*. 4*d*.	3*s* @3*s*. 3*d*.	3*s*. 2*d*. @3*s*. 6*d*.
Beef, American and Canadian *tierce*.	68*s*. @77*s*.	72*s*. 6*d*. @100*s*.	90*s*. @100*s*.
Butter, Cork – – – – *cwt*.	92*s*. @94*s*.	92*s*. @94*s*.	86*s*. @92*s*.
Bank of England circulation – –	£ 20,100,000	£ 20,500,000	£ 18,700,000
Bullion – – – – – – –	£ 14,800,000	£ 15,000,000	£ 12,400,000
Market rate of interest on first class bills – – – – –	4 to $4\frac{1}{2}$ per cent.	$3\frac{1}{2}$ per cent.	$4\frac{1}{2}$ to 6 per cent.

On the other hand, while the demand was thus much reduced, the supply was very generally increased; and that, in some instances, from a variety of causes operating concurrently. It can scarcely be necessary here to observe that commodities held in stock, upon credit, are liable to be thrown upon the market without any very close reference to the state of the current demand, whenever a general restriction of credit, or a material augmentation of the rate of interest, renders the retention of borrowed capital more difficult or expensive than usual. That there are few commodities requiring the investment of large amounts of capital which are not so held, to a considerable extent, is sufficiently well known; and the facts stated and alluded to in the foregoing pages, respecting the commercial failures which occurred in September, October, and November, 1847, afford ample evidence that considerable quantities of East India and colonial produce, in particular, were held upon credit at the period referred to.

The effect of a supply materially augmented by forced sales, being taken in conjunction with that of a reduced demand, it is not very difficult to account for the fall observed in the prices of such articles as tea, silk, indigo, cochineal, logwood, and others, between September and December 1847. Wool, cotton, and flax have suffered, more or less, throughout the year, and more especially towards its close, from a reduced demand for the factories; and iron has been similarly affected by a reduced demand for the railways; besides that, all these articles being held in large quantities, the limitation of credit and the pressure for floating capital must also have affected, more or less, the prices of each, by compelling their sale, or at least urging their holders to attempt to sell them, without giving the usual degree of consideration to the state of the demand for consumption.

The only article, not yet particularly referred to, the price of which has been materially reduced, is sugar. I deem it proper to treat this apart, as it is the article the fall in which was most remarkable, and attracted most attention; and also because, in examining the causes of the fall, I shall have an opportunity of exhibiting, in particular, the utter want of accordance between the fluctuations of prices and of the Bank note circulation observable in the last four months of 1847.

All the causes of reduced prices, already adverted to, bore upon that of sugar with extraordinary force. How far the supply was excessive, may be judged of from the following figures, extracted from the latest returns made up at the Board of Trade: —

Sugar (unrefined) imported into the United Kingdom, and entered for consumption.

	1845.	Gazette average Price.	1816.	Gazette average Price.	1847.	Gazette average Price.
	Cwts.	*s. d.*	*Cwts.*	*s. d.*	*Cwts.*	*s. d.*
In the 8 months ending 5th September.						
Imported – –	3,624,239		3,707,907		5,459,914	
Entered – –	3,383,161		3,355,115		4,012,233	
Excess of supply –	241,078	34 8	442,792	31 $4\frac{1}{4}$	1,447,681	25 10
In the 9 months ending 10th October.						
Imported – –	4,413,969		4,469,772		6,510,693	
Entered – –	3,888,923		4,020,488		4,581,492	
Excess of supply –	525,046	32 $5\frac{1}{4}$	449,284	32 $3\frac{1}{2}$	1,929,201	23 $5\frac{1}{2}$
In the 10 months ending 5th November.						
Imported – –	4,754,614		4,751,973		6,976,067	
Entered – –	4,228,113		4,467,330		4,959,980	
Excess of supply –	526,501	35 10	284,643	33 1	2,016,087	22 6
In the 11 months ending 5thDecember.						
Imported – –	5,038,546		5,028,446		7,414,351	
Entered – –	4,637,448		4,886,543		5,387,054	
Excess of supply –	401,098	36 8	141,903	33 $2\frac{1}{2}$	2,027,297	23 $4\frac{1}{2}$

Here the excess of supply would appear to have been quite sufficient to account for the low price observed to begin with. The fall of price between the 5th of September and the 5th of November, from 25*s*. 10*d*. to 22*s*. 6*d*. was, it will be observed, accompanied by an addition of 600,000 cwts. to the previous excess of supply; and the subsequent rise to 23*s*. $4\frac{1}{2}d.$, by the 5th of December, seems to be almost justified by the excess of supply having ceased to increase, without reference to any other circumstance. Such is the explanation derived from a consideration only of the extent of the supply in relation to the demand. But enormous as was the actual excess of supply, its effect upon the market is well known to have been materially increased by *forced sales*.

The prices of sugar, however, as of other articles, which fell with it, may be supposed, by the adherents of the currency theory, to have been affected by the variations in the amount of the Bank note circulation produced by the violent efforts of the Bank of England, and other banks, in the autumn of 1847, to comply with the restrictions imposed upon their issues. A reference to these variations, as they actually occurred, will show how far any such supposition is well founded.

For the week ending the 4th of September, the amount of Bank of England notes in circulation (including post bills) was 19,000,000*l*.; for the week ending the 6th of November, 21,300,000*l*.; and for the week ending the 4th of December it was 19,600,000*l*. Similarly, the Bank note circulation of the United Kingdom, which by the monthly return of the 11th of September, amounted to 33,778,000*l*., was returned, on the 6th of November, at 36,736,000*l*.; and on the 4th of December, at 34,605,000*l*.

So that the variations which took place in the price of sugar, as of other articles similarly affected by the severe restriction of credit in October, instead of agreeing with, were precisely the contrary of those which an adherent of the currency theory would have deduced from observation of the amount of Bank notes in use; while, as has been seen, a glance at the relation of supply and demand explains them at once.

If, however, further evidence be required of the extent to which the fall of prices observed, as to several articles of importance, in 1847, and particularly in the latter months of the year, is to be accounted for by reference simply to variations in the relation of supply and demand, it is to be found in abundance in the annual trade circulars issued in December, 1847, and January 1848. Subjoined are a few extracts from some of these papers: —

W. J. Thompson and Sons. *22nd December*, 1847.

Sugar —Sugar has suffered greater depression during the past month than any other article of importance, the greater ease of the money market not having afforded it any relief, the present stocks in this country are enormous as compared with last year, and the portion held by suspended houses has pressed rather heavily on the market added to which, the latest accounts from the colonies give prospect of a very abundant supply from most quarters, and the present low price of malt causes only a comparatively small quantity to be used for brewing and distilling purposes.

Coffee. —During the extreme depression which has now existed for some months past, and which has so seriously affected nearly all descriptions of produce, the coffee market, on the whole, has sustained itself tolerably well, and does not exhibit that great depreciation in value which is perceptible in some of our colonial produce. The stock of British West India amounts to about 2,400 casks, and 3,100 barrels and bags, against 2,300 casks and 1,950 barrels and bags, there is a falling off in the consumption of about 700 casks. The public sales of Ceylon, during the month, amount to 19,567 bags, and 400 cases and casks, of which 14,607 bags were of the plantation, and 4,960 bags of the native sorts. Owing to the large quantity of the former brought forward at an unusually dull period of the year, and consisting for the most part of inferior qualities, which generally compose the late shipments of the season, the sales have passed off very heavily, a concession in prices having been made in nearly all instances, showing a total decline during the month of 4*s*. to 5*s*. per cwt.

Lamp and Bruxner. *5th January*, 1848.

Isniao. —During the past year 55,523 chests have been brought forward at the four periodical sales, of which not more than 28,264 were actually sold, and not less than 5,000 chests of the former quantity taken out, without ever having been exposed for sale, proving beyond doubt that hitherto most unnecessary quantities have been exposed for sale, which circumstance itself is quite sufficient to depress the article, even in the face of a brisk demand, or even a rising market.

Cochineal. — As we fully anticipated in our last annual report, this article, immediately upon the opening of the market, attracted, from its peculiar position, (viz decreased stock and increasing demand,) a good deal of attention; and during the first three months a very large business was done, with a rapid advance in prices, more particularly during March and the beginning of April, when a purely speculative demand sprang up, and established an advance from the 1st of January, for all descriptions, of at least 6*d.* to 8*d.* per *l*b With this advance in price the demand fell off materially, and the importers, as well as holders, having shown at the same time great anxiety to realise, prices declined as rapidly as they had risen. The arrival of large supplies from Mexico in June, coupled with the early arrival of the Honduras crop, caused a still further depression, and so the article remained much depressed during the subsequent four months. With a brisk demand for export, a reaction took place during last month, and a considerable amount of business was done, with a gradual advance, and prices may now be generally quoted about 3*d.* above the lowest price, with a very firm market.

Coffee. — This article, like sugar, opened with great spirit on the 5th of January, and, like that commodity, rose up to the end of the month, and then gradually receded to the end of the year. The differential duty of 18*s.* 8*d.* per cwt has given such an impetus to the cultivation of *coffee*, in Ceylon, that the supplies thence have been sufficient to almost drive low foreign coffee out of this market. Forced sales have, however, caused, for some time past, panic prices; and we look with certainty for an advance in the price of good ordinary native of 3*s* to 4*s* per cwt, which the article will bear without affecting consumption Fine, fair, ordinary, and low middling Jamaicas, have also receded in price, having been pressed by the rapidly improving quality of Ceylon of the plantation kind Mochas have been particularly steady.

Manila Hemp—Owing to heavy arrivals in the summer, which were generally brought into the market, and sold without reserve, experienced a great fall in the value, and sales were effected from 28*l*. to 30*l*. per ton: the market being now completely bare, a great advance has been obtained, the current value being 40*l*. to 42*l*. per ton.

Norton, Kilburn, and Co. *1st January*, 1848.

Raw Silk —*Bengal.*—In the public sales in November but little business was done, the attendance of buyers being small, and a great indisposition shown by all parties to add to their engagements. Since that period very little has been done, and the deliveries for the last two months show a considerable decrease as compared with the previous year.

China. —An active demand continued for China silk until the month of August, but subsequent to that period prices gave way, owing to the disturbed state of the money market, and a consequent desire on the part of holders to effect sales.

Italian. —After the month of July, the demand was small, but uncertain, buyers not showing any disposition to add to their purchases more than was absolutely necessary, and the same feeling exists at the present time.

Haywood and M' Viccar. Liverpool, 31st December, 1847.

Cotton —1847. —The quantity actually consumed (supposing spinners to hold 50,000 bales against 100,000 last year) falls short of that in 1846 by 431,000 bales, or an average weekly of 8,290 bales. Throughout the whole of the year the complaints of spinners and manufacturers of the unremunerating state of business were general; so much so that some mills stopped working altogether, and many others reduced their working days by several hours. The quantity of cotton purchased by consumers in the months of September, October, and November, only averaged 14,500 bales weekly, against 29,500 bales during the same period in 1846; and prices declined in this time $2\frac{1}{4}$*d* per *l*b December brought accounts of open and more favourable weather in the United States for the growing crop than those previously received, and so completed the discouragement which existed.

Cunningham and Hinshaw. Liverpool, 31st December, 1847.

Cotton. —Consistently with the progressive development of the difficulties of the year, a review of prices shows us that the highest obtainable rates were current in the month of January last. Still, under the influence of limited stocks and the expectation of small supplies, an arduous struggle was carried on between importers, speculators, and the trade, even to a period so late as the end of August, when it became apparent to *all* that the difficulties of manufacturers were too great to admit of any other course than a greatly reduced consumption. We consequently find that from this period prices continued, with but few alternations, gradually to decline until the end of November, a fall of $2\frac{1}{2}$*d.* per lb on the most current qualities of bowed and Orleans being submitted to, middling cotton of these descriptions being respectively quoted at $4\frac{1}{8}d.$ to $4\frac{1}{4}d.$ and to $4\frac{3}{8}d.$ per lb. From this point there has been in these qualities a rally of fully $\frac{1}{4}d.$ per lb., the decline having induced a somewhat increased demand, and there appearing also no prospect of our receiving any but a very moderate supply for a month or two to come.

Hughes and Ronald. *Liverpool*, *1st January*, 1848.

Wool —We are happy to say that wc believe wool has suffered to a less extent than most of the raw materials of our leading manufactures, owing to the great caution displayed for a long time past. Prices are decidedly lower, say from 5 to 25 per cent under the quotations of this date last year. The fall is most evident in Australian, Cape of Good Hope, Russian-*Merino*, and Buenos Ayres wools, which is partly attributable to the undue quantities brought at one time on the market at the London public sales. In domestic and some of the useful qualities of low foreign, as East India and Egyptian, the fall is less marked, and will range from 5 to 15 per cent. The entries of foreign and colonial wool into this port during the past year, although less in number of bales by 8,000 than during 1846, is fully equal in weight, the excess in Buenos Ayres more than compensating for the deficiency from the West Coast of South America.

Gibson, *Ord*, *and Co.* *Leeds*, *21st January*, 1848.

"During the latter portion of the year the reduction in the price of home grown wool, suitable for the worsted trade, was from 10 to 15 per cent, the clothing wools experiencing even a still greater decline, say from 20 to 80 per cent. This difference in the value of the produce of the home and foreign grower is to be accounted for, by the fact that the former, taking no account of interest, is enabled to hold his clip for a much longer period, during the rule of low prices, than his foreign rival, who from the pressure of interest and charges generally finds himself unable to hold his goods and compelled to throw them upon the market, even at a sacrifice, in order to escape further loss by accumulation. Accordingly we find that though the stock of home grown wool in the country is now more extensive than it was in January, 1847, yet the amount held by the manufacturers and dealers is considerably less on the other the stock of foreign and colonial wool, suitable for clothing purposes, at present in the hands of the manufacturers is in a proportionable degree great.

M J Mahony. *London, 1st January*, 1848.

Iron —In the early part of the year a considerable business in railway bars took place at from 9*l*. 5*s* to 9*l*. 15s both for home and foreign supply, but towards the end of May it was evident a decline was about to take place, owing to the difficulty of many of the railway companies getting their proprietors to pay up their calls, this, followed by the pressure in the money market, brought the price in July and August last to 8*l*. 10*s*. to 8*l*. 15*s*, since which, the article has gradually declined to 7*l* per ton at the works, although some of the makers will not sell under 7*l* 10*s*. Bars, in Wales, owing to the principal ironmasters being fully employed on large orders for rails, commanded throughout the year almost as high a price as rails, in fact, at one period, higher prices were paid. The demand for bars, however, having been satisfied, the price has receded to about 7*l*. at the ports. Staffordshire bars, hoops, and sheets have maintained firm prices nearly throughout the year, and an extensive business has been done, notwithstanding the high rates for money latterly, however, a great falling off has taken place in the demand, and the general opinion of those conversant with the market is, that a decline of 2*l.* per ton will take place on quarter-day next. Foundry and forge pig iron were also in good demand throughout the year, but at present participate in the general dulness of the manufactured articles. As a matter of course, pig iron must fall in price as manfactured falls.

Scotch pig iron has been in great demand throughout the year, and the shipments large.

Thorburn and Co. *Glasgow, 31st December*, 1847.

Iron —The consumption and exports of pig iron hasp exceeded the make by 60,000 tons. It is gratifying to remark that so large a quantity has been exported this year, exceeding the last, or any former period, by fully 30,000 tons. The make this year has fallen off considerably, next year we may expect a further decrease, unless prices advance, as it is obvious that the present price will not pay the makers. It must be admitted that the home consumption this year has been less than the preceding, and this is accounted for, from the stoppage of a number of railways, &c.

Tables of prices of produce other than corn

The tables of prices in continuation of those appended to the previous volumes of this work, have been compiled, for the first six years (1840-1845), chiefly from Prince's Price Current; and for the last two years from the Price Current of The Economist newspaper.

The prices are taken in the first weeks of January, April, July and November respectively, or at the periods nearest to those at which a quotation of the article in question could be found.

As the principal purpose of these tables is to afford a comparative view of the variations of prices during long periods of time, it is obviously desirable that uniformity should be preserved in the method of their compilation. The plan adopted for the tables appended to the second volume has therefore been strictly adhered to, wherever a deviation from it, however otherwise advisable, appeared likely to interfere with this uniformity. The exceptions are few, and are readily explained. Some articles, as, for instance, oil of the northern fishery, and Russian pearl ashes, have now ceased to be quoted in price currents, regularly, if at all. The tables as to these have, therefore, been discontinued, and others substituted, containing the prices of similar articles which appear to have displaced them in the market. Others, as tea and foreign sugars, being imported and sold under new conditions, corresponding changes have necessarily been made in the mode of stating their prices. And one or two tables have been discontinued, either because the article referred to (as bristles) is practically of no importance, or because, as in the instance of oil and whalebone of the northern fishery, it has ceased to appear in the market. The distinction between "superior" and "inferior" descriptions of coffee, and of one or two similar articles, has been abandoned, as it does not appear to be in any degree essential to the purpose in view, and is likely rather to mislead than to aid the general reader, referring, as it does to a standard of quality, (amply sufficient, no doubt, for cotemporary uses, but) for the uniformity of which, (during long periods of time, there is no adequate security.

In reference to the changes made in the import duties during the eight years over which these tables extend, it is necessary to observe that there was a general addition of 5 per cent made to all the import duties, excepting those upon "corn, spirits, and timber and wood goods" (on which specific additional duties were imposed) from 15th May, 1840. In some instances, subsequent enactments, in dealing with the duties on particular articles, incidentally withdrew this addition. It is now applicable, however, to all those included in the following tables, excepting timber, spirits, and tallow; and in stating the rate of any particular duty for any period subsequent to May, 1840, the 5 per cent, and the resulting fractions, are taken into account.

14th Dec. 1847.

ASHES, Barilla, in Bond, per ton.					Import Duties.
1840	9*l* @9/10	8*l* @ 9*l*	8*l* @ 9*l*	10*l* @10/5	1812, July 9. Duty reduced. B.P. from $2\frac{1}{10}$ d. to $1\frac{1}{20}$ d.per lb.– Foreign,from $8\frac{2}{5}$ d. to $2\frac{1}{10}$d.per lb. 1845,March 19. Duty repealed.
1841	9/15 10*l*	9/15 10*l*	9/15 10/	9/15 10/	
1842	9/15 10*l*	9/15 10*l*	9/15 10/	9/15 10/	
1843	9/15 10*l*	9/15 10*l*	6/5	6/5	
1844	6/5	7/10 8/10	7/10 8/10	7/10 8/10	
1845	7/10 8/10	7/10 8/10	7/10 8/10	7/10 8/10	
1846	–	–	–	–	
1847	–	–	–	–	
ASHES, Canadian, Pearl, lst sort,per cwt.					
	s. *s.*	*s.* *s.d.*	*s.* *s.d.*	*s.* *s.*	
1840	31/ @ 32/	30/ @30/6	30/ @ 30/6	30/ @31/	
1841	30/ 31/	27/6 28/	28/ 29/6	32/6 33/	
1842	32/6 33/	34/ 34/6	34/ 34/6	27/ 28/	
1843	27/ 28/	32/ 32/6	27/ 29/	26/	
1844	28/ 28/6	25/ 26/6	27/ 30/	26/ 25/6	
1845	26/	24/6 25/6	25/ 26/6	22/9 23/	
1846	24/ 24/6	24/ 24/6	24/ 24/6	27/6 28/	
1847	29/ 29/3	29/3 29/6	30/ 31/	37/6 38/	
COFFEE, British Plantation, in Bond, (including Jamaica, I)emerara, Berbice, Dominica, St. Lucia, and Ceylon),per cwt.					
	s. *s.*	*s.* *s.*	*s.* *s.*	*s.* *s.*	
1840	86/ @ 155/	84/ @ 160/	81/ @ 150/	74/ @ 135/	1842,July 9. Duty reduced from $6\frac{3}{10}$ *d.*to $4\frac{1}{5}$ *d.*, per lb.
1841	69/ 135/	62/ 128/	65/ 150/	65/ 147/	
1842	47/ 144/	43/ 148/	40/ 148/	32/ 140/	
1843	32/ 135/	32/ 135/	32/ 135/	38/ 150/	
1844	30/ 150/	34/ 156/	19/ 133/	18/ 132/	
1845	18/ 132/	13/ 130/	16/ 127/	16/ 142/	
1846	25/ 130/	25/ 120/	25/ 115/	25/ 115/	
1847	25/ 115/	25/ 115/	25/ 128/	25/ 128/	

An Account of the Values of the Imports into, and Exports from the United Kingdom, in the Years 1838 *to* 1846 *inclusive*

Years.	Value of Imports into the United Kingdom, calculated at the Official Rates of Valuation.	Value of Exports from the United Kingdom, calculated at the Official Rates of Valuation.			Value of the Produce and Manufactures of the United Kingdom exported therefrom, according to the real or declared Value thereof.
		Produce and Manufactures of the United Kingdom.	Foreign and Colonial Merchandize.	Total Exports.	
	£	£	£	£	£
1838	61,296,513	92,453,967	12,711,512	105,165,479	50,061,737
1839	62,048,121	97,394,666	12,795,990	110,190,656	53,233,580
1840	67,492,710	102,706,850	13,774,165	116,481,015	51,406,430
1841	64,444,268	102,179,514	14,723,373	116,902,887	51,634,623
1842	65,253,286	100,255,380	13,586,422	113,841,802	47,381,023
1843	70,214,912	117,876,659	13,956,288	131,832,947	52,279,709
1844	75,449,374	131,558,477	14,398,177	145,956,654	58,584,292
1845	85,281,958	134,598,584	16,279,318	150,877,902	60,111,082
1846	75,953,875	132,288,845	16,296,162	148,584,507	57,786,876

An Account of the Quantities of the following Articles imported into the United Kingdom from 1838 *to* 1846 *inclusive.*

Years.	Cotton Wool.	Coffee.	Flax.	Hemp Undressed.	Sheep's Wool.	Silk, Raw and Waste.	Sugar, Haw.	Tallow.	Tea.	Tobacco Unmanu-factured.
	lbs.	lbs.	cwts.	cwts.	lbs.	lbs.	cwts.	cwts.	lbs.	lbs.
1838	507,850,000	39,932,000	1,626,276	730,376	52,594,000	4,404,354	5,035,373	1,122,449	40,413,000	30,162,000
1839	389,396,000	41,003,000	1,223,701	995,693	57,379,000	4,788,738	4,678,219	1,330,528	38,158,000	35,605,000
1840	592,488,000	70,250,000	1,253,240	684,068	49,436,000	4,459,542	4,035,845	1,200,489	28,021,000	36,680,000
1841	487,992,000	43,317,000	1,346,843	652,165	56,170,000	4,734,755	4,908,018	1,242,553	30,787,000	43,935,000
1842	531,750,000	41,444,000	1,145,759	585,905	45,881,000	5,388,100	4,756,011	1,011,370	40,742,000	39,526,000
1843	673,193,000	38,942,000	1,437,150	735,743	49,243,000	4,964,203	5,020,569	1,171,618	46,612,000	43,755,000
1844	646,111,000	46,523,000	1,583,494	913,233	65,713,000	5,899,187	4,880,075	1,079,486	53,147,000	37,610,000
1845	721,979,000	50,377,000	1,418,323	931,850	76,813,000	5,816,327	5,820,890	1,194,284	51,056,000	32,944,000
1846	467,748,000	51,634,000	1,146,743	880,810	65,117,000	5,280,000	5,613.847	1,114,761	54,768,000	52,787,000

The accounts of the bank of England, from 1840 to 1847 inclusive

In the following Table the four principal items of the accounts of the Bank, as published prior to September, 1844, are exhibited weekly for the whole period of eight years to which the present volume relates, with the exception of an interval of about six months, between March and September, 1844, the reason for which will be stated where it occurs.

In order to avoid the introduction of an unnecessary number of figures, as well as to afford additional facility of reference, five figures on the right hand of each item have been omitted, leaving the millions to stand as whole numbers, and the next figures as decimal parts of a million. For most purposes, requiring reference to the state of the Bank accounts in the past, the degree of accuracy thus attained will be found practically sufficient.

It may be necessary to observe that, throughout, the "circulation", includes the post bills.

Date.	Circulation.	Bullion.	Deposits.	Securities.
1840.	£	£	£	£
Jan. 7	15.5	4.5	14.5	28.4
14	17.8	4.4	9.3	28.5
21	18.1	4.5	8.0	24.6
28	17.7	3.9	7.6	24.2

Continued

Date.	Circulation.	Bullion.	Deposits.	Securities.
Feb. 4	17.6	3.9	7.0	23.7
11	17.2	4.0	6.9	22.9
18	16.8	4.2	6.8	22.4
25	16.5	4.3	6.5	21.6
March 3	16.4	4.4	6.5	21.6
10	16.2	4.6	6.5	21.0
17	16.0	4.7	6.9	21.1
24	15.9	4.4	6.8	21.2
31	16.3	4.4	6.4	21.3
April 7	16.5	4.3	10.5	25.5
14	17.8	4.1	8.1	24.6
21	17.5	4.1	8.0	24.2
28	17.4	4.2	7.5	23.6
May 5	17.2	4.2	7.3	23.3
12	17.2	4.3	6.6	22.3
19	16.8	4.4	6.3	21.6
26	16.8	4.5	6.0	21.1
June 2	16.7	4.5	6.1	21.0
9	16.4	4.6	5.9	20.5
16	16.2	4.7	6.3	20.5
23	16.0	4.8	6.9	20.9
30	16.6	4.8	7.2	21.9
July 7	16.4	4.6	14.2	28.9
14	18.1	4.4	9.1	25.9

Continued

Date.	Circulation.	Bullion.	Deposits.	Securities.
21	18.2	4.4	8.3	25.
28	17.9	4.4	8.0	24.4
August 4	18.0	4.4	7.3	24.
11	17.5	4.3	7.3	23.5
18	17.4	4.3	6.8	22.8
25	17.1	4.2	6.2	22.
Sept. 1	16.9	4.2	6.1	21.7
8	16.8	4.2	5.9	21.4
15	16.9	4.2	5.8	21.4
22	16.4	4.	5.8	21.2
29	16.5	3.8	5.7	21.4
Oct. 6	16.5	3.5	5.5	21.5
13	17.2	3.3	8.6	25.3
20	16.8	3.	7.1	23.8
27	16.4	3.	6.6	22.8
Nov. 3	16.6	3.	6.2	22.4
10	16.1	3.1	6.1	21.9
17	15.9	3.3	5.8	21.7
24	15.9	3.5	5.6	20.8
Dec. 1	16.1	3.6	6.2	21.4
8	15.8	3.8	6.6	21.5
15	15.5	4.	7.3	21.5
22	15.4	4.	7.9	22.1
29	15.5	4.	8.4	22.8

Continued

Date.	Circulation.	Bullion.	Deposits.	Securities.
1841.	£	£	£	£
Jan. 5	15.6	4.	8.4	22.8
12	17.2	3.9	9.8	26.
19	17.3	3.9	8.1	24.6
26	17.1	3.9	7.6	23.7
Feb. 2	16.9	3.9	7.1	23.
9	16.6	4.	6.9	22.5
16	16.5	4.1	6.5	21.7
23	16.3	4.3	6.4	21.3
March 2	16.4	4.5	6.5	21.3
9	16.2	4.7	6.6	21.1
16	16.1	4.7	6.7	21.
23	15.9	4.9	6.1	20.1
30	16.2	5.	6.2	20.4
April 6	16.4	5.	10.5	24.8
13	17.3	4.8	8.5	23.9
20	17.3	4.8	7.7	23.1
27	16.9	4.9	7.5	22.2
May 4	17.	4.9	7.2	22.1
11	16.7	5.	6.7	21.3
18	16.5	5.	6.6	20.9
25	16.5	5.1	6.6	20.7
June 1	16.4	5.2	6.3	20.3
8	16.3	5.2	6.3	20.3

Continued

Date.	Circulation.	Bullion.	Deposits.	Securities.
15	16.2	5.3	6.7	20.5
22	15.9	5.4	6.3	19.7
29	16.3	5.4	6.3	20.1
July 6	16.5	5.3	14.7	28.9
13	18.2	5.	10.1	26.4
20	18.6	4.8	8.6	25.5
27	18.3	4.8	8.2	24.7
Aug. 3	18.4	4.7	7.8	24.3
10	18.	4.7	7.6	23.9
17	17.6	4.7	7.2	23.2
24	17.5	4.8	7.	22.7
31	17.3	4.8	6.9	22.6
Sept. 7	17.	4.8	6.7	22.
14	16.9	4.8	6.5	21.7
21	16.9	4.7	6.4	21.6
28	17.1	4.6	6.6	22.3
Oct. 5	17.2	4.3	6.7	22.6
12	17.2	4.1	10.9	26.8
19	17.7	4.	8.	24.7
26	17.3	3.9	7.6	23.7
Nov. 2	17.5	4.	7.2	23.4
9	16.8	4.2	7.4	22.7
16	16.5	4.4	7.	21.9
23	16.3	4.7	6.9	21.4

Continued

Date.	Circulation.	Bullion.	Deposits.	Securities.
30	16.4	4.8	6.8	21.2
Dec. 7	16.3	5.1	7.1	21.3
14	16.	5.4	7.7	21.2
21	15.8	5.6	8.4	21.5
28	15.7	5.6	8.8	21.9
1842.	£	£	£	£
Jan. 4	16.1	5.6	9.	22.5
11	17.3	5.5	11.5	26.5
18	17.4	5.4	10.4	25.5
25	17.4	5.5	9.8	24.7
Feb. 1	17.5	5.6	9.3	24.4
8	17.1	5.7	9.	23.7
15	16.9	5.9	8.6	22.8
22	16.9	6.1	8.2	22.1
March 1	16.9	6.4	8.	21.5
8	16.6	6.6	7.5	20.9
15	16.6	6.7	7.1	20.
22	16.3	7.	6.8	19.2
29	16.6	7.1	6.6	19.2
April 2	17.	7.	7.3	20.1
9	18.	7.	10.5	24.1
16	18.5	7.	9.3	23.4
23	18.5	7.1	8.7	22.7
30	18.5	7.2	8.7	22.6

Continued

Date.	Circulation.	Bullion.	Deposits.	Securities.
May 7	18.2	7.2	8.1	21.8
14	18.	7.3	7.7	21.1
21	17.7	7.3	7.5	20.5
28	17.5	7.5	6.9	19.6
June 4	17.7	7.6	7.	19.8
11	17.4	7.6	7.2	19.7
18	17.2	7.8	7.9	20.
25	17.7	8.2	8.8	21.
July 2	18.2	8.5	8.6	21.
9	20.1	8.8	12.3	26.3
16	20.4	8.9	11.3	25.6
23	20.8	9.1	11.	25.4
30	20.7	9.4	10.9	25.0
August 6	20.3	9.5	11.	24.6
13	20.2	9.6	10.4	23.8
20	20.1	9.6	9.4	22.7
27	20.3	9.7	8.6	22.1
Sep. 3	20.2	9.8	8.5	21.8
10	19.7	9.8	8.4	21.2
17	19.3	9.8	8.2	20.5
24	19.	9.9	8.2	20.1
Oct. 1	19.3	9.8	7.7	20.2
8	19.2	9.7	7.5	19.8
15	20.3	9.5	10.5	23.8

Continued

Date.	Circulation.	Bullion.	Deposits.	Securities.
22	20.2	9.6	10.2	23.3
29	20.2	9.8	9.8	22.8
Nov. 5	20.1	9.9	9.7	22.4
12	19.6	10.1	9.6	21.8
19	19.1	10.2	8.8	20.3
26	18.8	10.4	8.7	19.7
Dec. 3	18.8	10.6	8.3	19.2
10	18.5	10.7	8.2	18.6
17	18.3	11.	8.2	18.
24	18.	11.1	8.8	18.3
31	18.2	11.1	8.8	18.6
1843.	£	£	£	£
Jan. 7	18.5	10.9	16.5	26.7
14	20.7	10.8	13.8	26.3
21	21.1	10.9	12.8	25.7
28	21.2	11.	12.5	25.4
Feb. 4	21.3	10.9	12.2	25.3
11	20.7	10.9	11.9	24.7
18	20.6	10.9	11.5	24.1
25	20.2	11.	11.5	23.5
March 4	19.7	11.	11.5	23.
11	19.3	11.1	11.3	22.4
18	19.6	11.3	10.8	22.

Continued

Date.	Circulation.	Bullion.	Deposits.	Securities.
25	19.6	11.5	10.2	21.5
April 1	19.5	11.6	10.	21.1
8	20.1	11.4	13.3	24.9
15	20.4	11.3	12.4	24.5
22	20.4	11.	11.4	23.7
29	20.2	11.3	11.4	23.2
May 6	19.8	11.1	10.8	22.5
13	19.5	11.2	10.1	21.5
20	19.1	11.4	9.7	20.6
27	19.	11.5	9.3	19.9
June 3	18.9	11.5	8.9	19.4
10	18.4	11.7	9.2	19.
17	18.1	12.	9.2	18.4
24	18.	12.1	9.5	18.6
July 1	18.3	12.	10.4	19.8
8	19.7	11.9	15.2	26.2
15	20.4	11.7	13.8	25.6
22	20.6	11.7	13.	25.1
29	20.6	11.8	12.6	24.5
August 5	20.2	11.8	12.5	24.1
12	19.6	12.	11.9	22.9
19	19.6	12.1	11.2	22.
26	19.4	12.1	10.5	21.
Sept. 2	19.4	12.2	11.	21.5

Continued

Date.	Circulation.	Bullion.	Deposits.	Securities.
9	18.9	12.2	10.9	20.8
16	18.7	12.2	10.3	20.
23	18.4	12.3	10.	19.4
30	19.	12.2	10.4	20.4
Oct. 7	18.9	12.	10.3	20.5
14	19.6	11.7	11.8	22.7
21	19.8	11.8	11.4	22.4
28	19.7	11.9	11.3	22.1
Nov. 4	19.5	12.	11.	21.6
11	19.1	12.3	11.	20.8
18	18.7	12.5	10.5	19.8
25	18.8	12.8	11.1	20.2
Dec. 2	18.9	13.1	11.7	20.6
9	18.5	13.4	12.2	20.4
16	18.3	13.9	12.9	20.4
23	18.6	14.3	13.2	20.5
30	19.3	14.9	13.7	21.2
1844.	£	£	£	£
Jan. 6	19.5	15.2	18.5	25
13	21.2	15.2	15.9	25.4
20	21.9	15.3	14.6	24.8
27	22.	15.5	14.3	23.9
Feb. 3	22.	15.6	14.	23.6

Continued

Date.	Circulation.	Bullion.	Deposits.	Securities.
10	21.7	15.8	13.4	22.6
17	21.5	15.9	13.2	22.
24	21.3	16.1	12.8	21.2
March 2	21.2	16.1	12.3	20.6

Thus far this Table is compiled from the Appendix to the Reports of the Select Committee on Banks of Issue, in 1840 and 1841, and from Parliamentary returns made subsequently, and preparatory to the renewal of the Bank charter in the session of 1844. From the last date given, until the Act of that session came into operation, only the usual monthly accounts were made public, showing the average amount of each item for the previous three months; and the results of these are given in the next page.

Periods to which the Averages refer.	Circulation.	Bullion.	Deposits.	Securities.
1844.	£	£	£	£
Jan. 27 to April 20	21.4	16.	13.6	22.1
Feb. 24 to May 18	21.3	16.	13.3	21.7
March 23 to June 15	21.3	15.9	13.4	21.9
April 20 to July 13	21.2	15.7	13.9	22.4
May 18 to August 10	21.3	15.5	14.	22.9

The Act of 1844, requiring a weekly publication of the accounts of the Bank in the London Gazette, came into operation in the first week of September in that year. These accounts vary materially, in form, from those previously published; but, to preserve the uniformity necessary to a ready comparison with the accounts at previous dates, the results are here presented, through the remainder of the Table, in the same shape as before.

Date.	Circulation.	Bullion.	Deposits.	Securities.
1844.	£	£	£	£
Sept. 7	21.2	15.1	12.2	21.8
14	20.9	15.1	12.8	22.1
21	20.6	15.1	13.8	22.8
28	20.9	15.	14.2	23.7
Oct. 5	21.1	14.6	14.4	24.5
12	21.3	14.3	16.3	26.3
19	22.1	14.1	12.4	23.5
26	22.3	14.	11.8	23.2
Nov. 2	22.2	14.	12.2	23.1
19	21.6	14.1	11.9	22.5
16	21.5	14.2	11.8	22.3
23	21.	14.3	12.6	22.5
30	20.7	14.5	13.5	22.9
Dec. 7	20.5	14.6	14.2	23.1
14	20.2	14.8	14.7	23.2
21	20.1	14.9	15.4	23.7
28	20.1	14.8	15.6	24.
1845.	£	£	£	£
Jan. 4	20.6	14.8	15.3	24.4

Continued

Date.	Circulation.	Bullion.	Deposits.	Securities.
11	21.4	14.7	12.9	22.8
18	21.6	14.7	11.8	21.9
25	21.7	14.8	11.4	21.5
Feb. 1	21.6	14.8	11.5	21.6
8	21.3	15.1	13.4	22.9
15	21.1	15.3	14.5	23.7
22	20.7	15.4	15.1	23.7
March 1	20.9	15.7	15.7	24.6
8	20.6	15.8	16.2	24.6
15	20.6	15.9	16.4	24.7
22	20.5	16.	17.3	25.4
29	20.7	16.2	18.	26.1
April 5	21.1	16.	17.3	26.
12	22.3	15.8	16.1	25.6
19	22.5	15.8	14.7	24.5
26	22.3	15.8	11.4	23.
May 3	22.4	15.8	13.	22.9
10	22.1	15.8	13.4	22.9
17	21.6	15.9	14.6	23.4
24	21.4	16.2	15.1	23.4
31	21.4	16.4	16.2	24.4
June 7	21.3	16.5	16.3	24.3
14	21.	16.6	16.5	24.1
21	21.2	16.6	17.	24.8

Continued

Date.	Circulation.	Bullion.	Deposits.	Securities.
28	21.3	16.6	17.5	25.4
July 5	21.6	16.4	17.3	25.7
12	22.6	16.1	14.8	25.5
19	22.5	15.8	13.7	23.7
26	22.3	15.7	13.6	23.5
August 2	22.4	15.7	14.1	24.2
9	22.5	15.6	14.2	24.4
16	22.9	15.6	13.9	24.5
23	22.5	15.6	13.7	24.1
30	22.1	15.5	14.4	24.5
Sept. 6	21.7	15.4	14.9	24.8
13	21.3	15.3	15.6	25.1
20	21.4	15.3	16.3	26.
27	21.6	15.1	16.8	26.9
Oct. 4	22.3	14.8	16.8	27.9
11	22.1	14.5	17.2	27.9
18	23.3	14.1	14.3	26.6
25	23.1	14.	13.2	25.5
Nov. 1	23.1	13.8	13.5	26.
8	22.8	13.7	14.4	26.8
1846.	£	£	£	£
Nov. 15	22.5	13.5	15.4	27.6
22	22.	13.5	16.3	28.1
29	21.8	13.2	16.6	28.5

Continued

Date.	Circulation.	Bullion.	Deposits.	Securities.
Dec. 6	21.5	13.	17.1	28.8
13	21.	13.2	17.7	28.7
20	21.	13.3	18.1	28.9
27	20.8	13.3	18.1	28.9
Jan. 3	21.2	13.2	17.7	28.9
10	21.8	13.1	15.8	27.8
17	22.1	13.1	15.9	28.3
24	22.1	13.1	18.6	30.9
31	22.4	13.2	21.4	34.
Feb. 7	21.3	13.3	23.9	35.4
14	21.	13.4	23.7	34.8
21	21.	13.6	24.2	35.1
28	20.9	13.7	24.9	35.8
March 7	20.3	13.7	24.3	34.6
14	20.2	13.8	23.2	34.5
21	20.1	13.9	24.3	34.3
28	20.5	13.9	24.4	34.7
April 4	20.8	13.8	23.8	34.6
11	21.2	13.5	22.2	33.3
18	21.5	13.6	20.9	32.1
25	21.5	13.6	19.6	30.8
May 2	21.6	13.7	19.3	30.6
9	21.3	13.8	19.2	30.
16	21.1	14.1	20.3	30.6

Continued

Date.	Circulation.	Bullion.	Deposits.	Securities.
23	21.1	14.4	20.7	30.6
30	20.8	14.7	21.3	30.9
June 6	20.7	14.9	21.6	30.7
13	20.4	15.3	22.	30.5
20	20.2	15.6	22.6	30.4
27	20.4	16.	22.8	30.6
July 4	20.9	15.9	22.1	30.6
11	21.7	15.8	19.3	28.5
18	22.	15.7	18.	27.7
25	21.7	15.9	17.	26.9
August 1	21.4	15.7	17.2	26.4
8	21.2	15.9	17.4	26.3
15	21.7	15.9	16.9	26.2
22	21.	16.1	16.9	25.4
29	21.2	16.3	16.3	24.8
Sept. 5	21.4	16.2	15.8	24.9
12	20.9	16.3	16.2	24.7
19	20.8	16.3	17.	25.4
26	20.7	16.2	18.	26.4
Oct. 3	21.4	15.8	17.9	27.4
10	21.7	15.5	18.1	27.6
17	22.3	15.1	14.3	25.
24	22.3	14.8	13.6	24.4

Continued

Date.	Circulation.	Bullion.	Deposits.	Securities.
31	22.3	14.8	13.3	24.4
Nov. 7	21.9	14.7	13.7	24.4
14	21.3	14.8	14.7	24.7
21	21.1	14.9	15.8	25.6
28	20.8	15.	16.4	25.8
Dec. 5	20.7	15.	16.9	26.1
12	20.6	15.1	17.1	26.1
19	20.4	15.1	17.4	26.1
26	20.5	15.	18.	26.9
1847.	£	£	£	£
Jan. 2	21.9	14.8	17.9	27.3
9	21.8	14.3	15.6	26.6
16	21.6	13.9	15.3	26.6
23	21.5	13.4	15.	26.6
30	21.4	12.9	14.1	26.2
Feb. 6	20.5	12.2	13.8	25.7
13	20.6	12.2	14.6	26.6
20	20.3	12.2	14.6	26.4
27	20.1	12.	15.2	27.2
March 6	20.1	11.5	15.8	28.3
13	20.	11.4	16.2	28.7
20	19.9	11.2	16.4	29.
27	20.7	11.	16.	29.2
April 3	20.8	10.2	15.5	30.
10	21.3	9.8	16.2	31.1

Continued

Date.	Circulation.	Bullion.	Deposits.	Securities.
17	21.1	9.3	13.	28.2
24	20.6	9.2	11.7	26.6
May 1	20.6	9.3	11.6	26.2
8	20.4	9.5	11.8	26.
15	19.9	9.8	13.	26.6
22	19.5	9.9	14.4	27.5
29	19.4	10.1	15.4	28.1
June 5	19.1	10.2	15.9	28.2
12	19.	10.3	16.9	29.
19	18.7	10.5	17.4	29.1
26	18.8	10.5	17.7	29.4
July 3	19.2	10.3	17.6	30.
10	19.8	10.	14.5	27.8
17	19.9	9.9	13.1	26.8
1847.	£	£	£	£
July 24	19.7	9.7	12.8	26.4
31	19.7	9.3	12.8	26.8
August 7	19.5	9.2	13.4	27.4
14	19.4	9.2	13.8	27.7
21	18.9	9.2	13.7	27.1
28	19.	9.1	14.2	27.8
Sept. 4	19.	8.9	14.5	28.5
11	18.6	8.9	15.1	28.8
18	18.7	8.8	15.9	29.8

Continued

Date.	Circulation.	Bullion.	Deposits.	Securities.
25	18.8	8.7	16.9	31.
Oct. 2	19.5	8.5	17.2	32.3
9	19.5	8.4	17.1	32.3
16	20.2	8.4	14.1	29.4
23	21.2	8.3	13.3	29.8
30	21.7	8.4	13.6	30.4
Nov. 6	21.3	8.7	13.7	29.9
13	20.9	9.2	14.3	29.5
20	20.1	10.	15.	28.8
27	19.8	10.5	15.9	28.9
Dec. 4	19.6	11.	16.2	28.4
11	19.1	11.4	16.6	28.
18	18.6	11.9	17.3	27.6
25	18.6	12.2	17.4	27.4

Bank Note Circulation of the United Kingdom.

Returns, uniform and periodical, of the note circulation of all the issuing Banks in the United Kingdom, were first required by the Act 4 & 5 Vict. c. 50. (passed 21st June, 1841.) They have since been made at the end of every four weeks. Quarterly returns were previously made of the circulation of the Country Banks of England and Wales, and these are given in the following Table for the first eighteen months. It will be observed that in the present, as in the foregoing Table, five figures on the right hand of each sum are omitted; and the reasons for this are in both cases the same:

	ENGLAND.			SCOT - LAND.	IRELAND.		Total.	Bullion in the Bank of England.
	Bank of England.	Private Banks.	Joint Stock Banks.	Chartered Private and Joint Stock Banks.	Bank of Ireland.	Private and Joint Stock Banks.		
Quarters ending —	£	£	£	£	£	£	£	£
1840. March 28	—	6.8	3.9	—	—	—	—	—
June 27	—	6.9	4.1	—	—	—	—	—
Sept. 26	—	6.3	3.6	—	—	—	—	—
Dec. 26	—	6.5	3.7	—	—	—	—	—
1841. March 27	—	6.3	3.6	—	—	—	—	—
June 25	—	6.4	3.8	—	—	—	—	—
Four weeks ending—	£	£	£	£	£	£	£	£
1841. July 24	17.9	5.9	3.4	3.1	3.0	19	35 4	5.0
Aug. 21	17.9	5.8	3.2	3.0	2.9	1.8	34.8	4.8
Sept. 18	17.0	5.7	3.3	3.0	2.8	1.9	34.0	4.8
Oct. 16	17.3	6.2	3.5	3 2	30	2.1	35.5	4.2
Nov. 13	170	6.2	3.4	3.1	3 3	2.6	36.1	4.2
Dec. 11	16.2	6.7	3 2	3.4	33	2.5	34.5	5.0
1842. Jan. 8	16.2	5.4	3.0	3.0	3.2	2.5	33.6	6-6
Feb. 5	17.4	5.5	3.0	2.9	3.2	2.5	34.7	5.6
March 5	16.8	5.2	2.9	2.8	3.8	2.4	33.5	6.2
April 2	16.6	5.0	3.0	2.6	3.0	2.2	33.0	7.0
April 30	18.4	3.4	3.1	2.5	3.1	2.1	34.8	7.0

Continued

	ENGLAND.			SCOT-LAND.	IRELAND.		Total.	Bullion in the Bank of England.
	Bank of England.	Private Banks.	Joint Stock Banks.	Chartered Private and Joint Stock Banks.	Bank of Ireland.	Private and Joint Stock Banks.		
May 28	17.8	5.3	3.1	2.9	3.0	19	34.3	7.3
June 25	17.5	4.9	2.8	2.8	2,9	1.7	32.9	7.8
July 23	19.9	5.1	2.9	2.7	2 8	1.6	35.3	8.8
Aug. 20	20.3	5.1	2.8	2.6	2.8	1.6	35.4	9.5
Sept. 17	19.9	5.0	2.8	2.6	2.8	1.9	34.9	9.8
Oct. 15	19.5	5.4	3.0	2.7	3.0	2.9	35.8	9.8
Nov. 12	20.1	5.4	3.1	2.8	S.1	2.1	36.9	9.9
Dec. 10	18.8	5.0	3.0	3.0	3.1	2.1	85.2	10.5
1843. Jan. 7	18.2	4.9	2.8	2.7	3.1	2.0	34.0	11.0
Feb. 4	21.1	5.0	2.9	2.6	3.1	2.1	36.9	11.9
March 4	20.3	4 7	2.8	2.5	3.1	2,0	35.8	10.9
April 1	19.5	4.7	2.8	2.4	3.0	20	34.6	11.4
April 29	20.3	4.9	3.1	2.4	3.1	1.9	36.0	11.3
May 27	19.1	4.7	3.0	2.8	32	1.8	35.1	11.3
June 24	18.4	4.3	2.8	2.8	3.3	1.7	33.4	11.8
July 22	19.8	4 4	2.3	2.6	3.0	1.6	34.5	11.8
Aug. 19	20.0	4.3	2.7	2.6	3.0	1.6	34.5	11.9
Sept. 29	19.1	4.2	2.7	2.6	29	1.6	33.5	12.2
Oct. 14	19.0	4.7	3.1	2.7	3.2	20	34.9	12.0

Continued

	ENGLAND.			SCOT - LAND.	IRELAND.		Total.	Bullion in the Bank of England.
	Bank of England.	Private Banks.	Joint Stock Banks.	Chartered Private and Joint Stock Banks.	Bank of Ireland.	Private and Joint Stock Banks.		
Nov. 11	19.5	4.9	3 3	2.9	3.5	2.4	36.6	12.0
Dec. 9	18.7	4 6	3.1	3.1	3.5	2.3	35.5	12.9
1844 Jan. 6	18.9	4.6	3 2	2.9	3 4	2.3	35.7	14.6
Feb. 3	21.8	4.9	3.4	2.7	3.5	2.4	39.0	15.4
March 2	21.4	4 9	3.4	2.6	3.0	2 4	38.6	16.0
March 30	20,8	4.9	3 5	2.6	3.5	2.1	37-9	16.3
April 27	21.8	5.2	37	2.7	3.6	2.3	39 5	15.8
May 25	21.5	5.1	3.0	3.0	3.6	22	39.2	15.7
Four weeks ending—	£	£	£	£	£	£	£	£
1841. June 22	20.6	4.7	3.6	3.1	3.4	2.0	37.7	15.8
July	21.4	4.6	3.3	2.9	3.4	1.9	37.7	15.4
Aug. 17	21.9	4.5	3.2	2.9	3.3	1.9	38.0	15.2
Sept. 14	21.2	4.3	3.1	2.9	3.3	2.0	37.1	15.2
Oct. 12	21.0	4.6	3.3	2.9	3.5	2.4	38.0	14.8
Nov. 9	21.9	4.6	3.2	3.2	3.8	2.8	39.8	14.1
Dec. 7	20.9	4.4	3.0	3.4	3.9	2.9	38.8	14.4
1845. Jan. 4	20.3	4.4	3.0	3.1	3.9	3.0	37.9	14.8
Feb. 1	21.6	4.5	3.1	3.0	3.9	3 1	39 5	14.8

Continued

	ENGLAND.			SCOT-LAND.	IRELAND.		Total.	Bullion in the Bank of England.
	Bank of England.	Private Banks.	Joint Stock Banks.	Chartered Private and Joint Stock Banks.	Bank of Ireland.	Private and Joint Stock Banks.		
March 1	21.0	4.4	3.0	2.9	3.9	3.1	38.6	15.4
March 29	20.6	4.4	3.1	2.9	3.9	3.1	38.2	16.0
April 26	220	4.6	3.3	3.0	4.0	3.0	40.1	15.9
May 24	21.9	4.6	3.2	3.3	4.0	2.8	40.1	15.9
June 21	21.2	4.3	3.1	3.4	3.8	2.7	38.9	16.5
July 19	22.0	4.4	3.1	3.3	3.8	2.6	39 5	16.2
Aug. 16	22.5	4.4	3.1	3.3	3.7	2.5	39.7	15.7
Sept. 13	21.9	4.3	3.1	3.3	3.7	2.5	39.0	15.6
Oct. 11	21.8	4.5	3.3	3.4	3.9	2.9	40.0	14.9
Nov. 8	23.1	4.7	3.3	3.5	4.3	3 4	42.6	13.9
Dec. 6	22.0	4.5	3.2	3.8	4.4	3.3	41.3	13.3
1846. Jan. 3	21.0	4.5	3.1	3.3	4.3	3.0	39.4	13.3
Jan. 31	22.1	4.6	3.2	3.1	4.3	3.1	40.6	13.2
Feb. 28	21.1	4.4	3.1	3.0	4.3	3.1	39.2	13.5
March 28	20.3	4.5	3.1	3.0	4.2	3.1	38.5	13.8
April 25	21.2	4.7	3.3	3.0	4.3	3.1	39.9	13.6
May 23	21.2	4.6	3.2	3.4	4.3	3 0	39.9	14.0
June 20	20.5	4.4	3 1	3.5	4.1	2.8	38.6	15.1
July 18	21.2	4.4	3.0	3.3	3.9	2.6	38.8	15.8

Continued

	ENGLAND.			SCOT – LAND.	IRELAND.		Total.	Bullion in the Bank of England.
	Bank of England.	Private Banks.	Joint Stock Banks.	Chartered Private and Joint Stock Banks.	Bank of Ireland.	Private and Joint Stock Banks.		
Aug. 15	21.5	4.3	3.0	3.3	3.8	2.6	38.8	15.9
Sept. 12	21.1	4.4	3.1	3.4	3.11	2.6	38.7	15.2
Oct. 10	21.1	4.6	3.2	3.6	4.1	3.0	40.0	1.5.9
Nov. 7	22.2	4.7	3.3	3.7	4.4	3.4	41.0	14.9
Dec. 5	21 0	4.5	3.1	3.9	4.3	3.4	40.6	14.9
1847. Jan. 2	20.6	4.5	3.1	3.7	4.2	3.3	39.5	15.0
Jan. 30	21.6	4.6	3.2	3.6	4.1	3.1	40.4	13.6
Feb. 27	20.4	4.5	3.1	3.5	4.0	3.0	38.6	12.2
March 27	20.0	4.5	3.2	3.3	3.8	2.8	373.9	11.3
April 24	21.0	4.7	3.3	3.3	3.8	2.7	38.9	9.6
May 22	20.1	4.5	3.2	3.5	3.6	2.3	37.5	9.6
June 19	19.0	4.3	3.0	3.6	3.3	2.1	35.6	10.3
July 17	19.4	4.3	3.0	8.4	3.2	2.0	35.5	10.2
Aug. 14	19.6	4.2	2.9	3.4	3.1	1.9	35.4	9.4
Sept. 11	19.9	4.1	2.9	3.4	3.0	2.0	34.5	9.0
Oct. 9	19.1	4.3	3.1	3.5	3.1	2.2	35.5	8.6
Nov. 6	21.1	4 2	3.0	3.6	3.2	2.2	37.6	8.4
Dec. 4	19.2	3.6	2.5	3.7	5.3		34.6	16.2

Correspondence between the government and the bank of England—25th Oct. 1847

"Downing Street, Oct. 25. 1847.

"Gentlemen — Her Majesty's Government have seen with the deepest regret, the pressure which has existed for some weeks upon the commercial interests of the country, and that this pressure has been aggravated by a want of that confidence which is necessary for carrying on the ordinary dealings of trade.

"They have been in hopes that the check given to transactions of a speculative character, the transfer of capital from other countries, the influx of bullion, and the feeling which a knowledge of these circumstances might have been expected to produce, would have removed the prevailing distrust.

"They were encouraged in this expectation by the speedy cessation of a similar state of feeling in the month of April last.

"These hopes have, however, been disappointed, and her Majesty's Government have come to the conclusion that the time has arrived when they ought to attempt, by some extraordinary and temporary measure, to restore confidence to the mercantile and manufacturing community.

"For this purpose, they recommend to the Directors of the Bank of England, in the present emergency, to enlarge the amount of their discounts and advances, upon approved security; but that, in order to retain this operation within reasonable limits, a high rate of interest should be charged. In present circumstances, they would suggest that the rate of interest should not be less than 8 per cent.

"If this course should lead to any infringement of the existing law, her Majesty's Government will be prepared to propose to Parliament on its meeting, a Bill of Indemnity.

"They will rely upon the discretion of the Directors to reduce as soon as possible the amount of their notes, if any extraordinary issues should take place, within the limits prescribed by law.

"Her Majesty's Government are of opinion that any extra profit derived from this measure should be carried to the account of tire public, but the precise mode of doing so must be left to future arrangement.

"Her Majesty's Government are not insensible to the evil of any departure from the law which has placed the currency of this country upon a sound basis; but they feel confident that, in the present circumstances, the measure which they have proposed may be safely adopted; and that, at the same time, the main provisions of that law and the vital principle of preserving the convertibility of the bank-note may be firmly maintained.

"We have the honour to be, Gentlemen,

"Your obedient humble Servants,

(Signed) "JOHN RUSSELL.

"CHARLES WOOD.

"The Governor and Deputy-Governor of the Hank of England."

(Reply.)

"Bank of England, Oct. 25. 1847.

"GENTLEMEN — We have the honour to acknowledge your letter of this day's date, which we have submitted to the Court of Directors, and we enclose a copy of the resolutions thereon; and

"We have the honour to be, Sirs,

"Your most obedient Servants,

(Signed) "JAMES MORRIS, Governor.

"H. J. PRESCOTT, Deputy-Governor.

"To the First Lord of the Treasury and the Chancellor of the Exchequer"

"Resolved— That this Court do accede to the recommendation contained in the letter from the First Lord of the Treasury and the Chancellor of the Exchequer, dated this day, and addressed to the Governor and Deputy-Governor of the Bank of England, which has just been read:

"That the minimum rate of discount on bills not having more than ninety-five days to run be 8 per cent:

"That advances be made on bills of exchange, on stock. Exchequer bills, and other approved securities, in sums of not loss than 2000*l*. , and for periods to be fixed by the Governors, at the rate of 8 per cent per annum."

Statement of the quantity of gold produced in Russia during the 28 years, 1819-1846

(From the *Journal de St. Petersburg*, *Samedi*, 23 *Janv.* 1847—6 *Févr.*)

Of the quantity of gold worked in 1846 in the Crown Mines and in the private mines of the Oural and Siberia, the mint has received to this date 1397 poods 15 liv. 13 zolotnicks, to which must be added 325 p. 14 liv. 74 zol. expected during the winter, thereby making the total production of 1846, 1722 p. 29 liv. 87 zol.

Formerly gold was only worked in the district of the mines of Catherinebourg, belonging to the Crown; in the mines of Reirzoff; and in the district of the mines of Kolyvano-Voskressewok, and of Nertchensk; and was extracted from silver which was worked in those mines: — the whole quantity extracted annually amounted to but 34 to 40 poods.

In 1819, some veins of auriferous sands (gisements de sables aurifères) were discovered in the Oural: — since that time the production of this precious metal has increased in the following proportions: —

				Poods.	Liv.	Zol.
In 1819	–	–	–	40	9	55
1820	–	–	–	44	3	0
1821	–	–	–	52	4	85
1822	–	–	–	79	21	36
1823	–	–	–	125	19	79
1824	–	–	–	228	13	38
1825	–	–	–	257	12	54
1826	–	–	–	257	25	15
1827	–	–	–	307	30	95
1828	–	–	–	317	39	44
		Total	–	1711	0	21

It was in 1829 that some veins of auriferous sands were also discovered in Siberia. At first the working was not very productive; but after a while, and more especially during the last six years, the results have been very brilliant; as the following figures will prove: —

				Poods.	Liv.	Zol.
In 1829	–	–	–	314	31	1
1830	–	–	–	378	15	79
1831	–	–	–	396	29	37
1832	–	–	–	410	8	61
1833	–	–	–	408	22	71
1834	–	–	–	406	4	64
1835	–	–	–	413	1	8
1836	–	–	–	426	3	74
1837	–		–	469	20	75
1838	–	–	–	524	36	69
1839	–	–	–	525	6	38
1840	–	–	–	585	15	60
1841	–	–	–	681	20	34
1842	–	–	–	950	26	68
1843	–	–	–	1283	2	60
1844	–	–	–	1341	25	60
1845	–	–	–	1386	6	41
1846	–	–	–	1722	29	87
			Total –	12,624	28	24

Thus since the discovery of the auriferous sands, *i. e.* since 1819, the working of the gold both in the Oural and in Siberia has produced, Poods 14,335 28 45.

Of this precious metal, the Crown Mines

in the Oural have contributed	–	2924	24	32
" those of Siberia –	–	1293	7	28
" the private mines in the Oural		4219	39	70

"and those in Siberia — 5897 37 11

Say, of Poods 14,335 28 45

The produce of the year 1846, which, as before stated, amounts to 1722 p. 29liv. 87 zol., forms more than one tenth of the whole quantity worked since 1819; and exceeds by 336 p. 23 liv. 46 zol., the result of the working of 1845.

Resume—From the Times. —(*Friday*, 26*th March*, 1847.)

Yield in 1846	Poods. 1722	Liv. 29	Zol. 87	Equal to oz. Troy. 907,284	Value at 77*s*. 9*d*. per oz. £ 3,527,066
Yield from 1819 (the period when some golden sands -were discovered in Oural) to 1828, inclusive.	1711	0	21	901,101	£ 3,503,029
Yield from 1829, (when a discovery was made in Siberia) to 1846, inclusive.	12,624	28	24	6,648,801	£ 25,847,215
Total Poods	14,335	28	45	Oz. 7,549,902	£ 29,350,244

Imperial manifesto

WE, NICHOLAS I., BY THE GRACE OP GOD, EMPEROR AND AUTOCRAT OP ALL THE RUSSIAS, ETC.

The various changes produced by time and the influence of

circumstances in our monetary relations have not only had the effect that the notes of the Imperial Bank, contrary to their original destination, have obtained the preference over the silver money, which is the proper standard of value in our empire, but also that hence a manifold agio has come into use, which has at length moulded itself differently in almost every locality.

Since we have become convinced of the necessity of putting an end, without further delay, to these fluctuations, which disturb the unity and conformity of our monetary system, and cause losses and difficulties of various kinds to all classes, we have, in our constant care for the welfare of our faithful subjects, thought it right to adopt decisive measures for the removal of the inconveniences which have thus arisen, and for their prevention in future.

For this purpose, and after special consideration in the Council of State of all the questions which the subject embraces, we decree as follows:——

Ⅰ. "In order to the restoration of the basis of the manifesto of the Emperor of Alexander L., of glorious memory, of June 20th, 1810, the Russian silver coinage is henceforth recognised as the money forming the principal medium for payments, and the silver ruble, according to its present value and existing subdivisions, is established as legal and unalterable chief metallic unit of the money current in the empire, in proportion to which all assessments, duties, and taxes, as well as different payments, and regulated State expenditures, shall at the time be reduced to silver value.

Ⅱ. "While the silver money will thus become the principal medium of payment, the notes of the Imperial Bank will, in conformity with their original destination, remain a more auxiliary sign of value, whereby for the present and future a more constant and unchangeable course in respect to the silver money will be assigned to the said notes, and, indeed, the silver ruble, as well in itself as in all its subdivisions, will be now at 3 rubles 50 copecs in bank paper.

Ⅲ. "According to the settled and unchangeable course, all persons will be at liberty to make the following payments either in silver or paper money: —

(A) "All imposts and duties accruing to the Crown or territorial jurisdictions, and other charges of that description, and in general all payments fixed by and due to the Crown.

(B) "All payments partaking of the nature of a tax, such as postage of letters, charge on post travelling, on salt, the farmed duties on liquors, stamps, passports, tobacco rolls, &c.

(C) "All payments to the several credit institutes of the empire, the savings banks, and private banks, established under the sanction of the Government.

Ⅳ. "In like manner all regulated state disbursements, all payments by the Crown and the Credit Institutes, the per centage on Treasury bills, and for the notes representing outstanding public debt securities, will be made good, in conformity with the same invariable course, in silver or in paper, as the one or the other kind of money may happen to exist in the coffers of the establishments.

Ⅴ. "All the above indicated payments and advances are, from and after the day of the publication of this manifesto, to be effected according to the above prescribed and unalterable course, nevertheless, the course for imposts, winch, awaiting the adoption of more discriminating measures respecting the monetary system, was for this year fixed at 3 rubles 60 copecs, must, as once sanctioned, subsist until the year 1840 at the same ratio; and so for assessments, duties, and all payments comprehended under letters (A) and (B) in article III.; as also for all regulated outlays and the like previously defined expenditures of the Crown. On this ground, and as it would be injurious to the commercial class to alter the tariff course in the middle of the year, the same will also be maintained until the year 1840.

Ⅵ. "All calculations, engagements, and in general all transactions between the Crown and individuals, as well as all bargains of private persons with each other, are to be contracted and completed in silver money only. As, however, in consequence of the wide boundaries of the empire, this regulation cannot be carried promptly into operation throughout the whole extent, the same is, therefore, to be considered as binding in full force only after the 1st of January, 1840, from which time forward no judicial authority, broker, or notary, shall, on their responsibility, take any part in the expediting or confirming of any settlements in paper money. However, all payments, as well for old contracts and stipulations in notes, as for the more recent in silver, may, without distinction, be completed in silver or paper money, according to the course established in article Ⅱ., and no one is entitled to refuse payments in silver or notes, without distinction, according to the said course.

Ⅶ. "The rule for loans from the Imperial Credit Institutes is henceforth also based on silver, and at the rate of 75, 60, or 45 silver rubles, on the revised registers of males.

Ⅷ. "In order to facilitate in all possible ways the exchange of money, it is hereby made the duty of the Rentist Chambers of Districts to exchange notes for silver, and silver for notes, in proportion to the state of their coffers, at the appointed rate of 3 rubles 50 copecs, and namely, the demand of every applicant to the extent, for one individual, of 100 rubles silver or notes, according to the circumstances.

Ⅸ. "To give to the paper money any other course than that fixed above is hereby strictly prohibited; as also is the giving to silver and notes an agio in the form of a percentage, or hereafter by new transactions to take advantage of the so-called settlement by account for specie. The course of exchange on the Bourse, as well as all quotations in the stock lists, price currents, and such-like advertisements, are henceforth to be expressed in silver. No notice of the course of bank notes shall in future be given on the Bourse.

Ⅹ. "The gold coinage is issued and received by the Crown and the Credit Institutes at 3 per cent. higher than the silver money—namely, the imperial, at 10 rubles 30 copecs; the half imperial, at 5 rubles 15 copecs silver.

Ⅺ "In order to prevent all disadvantage to persons making payments into the Crown offices and Credit Institutes, the officers of those establishments are required to consider it their duty in such transactions to reject no Russian money of the old or the present coinage under the pretext that the marks of the die are no longer perceptible, or that the weight is deficient, or the impression not recognizable. Thus, only coin which has been cut, filed, or which has holes in it, can be returned to the payers.

Ⅻ. "The copper money at present in circulation will be allowed to remain current until its conversion into silver value, in the following manner:

(A) "Three and a half copper copecs will be held equivalent to one silver copec, as well in respect of the copper coin which was struck on the footing of 36, as of that which was struck on the footing of 24 rubles to the pood.

(B) "The copper coin is receivable in the financial offices of the Crown in payment of taxes, duties, revenues, and other contributions, without limitation of quantity, with the exception, however, of those cases in which the amount receivable of copper money is fixed by contract. The Credit Institutes are not bound to receive more than to the value of 10 silver rubles of copper money. Among private persons the affair depends upon the stipulations entered into with each other."

(Under the Sign Manual)

"NICHOLAS.

"Given at St. Petersburg, on the 1st of July, in the year of grace, 1839, and of our reign the 14th."

Address of the Russian Minister of Finance, on presenting to the Council of State the Annual Accounts of the Imperial Ranks. — *10th July*, 1847.

Gentlemen, —In presenting to you the account returned of the banks of the empire, containing an exposition of their operations through the year 1846, I would previously inform you of some particular disposals which have been made in the course of this year.

1st. The want of money which has been felt during the last months of the past year in the principal places of Europe, accruing partly from what they were obliged to employ to buy corn, on account of the dearth experienced in different countries, and partly from the immense enterprises, having for their object the extension of railroads, allow not the hope that the loan destined to cover the expenses necessary in the present year for the construction of the railway from St. Petersburg to Moscow, can be realised in as advantageous a manner as the former loans; that is why, in the view of preparing in time secure resources to meet these expenses, an imperial *ukase* of the 21st January of the present year, prescribed the emission of the 8th and 9th series of the treasury bills of the empire, each worth 3,000,000silver rubles, besides the disbursement in reserve of the 10th and 11th series, in a case where it would become further difficult to open for this year a foreign loan for this purpose. Three of these series have already been put in circulation. The emission of the last, that is to say of the fourth, will probably be also indispensable. By this means guarantee will be found for the present year for the execution of the works of this construction, so important for commerce and industry.

2nd. Several proprietors of mines in the Ural chain of mountains, not having sufficient disposable capital to work these mines as they would wish, were forced, either to borrow money, sometimes at a high interest, or to sell their metal in advance at a great abatement in price, which paralysed the activity of these establishments, and put some of them in an awkward situation. To obviate this inconvenience, it has appeared necessary to found at Catherineburg, the centre of our metallic industry, a branch office of the Bank of Commerce to effect loans on the security of metals produced in the country. I cannot, on this occasion, pass over with silence the fact that the first idea of this useful institution belongs to S. A. I. Mgr. le Duc de Leuchtenburg, who visited personally the mines of Ural about the end of 1845.

This branch bank will forthwith commence its operations: we can then hope that before long the inconveniences will be overcome, and that the proprietors of the mines will be able to extend the circle of their operations.

At the same time that a branch of the bank was instituted at Catherineburg, not the least difficulty was found also to satisfy the desires of the merchants who frequented the Irbite fair, that a temporary office should be annually opened in imitation of the one at Niznei-Novgorod. It is to be hoped that this institution contributes to the greatest development of commerce in this remote country.

3rd. I do not think it superfluous to make mention here of the unexpected modification in the composition of the members of the council of the Bank of Issue of the empire named by the commercial body. Instead of five members entirely elected every three years among the merchants, it has been judged more convenient to designate as permanent members the president of the committee of the exchange, and the syndic of dealers: as to the other three members, their election will take place as in past times.

4th. The exchange of assignments of the bank and of bills of deposit actually in circulation against the bills of credit, having commenced the 1st of November, 1843, has continued till now with success without any coercive measures. On the number of 595,776,310 rubles ass., and of 48,551,198 rubles of bills of deposit, it has been exchanged till now for 498,139,025 rubles of the first, and 45,365,767 of the second. Rest, in circulation 97,637,285 rubles ass., and 3,185,430 of bills of deposit.

Seeing the *minimum* of this quantity, it has been judged necessary to take measures for the final debarment of the circulation, and the following adjournment has been irrevocably fixed: as general delay, the 1st of January, 1848; and as particular delay, for the government of Siberia, the 1st of July, 1848; and for the colonies of the company of North America, 1st of January, 1849.

5th. The use of a great part of the capital in Europe, in buying com, as I said above, and in railway speculations, ought necessarily to have a sensible influence on the minds of the public. You know, gentlemen, that they have considerably fallen in price, especially at the beginning of this year.

S. M. l' Empereur, in his constant solicitude for the progress of financial and commercial affairs, has condescended to order a previous examination in the committee of finance, and also with the advice of this last in the council of the empire of the following question: —"Ought they not, in the present depreciation of the price of the public funds, proceed to buy, employing for this purpose from 20 to 30,000,000 silver rubles of the funds of the Bank of Issue of notes of the empire, a like measure not being in the least in discord with the law on the inalienability of the funds of these notes, as in an exchange of metallic cash will be held a sum equivalent of other funds, which represent a capital bearing interest, and which, when it becomes necessary to reinforce the funds of the bank, will be able to be converted into gold and silver, by selling these securities, while, in the mean time, the interest sappertaining to them would enrich Russia?"

The committee of finance, examining the ground of this question, and taking it into consideration that in the banks of England and of France, enjoying the firmest credit, the game as in the other banks of the first class, the capital is composed partly in money of the precious metals, and partly in public funds —that in the employment of part of the capital of the banks of circulation, in the purchase of the public funds in Russia and elsewhere, will be more advantageous to the bank — the mass of transferable capitals will augment, and by that the transactions of commerce will become much easier and more extended; and that, not limiting the buying to the Russian funds, it will also be advantageous to acquire a certain quantity of funds of other states of the first order—so much more so, as the interests will be due in foreign countries — thus procuring to the minister of finance a considerable advantage, in liberating him from the necessary costs of the transmission to foreign countries of sums annually necessary for different payments, for the maintenance of legations, the payment of interests of foreign loans, as well as of different purchasse for the fleet and for the railway from St. Petersburg to Moscow; — the committee of finance, taking into consideration all these motives, has been entirely convinced that the execution of a like measure, not changing the terms of the manifesto of July the 1st, 1843, will not in the least disturb the solidity of our national credit, and in consequence, we have decided (February the 7th, 1847) to separate from the bullion representing the notes in circulation the sum of 30,000,000 silver rubles for the successive acquisition of Russian and foreign public funds, and to consign the operation itself to the minister of finance, who ought, in the necessary occurrences, to appeal to the special decision of his S. M. l' Empereur. The advice rendered by the council of the empire was sanctioned by his S. M. l' Empereur the 31st of March of the present year.

Regarding it as superfluous here to relate the particulars, I cannot help, Gentlemen, offering to your attention the fact that the above measure, not only has made no unfavourable public impression, but it has, on the contrary, strengthened the general confidence in the circulating notes of the empire, which is also confirmed by the following fact. At the time of its publication the capital in metallic money and ingots was 114,289,000 rubles; and now, after there has been taken from it 30,000,000, to purchase the public funds, the amount has risen to 110,590,000 rubles: it therefore follows that it has, since then, increased by 26,300,000 rubles.

Extracts from the evidence of Mr. Tooke before the select committee of the house of commons, on banks of issue, in 1840

28th July, 1840.

3292. *Mr. Hume.* Will you state what part of the currency or circulating medium affects prices, under the definitions which you have now given? —No one part of them affects the prices of commodities more than any of the other parts.

3293. *Mr. Grote.* Do you mean not more in degree, or not in any different way? —Not more in degree.

3294. You mean, that every portion, of that which you have described, under the name "circulating medium," is perfectly equal to every other portion in the effect which it produces upon prices? —Perfectly so.

3295. *Mr. Hume.* Do you mean that every transaction of purchase or sale, by any of the means which you have mentioned as included in the circulating medium, equally affects prices? —Yes, and that was my reason for caring so little about making a distinction among them. I doubt whether they operate upon prices at all.

3296. *Mr. Grote.* You mean, that none of those items which you have enumerated under the general term "circulating medium," have in your opinion any effect upon prices? —Yes, I mean that they are not operative causes of prices.

3297. *Mr. Hume.* What is it, then, which does affect prices? — *The cost of production limiting the supply on the one hand, and the pecuniary means of the consumer limiting the demand on the other.*

3298. Will not the variations in the quantity of the circulating medium affect prices? — No.

3299. Will it not if abundant be more at the disposal of individuals for purchasers than when it is scarce? — It will be more easily disposable, but it will not be necessarily so disposed of; *I believe that the amount of the circulating medium is the effect and not the cause of variations in prices.*

3300. *Mr. Warburton.* Suppose the supply of the precious metals in the world to be increased, and to go on doubling and trebling and so on, will not the prices of commodities estimated in the precious metals go on doubling and trebling and so on, in proportion to the increase of the precious metals? —Yes, they would undoubtedly; and *I took for granted that we were speaking of alterations in prices, as distinct from those of bullion-values in the commercial world.*

3301. Supposing the quantity of the precious metals in the world to remain constant, and that in any country you go on increasing the quantity of the notes payable on demand, will the prices of commodities estimated in those notes undergo a variation proportionate to the increase of the notes? — *Not if the notes are payable in gold on demand*, unless in the degree in which it may he supposed that the value of gold is affected in the commercial world by an extensive substitution of paper for gold; I consider that those points were distinctly understood as the only conditions by which the money prices of commodities were likely to be affected, independently of the circumstances affecting the articles themselves.

3302. Suppose, as before, the quantity of precious metals in the world to remain constant, and that the number of bills of exchange in the country is doubled, trebled, and so on, will the prices of commodities undergo a variation in proportion to the increase of bills of exchange? — *No, the increase of bills of exchange would not be the cause of any rise of prices or vice versa*; circumstances affecting the articles, or the opinions of persons dealing in the articles would affect prices.

3303. Suppose, as before, the quantity of the precious metals in the world to remain constant, and that the number of deposits in bankers' hands available to the purchase and sale of commodities is doubled, trebled, and so on, will the prices of commodities vary in proportion to that increase of deposits in bankers' hands? —*Not in the slightest degree.*

3304. *Mr. Grote.* Suppose an inconvertible paper money, such as the assignats which were issued by the French Government during the French Revolution, is it not your opinion that the quantity of paper money would have an influence upon prices? — A direct one, as has been the case with the French assignats and with some other issues of the continental Governments; and as was remarkably the case with the paper money in America during the war for independence. Perhaps I might be allowed to add, that *it is the analogy that has been commonly considered as subsisting between the paper issued by Government without liability to repayment, and paper issued upon securities and payable in gold upon demand, that has led to the very general and, as I believe, erroneous theory, which ascribes the alterations in the amount of the circulating medium so issued as the cause of a rise of prices.*

3305. *Mr. Warburton.* Do not you apprehend that all those other modes of payment, such as bills of exchange, notes payable on demand, deposits, and so forth, as the precious metals, are the ultimate commodity to which all those are referable, are limited in their amount and must bear a certain proportion to the coin specie of the country? — Unquestionably.

3306. And the precious metals being supposed to be invariable, the amount of bills of exchange, notes payable on demand, and so forth, can only fluctuate within certain moderate limits? —Within short periods, and before the principle of limitation can apply, there may be a very great fluctuation.

4th Aug. 1840.

3615. Have you seen a table contained in a work published by Mr. Porter, called "The Progress of the Nation," showing the comparative prices of fifty articles at different times during the years 1833-1834-1835-1836, and 1837, and also showing the amount of the Bank of England and country circulation during that period; and can you give any opinion as to its correctness? — Yes; I have seen the table, I am aware of the manner in which it has been constructed. The prices of fifty articles of merchandise have been taken monthly, for each month from January 1833 to the close of 1837; but the construction of the table is such, that, in my opinion, it can give no correct information of the kind which it professes to give. In forming this table, no reference is made to the comparative value of the articles contained in it; therefore, if the object of judging of the value of the currency, by the comparison of the prices of all or any of the articles contained in the list, were desirable or obtainable, it could not be done by this method. The comparisons are made, and the result drawn, without any reference whatever to the value of the articles compared. Thus, if I recollect rightly (for it is now four or five years since Mr. Porter showed me his manuscript framework of the tables), the article of Annatto, the whole annual importation of which is probably of a value not exceeding

20,000*l*. , is of equal influence in the result of the prices for the month or for the year as wheat, or cotton, or coffee, and sugar, articles which embrace as many millions as this does hundreds of pounds in value; and I rather think that the first five articles in the list, would not embrace the value of a hundredth part of five other articles that might he selected, yet those articles of low value enter into the same line of comparison with those of the highest value; and I believe that I might undertake to select twenty-five out of the fifty articles which would not constitute the value of one tenth of the remaining twenty-five. It is perfectly clear, taking as an instance dyeing materials, which are in small quantity, that there might be a rise, as in the ease of Annatto, of from 1s. to 2*s*. a pound, and this if carried through the year would make an advance as far as that article, out of the fifty told, of 100 per cent; and there might on the other hand be a fall in the price of wheat of 50 per cent; but, as the result of the two operating equally on the scale, while wheat had been falling only 50 per cent, you would have an apparent rise of prices of 50 per cent, and I think it must be perfectly clear that a table so constructed, although it would give a good deal of information to any body wanting to see the fluctuations in any particular article, and, although it certainly does great credit to the industry and ingenuity that has been employed in the construction of it, yet it is not only valueless but deceptive for the purpose for which it is proposed. The chances are against, rather than for, the result being one which is at all conformable to the tendency of the more valnable of the articles. Besides, on the face of the table there is a total discrepancy in the supposed coincidence between the circulation of bank notes and the progress of prices in the scale. Thus, for instance, in February 1835, when a rise of general prices, according to this table, of upwards of 16 per cent is indicated, there is no apparent increase in the circulation from February 1833, supposing the country circulation which is not there stated to be the same in both cases; and so I might go on in several other instances. There appears to me to be nothing approaching to a coincidence, even if that coincidence would of itself, if it existed, be sufficient to raise a presumption of cause and effect. The Bank of England notes in February 1833 were 18, 318, 000*l.*, and in February 18,099,000*l.*; at the same time, there is no doubt that in the early part of 1836 a very considerable number of articles, embracing a great value, and among those the articles that were referred to in my last examination, as introduced into the report of the Manchester Chamber of Commerce, were at an advance of prices compared with the period at which the scale commences. And it is equally true no doubt, that that set of articles did fall in *price* at different periods subsequently to 1836, but chiefly in the commencement of the summer of 1837. It will, however, be found on examination that in the case of each of those articles, which reached nearly, if not quite, their highest in the spring of 1836, there was a sufficient cause, from a reference to the supply and demand, for the rise that took place at that time; and also a very full and sufficient reason for the fall which subsequently succeeded, *without hating occasion to refer to any but the obvious mercantilc causes that operate upon markets, independently of any variations in the quantity of money appearing, as the originating cause of those variations in prices.*

3616. Are the prices of the five great articles, cottons, woollens, silks, linen, and hardware, included in those fifty articles of Mr. Porter's table? —The raw materials are, as I understand; the gentleman of the Manchester Chamber of Commerce, who have referred to this table in support of their views, consider that the raw materials are those which indicate the value of the currency. The articles that I understand to be in question, are cotton, wool, silks, flax, and iron.

3617. Do you happen to know whether the report of the Chamber of Commerce refers to the price of raw materials or of manufactured goods? —It is not quite clear that they make a distinction, but I think they refer to both in their estimate of loss; I imagine they include the losses the manufacturers have sustained in bringing the raw materials into a finished state; and also, the losses of the retail trade in the manufactured goods.

3618. Do you conceive that in those five articles there was a fall of from 25 to 30 per cent? — That will be seen by the list of prices, without going into each of them. The fall was in no one of the articles so much as 50 per cent. The extreme depression did not last many days, nor apply to any considerable sales; and the general range of prices in 1837 as compared with 1836, does not indicate a fall greater in any particular article than was warranted by the state of supply and demand.

3619. Can you make any statement to the Committee in confirmation of this opinion of yours? —Yes. Of the quantity of iron produced there are no statistical returns; at the same time it is quite matter of notoriety that there was at that time a great increase of furnaces put into blast, and a vast increase of the quantity of iron produced. Of the remaining four articles I have here a statement, which will show the quantities imported for four years, during 1833, 1834, 1835, and 1836; I have added to the table two other articles to which a similar mode of reasoning applies.

The witness delivered in the same, which was as follows:

Years.	Cotton twist.	Sheep's Wool	Silk, raw and thrown.	Flax.	Indigo.	Tea.
1833	303,656,887	380,46,087	3,014,228	126,550,896	6,635,436	31,709,016
1834	326,875,425	464,55,232	3,835,661	88,958,464	4,155,296	33,613,980
1835	363,702,963	421,74,496	3,953,363	183.182,960	4,168,396	44,360,550
1836	406,959,057	642,39,952		1151,590,720	7,710,544	49,307,710

And whereas, the stocks of cotton, notwithstanding the increase of importation down to 1835, were progressively diminishing; at the close of 1836 it turned out that there was a very large increase of stock, compared with the preceding three years, which of itself would account for a considerable fall of price. With respect to that and other articles which have been particularly referred to, I should observe, that while the state of the supply would account for a great part of the rise in 1836, and the subsequent fall, there were circumstances affecting the demand which were calculated to increase all the effects that might be anticipated from a view of excess in the supply. Of the circumstances I allude to as affecting the demand, the most extraordinary was an increasing extent, from 1833 to 1836, of shipments to America. The importations into the United States, which are chiefly from this country, in 1833 were 108,118,311 $: in 1836 they had increased to 189,880,935 $. Of the causes of that increased demand, it may be of interest to the Committee to have an authentic and very concise account: it is contained in an extract of the Message of the President of the United States of America to Congress, dated Washington, 4th September 1837, which with the permission of the Committee I will read:

"The history (says the Message,) of the trade in the United States for the last three or four years, affords the most convincing evidence that our present condition is chiefly to be attributed to over-action in all the departments of business; an overaction, deriving, perhaps, its first impulse from antecedent causes, but stimulated to its destructive consequences by excessive issues of bank paper, and by other facilities for the acquisition and enlargement of credit. At the commencement of the year 1834, the banking capital of the United States, including that of the National Bank then existing, amounted to about 200,000,000 $; the bank notes then in circulation to about 95,000,000 $; and the loans and discounts of the banks, to 324,000,000 $. Between that time and the 1st of January, 1836, being the latest period to which accurate accounts have been received, our banking capital was increased to more than 251,000,000 $;our paper circulation to more than 140,000,000 $; and the loans and discounts to more than 457,000,000 $. To this increase are to be added the many millions of credit acquired by means of foreign loans, contracted by the states and state institutions, and, above all, by the lavish accommodations extended by foreign dealers to our merchants. The consequence of this redundancy of credit, and of the spirit of reckless speculation engendered by it, was a foreign debt contracted by our merchants, estimated in March last at 30,000,000 $; the extension to traders in the interior of our country, of credits for supplies greatly beyond the wants of the people; the investment of 39,500,0005 $ in unproductive public lands, in the years 1835 and 1836, whilst in the preceding years the sales only amounted to 4,500,0005 $, the creation of debts to an almost countless amount, for real estate, in existing or anticipated cities and villages equally unproductive, and at prices now seen to be greatly disproportionate to their real value; the expenditure of immense sums in improvements, which in many cases have been found to be ruinously improvident."

Perhaps the Committee will allow me to lay before it in illustration of the very extraordinary impulse that was given to the extension, and, apparently, the undue extension of trade, by the system of credits which prevailed in the five or six years preceding 1836, the following statement, showing what had been the exports and imports from 1824 to 1830, and comparing those with the imports and exports from 1831 to 1837 inclusive.

(The witness delivered in the same, which was as follows.)

From 1824 to 1830 inclusive, the imports and exports of the Union were about on a balance, and stood as follows: —

Years	Imports.	Exports.
1824	80,549,007	75,986,657
1825	96,340,075	99,535,388
1826	84,974,477	77,595,322
1827	79,484,068	82,324,827
1828	88,509,824	72,264,686
1829	74,492,527	72,358,671
1830	70,876,920	73,849,508

But thenceforward the case was different, as the following results will show:

Years	Imports.	Exports.
1831	103,191,124	81,310,583
1832	101,029,266	87,176,943
1833	108,118,311	90,140,433
1834	126,521,332	104,346,973
1835	149,895,749	121,693,577

1836	189,880,035	128,663,040
1837	140,989,217	117,419,376

Under a system of credit like that which seems to have prevailed, and have been acted upon to so extraordinary an extent in the United States at the period under consideration, it is hardly to be wondered at that the manufacturers of this country should receive a prodigious impulse, and that they should have carried on, as long as credit was entire, a most beneficial and prosperous business. Indeed, so sound and solid did the business naturally appeal to the manufacturers to be, that it is not to be wondered at that they should have relied upon its continuance, and availed themselves of all their means of capital and credit to extend their manufacturing establishments; for the credits they received, against the orders that were sent to them, were of the very best description, being upon houses here whose reputation for wealth left no question at all about their responsibility; but having in these prosperous times so extended their power of manufacture, and probably having had gains in a much larger proportion than would be indicated by a mere rise in the price of the law materials, it is perfectly obvious that upon the cessation or great curtailment of that demand, the loss on the manufactured goods would be in a greater proportion than the fall upon the raw material; and, as far as I can learn from general information, the price of manufactured goods had, in point of fact, fallen in a greater proportion than the price of raw materials. At the same time I beg leave to disclaim any particular knowledge of the markets for manufactured goods. While, through 1836, so extensive a demand for export had existed, the falling off in 1837 was very great. In proof of this, is the following statement of the number of packages sent from Liverpool to the Northern Atlantic towns, from the month of April to the month of September inclusive, in each of the years 1836 and 1837. Of cotton goods in 1836, 20,140; in 1837, 1842. Of worsted stuffs in 1836, 6687; in 1837, 2990. Of woollen goods in 1836, 18,096; in 1837, 4,400. I think, therefore, without going into further details, which would he fatiguing to the Committee, *a very clear caste it made out to account for the rise of prices of the articles alluded to in the period ending in the spring of* 1836, *and for their subsequent fall in the spring and summer of* 1837, *without reference to the. state of the circulation.*

3620. Can you in the years which have elapsed, subsequently to 1837, trace any effect produced upon prices by the variations in the amount of bank notes in circulation? —*Not any.*

3621. Are the Committee, then, to understand, that so long as the paper is convertible into, specie, you cannot attribute any effect whatever upon prices to the variations in the amount of the bank notes in circulation? —*I am perfectly satisfied that no alteration in the prices can be traced in any way to the amount of the circulation.*

3622. It appears by the evidence given by you in 1832, that you gave this answer (3821). "If an enlarged issue takes place, coincidently with circumstances favouring speculation and general over-trading, there can be no question but that it contributes to increase that tendency, and to aggravate very considerably the consequent revulsion." Do you still retain that opinion? *I do not*, I had not then divested myself of the opinion which had been, and I believe is, the prevailing one, that there is a connection between the amount of bank notes in the hands of the public and the state of prices. I do not ascribe any variation in prices to variations in the amount of circulation, as their originating cause.

3623. Do you not suppose that an increase in the amount of bank notes in circulation, will afford facilities for the enlargement of the circulating medium, and of credit generally, so as to facilitate an increase of prices? —Not at all. *I conceive that it is the enlargement of credit, under the influence of opinion respecting prices, that, by entailing an increase of transactions, may, according to the nature of the transactions, rather than the amount of them, call out an additional amount of bank notes.*

5th August, 1840.

3722. Have you any observations to make upon the conduct of the Bank in the course of the year 1836?

That question involves considerations that would diverge, probably, into a very extensive discussion upon the propriety of the Bank interfering, as it did, in the case of the accommodation afforded to the Northern and Central Bank, and likewise to the American Houses. In my opinion the Bank did not take measures early enough to keep down or reduce its securities so as to counteract the efflux of bullion at the time when it was in a low proportion to their liabilities, and when, in contemplation of circumstances, of no improbable occurrence, their power of maintaining the convertibility of their paper might have been involved.

3723. Do you conceive that the variations in the amount of the bullion, depend upon the variations in the amount of the securities? —*Clearly, that is the only mode in which the Bank can operate, viz., by the securities. The circulation is independent of the Bank operations, within certain extensive limits.* As I have before observed, until the amount of the deposits is reduced so much as to admit of no further claim on the part of the depositors for bank notes against them, the Bank may not be in a position in which they can with certainty operate upon the amount of the circulation.

3724. Do you conceive, then, that an increase of securities necessarily tends to an efflux of bullion, and a diminution of securities to an influx of bullion? —*Certainly, according to the degree.*

3725. Do you conceive that to be independent of the variations in the amount of bank notes in circulation at the time? —*As nearly as may be independent of it, that is within very extensive limits; I mean that the limit to the reduction would be that degree of it which would operate upon the minimum of the reserve of the bankers within the district to which the exclusive privilege of the Bank of England is limited. Until the reduction reach that amount, it is not at all clear that there is any immediate connection between the state of the circulation and the tendency to an influx or any efflux of bullion.*

3726. Does it appear that the extraordinary increase of securities in the autumn of 1835, had any tendency to check the influx of bullion? —*I have no doubt that it did check the influx, and that is one of my objections to it.*

3727. Did not the bullion increase more rapidly than before, towards the close of 1835, and in the early part of 1836? Unquestionably it did.

3728. Does it appear that the diminution of securities in the first quarter of 1836, produced any subsequent increase of the bullion? — *It is only as operating upon the rate of interest that the amount of securities is important in one way or the other. I do not mean to say that there is any fixed proportion between the securities and the amount of bullion.* There may be certainly a diminution of the bullion coincident, or contemporaneous with, a reduction of securities; in that case it is clear that the rate of interest is not sufficiently high, and that a further reduction of securities is necessary.

3729. Does it not appear that, in the autumn of 1835, the influx of bullion was accompanied by a diminution of circulation, and an increase of securities? — Yes; but my objection to any increase of securities still is, that if there had been a moderate pressure on the money market at that time, which would have been effected by withholding the reinvestment, the influx of bullion would have been more considerable; and then, when the turn came in May 1836, the Bank would have been in a better position to have met it. *There is a degree of reduction of the amount of bank notes which would operate immediately and violently the moment that, through the operation of the forcible reduction of the securities, the circulation should be reduced below that winch would be consistent with the regular payments of the metropolis; there would be a very considerably increased value of the circulating medium, probably a very great rise in the rate of interest, and a considerable contraction of transactions upon credit, and an inevitable tendency to produce an influs, or to stop a drain, if any previously existed, of bullion.*

3730. Would not, on your principle, the rapid reduction of securities which took place in the first quarter of 1836, have tended to produce an influx of bullion instead of a drain, which notoriously took place from that time? —No: I must be misunderstood if I have said anything (for I certainly did not intend to do so) which would lead to the supposition that the mere numerical amount of securities is to be looked to, as certainly indicating whether it favoured the influx or the efflux of bullion; but I certainly conceive, looking at the table as it is before me, that if the Bank had adhered to its rule (upon which I am not at present called upon to give any opinion) of keeping its securities even, the chance is that there would not have been so low a state of their treasure through 1835 as really did exist.

3731. Did you not state that you conceived that the variations of bullion, depend upon variations of securities; that an increase of securities tended to produce an efflux of bullion, and that a diminution of securities tended to produce an influx of bullion? — That might be the general tendency, but it might be counteracted by other circumstances.

3732. If that be so, do you not conceive that so considerable a diminution of securities as 5,000,000*l*. in three months, would tend to produce, according to your principle, an influx of bullion? —Not unless it was a designed operation of the Bank. If it was merely the effect of the running off of the securities, I am not clear that it would; it would require an operation upon the rate of interest. There might be such a state of credit as for some time would interfere with any operation by the Bank, unless carried to a considerable extent, on the rate of interest.

3733. Do you conceive that so large a reduction as 5,000,000*l*. in the amount of circulation, by whatever cause produced, would not lead to an influx of bullion? —I can hardly conceive any short period, and taking corresponding periods of the quarter in which a reduction of 5,000,000*l*. would not operate in the way I have stated, of interfering with the regularity of the payments of the metropolis; and, in that case, I have no doubt it would have a great effect, in either inducing or increasing an influx of bullion.

3734. If then, according to your last statement, a reduction in the amount of the circulation would produce an influx of bullion; and, according to your previous answer, a reduction in the amount of securities might or might not produce that effect, is it not probable that an influx or efflux of bullion depends upon the variations in the amount of the circulation, more than upon the variations in the amount of the *securities?* —*The variations in the amount of the circulation unquestionably, if operated upon distinctly to that extent, would produce it; but I conceive, that under the action of the public as we have seen it, there is no direct influence of the amount of the circulation upon the efflux or influx of bullion.*

3735. Mr. Grote. Your opinion is that so soon as the reduction in the circulation is carried to the extent of affecting the reserves of the private London bankers, it then does tend to exercise a direct influence upon the efflux or influx of bullion? —Yes, that is the limit within which I consider that a reduction of the circulation would operate.

3736. Do not you conceive that, in point of fact, the limit is very soon reached, even by a very moderate reduction in the amount of the aggregate circulation? —*Whatever limit that may be, there is no reduction in modern times that seems to have reached that limit.*

3737. Do you conceive that the utmost actual reduction which has taken place in the Bank circulation at any period within the last ten years, has been so small as not to affect practically the management of the London bankers and the amount of reserves? —When I said the amount of their reserves, perhaps I did not express myself with sufficient accuracy. *What I meant is the minimum of their reserves, that amount below which they would not consider themselves as being in a state of security in opening for business.*

3738. Is it not reasonable to suppose that the London bankers hold in general such reserve as is sufficient for their ordinary wants for the present time, and for such time as may be within the compass of reasonable anticipation and no more? —I should say that there must be much more latitude than that, otherwise the payments of London would never have been effected with the regularity with which they have been; the state of credit would not have been so generally maintained as it has been. *I conceive that London bankers can very rarely be in a state that does not admit of a very considerable latitude or surplus beyond a fair computation of their necessary wants for the supply of the demand by the public for bank notes.*

3739. Is it not a fact that in times of contraction of the aggregate circulation, and a drain of bullion, the feelings of caution naturally operating upon the London bankers lead them at such moments to require a larger proportional reserve than they would think necessary in times of ease and plenty? — Whenever the reduction in the amount of hank notes is carried to the extent, that would induce the London bankers to reduce their advances, I am quite ready to admit that it would operate upon the value of the circulation, and in so far tend to favour the influx of bullion or to prevent its efflux. *I only speak of the obvious want of coincidence between the amount of the circulation and the variations in the other points, or, what I have called, the elements of the position of the Bank; namely, the apparent steadiness of the amount of the notes in circulation during certain periods, compared with the deposits and the securities, or the bullion; and that comparative uniformity indicates a very great degree of regularity in the demand for bank notes.*

3740. But do not you think that the actual fluctuations which take place, on ordinary periods throughout the quarter, in the amount of the bank circulation, are quite sufficient to affect very considerably the conduct of the private London bankers, that is to say, that in the scarce times of the quarter, London bankers are less free in their advances than they are in the plentiful times of the quarter immediately after the payment of the dividends? —I had understood that that had ceased to be the fact since the practice of the Bank in making the quarterly advances; but, however, I am not sufficiently acquainted with the details of banking to be justified in giving a confident opinion upon that point. I only observe, and I would take this very instance of the reduction in the amount of the circulation at the close of 1835, and the commencement of 1836, when it was quite notorious that the extension of credit, and of business generally, and of fresh enterprises, was on an extraordinarily enlarged scale, *in proof of the absence of any direct or necessary influence of the amount of the circulation the amount of the circulation was then less than it had been for several years before*; *and*, *according to my former answer*, *in* 1833 *and* 1834, *when trade and credit were in a remarkably quiet state*, *the circulation stood very much higher*.

3741. Have yon any positive reasons for your conclusion that the London bankers hold in general the large surplus reserve, to which you have alluded in former answers, which prevents them from being affected by any reduction in the aggregate circulation of the Bank of England, till that reduction has been carried to a very considerable extent? —As I said before, I am not sufficiently acquainted with the practice of London bankers to be able to give a confident opinion upon that point; all I mean to say is, that there have been considerable variations in the amount of the circulation, which seem not to have been accompanied with any corresponding influence upon the facilities of the money market.

3742. Do you think it wise or practicable for the Bank, keeping as it docs a large amount of deposits in conjunction with its functions as an issuing body, to adopt the rule of keeping the amount of its securities fixed and un-changeable? — I am not prepared to give a decided opinion as to either the power of the Bank, or the expediency of the exercise of that power, to keep its securities under all circumstances even. *The view that I have of the best regulation of its securities by the Bank, is that which shall enable it to preserve most constantly a very considerable reserve of bullion compared with its liabilities.*

3743. Are you of opinion that a mixed circulation of paper and coin ought to fluctuate in amount in the same manner and proportion as a metallic currency, if we had a metallic currency, would fluctuate? — I am not at all clear that in a mixed circulation of coin and paper, it is desirable that the fluctuations in the amount of the aggregate paper circulation should vary exactly with the variations in the amount of bullion; on the contrary, I believe that a variation in the amount of the circulation, corresponding exactly, or as nearly as might be, with the variations in the amount of bullion, would be exceedingly inconvenient, and occasion very frequent, and sometimes violent, oscillations in the rate of interest, or, as it is technically called, the money market.

3744. If the paper circulation is to be preserved constantly conformable in value to gold, must it not conform in quantity constantly also to gold? — *Not at all; as long as the paper is strictly convertible into gold, it cannot be said that the value of the currency is impaired; there may be a very considerable occasional demand for the export of the precious metals, without any ground of inference that the originating cause of it has been any excess of the circulation of this country; with a sufficient reserve of bullion on the part of the Bank, the probability is that the gold would in such a case return, and that there may have been no intermediate disturbance of that amount of the circulation which was previously not in excess as compared with the ordinary transactions of the country.*

3745. Do not you think that however large the reserve of gold in the hands of the Bank might be at the period when the foreign drain began, if the Bank were either to increase the quantity of bank notes in circulation, or even to decline contracting them during the course of that drain, the probability is very much indeed increased of the drain continuing to such an extent as to exhaust the Bank reserve of bullion, and thus to frustrate the possibility of maintaining the convertibility of the bank notes? —I believe that, with a large reserve of bullion at the commencement of any drain, if the Bank simply kept their securities from increasing beyond the amount, which, previously to the drain, they found that they bad been able to preserve, without any obvious effect in causing an extreme depression of the rate of interest, they might retain that amount of securities; and then, consequently, in all probability there would be no material alteration of the circulation. The Bank might allow, to some extent, the drain to proceed without any forced operation, beyond a very moderate rise in the rate of interest. I can conceive of hardly any eircumstances which would not enable it, always supposing a large average reserve, to maintain very nearly the same amount of the circulation, except in as far as it might be acted upon by the public, consistently with admitting of a reflux of bullion.

3746. Does it not seem to you if the Bank were to permit the circulation of bank notes to be diminished, in exact proportion with the bullion which was demanded from them for export, that such diminution would have the effect of causing the demand for export to subside much sooner; in as much as a smaller quantity of gold would suffice for the purpose of assimilating the value of the currency of this country to that of foreign currencies? — Yes, I believe that might be the case; but it would be attended with more frequent and greater fluctuations in the late of interest: and I should say, as a general position, that the management of the amount of the paper circulation will be attended with greater or less uniformity in the rate of interest, according as the proportion of bullion is greater or less. I remember perfectly that the late Mr. David Ricardo supposed that you might maintain a circulation of paper by bullion payments, in the proportion of 25,000,000*l.*[①] of paper to 3,000,000*l.* bullion. Now, taking that as a possible case in theory, it would, if attempted to be acted upon, be attended with variations in the rate of interest which I think would hardly be less, than occasionally down to 3 and 4 per cent., and sometimes up to 30 and 40 per cent. *In the management of a convertible paper currency, whether you have separate departments or not, you must have a large reserve of bullion in order to obviate very great fluctuations in the rate of interest*; *and, with a sufficiently large amount of bullion, I still repeat, habitually preserved*, (that is supposing that the Bank should undertake to regulate its issues upon a reserve of bullion much larger than has been thought necessary, particularly in the interval between 1834 and 1838,) *there would be much fewer violent alterations in the rate of interest than if there were a separation of the departments, and the deposit*

---

① Speaking as I did from memory, I have made a mistake in stating 25,000,000*l.*. it should have been 24,000,000*l.* according to his evidence before the Committee of the House of Commons on Cash Payments, in 1819. The following is the passage in Mr. Ricardo's evidence in which the statement occurs—

Q 28 —What in your judgment would be the necessary reserve of coin for the larger notes, according to the old plan and what would be the amount of bullion to answer the demand, according to your plan?

A.—I have already observed they would in my opinion be equal, and must depend upon the knowledge of the Bank of the principles of money i should think that a reserve of *three millions* would, under good management, be amply sufficient, upon a supposition of twenty-four millions of Bank of England notes in circulation.—(*Commons' Committee on Cash Payments*, 1819. p. 187.)

department of the Bank of England were not to be considered bound to hold so large a reserve in proportion, as would be considered requisite for the two departments as they are at present united; and, under the union with that increased habitual reserve, the variations would be less than under a separation; even supposing the deposit department had in the latter case a much larger habitual reserve, than it is likely that any mere bank of deposit would have.

3747. Is it your opinion that it is possible to name any amount of reserve which will be sufficient, under all circumstances, to protect the country against the danger of suspension of specie payments, on the supposition that the Bank, during a foreign drain, abstained from any measures of contraction, and suffer their circulation to remain unaltered in point of amount? —I do not go the length of saying that the Bank should be perfectly passive under a drain, I only mean to say, that, giving it credit for sufficient prudence upon the ordinary principles of banking, where a certain amount of reserve is assumed to be requisite it might take measures which would have the effect of moderating, if not stopping the drain: and yet not act very forcibly upon the money market, and not in the slightest degree affect the amount of the circulation.

3748. Will you have the goodness to explain what you moan by not being perfectly passive, upon the supposition that the amount of the circulation is left unaltered? —I should take, as an instance, the passive state of the Bank under a drain; their conduct during the two drains that occurred in 1828 and 1829, and again from 1830 to 1832. Under the latter drain, particularly, they sustained a very great diminution of treasure without the slightest forced operation on their part to counteract it; and yet you cannot conceive a state of things upon the whole more threatening a continuance of a severe drain than that, for it was during a state of partial war upon the continent of Europe; there was also a very large importation of foreign corn, and there was a great deal of internal insecurity; *and yet the Bank, without the slightest effort, allowed the drain to proceed to a very considerable extent, and to the loss of* 6,000,000*l. of treasure, which returned spontaneously with nearly as full a tide as that with which it wait out.*

3749. *Mr. Warburton.* What course do you apprehend the Bank did take in the drain from 1830 to 1832? —*It allowed the public to act exclusively upon its position.*

3750. Did it allow its paper circulation to diminish at the same time that its bullion diminished? — *They took no measures to cause a diminution.*

3751. *Mr. Grote.* Was the paper circulation diminished at the time that the bullion was in the course of diminution? — *The circulation was diminished, but it was diminished by an internal demand, and not by any act of the Bank.*

3752. (*Chairman.*) Was the amount of bank notes in circulation diminished by an internal demand? —What is meant by the expression "internal demand," was the "action of the public." "*The Bank took no measures whatever in* 1828, *or* 1832, *as far as I can understand, to counteract the drain in either of those two periods.*

3753. *Mr. Grote.* Then would it be a course of conduct that you would recommend to the Bank Dircctors that, during the pressure of a foreign drain, they should take no measures for diminishing the amount of bank notes in circulation in any way corresponding to the efflux of bullion? —*I should have no idea of the propriety of their operating distinctly with a view to the circulation, but I think that they should take measures for a moderate pressure upon the money market; that is, to raise the market rate of interest; the rate of interest being the great medium through which the efflux or influx of bullion in the first instance takes place.*

3754. Do you conceive that the Bank Directors could, to any considerable degree, raise the rate of interest without at all diminishing the number of notes in circulation? — *I conceive that they might raise the rate of interest within a moderate degree, and yet not affect the amount of notes in circulation.*

3755. But is it your opinion that they could, to any considerable degree, raise the rate of interest, without diminishing the amount of notes in circulation? —*To a considerable degree, perhaps not; but it is difficult to form a very distinct opinion, and still more so to deliver a judgment upon questions of degree.*

3756. Unless the rate of interest were considerably raised, does it appear to you that much effect could be produced for the purpose to which these questions have been referred, namely, that of arresting the drain of bullion for export? —*With a very large reserve at the commencement of the drain, I do think that they might abate it without any violent operation on the rate of interest.*

3757. But in point of fact, according to the course which you recommend, there would be no abatement of the drain at all, excepting that which arose from the positive paying away of so much gold to foreign countries; there would be no abatement arising from any diminution in the circulation of this country? — No; exactly.

3758. That being the state of the case, does it seem to you that a moderate rise in the rate of interest, such as the Bank might possibly produce without any contraction of its circulation, could have any sufficient effect in arresting the drain of bullion under those circumstances? — I think it could always; *assuming that there was a very large reserve at the outset*; for very considerable effect is constantly produced in variations, within short periods, of the treasure, by variations in the rate of interest; inasmuch *as those variations, although only within a moderate degree, are attended with a greater or less inducement to negotiation of foreign securities in this country, or to the influx of foreign capital into this country for investment, every fluctuation in the rate of interest that can be said to have any perceptible influence at all, operates directly in that way.*

3759. Would it not be the natural consequence of the course of management which you recommend, that the drain for bullion for export would proceed much further than if measures of contraction were resorted to on the part of the Bank; therefore, assuming that the Bank reserve of bullion was not entirely exhausted, would there not be at any rate a corresponding difficulty in recovering the bullion so lost? — *I should apprehend not. because, by the supposition the export of bullion does not arise from any previous excess in the amount or value of the circulation of this country, but simply from some casual payments which can only be effected through the medium of the export of the precious metals.*

3760. Then, is it your opinion that the course of action to be pursued by the Bank, whenever a drain of bullion arises, would depend upon its being able to determine with accuracy what the causes are from which that drain proceeds? —I presume that the Directors must have some general knowledge of the nature and causes of the drain; at the same time, my answer would not absolutely depend upon that. I beg not to be understood as saying that the Bank ought to be perfectly passive under a drain. *All I mean to say, is, that with a large amount of treasure at the outset of it, there would be very little occasion for a violent effort on the part of the Bank, in order to abate or stop the drain by operating upon its securities.*

3761. My question referred not to the amount of the securities, but to the amount of circulation. I understand, that, in certain cases where the Bank could determine with accuracy that the drain of bullion arose from no cause connected with the previous excess in the currency, you are of opinion that the Bank need not diminish the amount of its notes in circulation, even though the drain might proceed to a very considerable extent? —I should still say that *the only view I have of the power of the Bank, is that of operating upon its securities, and that it is on the rate of interest, and not on the amount of the circulation, that it would operate in abating or stopping a drain.* And far from saying that the Bank ought to be perfectly passive, I think that, looking to whatever may be the reduction which their treasure is undergoing, they should take the precautions which would obviously present themselves as means of increasing the rate of interest, or, in other words, of some forcible action upon the securities. *The utmost extent of the view that I entertain upon the subject is, that, with a large amount of treasure, and under a union of the departments of banking and issue as at present conducted, a very much less violent operation upon the securities would be requisite, than would be requisite if the Bank was separated as a bank of deposit from a bank of issue*

3762. It appears, by the returns laid before the committee of 1832, that the stock of bullion in the hands of the Bank on the 31st August, 1824, was 11,787,000*l.*; does it not appear to you that the Bank, having so far relied upon that large store of bullion as to have refrained from taking any steps for contracting the circulation during the course of 1825, adopted an unfortunate course of policy, and one which contributed in a considerable degree to aggravate the commercial misfortunes which arose at the end of 1825? —I conceive that the great error of the Bank in 1824 and 1825, was not so much in not acting forcibly in a reduction of their securities in 1825, as in having added, by a very violent operation, to the securities at the close of 1824, which had the effect of allowing the very much greater extension of the spirit of speculation and of general overtrading which prevailed in the spring of 1825. I am not at all sure that if they had made any forced action on the securities in 1825, they would not have been charged with all the consequences which ensued, as resulting from an act of theirs. At the same time, seeing the extent to which the drain was going, they ought, in point of strictness, unquestionably to have taken measures for reducing their securities more rapidly than they did. But nothing after the spring of 1825 could possibly have prevented the catastrophe which eventually occurred. They would probably have hastened it, and so far have hastened the reflux of bullion. *But after the spring of* 1825, *I have no idea that any act of the Bank could have prevented the great destruction of private credit which then occurred.*

3763. Do not you think that measures for diminishing the amount of bank notes in circulation somewhat in proportion to the efflux of bullion, if such measures are taken at the time when the efflux of bullion first begins, are attended with a less degree of inconvenience and pressure upon the money market than if such measures are postponed until the drain shall have continued for a considerable time and abstracted a considerable quantity of bullion? —I should say that that would very much depend upon the circumstances of the case. It would depend very much upon the state of trade and of credit at the time. But, as a general proposition, I should imagine that variations of the money market to some extent would be, as I said before, very frequent; and after all it would be very requisite to state some line which should constitute what is called the commencement of a drain; because there may be a demand for foreign payment that would not in all probability extend beyond a million or two; that is constantly occurring, and I apprehend there would be a good deal of inconvenience if the Bank attempted to operate upon the circulation to that extent upon every variation occurring in the amount of bullion.

3764. Is it not the fact, that the longer the measures of contraction and protection of the Bank are postponed, the more stringent they must be made in order to accomplish the object; and is there not, in point of fact, a degree of alarm, which arises out of the very fact of the stock of bullion having decreased very much, which, to a great degree, aggravates the effect of the measures of precaution taken by the Bank, if they are applied for the first time during a low state of the bullion? —Yes; I am perfectly ready to acquiesce in all that is stated in the question At the same time, I conceive that, always supposing that the Bank regulate their management with a view to the preservation of a large amount of bullion, they would take such measures as would abate the drain before it leached such a point as should cause the alarm which is supposed in the question. For instance, if at the commencement of the drain in 1838, instead of apparently favouring, but, at all events, not taking any measures to counteract it, under the threatening circumstances which were in prospect, they had taken earlier measures to raise the rate of discount, or to reduce their securities, the subsequent drain would probably have been abated; and, according to my supposition, if they had 15, 000, 000*l.* instead of 10,000,000*l.* at the commencement of 1838, and they had acted as they did in the instance of the drain from 1830 to 1832, there would not have been a reduction of treasure sufficient to have excited any thing of alarm, or any of the inconve-niencies that attended the state of uneasiness which the reduced treasure of the Bank towards the close of 1839 occasioned.

3765. Then, do you think that at the time when a foreign drain commences, although the Bank of England ought not to take any measures for suffering its circulation to diminish, it ought to take measures for correcting that drain by raising the rate of interest? —Yes; within certain limits. I have no hesitation in saying practically, as a matter of business, what I imagine would be the case, that, in ordinary fluctuations, such as would be constantly occurring in the negotiation of foreign loans, and other circumstances causing a demand for bullion, there might be an efflux to the extent of 5,000,000*l*, and between the limits of 15,000,000*l*. and 10,000,000*l*. the Directors would take no active measures, but when the treasure got below 10,000,000*l*. they would take such measures as, under the present system of considering 10,000,000*l*. as their maximum, they were proposing to take when the bullion was reduced to 5,000,000*l*.

3766. How can you be sure, upon your system, that, the foreign drain shall never commence except at the moment when the Bank reserve of bullion is at its maximum? — I imagine that the Bank Directors would be able to explain that point. If they could not undertake to regulate their issues upon an amount of bullion that was very considerably larger than that, which, judging from the management between 1834 and 1836, they seemed to have thought sufficient, then I should say there is no security against exhaustion.

3767. In ease the drain should commence at a period when the Bank reserve of bullion was short of 15,000,000*l*., would you consider that it would be requisite for the Bank to suffer the circulation to diminish in proportion to the efflux of gold? —*I still do not think that introducing the circulation as a distinct part of the action of the Bank gives the correct view of it. I conceive that the whole question, whether the Bank can or cannot maintain a certain average amount of reserve, which is in bullion, turns upon their management of the securities. The circulation mag in some cases be affected by it, or not, but the Bank directors can only look to variations in the amount of their securities.*

3768. But ought they not to consider the variations in the amount of securities as a means of operating upon the amount of circulation? — There may be a very considerable improvement in the value of the circulation without any reduction in the amount of it. *The Bank may operate within considerable limits upon the rate of interest without affecting the circulation in amount, but considerably in point of value.*

3769. (*Mr. Warburton.*) Would the raising of the rate of interest produce any effect upon the exchanges, unless it occasioned a diminution in the application for discounts, and therefore in the amount of the circulation? — It would produce a decided effect upon the exchanges, at the same time that there would, in all probability, be an increase in the amount of the issues①, through the medium of discounts: the effect upon the exchanges of a rise in the rate of interest would be that of inducing foreign capitalists to abstain from calling for their funds from this country to the same extent as they otherwise might do, and it would operate at the same time in diminishing the inducements to capitalists in this country to invest in foreign securities or to hold foreign securities, and it might induce

① This must clearly have been an inadvertence on my part. According to the whole tenour of my evidence, I must either by the word "issue" have meant securities, or, if it meant circulation, my answer should have been in the negative.

them to part with foreign securities in order to make investments in British stocks or shares. It would likewise operate in restraining credits from the merchants in the country by advances on shipments outwards, and it would have the effect of causing a larger proportion of the importations into this country to be earned on upon foreign capital.

3770. Then you apprehend that would increase the number of applications for discount? —Yes; supposing that the market rate was raised up to or beyond the Bank rate.

3771. Then do you mean that the more a man has to pay for the use of money, the more likely he is to apply for it? —No; that is not my view of it; by the supposition the market rate would be raised up to or beyond the Bank rate. In that ease, even supposing the total number requiring discounts not to be increased, a larger proportion of them would apply to the Bank. And, in point of fact, it lias invariably happened that, when the market rate of interest has been low, there have been few applications to the Bank for discount, while they have increased with every advance of the Bank rate, provided that such advance was kept within the market rate.

3772. (*Mr. Grote.*) Does not the course of management which you recommend amount to this, that, if a foreign drain begins when the Bank has in its coffers a reserve of 15,000,000*l*. of bullion it can afford to pay out and should pay out 5,000,000*l*. of that reserve previously to resorting to any measure for contracting the currency; but that if the drain should proceed beyond the 5,000,000*l*. their measures of contraction and of protection to the Bank treasure must be resorted to? — Yes; that is my opinion.

3773. Then after the 5,000,000*l*. are away, it is your opinion that the Bank ought to contract its currency? — Yes, I admit that the Bank ought to take measures when it has got below that which should be considered as the medium which it should conduct its management upon, and that the probability is that the sending abroad of so large a sum as 5,000,000*l*., would of itself be sufficient to meet *any ordinary fluctuation* in international payments, requiring bullion as the mode of effecting them without any material disturbance in the amount of our circulating medium.

3774. But still, if it should happen that the drain goes on to an extent to carry the reserve of the Bank below 10,000,000*l*., you would be of opinion that contraction on the part of the Bank ought not to be any longer postponed? — Exactly.

3775. Consequently, under the supposition that a foreign drain began at a period when the Bank reserve was only 10,000,000*l*., you would consider that the Bank ought to contract the circulation for the purpose of protecting itself without delay? — Yes; that it ought to operate upon the securities, *at the same time it might do so without necessarily affecting the circulation.*

3776. But that it ought to take some positive precautionary measures? — Yes; such as the bank directors would say it would be in the power of the Bank to take, *just as any prudent private, banker, having, generally speaking, a large reserve, would be able to take measures of precaution whenever he saw that the tendency was to a larger demand upon him than usual.*

3777. Would it be possible for any private banker to take precautions without diminishing the extent of accommodation which he afforded to the public? — I should say that they might diminish their liabilities; but they could only do that by parting with their securities, or not renewing those which were running off.

3778. Would not the direct effect of such parting with the securities be to contract the circulation? — *It might or might not: it would diminish their liabilities, but it would not necessarily operate upon that part of the liabilities which consists of circulation.*

3779. Does it not seem to you, then, that the scheme of management which you recommend for the circulation of the Bank would be, that the Bank should artificially keep up the rate of interest, and contract its circulation during a period when there was an influx of bullion for the purpose of making that influx of bullion last still longer, and go to a greater extent than it would naturally do under a metallic currency, in order that the Bank might be able, when an efflux of bullion commenced, to postpone the necessity of contracting until that effect had been carried to a certain extent? — Precisely. I would beg leave to observe that that state of the circulation, and, as I conceive, the benefits arising from it, were exhibited in a very striking degree in the interval of five years, corresponding, in some respects, with the years from 1833 to 1837. Those five years occurred fifty years ago. After the severe drain which the Bank experienced in the year 1783,—during the progress of which drain they were under the necessity of operating very violently upon the securities, because they had rather a low amount of treasure,—the reflux of bullion was such, that, having in 1783 been reduced to 590,000*l.* or thereabouts, it reached, in 1788, 5,743,740*l.*; in 1790 it was 8,633,000*l.*, and it continued at upwards of 6,000,000*l.* till February 1702. Now, if you double the amount of the circulation and deposits as they stood in February, 1790, it would make the liabilities amount to what they were at the close of and during several periods in 1834 and 1835. In 1834, I see they reached above 34,000,000*l.*; in February, 1790, the liabilities were 16,263,000*l.*: the securities were 10,332,000*l.* Now, if you double the liabilities, you will find that they would amount to 32,526,000*l*, and the securities to a little above 20, 000, 000*l*. , and the bullion would, if doubled, be 17,200,000*l*. The bullion continued at about 8,000,000*l*. till 1792 the foreign exchanges took an adverse turn in that year, and there was a drain down to 5,000,000*l*. In the autumn of 1792, and the early part of 1793, there occurred a total derangement of the country circulation; but the Bank then was in a state of such perfect ease, that, without any special interference, and without any alteration in the rate of its discount, it was enabled to increase its discounts, which, in August, 1791, amounted to 1, 898, 000*l* to 6, 456, 000*l*. in February, 1793; and to supply guineas, there being no Bank of England notes at that time under 10*l*. , the bullion was reduced to 4,010,000*l*. : but that would have been equal compared with their general liabilities to 8,000,000*l*. of bullion in 1836. The period of discredit and derangement went off, and there was soon after a reflux of bullion, the increase between February and August, 1793, having been 1,300,000*l*. I ought to have mentioned that the Bank did not alter its rate of discount from 5 per cent, during the whole of that period. The increase in the discounts was very nearly 5,000,000*l*. during the period of discredit, without any disturbance of the feeling of security respecting the position of the Bank, as to the power of maintaining the convertibility of its paper. Now, I should beg to contrast that state of things with that which occurred in 1836. If the Bank, instead of being reduced to about 4,000,000*l*. in the autumn of 1836, or the spring of 1837, had only been reduced to 8,000,000*l*. of bullion, its position would have been in every respect very different, and the general state of things would have been different; because there is no doubt, that the reduced state of bullion at that time operated as a great cause of general uneasiness. Will the committee allow me to put in this paper, containing a statement of the position of the Bank in the former period that I have alluded to.

(The witness delivered in the same, which was read as follows:)

	Circulation.	Deposits.	Liabilities.	Securities.	Bullion.	Assets.	Rest.
	£	£	£	£	£	£	£
1788 Feb.	9,561,120	5,177,050	14,738,170	11,864,510	5,743,440	17,607,950	2 860,780
August	10,062,880	5,528,640	15,531,520	11,570,320	6,899,160	18,469,480	2,937,960
1789 Feb.	9,807,210	5,537,370	15,344,580	10,960,690	7,228,730	18,189,420	2,844,840
August	11,121,800	6,402,450	17,524,250	11,697,760	8,645,860	20,343,620	2,819,870
1790 Feb.	10,040,540	6,223,270	16,263,810	10,332,120	8,633,000	18,965,120	2,701,310
August	11,433,340	6,199,200	17,632,540	12,003,520	8,386,330	20,389,850	2,757,310
1791 Feb.	11,439,200	6,364,550	17,803,750	12,602,640	7,869,410	20,472,050	2,668,300
August	11,672,320	6,437,730	18,110,050	12,819,940	8,055,510	20,875,450	2,765,400
1792 Feb.	11,307,380	5,523,370	16,830,750	13,068,560	6 468,060	19,536,620	2,705,870
August	11.0 6,300	5,526,480	16,532,780	13,905,910	5,357,380	19,263,290	2 730,510
1793 Feb.	11,888,910	5,346,450	17,235,360	16,005,250	4,010,680	20,015,930	2,780,570
August	10,865,050	6,442,810	17,307,860	14,809,680	5,322,010	20,131,690	2,823,830

3780. Is it not essential to your system, that, during a period of influx of bullion, the Bank should have it in its power to keep up the rate of interest; and could the Bank possibly do this during such a period without a very violent action upon its securities, and upon the circulation, during a period which is usually called one of great plenty of money? —I conceive that that is a period generally in which the Bank may manage with the greatest ease, either to preserve or to replenish the amount of its treasure, by simply allowing its securities to run off without re-investment, as long as it is desirable to accomplish that object; and that appears to me to have been very much the state of the case in the period of the last century to which I have alluded.

3781. But has not it happened during several periods that, the Bank rate of discount having been kept above the market rate, nearly all the discounts in the Bank of England have run off, and still the market rate of discount did not rise up to the Bank rate? —Certainly; that was the case in 1822.

3782. And, that being the case, would it be practicable for the Bank, under such circumstances, to raise the rate of interest, so as artificially to produce a greater influx of bullion, without very violent action upon the remainder of its securities, and a corresponding contraction of the circulation? —*I do not think it would act upon the circulation at all: I think the circulation would be kept up in a great measure by the* influx of the gold: the gold would naturally go into the Bank, as a deposit, or in exchange for notes; and in that case, taking the supposition in the question, there would be every inducement to take it out in notes.

3783. The object of the question is to know, what means the Bank would have of artificially keeping up the rate of interest, which is the means by which you. suppose the Bank is to produce a large import of bullion? — I conceive that if they reduced their securities sufficiently low, it is impossible but that the gold must more or less flow in to preserve the general value of the circulation: the general value of the circulation is not determined by the amount of Bank notes — the general value of the circulation is determined by the exchanges.

3784. Under those circumstances, if the Bank could by any means raise the rate of interest up to such a point as to cause the influx of bullion to continue beyond its natural amount; if they could do it by any means, would it not be requisite that they should operate in a very violent manner by the sale of Exchequer bills, or the securities independently of discounts? — No; it does not appear to me that that would be necessary at all. So far from a violent action, it appears to me, that it would require them to be passive. If upon the efflux of some of their existing securities no re-investment took place, which could not be supposed to produce any violent action, I have no idea that there would be any material disturbance of the value of the circulation as connected with internal purposes in the process that is supposed in the question.

3785. But in the case which you supposed, and according to the system which you propose, would it not be the duty of the Bank of England not to be passive, but to interfere actively for the purpose of prolonging the influx of bullion beyond its natural extent? — I doubt the propriety of the term "actively" used in the question. I think, simply, by keeping down the amount of its existing securities, and allowing the efflux of those which were running off without re-investment, the effect would he produced without any effort on the part of the Bank. I am supposing that the circumstances of trade are such as not of themselves to entail any disturbance one way or the other. I will, for instance, take the period that has been alluded to, namely, 1834. I contend that, if the Bank had kept its securities (not that I wish to commit myself to a general opinion as to the propriety of keeping the securities even or not) rather below than above 24,000,000*l*., the probability is that, through that and the following year, they would have maintained a larger amount of bullion. At the same time, if it had required a reduction of the securities to 22,000,000*l*. or 20,000,000*l*., I should still say that it was incumbent upon the Directors to have effected that upon the system which I have suggested, supposing they had been acting upon that before. I do not mean to say that they ought to have done it: but, in supposing, as a distinct opinion which I entertain, that they cannot conduct such an amount of liabilities as they have had during the last three or four years with so small an amount of bullion as they have had, for a considerable part of that interval, I have assumed, that, if they found, with an amount of 24,000,000*l*. of securities, the bullion either went out or did not come in to a sufficient extent, they would reduce the securities. I consider that, with, a view of maintaining the proper amount of bullion, they should not in all cases retain the same amount of securities; and if a designed reduction of securities be desirable with that view, it will be most conveniently effected by sales on the part of the Bank when the puces are high, or, in other words, when the market rate of interest is low.

3786. (*Mr. Warburton.*) Then your plan is, that they should not commence operating upon the exchanges the moment they saw that there was a turn in them, but that they should allow the drain to run on for a considerable period before they took any step whatever? — Yes; that is what I should distinctly suggest as the more convenient mode of management, *provided always they had in view so to regulate their securities, as to preserve on an average a very considerable amount of treasure.*

3787. Do you not believe that the exchanges would be kept more steady, and would not run so much into extremes, if, at an earlier period than you recommend, they endeavoured to alter the course that the exchanges were taking? —The exchanges would, doubtless, in that case, not undergo the same extent of variation; but the circulating medium and the general scale of transactions in the country would be interfered with or disturbed in a much greater degree, by the Bank operating upon its securities upon every turn of the exchanges.

3788. Do you mean to say that the inconvenience produced to the mercantile interest, the monetary pressure would be less in amount than it now is, or less frequent? — Both.

3789. Do not you apprehend that the monetary pressure, in case of a drain, depends in extent very much in the degree to which the exchanges are adverse? —I do not apprehend so, excepting so far as the continuance of that state involves ultimately the necessity of strong counteracting measures on the part of the Bank.

3790. Then do you not apprehend, if the drain is allowed, as you propose, to run on for a considerable time, that, supposing the drains till to continue after the Bank treasure has been reduced 5,000,000*l*., stronger counteracting measures are necessary in that case, than if the counteracting measures had been had recourse to at the moment the exchanges began to turn? — I do not think that the consequences involved in the question would follow. A reduction of 5,000,000*l*. might take place and no further drain ensue. If restrictive measures were only to commence when the Bank treasure had got down to 10,000,000*l*., they would be very different in effect, or in the chance of disturbance of the general mercantile course of affairs, from what they would be if the drain, as heretofore, were allowed to proceed till the treasure was reduced to 5,000,000*l*. A very moderate exercise of precautionary measures would, in my opinion, be requisite, after the efflux of 5,000,000*l*., to prevent such a further efflux as would place the Bank under the necessity of eventually adopting any very violent measures.

3791. The reason you have given for not commencing to reduce the circulation immediately that the exchanges turned, is, that it would occasion inconvenience to the mercantile interests. Is not that so? — No; I might have said so; but what I meant was, that it would occasion a disturbance in the general scale of transactions in the country, in as far as uniformity of the circulating medium in con-nexion with the ordinary transactions of the country was concerned. I should use the term general convenience rather than strictly mercantile convenience, for I consider it to be a matter of general convenience that fluctuations, in the rate of interest, should not be either abrupt or violent.

3792. Which do you consider to be the principal duty of the Bank, to occasion an uniform rate of interest in the country, or to look to the preserving of the convertibility of its notes as its primary duty? — *I consider maintaining the convertibility of its notes is its priming duly*; *and, if the preservation of a moderate uniformity of the rate of interest were incompatible with the perfect security of the convertibility of the paper, I should without hesitation say, that every consideration of convenience ought to give way to the preservation of the principle of convertibility.*

3793. Have you not said that the fluctuations in treasure would be much less if the Bank commenced to operate immediately, than if it allowed the drain to proceed before it commenced its measures of contraction? — Yes.

3794. Then do you not think, that if it operated immediately the momentary deviation from the mean in the amount of the circulation would be much less than the deviations that did take place, or which would take place according to the system you recommend? — In the first place, I should think it hardly possible to prescribe or define exactly the line which you should call the commencement of a drain, and, therefore, a forcible operation by the Bank upon its securities such as proposed, would, I believe, be infinitely more inconvenient than the application of precautionary measures, when it should appear that the drain was one that, from its general appearance, threatened a continuance below the amount at which I consider that precautionary measures might be dispensed with. *But there is one point which seems to me to be assumed in all the questions hitherto upon this point; that the amount of the circulation is that part of the position of the Bank which should be looked to for redressing the exchanges*: whereas, in point of fact, if the bankers generally, or the deposit department of the Bank, happened at the time that the demand for foreign payments occurred to have large reserves, the circulation might be preserved without alteration, notwithstanding a considerable efflux of the metals. I can easily imagine a state of things in which, even supposing that there was a separate Bank of issue from the banking department, there might be a drain for foreign payment to the amount of 3,000,000*l*. or 4,000,000*l*., requiring an efflux of the precious metals to that amount, which would be supplied entirely out of such reserve, and therefore would leave the circulation without any alteration at all. I never understood whether that case was included in the theory of the fluctuation of the circulation corresponding with the variation that would take place in a metallic currency.

3795. Docs not your supposition depend entirely upon this, that you assume the reserves which the London bankers held as deposits in the Bank of England greatly exceed the amount which it is necessary for them to keep as reserves, to meet the demands of their own depositors? — It may be so; and I raised the question for the very purpose of stating that, on the supposition that the reserves of the bankers, and more especially the reserve of the deposit department of the Bank of England, happened to be low coincidentally with the commencement of a drain, and taking the rule proposed for variation as in the metallic circulation, the pressure would be extreme.

3796. Does it make any great difference as it regards the facilities of the money market, whether the Bank reduces its circulation by the sale of securities, or by diminishing the amount of its discounts? — The forcible diminution of its discounts, by which I mean limiting the amount to be discounted, or shortening the period of the bills, would have a very much more violent operation than the sale of public securities; but that would be only in so far as the public bad previously been accustomed to an unlimited extent of discount, varying only in the rate.

3797. By selling its securities, does it not diminish the amount of the circulation held by the bankers? —I do not mean in the slightest degree to question the correctness of the general principle, that if, with a view to contraction, and to increasing the value of the circulating medium, the Bank wish to reduce their securities, it is immaterial, for the main purpose, whether it is done through commercial discounts or by the sale of public securities: I only mean, that, considering that the Bank are looked to as a constant resource by the great discount brokers, it would have a prodigious effect if there were to be any forcible narrowing of the discounts.

3798. Are you of opinion that it is the duty of the Bank to do what is called "*uphold the credit of the country*," in times of monetary pressure, to such an extent as to lessen the convertibility of its own notes? —Certainly; that is not the duty of the Bank. I conceive that its first care should be the convertibility of its paper.

3799. And, therefore, whatever degree of pressure may arise to the mercantile interests by the Bank adhering to the principles of maintaining the convertibility of its notes, that pressure ought rather to be undergone than that the convertibility should be endangered? —I have no question but that it is the duty of the Bank, at all events, to maintain inviolable the fulfilment of its own engagements, that is the first duty of all bankers.

3800 What is your opinion of the recent act for suspending the operation of the usury laws with regard to bills of exchange? —I have not, nor ever had, any doubt that the working of the recent act has been of unmixed advantage.

3801. And, according, to your view of the working of the currency, the allowing so large a margin to the rate of interest which the Bank may charge is eminently conducive to the proper working of the Bank? — Yes; at the same time I beg leave to observe, that, if the Bank manage their securities with a view to the preservation of a large average amount of bullion, their operation on the market rate of interest, by alterations in their rate of discount, will be comparatively on a very small scale.

3802. Admitting that the Bank may produce an influence upon the market rate of interest for short periods, do you believe that the Bank has it in its power to regulate the rate of interest altogether? — No; certainly not for a length of time.

3803. Therefore, if, during considerable periods, the market rate of interest is high or low, yon do not consider that the Bank is to be blamed for that? — No; not at all.

[My evidence from question 3624 to 3720 inclusive has been omitted, because, —

1. The length of it is such, that, if added to these extracts, the space that the whole would occupy would be altogether disproportioned to the other contents of this volume, insomuch that, doubtful as I have been whether the extracts I proposed to insert were not too long, I should, if the only alternative bad been to give the whole or none, have determined on the latter.

2. The points involved in the parts omitted, although important with

reference to the questions as to the management of the Bank in the interval between 1832 and 1836, and especially to that part of its management which related to its employment of the surplus funds of the East India Company, and of the deposits on account of the West India loan in 1835, have no immediate bearing upon the purpose for which the portion of the examination here introduced is given.

That purpose is to exhibit my views as stated to the Committee, on the following points: —

1. That prices are the consequence, and not the cause, of variations in the circulation, that is, of bank notes in the hands of the public.

2. That the Bank had not the power of acting directly on the amount of its circulation.

3. That it was exclusively through the medium of its securities, that the Bank could operate on the foreign exchanges.

4. That the management of the Bank would be best regulated, with a view of the convenience of the public, consistently with the constant maintenance of its payments in cash, by the possession of a very large average amount of treasure.

It can hardly fail of being observed, on the perusal of this examination, how totally inaccessible the Committee were to the points of view which I endeavoured to impress upon them. Sir Robert Peel was not present at any part of my examination.]

Extract from the report of the select committee on the state of commercial credit—April 25th, 1793

A SPIRIT of commercial speculation and commerce had been for some time increasing in every part of the kingdom, and had now got to such a height as to threaten public credit with very serious danger.

The circulating specie being by no means sufficient to answer the very increased demands of trade, the quantity of paper currency brought into circulation, as a supplying medium, was so great and disproportionate, that a scarcity of specie was produced, which threatened a general stagnation of the commercial world.

In consequence of this alarming state of public credit, on the motion of Mr. Pitt, a select committee was this day appointed to take into consideration the present state of commercial credit, and to report their opinion and observations thereupon to the House.

April 29. — The Lord Mayor reported from the said Committee, That the Committee had made a progress in the matter to them referred, and had directed him to make the following Report: —

Your Committee have thought it incumbent on them, in proceeding to execute the orders of the House, to direct their attention to three principal points.

1st. Whether the difficulties at present experienced, or the probability of their continuance and increase are of such urgent importance to the public interest as to require the interposition of the Legislature?

2nd. On the supposition that such interposition should be deemed necessary, what is the most practicable and effectual plan which can be adopted for giving relief?

3rd. What means can be suggested for preventing the renewal of similar inconveniences?

The consideration of the first and second heads appeared in some measure blended together; and the third, though of great importance, appearing to be less urgent in point of time, your Committee have thought it proper to submit to the House such considerations as occurred to them upon the two first points, reserving the latter for a separate report.

Under the first of these heads, the notoriety of failures to a considerable extent, the general embarrassment and apprehension which has ensued, the consideration of the necessary connection between different mercantile houses, and their dependence on each other, and the influence which the state of commercial credit must have upon the trade, the revenue, and general interests of the country, appeared sufficient, without minute examination, to satisfy your Committee that the present situation strongly called for an immediate and effectual remedy, if any practicable plan could be suggested for that purpose.

In addition to this, the Committee had an opportunity of collecting from several of their own members information, grounded either on their general observations upon the subject, or on their own immediate and personal knowledge.

Your Committee, understanding that some suggestions on this subject had been laid before the Chancellor of the Exchequer, on the part of several persons of great eminence and respectability in the city of London, were of opinion, that a communication of these suggestions would be very material to the objects of their inquiry, with a view of ascertaining the opinion of persons of this description, both with respect to the necessity of some remedy, and to the particular mode in which it might be applied.

The Chancellor of the Exchequer accordingly laid before the Committee a paper which had been delivered to him on the 23rd instant by the Lord Mayor and Mr. Bosanquet, which is inserted in the Appendix to this Report: he also stated to the Committee the circumstances which had led to this paper being drawn up. That he had received representations from many different quarters, which induced him to believe that the failures which had taken place had begun by a run on those houses who had issued circulating paper without being possessed of sufficient capital; but that the consequences had soon extended themselves so far as to affect many houses of great solidity, and possessed of funds ultimately much more than sufficient to answer all demands upon them, but which had not the means of converting those funds into money or negotiable securities in time to meet the pressure of the moment.

That the sudden discredit of a considerable quantity of paper which had been issued by different banks, in itself produced a deficiency of the circulating medium, which, in the ordinary course of things, could not be immediately replaced, and that this deficiency occasioned material inconvenience in mercantile transactions. That, in addition to this immediate effect, these circumstances also were represented to have induced bankers and others to keep in their hands a greater quantity of money than they thought necessary in the usual train of business, and that large sums were thus kept out of circulation, and great difficulty arose in procuring the usual advances on bills of exchange, particularly those of a long date. That many persons were said to be possessed of large stocks of goods which they could not at present dispose of; and on the credit of which they could not raise money. That this occasioned an interruption of the usual orders to manufacturers, which, circumstanced together with the interruption of the means by which they were enabled to make their weekly payments, tended to prevent the employment of a number of persons engaged in different manufactures.

That those evils were represented as likely rapidly to increase to a very serious extent, if some extraordinary means were not adopted to restore credit and circulation.

That, in consequence of these representations, he had desired a meeting of different gentlemen, in order to obtain the best information in his power respecting the extent of the evil, and the possibility and propriety of any measure to remedy it. That after much discussion, all the gentlemen present seem to agree in a very strong opinion of the extent of the evil; though many objections at first occurred to any plan for remedying it. That in the result it was agreed to desire the gentlemen, whose names were mentioned in the paper now delivered, to meet the next day at the Mansion House, to consider more particularly the proposal for the issue of Exchequer Bills to a certain amount, to be advanced under proper regulations for the accommodation of such persons as might apply for the same, and likewise the objections to which such a proposal might be liable, and that the paper which he had laid before the Committee contained the opinion of this second meeting. The Lord Mayor informed the Committee, that, in conformity to the statement mentioned by the Chancellor of the Exchequer, eleven gentlemen met at the Mansion House on the 23rd, selected principally from that part of the preceding meeting who had expressed the greatest difficulty in finding out a remedy, and, after a long discussion upon the subject, they unanimously were of opinion, that the interposition of parliament was necessary, and that an issue of Exchequer Bills under certain regulations and stipulations was the best practical remedy.

The following is the account given by Macpherson in his *Annals of Commerce* of the events of this remarkable period: —

" Of the wealth accumulated in nine peaceful years of successful commerce, a very considerable portion was invested in machinery and in land navigation; objects which, though generally very productive in due time, require a heavy advance of capital, and depend for their productiveness entirely upon the general prosperity of the trade of the country. At this time also the concerns of both merchants and manufacturers were much more widely extended, and were much greater than at any former period; a natural effect of increasing prosperity, and sometimes a cause of ensuing calamity. From the operation of causes which I shall not pretend to explain, the unprecedented number of bankruptcies in November 1792, was prodigiously exceeded in number and amount by those which took place in the spring and summer of this year; 105 in March, 188 in April, 209 in May, 158 in June, 108 in July. Many houses of the most extensive dealings and most established credit failed; and their fall involved vast numbers of their correspondents and connections in all parts of the country. Houses of great respectability and undoubted solidity, possessing ample funds, which actually did in a short time enable them to pay every shilling of their debts, were obliged to stop payment; and some bankers, who, almost immediately on recovering from the first panic, resumed their regularity of their payments, were obliged to make a pause. Many, whom the temporary assistance of even a moderate sum of money would have enabled to surmount their difficulties, could not obtain any accommodation; for in the general distress and dismay every one looked upon his neighbour with caution, if not with suspicion. It was impossible to raise any money upon the security of machinery or shares of canals, for the value of such property seemed to be annihilated in the gloomy apprehensions of the sinking state of the country, its commerce and manufactures; and those who had any money, not knowing whom they could place it with safety, kept it unemployed, and locked up in their coffers.

"In consequence of an interview of several of the principal merchants and traders with Mr. Pitt, the Prime Minister, a meeting was held at the Mansion House, April 23rd, to concert measures for putting a stop to this terrible calamity; when the Lord Mayor, Messrs. Anderson, Bosanquet, Forster, Baring, Cheawell, Thornton, Harman, Winshrop, Boddington, and Hunter, after much deliberation, drew up the outlines of a plan for the revival of commercial credit and the restoration of confidence, by a parliamentary advance of Exchequer Bills, under proper regulations, to houses of real capital, a copy of which was immediately laid before Mr. Pitt.

"On the 8th May, in compliance with the recommendation of the Committee, this was agreed to, and the advances were to be made to such of the merchants, traders, bankers, &c., as should apply for them in sums not under 4000*l*. on security approved, or on the deposit of goods of double the value of the sums advanced, at 5 per cent. This was not one of those officious and ill-concerted interferences by which some governments ruin the interests of commerce while they profess themselves the protectors of it. The very first intimation of the intention of the legislature to support the merchants operated all over the country liken charm, and in a great degree superseded the necessity of the relief, by an almost instantaneous restoration of mutual confidence.

"Some of the principal people of Liverpool had digested a plan for supporting the credit, of the merchants and traders of that town, whose very extensive and complicated concerns had involved them in perhaps a greater share of the general calamity than any other place except London.

This proposal was to issue negotiable notes secured on the estate of the Corporation, which is sufficiently ample, and to employ them in support of the credit of individuals, and it received the sanction of Parliament, who authorised the Corporation of Liverpool to issue notes to the amount of 200,000*l*."

THE END.